Yucatán

Ben Greensfelder

LONELY PLANET PUBLICATIONS
Melbourne • Oakland • London • Paris

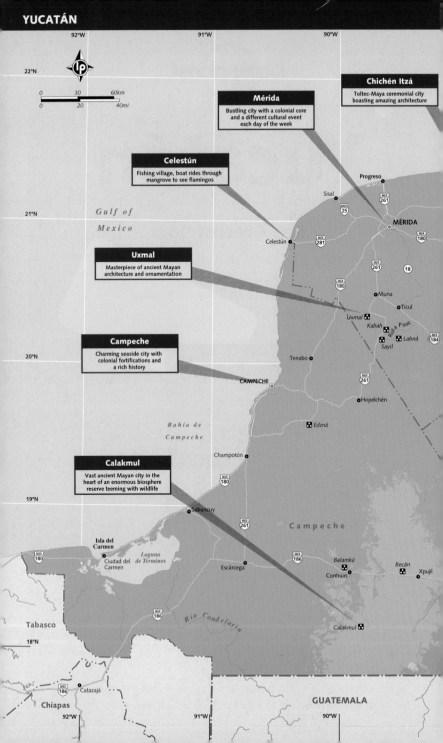

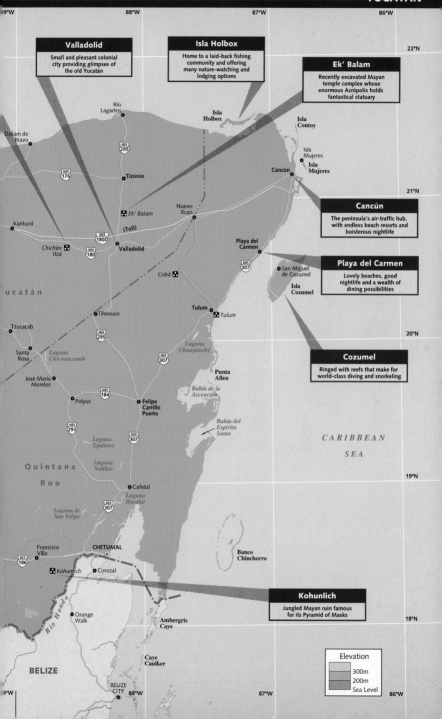

YUCATÁN

Valladolid
Small and pleasant colonial city providing glimpses of the old Yucatán

Isla Holbox
Home to a laid-back fishing community and offering many nature-watching and lodging options

Ek' Balam
Recently excavated Mayan temple complex whose enormous Acrópolis holds fantastical statuary

Cancún
The peninsula's air-traffic hub, with endless beach resorts and boisterous nightlife

Playa del Carmen
Lovely beaches, good nightlife and a wealth of dining possibilities

Cozumel
Ringed with reefs that make for world-class diving and snorkeling

Kohunlich
Jungled Mayan ruin famous for its Pyramid of Masks

22°N
21°N
20°N
19°N
18°N

89°W
88°W
87°W
86°W

Río Lagartos
Dziam de Bravo
Tizimín
Ek' Balam
Kantunil
Chichén Itzá
(Toll)
Valladolid
Cobá
Tihosuco
Tzucacab
Santa Rosa
José María Morelos
Polyuc
Felipe Carrillo Puerto
Cafetal
Francisco Villa
CHETUMAL
Kohunlich
Corozal
Orange Walk
Ambergris Caye
Caye Caulker
BELIZE CITY
BELIZE

Isla Holbox
Isla Contoy
Isla Mujeres
Isla Mujeres
Cancún
Nuevo Xcan
Playa del Carmen
San Miguel de Cozumel
Isla Cozumel
Tulum
Tulum

Laguna Chunyaxché
Punta Allen
Bahía de la Ascención
Bahía del Espíritu Santo
CARIBBEAN SEA
Banco Chinchorro

Yucatán
Laguna Chicnanconab
Laguna Xpaitoro
Laguna Nohbec
Quintana Roo
Laguna Bacalar
Laguna de San Felipe
Río Hondo

MEX 295
MEX 176
MEX 180D
MEX 180
MEX 295
MEX 307
MEX 184
MEX 293
MEX 307
MEX 307
MEX 186

Elevation
300m
200m
Sea Level

Contents – Text

YUCATÁN STATE   154

CAMPECHE STATE   207

LANGUAGE   225

GLOSSARY   234

INDEX   243

MAP LEGEND   back page

METRIC CONVERSION   inside back cover

Contents – Maps

YUCATÁN MAP INDEX

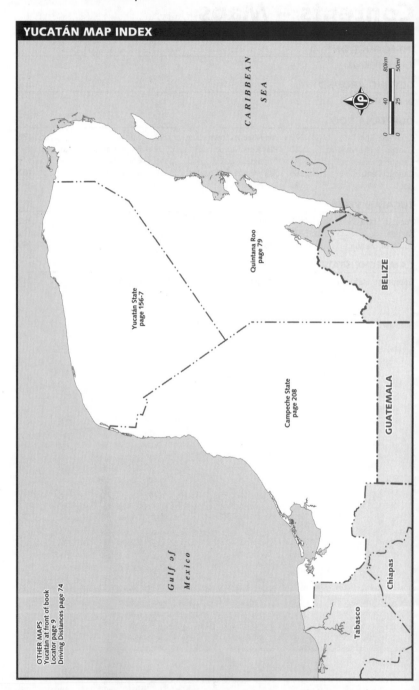

CARIBBEAN SEA

80km
50mi

40
25
0
0

Quintana Roo
page 79

Yucatán State
page 156-7

BELIZE

Campeche State
page 208

GUATEMALA

Chiapas

Tabasco

Gulf of Mexico

OTHER MAPS
Yucatán at front of book
Locator page 9
Driving Distances page 74

The Author

Ben Greensfelder

This is Ben's third time covering the Yucatán for Lonely Planet, which should mean you're holding a charmed book. When not trotting the globe for LP or to help his wife (the inimitable Sandra Bao) with her authoring trips for the company, Ben holes up in Oakland, California. When last spotted he was spending a lot of time shouting at the television, the radio and the occasional newspaper, plotting a US regime change and taking mountain-bike rides in a vain attempt to stay sane.

FROM THE AUTHOR

Warmest thanks to all of the following: in Mérida, Raúl Li Causi, for his continuing updates and constant efforts to improve the Mexican travel experience, and Nicole and Nelson for their delightful hospitality. In Cancún, Antonio Laviada and crew for among other things, the many insights into the Yucatán, and the trip to Banco Chinchorro; as well as to Linda Sosa at the Belizean consulate. Kelly Mattheis in Cozumel: for everything! In Playa del Carmen to Horst, Gary, Pamela and Tom. And to Susana Escobar in Campeche, as well as everyone else on the peninsula who helped out.

A big *¡gracias!* to all the Lonely Planet readers who sent letters and email, including Aristea Parissi of Thessaloniki.

At Lonely Planet, my gratitude to Elaine Merrill for hiring me and being a joy to work with, which goes double for Gabrielle Wilson in Melbourne. Thanks also to Susannah Farfor and cartographer Herman So for all their efforts.

Michael Hesson, *dios bo'otik* for writing the Mayan language section. Many thanks to John Noble, coordinating author of Lonely Planet's *Mexico,* which was the basis for several sections of this book's front chapters. Sandra, thanks for chauffeuring the lawless roads – happy 10th anniversary! Finally, I'd like to dedicate this book to my mother, Jean Margaret Greensfelder.

This Book

The first edition of Yucatán was written by Scott Doggett. Some of the information in this edition was based on the eighth edition of *Mexico* and the fourth edition of *Belize, Guatemala and Yucatán*. This edition was written by Ben Greensfelder.

FROM THE PUBLISHER

This edition of *Yucatán* was commissioned and developed in Lonely Planet's Oakland office by Elaine Merrill with assistance from Valerie Sinzdak. Graham Neale commissioned and developed the maps. The book was produced in LP's Melbourne office. Gabrielle Wilson coordinated the editing with assistance from Susannah Farfor. Herman So coordinated the mapping with assistance from Anneka Imkamp. Justin Flynn helped out with proofreading. The book was designed and laid out by John Shippick and Cris Gibcus. The cover was designed by Pepi Bluck and David Kemp, and produced by Ruth Askevold. Karen Fry provided the climate charts. Pablo Gastar produced the enticing color wraps from photographs supplied by Lonely Planet Images. A special thanks to Michael Hesson at the University of Pennsylvania who wrote the Mayan language section. The language chapter was produced by LP's Emma Koch and Quentin Frayne. The entire process was overseen by project manager Celia Wood.

Thumbs up to author Ben Greensfelder for the lively text and his great sense of fun. *Arriba y adelante.*

Thanks

Lonely Planet would like to thank the following readers for their anecdotes, suggestions and recommendations:

June Arber, David Arlt, Judy Avisar, Dr Klaus Bajohr-Mau, Amanda Bayliss, Aggie Black, Julia Blanc, Dick Blom, Susann Blum, Duane Bong, Shirley Boudewijns, Charlotte Brauer, Michael Bray, Sharon Bray, Eleanor Bridger, Catja Caemmerer, Robey Callahan, Kate Camp, Douglas Campbell-Smith, Nelita Castillo, Anthony Cawthorne, Iona Chamberlin, Rafael Clifford, E Coder, Karin Cohn, Stephaney Cox, Irene Czurda, Stijn Dekeyser, Frank de Roeck, M Digel, Debbi Dolan, Anouk Donker, Joyce Edling, Caroline Edwards, Robert Ettinger, Lauren Farber, Ben Flower, Andreas Foerster, Chris Ford, Brian Fowler, Mirit Friedland, Carlos R Galan Diaz, Richard Garcia, Belen Gavela, Stefan Goeddertz, Denis Grady, Shamir Gurfinkel, Steve Guthrie, Manuela Gutierrez Rebollo, Julie Hatfield, Jacob Hegner, Freddie Heitman, Jeff Hicks, Daniel Houghton, Natasha Hynes, Michael Irwig, Nadler Ishay, Soames Job, Karen Judge, Ali K, Joanne Kitson, Peter Krijger, Peter & Anabel Krijger, Agniesia Kulik, Daniel Lavoie, Dan Leach, Milton Lever, Nicolai Leymann, Edwin Lipscomb, Andreas Lots, Brenda Lyon, Silvia Makovnikova, Birgit Maris, Jeff Marshall, Nadeige Martelly, Sibylle Mau, Ernest Maxwell, Beth McCall, Rory McCall, Sherry McCarnan, Dan McDougall, Phillip McRoberts, Phillip & Shona McRoberts, Amy McVay, Andrea Medovarski, Lilia Mendoza, Aditya Menon, Peter Milec, Carolina Miranda, Gail Morton, Detlev Mueller, Jobst Muhlbach, Jeanne Nash, Saskia Neuijen, Guido Paola, Aristea Parissi, Paul Pinn, Edna Platzer, Jim Premeaux, Jurgen Rahmer, Suma Ramzan, Archie Reid, Charles Renn, Pamela Rey, Rolf Richardson, Sally T Ringe, Nicola Rizzi, Eric Robette, Valerie Roedenbeck-Galli, Benzi Ronen, Marvin Rosen, Bengt Sagnert, Rajasi Saha, Joerg Schnabel, Martina Schoefberger, Malte Schumacher, David Scott, Roland & Bettina Shulze, Amit Irit Shwartz, Luc Sicard, Laura Siklossy, Hana Skockova, David Smallwood, Mike Smet, Samuel Smith, John Snead, Laurie Snead, Helen Stack, Cecilia Stranneby, Josip Svoboda, Peter Tavoly, Elizabeth Thompson, Dan Unger, Roel van den Berkmortel, Ron van Rooijen, Bob Villier, Katrin Wanner, Caroline Wexler, Fiona Whiddon, Krsita Willeboer, Ralph Winkelmolen, Katy Witkowski, Erik Wolfers, Rick Woods, Holly Worton, Lalita X, Basil Yokarinis

Foreword

ABOUT LONELY PLANET GUIDEBOOKS

The story begins with a classic travel adventure: Tony and Maureen Wheeler's 1972 journey across Europe and Asia to Australia. There was no useful information about the overland trail then, so Tony and Maureen published the first Lonely Planet guidebook to meet a growing need.

From a kitchen table, Lonely Planet has grown to become the largest independent travel publisher in the world, with offices in Melbourne (Australia), Oakland (USA), London (UK) and Paris (France).

Today Lonely Planet guidebooks cover the globe. There is an ever-growing list of books and information in a variety of media. Some things haven't changed. The main aim is still to make it possible for adventurous travelers to get out there – to explore and better understand the world.

At Lonely Planet we believe travelers can make a positive contribution to the countries they visit – if they respect their host communities and spend their money wisely. Since 1986 a percentage of the income from each book has been donated to aid projects and human rights campaigns, and, more recently, to wildlife conservation.

Although inclusion in a guidebook usually implies a recommendation we cannot list every good place. Exclusion does not necessarily imply criticism. In fact there are a number of reasons why we might exclude a place – sometimes it is simply inappropriate to encourage an influx of travellers.

UPDATES & READER FEEDBACK

Things change – prices go up, schedules change, good places go bad and bad places go bankrupt. Nothing stays the same. So, if you find things better or worse, recently opened or long-since closed, please tell us and help make the next edition even more accurate and useful.

Lonely Planet thoroughly updates each guidebook as often as possible – usually every two years, although for some destinations the gap can be longer. Between editions, up-to-date information is available in our free, monthly email bulletin *Comet* (W www.lonelyplanet.com/newsletters). You can also check out the *Thorn Tree* bulletin board and *Postcards* section of our website, which carry unverified, but fascinating, reports from travellers.

Tell us about it! We genuinely value your feedback. A well-traveled team at Lonely Planet reads and acknowledges every email and letter we receive and ensures that every morsel of information finds its way to the relevant authors, editors and cartographers.

Everyone who writes to us will find their name listed in the next edition of the appropriate guidebook. The very best contributions will be rewarded with a free guidebook.

We may edit, reproduce and incorporate your comments in Lonely Planet products such as guidebooks, websites and digital products, so let us know if you don't want your comments reproduced or your name acknowledged.

How to contact Lonely Planet:
Online: e talk2us@lonelyplanet.com.au, W www.lonelyplanet.com
Australia: Locked Bag 1, Footscray, Victoria 3011
UK: 72-82 Rosebery Ave, London, EC1R 4RW
USA: 150 Linden St, Oakland, CA 94607

Introduction

The Yucatán Peninsula is home to some of the most impressive archaeological sites in the world, including the ancient Mayan cities of Chichén Itzá, Uxmal and Calakmul. The peninsula – often referred to simply as 'the Yucatán' – also contains numerous colonial cities, captivating Franciscan churches and stately government buildings that date back to the earliest years of the Spanish conquest of the Americas.

The Yucatán lies squarely within the *mundo Maya,* or Mayan world – a vast realm that includes portions of Mexico, Guatemala, Belize, Honduras and El Salvador. Not only are more Mayan ruins located in the Yucatán than anywhere else, but the Mayan way of life has endured here despite the best efforts of Spanish missionaries to destroy it. Mayan villages dot the peninsula like scattered kernels of corn, and in them the residents continue to live off the land and worship their gods as they have for at least 1800 years. The great cities mostly lie in ruin, but many aspects of Mayan culture live on.

Although humans have occupied the Yucatán for thousands of years, most of the peninsula remains blanketed by tropical lowland forest. The forest is not the snake-dripping jungle of Amazonia, but it is home to jaguars, tapirs and crocodiles, hundreds of species of exotic birds and a dazzling array of butterflies. It is here, too, that Mexico's two largest flamingo sanctuaries can be found, and a trip to either is an unforgettable experience. Also found throughout the Yucatán are spectacular caves ripe for exploring and freshwater pools that take the bite out of the tropical midday sun.

The Yucatán's Caribbean coast, bordered nearly its entire length by a barrier reef and boasting warm crystalline waters with an amazing array of sealife, offers truly world-class snorkeling and scuba diving. And the more turbid waters at the peninsula's northern tip, off Isla Holbox, offer a chance for snorkelers and divers to see concentrations of whale sharks unknown elsewhere in the world. Visitors can also swim, fish or kayak

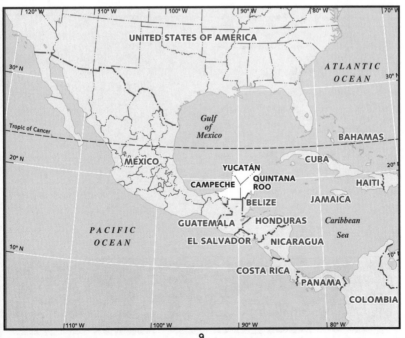

through mangroves, on the reef-sheltered sea or in limestone-bottomed lakes.

Sun-worshippers and party animals the world over have at the very least heard of Cancún, a long and narrow resort-lined island that is shaped like a Lucky 7 and hugs the eastern coast of the Yucatán. Mexico is home to Acapulco, Mazatlán and Cabo San Lucas, but Cancún receives more visitors each year than those three famous spots combined. Cancún's sugary beaches, scandalous nightlife and lengthy menu of restaurants draw people from around the world, and nearby Isla Mujeres and Playa del Carmen hold mellower alternatives and their own brands of nightlife and culinary offerings.

Shoppers will appreciate the handicrafts found on the peninsula. In their handmade goods, the modern-day Maya have fused Old and New World forms and materials. Among the handicrafts produced in the Yucatán are exquisite silver ornaments that reflect the filigree technique introduced by the Spanish, wonderful models of galleons carved from mahogany and panama hats so tightly woven that they can hold water. Some of the world's best hammocks and finest guayaberas come from the Yucatán.

Mexico is famous for its cuisine, which varies considerably from one part of the country to another. Even if you've eaten scores of Mexican dishes, chances are you're unfamiliar with Yucatecan food. Among the better-known regional dishes are *cochinita pibil* (pork slow-cooked in banana leaves and flavored with *achiote* paste, oregano leaves, salt, pepper, garlic, onion, sour orange and a single habanero pepper) and *pavo en escabeche oriental* (turkey marinated in sour orange juice, garlic and chilies, slow-cooked to perfection, then sliced and cooked in green oil and garlic).

Splendid colonial architecture. Magnificent Mayan ruins. History galore. A fascinating people. Culture at every turn. Sun-soaked beaches lapped by clear, warm tropical waters. Great food. Good shopping. Superb snorkeling. Vast cave systems. Refreshing natural pools. World-class diving. The Yucatán has something for most everyone.

Facts about the Yucatán

HISTORY
Early Americans

The date of arrival of *Homo sapiens* in the Americas is the subject of much debate among scientists. Carbon dating in 2002 of several skulls found in Mexico put their age at 13,000 years, making them the earliest known human remains found in the country.

The generally accepted belief is that humans arrived in several migratory waves from Siberia via a land bridge that connected present-day Alaska with Asia, exposed when the Pleistocene epoch's huge glaciers bound up water and lowered the level of the seas. Some of the earlier waves may have died out completely, leaving the Americas to be repopulated by later arrivals.

By around 8000 BC, human settlements were widespread throughout the Americas. By this time, the last ice age was over and rising temperatures had resulted in climate changes everywhere. In Mexico, drier weather had caused grasslands to dwindle, along with the large herds of animals that grazed them. This forced the people living there to derive more of their food from plant sources, and most likely stimulated the development of agriculture. By about 6500 BC, in the Tehuacán valley in what is now Puebla state, people were planting seeds of chili and a kind of squash. By about 5000 BC, Native Americans on the Gulf Coast were cultivating maize (corn), believed to have originated in the region of present-day Panama.

As 2000 BC neared, many Mesoamericans (peoples in the area between central Mexico and present-day Nicaragua) were cultivating corn, squash, avocados and beans, and raising chickens, turkeys and dogs. They continued to hunt and fish as they had for generations, but they became heavily dependent upon crops.

Mexico's ancestral civilization arose near the Gulf Coast, in the humid lowlands of southern Veracruz and neighboring Tabasco. These were the mysterious Olmecs, who developed a writing system of hieroglyphics. The Olmecs developed many religious rituals, including human sacrifices to assuage a number of blood-thirsty gods.

The Olmecs' jaguar-god art became widespread through Mesoamerica. The huge, mysterious basalt heads they carved weighed up to 60 tons. How the heads were hewn without metal tools and moved some 100km from basalt quarries to the Olmecs' capital city of La Venta remains a mystery.

Eventually the Olmecs disappeared; historians assume they were trampled by waves of invaders. But aspects of Olmec culture lived on among their neighbors, paving the way for the later accomplishments of Mayan art, architecture and science.

Around 500 BC the Zapotecs of Oaxaca, who lived on the Pacific coast southwest of the Olmec territory, borrowed considerably from the Olmec culture, and in many ways took it a step further. Like the Olmecs, the Zapotecs built stone structures for religious uses, but they also produced fine headdresses and highly detailed terra-cotta objects with significant cult meanings. The same can be said for the Teotihuacán and El Tajín cultures that existed from AD 250 to 900, hundreds of kilometers north of the Zapotecs, who disappeared around AD 800.

Enter the Maya

Around the same time the Teotihuacán and El Tajín civilizations flourished, another civilization was having its day in the sun on the Yucatán Peninsula and in the highlands to the south. These people were the ancient Maya, who existed as a civilization from about AD 250 to 1524. The latter date is the year the last major Mayan group, the Quiché Maya, was conquered by Spanish troops (at the Battle of Utatlán, in Guatemala).

Archaeologists believe Mayan-speaking people first appeared in the highlands of Guatemala as early as 1500 BC, and that groups of Mayan farmers relocated to the lowlands of the Yucatán Peninsula between 1200 BC and 1000 BC. In the lowlands, the Maya formed villages and tended crops just as they had done in the highlands. For the next 400 to 600 years they did little of archaeological value, though it was during this period that the early Maya invented the *na* (thatched Mayan hut), which is still used today throughout the Yucatán. It was also between 1200 BC and 300 BC that the Maya placed a high value on cacao beans, using them to make chocolate and as a currency.

As agriculture played an increasing role in Mayan life, so too did the climate in which the Maya lived. By 300 BC, most Mayan villages were heavily dependent upon regular rains to feed their crops. A dry spell was cause for panic; a drought brought widescale death. Understanding when the rains came became a Mayan preoccupation, and perhaps stimulated by this, they developed a calendar that featured a year of 18 months, each 20 days long, with five days left over. This is known as the vague year calendar.

Late Pre-Classic Period (300 BC to AD 250)

As the Maya got better at agriculture, the food surpluses they generated allowed them time for other activities. Their society diversified into various classes, and they began to build temples. The first temples consisted of raised platforms of earth topped by a thatch-roofed shelter very much like a normal *na*.

As had been the practice with the *na*, the local potentate was buried beneath the shelter. In the lowlands, where limestone was abundant, the Maya began to build platform temples from stone. As each succeeding local potentate had to have a bigger temple, larger platforms, and more of them, were put over other platforms, forming huge step pyramids with a *na*-style shelter on top. The potentate was buried deep within the stack of platforms. Sometimes the pyramids were decorated with huge stylized masks.

More and more pyramids were built around large plazas, much as the common people clustered their thatched houses in family compounds facing a common open space. The stage was set for the flourishing of Classic Mayan civilization.

Early Classic Period (AD 250 to 600)

Armies from Teotihuacán (near modern Mexico City) invaded the Mayan highlands, conquered the Maya and imposed their rule and their culture for a time, but they were finally absorbed into Mayan daily life. The so-called Esperanza culture, a blend of Mexican and Mayan elements, was born of this conquest.

The great ceremonial centers at Copán, Tikal, Yaxchilán, Palenque and especially Kaminaljuyú (near present-day Guatemala City) flourished during this time.

Late Classic Period (AD 600 to 900)

At the height of this period, the Mayan lands were ruled not as an empire but as a collection of independent, but also interdependent, city-states. Each city-state had its noble house, headed by a king who was the social, political and religious focus of the city's life. The king propitiated the gods by shedding his blood in ceremonies where he pierced his tongue or penis (or both) with a sharp instrument. (There's nothing new under the sun.) He also led his city's soldiers into battle against rival cities, capturing prisoners for use in human sacrifices. Many a king perished in a battle he was too old to fight; but the king, as sacred head of the community, was required to lead in battle for religious as well as military reasons.

King Pacal ruled at Palenque and King Bird-Jaguar at Yaxchilán during the early part of this period, marking the height of civilization and power in these two cities. Mayan civilization in Tikal was also at its height during the late Classic period. By the end of the period, however, the great Mayan cities of Tikal, Yaxchilán, Copán, Quiriguá, Piedras Negras and Caracol had reverted to little more than villages. The focus of Mayan civilization shifted to northern Yucatán, where a new civilization developed at Chichén Itzá, Uxmal and Labná, giving us the artistic styles known as Toltec-Maya, Puuc, Chenes and Río Bec.

Early Post-Classic Period (AD 900 to 1200)

The collapse of Classic Mayan civilization is as surprising as it was sudden. It seems as though the upper classes demanded ever more servants, acolytes and laborers, and though the Mayan population was growing rapidly, it did not furnish enough farmers to feed everyone. Thus weakened, the Maya were prey to the next wave of invaders from central Mexico.

The Toltecs of Tula (near Mexico City) conquered Teotihuacán, then marched and sailed eastward to Yucatán. They were an extremely warlike people, and human sacrifice was a regular practice. Legend has it that the Toltecs were led by a fair-haired, bearded king named Quetzalcóatl (Plumed Serpent), who established himself in Yucatán at Uucilabnal (Chichén Itzá). The story was told that he would one day return from the direction of the rising sun. The culture at Toltec Uucilabnal flourished after the late 10th century, when all of the great buildings were constructed, but by 1200 the city was abandoned.

Late Post-Classic Period (1200 to 1530)

The Itzáes After the abandonment of Uucilabnal, the site was occupied by a people called the Itzáes. Probably of Mayan race, the Itzáes lived among the Putún Maya near Champotón in Campeche until the early 13th century. Forced by invaders to leave their traditional homeland, they headed southeast into El Petén to the lake that became known as Petén Itzá after their arrival. Some continued to Belize, later making their way north along the coast and into northern Yucatán, where they settled at Uucil-abnal. The Itzá leader styled himself Kukulcán (the Mayan name for Quetzalcóatl), as had the city's Toltec founder, and recycled lots of other Toltec lore as well. But the Itzáes strengthened the belief in the sacred nature of cenotes (the natural limestone sinkholes that provided the Maya with their water supply on the riverless plains of the northern Yucatán Peninsula), and they even named their new home Chichén Itzá (Mouth of the Well of the Itzáes).

From Chichén Itzá, the ruling Itzáes traveled westwards and founded a new capital city at Mayapán, which dominated the political life of northern Yucatán for several hundred years. From Mayapán, the Cocom lineage of the Itzáes ruled a fractious collection of Yucatecan city-states until the mid-15th century, when a subject people from Uxmal, the Xiú, overthrew Cocom power. Mayapán was pillaged, ruined and never repopulated. For the next century, until the coming of the conquistadors, northern Yucatán was alive with battles and power struggles among its city-states.

The Spaniards Since Christopher Columbus' arrival in 1492, the Spaniards had been in the Caribbean with their main bases on the islands of Santo Domingo (Hispaniola, now home to Haiti and the Dominican Republic) and Cuba. While searching for a passage to the East Indies through the landmass to their west, they heard tales of an empire rich in gold and silver. Trading, slaving and exploring expeditions from Cuba were led by Francisco Hernández de Córdoba in 1517 and Juan de Grijalva in 1518. When these expeditions attempted to penetrate inland from Mexico's Gulf Coast, they were driven back by hostile natives.

In 1518 the governor of Cuba, Diego Velázquez, asked Hernán Cortés to lead a new expedition westward. As Cortés gathered ships and men, Velázquez became uneasy about the costs of the venture and about Cortés' questionable loyalty, so he canceled the expedition. Cortés ignored the governor and set sail on February 15, 1519, with 11 ships, 550 men and 16 horses.

Landing first at Cozumel, off Yucatán, the Spaniards were joined by Jerónimo de Aguilar, a Spanish priest who had been shipwrecked there several years earlier. With Aguilar acting as translator and guide, Cortés' force moved west along the coast to Tabasco. After defeating an Indian group there, the expedition headed inland, winning more battles and some converts to Christianity as it went.

At this time, central Mexico was dominated by the Aztec empire from its capital of Tenochtitlán (now Mexico City). The Aztecs, like many other cultures in the area, believed that Quetzalcóatl would one day return from the east. Cortés' arrival coincided with their prophecies of Quetzalcóatl's return. Fearful of angering these strangers who might be gods, the Aztecs allowed the small Spanish force into the capital rather than slaughtering them outright.

By this time thousands of members of the Aztecs' subject peoples had allied with Cortés, eager to throw off the harsh rule imposed by their overlords. Many Aztecs died of smallpox introduced by the Spanish, and by the time they resolved to make war against Cortés and their own erstwhile subjects, they found themselves outnumbered and were defeated, though not without putting up a tremendous fight.

A detailed firsthand account can be found in *True History of the Conquest of New Spain* by one of Cortés' soldiers, Bernal Díaz del Castillo. *The Broken Spears,* by Miguel León-Portilla, relates the Aztecs' version of events and is drawn largely from codices written after the conquest.

Cortés went on to conquer central Mexico, after which he turned his attentions to the Yucatán.

Conquest & the Colonial Period (1530 to 1821)

Francisco de Montejos Despite the political infighting among the Yucatecan Maya, conquest by the Spaniards was not easy. The Spanish monarch commissioned Francisco de Montejo (El Adelantado, or the Pioneer) with the task, and he set out from Spain in 1527 accompanied by his son, also named Francisco de Montejo (El Mozo, or the Lad). Landing first at Cozumel off the Caribbean coast, then at Xel-Há on the mainland, the Montejos discovered (perhaps not to their surprise) that the local people wanted nothing to do with them. The Maya made it quite clear that the two would-be conquerors should go conquer somewhere else.

The father and son team then sailed around the peninsula, conquered Tabasco (1530) and established their base near Campeche, which could easily be supplied with provisions, arms and troops from New Spain (central Mexico). They pushed inland to conquer, but after four long, difficult years they were forced to retreat and to return to Mexico City in defeat.

The younger Montejo took up the cause again, with his father's support, and in 1540 returned to Campeche with his cousin named (guess what?) Francisco de Montejo. The two Montejos pressed inland with speed and success, allying themselves with the Xiús against the Cocomes, defeating the Cocomes and converting the Xiús to Christianity.

When the Xiú leader was baptized, he was made to take a Christian name, so he chose what must have appeared to him to be the most popular name of the entire 16th century and became Francisco de Montejo Xiú.

The Montejos founded Mérida in 1542 and within four years subjugated almost all of Yucatán to Spanish rule. The once proud and independent Maya became peons, working for Spanish masters without hope of deliverance except in heaven. The conquerors' attitude toward the indigenous peoples is graphically depicted in the reliefs on the facade of the Montejo mansion in Mérida: in one scene, armor-clad conquistadors are shown with their feet holding down ugly, hairy, club-wielding savages.

The Mayan lands were divided into large estates, or *encomiendas,* and the Maya living on the lands were mercilessly exploited by the landowning *encomenderos.*

With the coming of Dominican friar Bartolomé de Las Casas and groups of Franciscan and Augustinian friars, things improved for the Maya. In many cases the friars were able to protect the local people from the worst abuses, but exploitation was still the general rule.

Friar Diego de Landa The Maya recorded information about their history, customs and ceremonies in beautiful painted picture books made of beaten-bark paper coated with fine lime. These codices, as they are known, must have numbered in the hundreds when the conquistadors and missionary friars first arrived in the Mayan lands. But because the ancient rites of the Maya were seen as a threat to the adoption and retention of Christianity, the priceless books were set aflame upon the orders of the Franciscans. Only a handful of painted books survive, but these provide much insight into ancient Mayan life.

Among those Franciscans directly responsible for the burning of the Mayan

The Last Mayan Kingdom

The last region of Mayan sovereignty was the city-state of Tayasal, in Guatemala's department of El Petén. A group of Itzáes, driven out of Chichén Itzá, moved south and settled on an island in Lago Petén Itzá, at what is now the town of Flores. They founded a city named Tayasal and enjoyed independence for over a century after the fall of Yucatán. The intrepid Cortés visited Tayasal in 1524, while on his way to conquer Honduras, but did not make war against King Canek, who greeted him peacefully. Only in the late 17th century did the Spanish decide that this last surviving Mayan state must be brought within the Spanish empire; in 1697 Tayasal fell to the latter-day conquistadors, some 2000 years after the founding of the first important Mayan city-states.

It's interesting to consider that the last independent Mayan king went down to defeat only a decade before the union of England and Scotland (1707) and at a time when Boston, New York and Philadelphia were small but thriving towns.

Tom Brosnahan

books was the inquisitor Friar Diego de Landa, who, in July of 1562 at Maní (near present-day Ticul in Yucatán), ordered the destruction of 27 'hieroglyphic rolls' and 5000 idols. He also had a few Mayas burned to death for good measure. Landa went on to become bishop of Mérida from 1573 until his death in 1579.

Ironically, it was Friar Diego de Landa, the great destroyer of Mayan cultural records, who wrote the most important book on Mayan customs and practices – the source for much of what we know about the Maya. Landa's book, *Relación de las Cosas de Yucatán,* was written about 1565. It covers virtually every aspect of Mayan life as it was in the 1560s, from Mayan houses, food, drink and wedding and funeral customs, to the calendar and the counting system. The book is available in English as *Yucatán Before and after the Conquest.* You can buy it at a number of bookstores as well as shops at archaeological sites in the Yucatán.

Independence Period (1810 to 1821)

During the colonial period, society in Spain's New World colonies was rigidly and precisely stratified. Native Spaniards were at the very top; next were the criollos, people born in the New World of Spanish stock; below them were the mestizos or ladinos, people of mixed Spanish and Indian blood; and at the bottom were the Indians and blacks of pure race. Only the native Spaniards had real power – a fact deeply resented by the criollos.

The harshness of Spanish rule resulted in frequent revolts, none of them successful for long. In 1810, Mexico's Miguel Hidalgo y Costilla gave the Grito de Dolores, or Cry (of Independence) at Dolores, at his church near Guanajuato, inciting his parishioners to revolt. With his lieutenant, a mestizo priest named José María Morelos, he brought large areas of central Mexico under his control. But this rebellion, like earlier ones, failed. The power of Spain was too great.

Napoleon's conquests in Europe changed all that, destabilizing the Spanish empire's foundations. When the French emperor deposed Spain's King Ferdinand VII and put his brother Joseph Bonaparte on the throne of Spain (1808), criollos in many New World colonies took the opportunity to rise in re-

volt. By 1821 both Mexico and Guatemala had proclaimed their independence.

Independent Mexico urged the peoples of Yucatán, Chiapas and Central America to join it in the formation of one large new state. At first Yucatán and Chiapas refused and Guatemala accepted, but all later changed their minds. Yucatán and Chiapas joined the Mexican union, and Guatemala led the 1823 formation of the United Provinces of Central America, which included Guatemala, El Salvador, Nicaragua, Honduras and Costa Rica. Their union, torn by civil strife from the beginning, lasted only until 1840 before breaking up into its constituent states.

Though independence brought new prosperity to the criollos, it worsened the lot of the Maya. The end of Spanish rule meant that the Crown's few liberal safeguards, which had afforded the Indians minimal protection from the most extreme forms of exploitation, were abandoned. Mayan claims to ancestral lands were largely ignored and huge plantations were created for the cultivation of tobacco, sugarcane and henequen (a plant yielding rope fiber). The Maya, though legally free, were enslaved by peonage to the great landowners.

War of the Castes

Beginnings Divisions between the liberals of Campeche and the conservatives of Mérida led several times to fighting on the peninsula (Campeche and its surrounding area eventually broke away from Yucatán, achieving statehood in 1863). At the same time there were those who entertained the notion of declaring independence from Mexico and perhaps forming a union with the USA, and who anticipated that such a move would lead to invasion by Mexico. In order to wage these battles, the hacendados (landholders) made the mistake of arming and training their Mayan peons as local militias. The Maya seized the opportunity to plot a rebellion against their Yucatecan masters.

In July 1847 a Mayan cacique (chief) was caught with a letter detailing a plot to attack Tihosuco (in the present-day state of Quintana Roo). He was taken to Valladolid and shot, to discourage the plotters, who, interestingly enough, were led by Don Jacinto Pat, the mulatto cacique of Tihosuco, Bonifacio Novelo, a mestizo, and Cecilio Chi, a full-blooded Maya. Rather than be discouraged, they attacked the town of Tepich, south of Tihosuco, killing several criollo families. Thus began the War of the Castes, which the rebels next took to Tihosuco. Supplied with arms and ammunition by the British through Belize, they spread relentlessly across the Yucatán, and in March 1848 attacked Valladolid itself. The rebels quickly gained control of the city in an orgy of killing, looting and vengeance.

In little more than a year, the Mayan revolutionaries had driven their oppressors from every part of the Yucatán except Mérida and the walled city of Campeche. Seeing the whites' cause as hopeless, Yucatán's governor was about to abandon Mérida when the rebels abandoned the attack and went home to plant the corn they would need to carry on the fight. This gave the whites and mestizos time to regroup and receive aid from their erstwhile adversary, the government in Mexico City.

The Talking Cross The counterrevolution against the Maya was without quarter and vicious in the extreme. Between 1848 and 1855 the Indian population of Yucatán was halved. Some Mayan combatants sought refuge in the jungles of what is now southern Quintana Roo. There, they were inspired to continue fighting by a religious leader working with a ventriloquist, who, in 1850 at Chan Santa Cruz, made a sacred cross 'talk' (the cross was an important Mayan religious symbol long before the coming of Christianity). The talking cross convinced the Maya that their gods had made them invincible, and they continued to fight, overwhelming the Mexican garrison in Bacalar's Fuerte de San Felipe in 1858. By about 1866 the governments in Mexico City and Mérida gave up on the area and the war was reduced to the occasional skirmish between Mayas and Mexican patrols who wandered too far into their territory.

Toward the end of the 19th century, Mexican president Porfirio Díaz launched an assault, sending troops with modern weapons to fight the rebels, who stood in the way of his plans to exploit the region's chicle and hardwoods, and to cultivate sugarcane. In June 1901 the last of the rebel chiefs were taken prisoner in Muyil and executed by firing squad in Xcán. The shrine of the talking cross at Chan Santa Cruz was destroyed, and the town was renamed Felipe Carrillo Puerto, in honor of a progressive Yucatecan governor. But the local Maya continued to harass and interdict the Mexicans guerrilla-style for decades. An official, negotiated surrender was signed in 1936, but even then many refused to recognize the document signed by representatives they considered traitors. Incidents of resistance, though very few, continued into the 1950s. In the year of the surrender the region was declared a Mexican territory; it didn't become a state until 1974. Today, if you visit Felipe Carrillo Puerto, you can visit the restored shrine of the talking cross above a dried-up cenote in what is now a city park, though the local Maya are very protective of it. Many of them maintain a strong sense of Mayan cultural identity, as well as the spirit of resistance and independence.

Revolution, Rope & Reform

Porfirio Díaz, who definitively reclaimed Quintana Roo for Mexico, ruled the country from 1876 to 1911 as a dictator, banning political opposition and free press. During this period, known as the porfiriato, Díaz brought the country into the industrial age, hugely expanding the railroad network, stringing telephone and telegraph lines, and instituting many other public-works projects. Ruthless in his use of force to maintain power, Díaz also passed unfair laws that created an even larger class of landless peasants and concentrated wealth in the hands of an ever-smaller elite.

In the Yucatán, enormous fortunes were made by the owners of haciendas producing henequen and sisal, plants in the agave family yielding fibers that can be made into rope, twine and other products. (For a detailed description of this spiky plant and its cultivation, see the boxed text 'Henequen: A Smelly, Bitter Harvest' in the Yucatán State chapter.) The Mayan laborers on these haciendas were basically serfs in a patronage system, paid in scrip that they spent in the 'company store.' Meanwhile, wealthy plantation owners sent their children to schools in Europe and built grand houses on their estates as well as opulent town mansions, particularly in Mérida, where many still stand.

Díaz was brought down by the Mexican Revolution, which erupted in 1910 and

Catedral de la Concepción Inmaculada, Campeche

Palace of the Masks, Kabah

Magician's House, Uxmal

El Castillo, Chichén Itzá

Santuario de la Virgen de Izamal, Izamal

Temple of the Warriors, Chichén Itzá

plunged the country into chaos for the next 10 years. Several factions fought first the government, then among themselves, and as many as 2 million Mexicans lost their lives. Resentment against the ruling institutions boiled over in the Yucatán: many churches were stripped bare and henequen haciendas were attacked or sabotaged.

In the decades following the revolution, agrarian reforms redistributed much of the peninsula's agricultural land, including many of the haciendas, into the hands of peasant cooperatives called *ejidos*. Some of these carried on henequen production even after demand for the product dwindled with the development of synthetic fibers following WWII.

The Yucatán Today

Starting with the development of Cancún in the early 1970s, tourism on the peninsula has been wreaking radical changes. All of the three states – Quintana Roo, Yucatán and Campeche – are undergoing transformation, and many of the region's Maya have left their villages to find work in Cancún, Cozumel, Playa del Carmen and other tourist haunts, usually as service personnel or in construction. Mexico's 1982 debt crisis led to the government's restructuring the legal framework of the *ejido* system to allow outside investment as well as privatization and sales of cooperative land. These days you can see advertisements in Playa del Carmen and elsewhere offering building lots and houses on land within *ejido* boundaries.

The governor of Quintana Roo from 1993 to 1999, Mario Villanueva, allowed the sale of all state-owned coastal lands to private interests. Much of the land had recently been transferred from federal control, and much of it sold for a fraction of its actual value. Just before his term (and his immunity to prosecution) expired, Villanueva fled, accused of helping drug traffickers move tons of cocaine through the state. He remained out of sight for two years, variously reported to be living in Cuba, Costa Rica and Belize. During that time he admitted to accepting millions of dollars in bribes from developers, but denied the drug charges. In May 2001 he was arrested at his ranch near Cancún, and at the time of research was still facing extradition to the United States on the drug charges.

GEOGRAPHY

The Yucatán Peninsula is a vast limestone shelf, sloping slightly downwards from its east–west center. In its northern section it rises no more than a dozen meters above sea level. The shelf extends outward below sea level from the shoreline for more than 100km to the north and west, while on the eastern (Caribbean) side it reaches only a fraction of this. Approaching the Caribbean side by air, you should have no trouble seeing the barrier reef that parallels the coastline at a distance of a few hundred meters to about 1.5km. Known variously as the Great Maya, Mesoamerican or Belize Barrier Reef, it's the longest of its kind in the Northern Hemisphere, extending from southern Belize to Isla Mujeres off the northern coast of Quintana Roo. On the landward side of the reef, the water is usually no more than 5m to 10m deep. On the seaward side of the reef, the water is deeper, plunging in spots to depths of more than 2000m only 10km out, in the Yucatán Channel running between the peninsula and Cuba.

The underwater shelf makes Yucatán's coastline wonderful for aquatic sports, keeping the waters warm and the marine life (fish, crabs, lobsters, tourists) abundant, but on the west side it makes life difficult for traders, who cannot bring their oceangoing vessels near shore to dock.

About 60km south of Mérida, near Ticul, the flat Yucatán plain gives way to the rolling hills of the Puuc ('hill' in Maya) region, which reach an altitude of about 100m. Campeche state is also hilly, especially in its southern interior, where altitudes reach over 300m.

Many subterranean pools have formed in the peninsula's porous limestone, and rivers flow only underground, except in short stretches near the sea where their roofs have collapsed and in the southernmost reaches of the region where the peninsula joins the rest of Mexico (and Guatemala). Some underground streams don't release their water until well offshore; others empty into lagoons near the sea. The peninsula has a few lakes (usually called *lagunas*), including the long and lovely Laguna Bacalar in southern Quintana Roo. Most Yucatecans have traditionally gotten their freshwater from cenotes (limestone caverns with collapsed roofs), which serve as natural cisterns. South of the Puuc region, in the Chenes region, the inhabitants draw water from the *chenes* (limestone pools), more than 100m below ground.

CLIMATE

It is nearly always humid in the Yucatán, even when it's not hot. The coolest temperatures occur from November through February or March, the season of *nortes* (relatively cold storms bringing wind and rain from the north). The 2002–03 season saw an unusually high number of *nortes* roll in, some of which blew for days. Apart from these, you can expect hot, sunny days in that time of year.

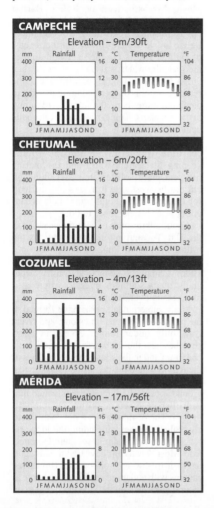

November through April is the driest season, but those darn *nortes* can dump a lot of rain, at times even flooding the streets of Mérida, Cancún and other cities. The rainy season runs from May through October, and temperatures as well as humidity soar, particularly in May and June. You can expect heavy rains for an hour or two most afternoons, but generally clear weather otherwise.

The official Atlantic hurricane season lasts from June 1 to November 30, with most of the activity from mid-August to mid-September; about once every decade, some part of the region gets hits hard. In 1998, Hurricane Mitch killed more than 10,000 people in Central America and southeastern Mexico. In 2002, milder Hurricane Isidore caused considerable damage, knocking down trees, houses and power poles in Yucatán and Campeche states, and killing a lot of chickens and pigs, but no humans.

If a full-blown hurricane is predicted for where you are, go somewhere else – fast! Sitting out a hurricane may look exciting in the movies, but hurricanes are almost always followed by shortages of housing, transportation, electricity, water, food, medicine etc, which can be unpleasant if not perilous.

Should it not be possible to leave, at the very least go inland – far from the dangerous sea swell that usually accompanies hurricanes. Try to stock up on enough items to meet your needs for at least a week. And though it may sound obvious, avoid the temptation to look out a window, as it may be hit by flying debris, and shatter.

ECOLOGY & ENVIRONMENT

The Yucatán is home to some truly spectacular wildlife, both on land and in sea, but until recently very little was done to protect it. Large-scale tourism developments are affecting fragile ecosystems, especially along the 'Riviera Maya' south of Cancún. Many hectares of vital mangrove swamp have been bulldozed, and beaches where turtles once laid eggs are now occupied by resorts and vacationers, or permanent housing. Large sections of coral reef are likely to die off, along with the marine life they support. Many of these developments were done without permits, some through bribes paid to officials as high ranking as the former governor.

Steps have been taken to preserve vast tracts of tropical forest in the region. Mexico,

Hurricanes

Hurricanes that strike the Yucatán Peninsula originate off the coast of Africa, forming when winds rush toward a low-pressure area and swirl around it due to the rotational forces of Earth's spin. The storms move counterclockwise across the Atlantic, fed by warm winds and moisture, building up force in their 3000km run toward Central and North America.

A hurricane builds in stages, the first of which is called a tropical disturbance. The next stage is a tropical depression. When winds exceed 64km/h, the weather system is upgraded to a tropical storm and is usually accompanied by heavy rains. The system is called a hurricane if wind speed exceeds 120km/h and intensifies around a low-pressure center, the so-called 'eye of the storm.'

Hurricane systems can range from 80km in diameter to devastating giants more than 1600km across. Their energy is prodigious – far more than the mightiest thermonuclear explosions ever unleashed on earth. The area affected by winds of great destructive force may exceed 240km in diameter. Gale-force winds can prevail over an area twice as great.

The strength of a hurricane is rated from one to five. The mildest, a Category 1 hurricane, has winds of at least 120km/h. The strongest and rarest hurricane, the Category 5 monster, packs winds that exceed 250km/h. Hurricane Mitch, which killed more than 10,000 people in Central America and southeastern Mexico in late 1998, was a rare Category 5 hurricane. Hurricanes travel at varying speeds, from as little as 10km/h to more than 50km/h.

For current tropical-storm information, go to the US National Oceanic and Atmospheric Administration's **National Hurricane Center** (W *www.nhc.noaa.gov*).

---

sometimes with funding from the United Nations, has established biosphere reserves in which hunting, fishing and the cutting or burning of forest are restricted by law. These protect coral reefs and breeding grounds for rare and endangered species.

Unfortunately, oversight in many of these reserves is limited or nonexistent, and illegal fishing, hunting and logging (as well as poor boating and diving practices resulting in damage to reefs) are common occurrences. But the reserves on the whole fare better than other land.

A growing number of nongovernment environmental groups around the country have scored victories, some with support from outside Mexico. Bright spots include the cancellation in 2001 of a large hotel project at the beach of Xcacel in Quintana Roo, an important nesting ground for sea turtles, and the reduction in size of a mammoth project planned for Puerto Morelos, just south of Cancún.

See Responsible Tourism in the Facts for the Visitor chapter for details on how you can do your bit by being a responsible traveler.

FLORA & FAUNA
Plants

The plants found on the peninsula fall into four main categories: aquatic and subaquatic vegetation, and humid and subhumid forests. In other words, the Yucatán has got mangroves, it's got sea plants, and it's got tropical forests.

You can expect to see a wide variety of flora on the peninsula, ranging from swampy-looking mangrove forest along some stretches of the coast to a fairly dense forest characterized by mostly lower trees that shed their leaves in the winter, to a jungle-like forest with tall trees and climbing vegetation and more than a few air plants (but without the soggy underbrush and multiple canopies you'd find farther south).

In the Yucatán you can also see a wide variety of palms, many mango and avocado trees, and lots of annuals and perennials, such as the flamboyant tree (also called the royal poinciana) with its red-orange flowers, and the purple-flowering jacaranda. There are 75 known species of orchid in the taller trees found on the southern half of the peninsula; for the really spectacular blooms, the avid orchid hunter will need to head into the highlands of Chiapas, where the exotic plants thrive at an elevation of about 1000m.

Birds

What the Yucatán lacks in plant life, relative to the spectacular jungle foliage found in Chiapas and in many parts of Central America, it more than makes up for in bird life. The peninsula is home to many regional endemics (such as birds found only on Cozumel), a startling variety of waterbirds and an impressive list of tropical species.

In her 2002 *Check-List of the Birds of the Yucatán Peninsula,* Barbara MacKinnon states that there are some 537 known species of bird on the peninsula and nearby islands. This figure represents 50% of the total number of bird species that have been recorded in all of Mexico. What's more, MacKinnon notes that most of the 537 species were recorded in areas set aside for conservation.

Among some of the species birders on the peninsula would want to squint for are the yellow-lored Yucatán parrot, the white-lored gnatcatcher, the black-throated blue warbler, and the Yucatán bobwhite. Don't forget the wading birds: flamingos, herons (great blue, tiger and others), snowy egrets, white ibis and roseate spoonbills among them. In addition to MacKinnon's field checklist, which can often be found in Cancún bookstores, serious birders will want to purchase a copy of Steve NG Howell's *A Bird-Finding Guide to Mexico* (1999, Cornell University Press), in which he devotes 30 information- and map-packed pages to 10 of the best birding sites in the Yucatán.

Land Animals

Jaguars still roam the forests of the peninsula, but you are unlikely to see one except in a cage, as they're rare and very seclusive. Despite the Maya's traditional fascination with the New World's largest cat, poaching has all but wiped them out in southeastern Mexico. Your best chances of spotting one in the wild are probably in the Reserva de la Biósfera Calakmul (Calakmul Biosphere Reserve) in Campeche state.

The puma, the ocelot, the margay and the peninsula's other native wildcat, the jaguarundi, are also endangered, but sightings of pumas in the southern portion of the peninsula aren't all that unusual.

The agile spider monkey inhabits some forested areas of the region. It looks something like a smaller, long-tailed version of the gibbon, an ape native to southwest Asia. The howler monkey is another elusive primate, frequenting forest around the ruins of Calakmul and in isolated pockets else-

where. Howlers are more often heard than seen, but you have a fair chance of seeing both them and spider monkeys at Punta Laguna (see Punta Laguna in the Quintana Roo chapter).

Crocodiles still ply the mangroves near the towns of Río Lagartos and Celestún (home to two of Mexico's largest flamingo colonies) in Yucatán state, but their numbers are a fraction of what they were just 30 years ago. There are still plenty of the beady-eyed amphibious reptiles at the Reserva de la Biósfera Sian Ka'an (Sian Ka'an Biosphere Reserve), and small numbers elsewhere up and down the Caribbean coast, including at Laguna Nichupté, which backs onto Cancún's Zona Hotelera.

Other regional natives include tapirs and pig-like peccaries (javelinas), as well as armor-plated armadillos. The anteater is a cousin of the armadillo, though it's difficult to see the resemblance. There are several species, all with very long, flexible snouts and sharp-clawed, shovel-like front paws – the two tools needed to seek out and enjoy ants and other insects. Unlike the armadillo, the anteater is covered in hair and has a long bushy tail. Its slow gait and poor eyesight make it a common roadkill victim.

The *tepezcuintle* (paca) and *sereque* (agouti) are large, tailless rodents (much cuter than that sounds) found on the peninsula. A few species of deer can be found as well, including the smallest variety in North America.

Unless you're looking for it, you're not likely to see the Western diamondback rattlesnake except as roadkill. Whatever they do, don't touch one – not even a dead one. Biting is a reflex action that takes a while to shut down in rattlesnakes.

Sea Creatures

The Great Maya Barrier Reef, which runs parallel to the length of Quintana Roo's coast, is home to some of the finest snorkeling and diving in the world. What makes the snorkeling so incredible is the tremendous variety of colorful marine life that exists here. At times the fish look lit up. The coney grouper, for example, is impossible to miss in its bright-yellow suit (it varies in color from reddish brown to sun yellow). The redband parrot fish is easy to recognize by the striking red circle around the eye and the red band that runs from the eye to the gills. As their name suggests, butterfly fish are brilliantly colored (there are six species in the area), and the yellow stingray is covered with attractive spots that closely resemble the rosettes of a golden jaguar.

Providing an extraordinary backdrop to the colorful stars of the sea is a vast array of corals, which come in two varieties: hard corals, such as the great star coral, the boulder coral and numerous brain corals; and soft corals, such as sea fans and sea plumes, which are particularly delicate and sway with the current. Successive generations of coral form a skin of living organisms over the limestone reef.

Complementing the experience is a water temperature that seldom dips below 27°C (77°F) and visibility that's often simply amazing. Because this coast contains not a single exposed river (many underground rivers do present themselves as they near the sea, but they carry very little soil), there's practically no sediment to muck up the water. Visibility is compromised only during or after a storm, and for several weeks around April–May and September–October, when reef animals and plants release zillions of eggs and droplets of sperm.

Endangered Species

Pollution, poaching, illegal traffic of rare species and the filling in of coastal areas for yet another resort are taking an enormous toll on the Yucatán's wildlife. However, the biggest killer of all is deforestation. Since 1960, more than 5 million hectares of forest have been felled in the Yucatán. The lives of all the plants and animals that depend on the forest have also passed to another world. Species on the peninsula that are threatened with extinction include five species of cat, four species of sea turtle, the manatee, the tapir and hundreds of species of bird, including the harpy eagle, the red flamingo and the jabiru stork.

Parks & Reserves

There are several national parks on the peninsula, some scarcely larger than the ancient Mayan cities they contain – Parque Nacional Tulum is a good example of this. Others, like Parque Nacional Isla Contoy, a bird sanctuary northeastern Quintana Roo, are larger and have been designated to protect wildlife.

The fact that former president Ernesto Zedillo was an avid scuba diver was likely a factor in the creation of several *parques marinos nacionales* (national marine parks) off the coast of Quintana Roo: Arrecifes de Cozumel; Costa Occidental de Isla Mujeres, Punta Cancún y Nizuc; and Arrecifes de Puerto Morelos.

Very large national biosphere reserves surround Río Lagartos, Celestún (both in Yucatán state) and Banco Chinchorro (Quintana Roo), spreading across thousands of hectares. The Reservas de la Biósfera Ría Lagartos and Celestún are well known for their diversity of bird and animal species, including large colonies of red flamingos, while Banco Chinchorro contains a massive coral atoll, many shipwrecks and a host of marine species.

Even more impressive are the two colossal Unesco-designated biosphere reserves found in the Yucatán: the Reserva de la Biósfera Calakmul, covering more than 7230 sq km in Campeche, Quintana Roo and Chiapas, as well as parts of Belize and Guatemala, is home to more than 300 species of birds and to jaguars, pumas, tapirs coatis, peccaries and many other animals. The Reserva de la Biósfera Sian Ka'an, beginning 150km south of Cancún, covers 6000 sq km, including 100 sq km of the Great Maya Barrier Reef. Its life forms range from more than 70 species of coral to 350 species of bird (by comparison, there are only 400 species of bird in all of Europe). Crocodiles, pumas, jaguars and jabirus are among the animals calling Sian Ka'an home.

GOVERNMENT & POLITICS

The United Mexican States (Estados Unidos Mexicanos) is a multiparty democracy with an elected president, a bicameral legislature and an independent judiciary. The legislatures and governors of Mexico's states are elected by their citizens, as are the *ayuntamientos* (town councils), which run the *municipios* (townships), and their alcaldes (mayors).

Such is the theory. In practice, Mexican political life was dominated for most of the 20th century by one party, the Partido Revolucionario Institucional (PRI; Institutional Revolutionary Party), and its predecessors, with the national president ruling in the tradition of strong, centralized leadership.

Accusations of fraud, corruption, bribery, intimidation and violence long accompanied the all-conquering PRI's election tactics and style of governing at every level.

In 2000, Mexican politics celebrated its equivalent of the dismantling of the Berlin wall, when Vicente Fox Quesada of the Partido de Acción Nacional (PAN; National Action Party) was elected president; he was the first non-PRI president since the PRI was invented (under a different name, PNR) in 1929. All three main parties broke new ground by using a primary-election system to choose their presidential candidates. This was particularly historic in the case of the PRI, whose candidates had previously been picked by the *dedazo* (fingering) method in which the outgoing president, who is forbidden by law from serving more than one *sexenio* (six-year term), chose a candidate to succeed him from within PRI ranks. That candidate had invariably become president.

Democratization, meanwhile, continued at other levels of Mexican politics too; by 2003 there were 15 state governorships in non-PRI hands (eight PAN, including the state of Yucatán, five PRD and two PAN–PRD alliances).

Fox has made efforts to clean up corruption in Mexico's police and security forces and its prison system, and has pledged to better the lot of indigenous groups. Critics say he hasn't gone far enough, while supporters say he is handcuffed by decades of entrenched corruption. He may find redemption in his handling of the 'Pemexgate' scandal that broke in late 2002, when it was learned that Pemex, the state oil monopoly, funneled some US$110 million to PRI campaign coffers in 2000.

However successful Fox's *sexenio* turns out, his election as president was the biggest event in Mexican politics since the forming of the PRI in the chaotic aftermath of the revolution in the early 20th century.

ECONOMY

Tourism is the top industry in the states of Quintana Roo and Yucatán, and both enjoy higher rates of employment than most of the rest of Mexico. Though tourism is gaining steam in Campeche, oil production and fishing remain its main revenue generators.

Agricultural activities on the peninsula include the raising of citrus and sugarcane crops, poultry, hogs, and cattle (especially big in the northern section of Quintana Roo). Many Mayas still raise bees as their ancestors did, and sell the honey.

The state of Yucatán contains some 99 maquiladoras – factories where foreign companies are allowed to import raw materials duty-free for processing or assembly by inexpensive Mexican labor, and then re-export the finished products. Once seemingly restricted to border towns, foreign-owned and -operated factories, mostly producing textiles, shoes and clothing, employed 28,000 people in January of 2003. The pay is poor and turnover is very high.

POPULATION & PEOPLE

For more than a millennium, the Maya of the Yucatán have intermarried with neighboring and invading peoples. The descendants of Mayan and Spanish stock are called mestizos.

Most of Mexico's population is mestizo, but the Yucatán has an especially high proportion of pure-blooded Maya. In some parts of the region, Mayan languages prevail over Spanish, or Spanish may not be spoken at all. In remote jungle villages, some modern cultural practices descend almost directly from those of ancient Mayan civilization.

Thanks to the continuation of their unique cultural identity, the Maya are proud without being arrogant, confident without the machismo seen so frequently elsewhere in Mexico, and kind without being servile. And with the exception of those who have become jaded by the tourist hordes that descend on Cancún, Cozumel and other cities on the peninsula, the Maya have a welcoming attitude toward foreign visitors.

Quintana Roo has surpassed the state of Yucatán in employment opportunities and consequently has become the fastest-growing of the three states on the peninsula, attracting job-seekers from all over the republic. Many middle-class *chilangos* (natives of Mexico City) have made their way to Quintana Roo to escape the pollution and skyrocketing crime rate. The state has about 984,000 inhabitants, just under half of them in Cancún; another nearly 130,000 people reside in Chetumal, the capital.

Yucatán contains just over 1.7 million inhabitants, about 690,000 of whom live in the bustling capital of Mérida.

Though covering more than 51,000 sq km, Campeche is the peninsula's least progressive and least populated state, with 713,000 residents, only 198,000 of whom live in the capital city of Campeche.

If you haven't done the math yet, that totals to about 3.2 million people living in the peninsula's three states.

ARCHITECTURE & ARCHAEOLOGY

Mayan architecture is amazing for its achievements but perhaps even more amazing for what it did not achieve. Mayan architects never seem to have used the true arch (a rounded arch with a keystone), and never thought to put wheels on boxes for use as wagons to move the thousands of tons of construction materials needed in their tasks. They had no metal tools – they were technically a Stone Age culture – yet could build breathtaking temple complexes and align them so precisely that windows and doors were used as celestial observatories of great accuracy.

The arch used in most Mayan buildings is the corbeled arch (or, when used for an entire room rather than a doorway, corbeled vault). In this technique, large flat stones on either side of the opening are set progressively inward as they rise. The two sides nearly meet at the top, and this 'arch' is then topped by capstones. Though they served the purpose, the corbeled arches severely limited the amount of open space beneath them. In effect, Mayan architects were limited to long, narrow vaulted rooms.

The Maya also lacked draft animals (horses, donkeys, mules, oxen). All the work had to be done by humans, on their feet, with their arms and with their backs, without wagons or even wheelbarrows.

The Celestial Plan

Every major work of Mayan architecture had a celestial plan. Temples were aligned so as to enhance celestial observation, whether of the sun, moon or certain stars, and planets, especially Venus. The alignment might not be apparent except at certain conjunctions of the celestial bodies (eg, an eclipse), but the Maya knew each building was properly 'placed' and that this enhanced its sacred character.

Temples usually had other features that linked them to the stars. The doors and

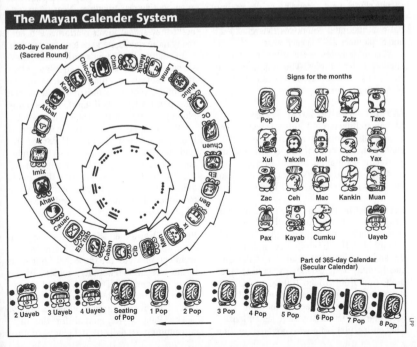

The Mayan Calender System

260-day Calendar
(Sacred Round)

Signs for the months

Pop Uo Zip Zotz Tzec

Xul Yakxin Mol Chen Yax

Zac Ceh Mac Kankin Muan

Pax Kayab Cumku Uayeb

Part of 365-day Calendar
(Secular Calendar)

2 Uayeb 3 Uayeb 4 Uayeb Seating of Pop 1 Pop 2 Pop 3 Pop 4 Pop 5 Pop 6 Pop 7 Pop 8 Pop

windows might be aligned in order to frame a celestial body at an exact point in its course on a certain day of a certain year. This is the case with the Palacio del Gobernador (Governor's Palace) at Uxmal, which is aligned in such a way that from the main doorway, Venus would have been visible exactly on top of a small mound some 3.5km away, in the year AD 750. At Chichén Itzá, the observatory building called El Caracol was aligned in order to sight Venus exactly in the year AD 1000.

Furthermore, the main door to a temple might be decorated to resemble a huge mouth, signifying entry to Xibalbá (the secret world or underworld). Other features might relate to the numbers of the calendar round, as at Chichén Itzá's El Castillo. This pyramid has 364 stairs to the top; with the top platform, this makes 365, the number of days in the Mayan vague year. On the sides of the pyramid are 52 panels, signifying the 52-year cycle of the calendar round. The terraces on each side of each stairway total 18 (nine on either side), signifying the 18 'months' of the solar vague year. The alignment of El Castillo catches the sun and makes a shadow of the sacred sky-serpent ascending or descending the side of El Castillo's staircase on the vernal and autumnal equinoxes (March 20–21 and September 21–22) each year.

Mayan temples were often built atop smaller, older temples. This increased their sacredness and preserved the temple complex's alignment.

Mayan Architectural Styles

Mayan architecture's 1500-year history saw a fascinating progression of styles. Styles changed not just with the times, but with the particular geographic area of Mesoamerica in which the architects worked. Not all of the styles can be seen in the Yucatán.

Late Pre-Classic This style is perhaps best exhibited at Uaxactún, north of Tikal in Guatemala's Petén department. Uaxactún's Pyramid E-VII-sub is a fine example of how the architects of what is known as the Chicanel culture designed their pyramid-temples in the time from around 100 BC to AD 250. It's a square stepped-platform pyramid with central stairways on each of the four sides, each stairway flanked by large jaguar masks. The entire platform was covered in fine

white stucco. The top platform is flat and probably bore a temple *na* made of wooden poles topped with palm thatch. This temple is well preserved because others had been built on top of it; these later structures were ruined by the ages and were cleared away to reveal E-VII-sub. Chicanel-style temples similar to this one were built at Tikal, El Mirador and Lamanai (in Belize) as well.

Early Classic The Esperanza culture typifies this phase. In Esperanza-style temples, the king was buried in a wooden chamber beneath the main staircase of the temple; successive kings were buried in similar places in the pyramids built on top of the first one.

Of the surviving early Classic pyramids, perhaps the best example is the step-pyramid at Acanceh, just south of Mérida.

Late Classic The most important Classic sites flourished during the latter part of the period. By this time, the Mayan temple-pyramid had a masonry building on top, replacing the *na* of wooden poles and thatch. Numbers of pyramids were built close together, sometimes forming contiguous or even continuous structures. Near them, different structures now called palaces were built; they sat on lower platforms and held many more rooms, perhaps a dozen or more.

In addition to pyramids and palaces, Classic sites have carved stelae and round 'altarstones' set in the plaza in front of the pyramids. Another feature of the Classic and later periods is the ball court, with sloping playing surfaces of stone covered in stucco.

Of all the Classic sites, Tikal in Guatemala is the grandest restored so far. Here the pyramids reached their most impressive heights and were topped by superstructures (called roofcombs by archaeologists) that made them even taller. As in earlier times, these monumental structures were used as the burial places of kings.

Puuc, Chenes & Río Bec Among the most distinctive of the late Classic Mayan architectural styles are those that flourished in the western and southern regions of the Yucatán Peninsula. These styles valued exuberant display and architectural bravado more than they did proportion and harmony.

The Puuc style, named for the hills surrounding Uxmal, used facings of thin limestone 'tiles' to cover the rough stone walls of buildings. The tiles were worked into geometric designs and stylized figures of monsters and serpents. Minoan-style columns and rows of engaged columns (half-round cylinders partly embedded in a wall) were also a prominent feature of the style; they were used to good effect on facades of buildings at Uxmal and at the Puuc sites of Kabah, Sayil, Xlapak and Labná. Puuc architects were crazy about Chac, the rain god, and stuck his grotesque face on every temple, many times. At Kabah, the facade of the Templo de los Mascarones is completely covered in Chac masks.

The Chenes style, prevalent in areas of Campeche south of the Puuc region, is similar to the Puuc style, but Chenes architects seem to have enjoyed putting huge masks as well as smaller ones on their facades.

The Río Bec style, epitomized in the richly decorated temples at the archaeological sites between Escárcega and Chetumal, used lavish decoration, as in the Puuc and Chenes styles, but added huge towers to the corners of its low buildings, just for show. Río Bec buildings look like a combination of the Governor's Palace of Uxmal and Temple I at Tikal.

Early Post-Classic The collapse of Classic Mayan civilization created a power vacuum that was filled by the invasion of the Toltecs from central Mexico. The Toltecs brought with them their own architectural ideas, and in the process of conquest these ideas were assimilated and merged with those of the Puuc style.

The foremost example of what might be called the Toltec-Maya style is Chichén Itzá. Elements of Puuc style – the large masks and decorative friezes – coexist with Toltec warrior atlantes (male figures used as supporting columns) and *chac-mools,* odd reclining statues that are purely Toltec and have nothing to do with Mayan art. Platform pyramids with broad bases and spacious top platforms, such as the Temple of the Warriors, look as though they might have been imported from the ancient Toltec capital of Tula (near Mexico City) or by way of Teotihuacán, with its broad-based pyramids of the sun and moon. Because Quetzalcóatl was so important to the Toltecs, feathered serpents are used extensively as architectural decoration.

Late Post-Classic After the Toltecs came the Cocomes, who established their capital at Mayapán, south of Mérida, and ruled a confederation of Yucatecan states. After the golden age of Tikal and Palenque, even after the martial architecture of Chichén Itzá, the architecture of Mayapán is a disappointment. The pyramids and temples are small and crude compared to the glorious Classic structures. Mayapán's only architectural distinction comes from its vast defensive city wall, one of the few such walls ever discovered in a Mayan city. The fact that the wall exists testifies to the weakness of the Cocom rulers and the unhappiness of their subject peoples.

Tulum, another walled city, is also a product of this time. The columns of the Puuc style are used here, and the painted decoration on the temples must have been colorful. But there is nothing here to rival Classic architecture.

Cobá has the finest architecture of this otherwise decadent period. The stately pyramids here had new little temples built atop them in the style of Tulum.

Spanish Colonial Architecture

The conquistadors and Franciscan and Dominican priests brought with them the architecture of their native Spain and adapted it to the conditions they met in the Mayan lands. Churches in the largest cities were decorated with baroque elements, but in general the churches are simple and fortresslike. The exploitation of the Maya by the Spaniards led to frequent rebellions, and the strong, high stone walls of the churches worked well in protecting the upper classes from the wrath of the indigenous people.

As you travel through the region, you'll see that many churches are plain, both inside and out. These crude and simple borrowings from Spanish architecture are eclipsed by the richness of the religious pageantry that takes place inside the buildings – including many half-Mayan, half-Catholic processions, rituals, decorations and costumes.

ARTS

The arts and crafts scene on the Yucatán is enormously rich and varied. The influence of the Mayan or Spanish cultures (or both) appears in almost every facet of Yucatecans' art, from their dance and music to the clothes they wear, such as the *huipiles,* the colorfully embroidered white cotton tunic-dresses Mayan women have been wearing for centuries, and *panamás* (panama hats), which were being woven in the state of Campeche long before their famous namesake received worldwide acclaim as stylish and practical headgear for the Tropics.

Pre-Hispanic Art

The Classic Maya, at their cultural height from about AD 250 to 800, were perhaps ancient Mexico's most artistic people. They left countless beautiful stone sculptures, of complicated design and meaning but possessing an easily appreciable delicacy of touch – a talent also expressed in their unique architecture. Subjects are typically rulers, deities and ceremonies.

Dance

The Spanish influence on Mayan culture is quite evident in the *jarana,* a dance Yucatecans have been performing for centuries. In this dance, the men and women move separately, facing each other in two lines. At different stages of the *jarana,* the couples raise their arms and snap their fingers. The dancers move in precision to the music.

Although the music is different, the dance is quite similar to the *jota,* a folkloric dance performed in Spain's Alto Aragón region. The movements of the dancers, with their torsos held rigid and a formal distance separating men from women, are nearly identical; however, whereas the Spanish punctuate elegant turns of their wrists with clicks of their castanets, the Mayan women snap their fingers.

Music

Latin jazz, Caribbean reggae, and English-and Spanish-language rock and roll is often performed in the tourist haunts of Cancún, Mérida and Playa del Carmen, while the latest popular dance music fills the dance halls from Mérida to Chetumal, near the Belize border. These days *música tropical,* including salsa, merengue, mambo and the galumphing cumbia, is quite the rage.

To hear traditional Yucatecan music you must attend one of the folkloric shows put on for tourists in Cancún, or a *vaquería* (traditional Yucatecan parties where couples dance in unison to a series of songs) in the lovely colonial city of Mérida, the cultural capital of the peninsula and the capital of Yucatán state. *Vaquerías* are held every Monday night in front of Mérida's Palacio Municipal.

Jarana music is generally provided by an orchestra consisting of at least two trumpets, two trombones, violins, kettledrums and a guiro (a percussion instrument made out of a gourd). A *jarana* orchestra always ends its performances with the traditional *torito,* a vivacious song that evokes the fervor of a bullfight. If you are in Mérida for a *vaquería,* make sure that you stay until the very end.

Textiles

Women throughout the Yucatán Peninsula traditionally wear straight, white cotton dresses called *huipiles,* the bodices of which are always embroidered. These tunics generally fall just below the knee; on formal occasions, a lacy white underskirt that reaches the ankle will be added to the dress. *Huipiles* are never worn with a belt, which would defeat its airy, cool design.

Also commonly worn on the peninsula (and similar to the *huipil* in appearance) is the *gala terno,* which is a straight, white, square-necked dress with an embroidered overyoke and hem, worn over an underskirt which sports an embroidered strip near the bottom. It is fancier than a *huipil* and is often accompanied by a delicately hand-knitted shawl.

In addition to *huipiles, galas ternos* and shawls, Mayan women throughout the peninsula are known for weaving lovely sashes, tablecloths and napkins.

Panama Hats

The classic woven straw hat that most people associate with Panama was made internationally famous in the late 19th century by Ferdinand de Lesseps, builder of the Suez Canal and the brains behind the failed French attempt to build a canal in Panama.

The much-photographed Lesseps was balding when he arrived in Panama, and he found that the light but durable hat provided excellent protection against the sun. Most newspaper photographs taken of him here showed the larger-than-life figure looking even more worldly in his exotic headgear. Soon men around the globe began placing orders for the 'panama hat.'

The original hat was made in Ecuador and exported to Panama. However, at least as early as the 1880s, residents of Bécal in the Mexican state of Campeche were producing the same style hat. Today, more than 1000 people in the small, quiet town of Bécal are still making the hats, which they variously call *panamás* or jipijapas (the Mexican hats are made from jipijapa palm fronds).

Wooden Crafts

In handicrafts shops across the peninsula, you'll come across beautiful wooden crafts, such as carved wooden panels and wooden galleons.

The ancient Maya made wood carvings of their many gods, just as they carved the images of their deities in stone. The skill and techniques associated with the artistry survive to this day. The wooden panels are often a meter or more in height and feature a strange looking character of unmistakably Mayan imagination – the image will resemble figures you've seen at Mayan ruins. If the carved image is one of a heavily adorned man raising a chalice, most likely you're looking at a representation of Itzamná, lord of the heavens; he's a popular figure on the wooden panels of contemporary Maya.

Mayans – so impressed with the Spanish galleons that arrived on their shores that they made meter-long models of the ships, complete with tiny sails – have been making wooden galleons for generations. Today, the galleons that used to haul cargoes of hardwood back to Europe are gone, but the craft of galleon model-making is alive and well in the Yucatán.

You can usually find carved wooden sailfish, carved wooden turtles and carved wooden parrots at the same craft shops where you find the lovely wooden models of galleons. Campeche is the state most associated with such items, but they are made by artisans in the states of Yucatán and Quintana Roo as well.

RELIGION
The Ancient Maya

World-Tree & Xibalbá For the Maya, the world, the heavens and the mysterious 'unseen world' or underworld, called Xibalbá (shi-bahl-**bah**), were all one great, unified structure that operated according to laws of astrology and ancestor worship. The towering ceiba tree was considered sacred. It symbolized the Wakah-Chan or Yaxché, or World-Tree, which united the 13 heavens, the surface of the earth and the nine levels of the underworld of Xibalbá. The World-Tree had a sort of cruciform shape and was associated with the color blue-green. In the 16th century, the Franciscan friars required the Indians to venerate the cross; this Christian symbolism meshed easily with established Maya beliefs.

Points of the Compass In Mayan cosmology, each point of the compass had special religious significance. East was most important, as it was where the sun was reborn each day; its color was red. West was black because it was where the sun disappeared. North was white and was the direction from which the all-important rains came, beginning in May. South was yellow because it was the sunniest point of the compass.

Everything in the Mayan world was seen in relation to these cardinal points, with the World-Tree at the center, but the cardinal points were only the starting point for the all-important astronomical and astrological observations that determined fate.

Bloodletting Humans had certain roles to play within this great system. Just as the great cosmic dragon shed its blood, which fell to the earth as rain, so humans had to shed blood to link themselves with Xibalbá.

Bloodletting ceremonies were the most important religious ceremonies, and the blood of kings was seen as the most acceptable for these rituals. Thus when the friars said that the blood of Jesus, the King of the Jews, had been spilled for the common people, the Maya could easily understand the symbolism.

Sacred Places Mayan ceremonies were performed in natural sacred places as well as in their human-made equivalents. Mountains, caves, lakes, cenotes, rivers and fields were all sacred and had special importance in the scheme of things. Pyramids and temples were thought of as stylized mountains; sometimes they had secret chambers within them, like the caves in a mountain. A cave was the mouth of the creature that represented Xibalbá, and to enter it was to enter the spirit of the secret world. This is why some Mayan temples have doorways surrounded by huge masks: as you enter the door of this 'cave,' you are entering the mouth of Xibalbá.

The plazas around which the pyramids were placed symbolized the open fields or the flat land of the tropical forest. What we call stelae were to the Maya 'tree-stones'; that is, sacred tree-effigies echoing the sacredness of the World-Tree. These tree-stones were often carved with the figures of great Mayan kings, for the king was the World-Tree of Mayan society.

As these places were sacred, it made sense for succeeding Mayan kings to build new and ever grander temples directly over older temples, as this enhanced the sacred character of the spot. The temple being covered over was not seen as mere rubble to be exploited as building material, but as a sacred artifact to be preserved. Certain features of these older temples, such as the large masks on the facades, were carefully padded and protected before the new construction was placed over them.

Ancestor worship and genealogy were very important to the Maya, and when they buried a king beneath a pyramid, or a commoner beneath the floor or courtyard of his or her *na*, the sacredness of the location was increased.

The Mayan 'Bible' Of the painted books destroyed by Friar Diego de Landa and other Franciscans, no doubt some of them were books of sacred legends and stories similar to the Bible. Such sacred histories and legends provide a worldview to believers and guide them in belief and daily action.

One such Mayan book, the *Popol Vuh*, survived not as a painted book but as a transcription into the Latin alphabet of a Mayan narrative text. In other words, it was written in Quiché Maya, but in Latin characters, not hieroglyphs. The *Popol Vuh* was apparently written by Quiché Maya Indians of Guatemala who had learned Spanish and the Latin alphabet from the Dominican friars. The authors showed their book to Francisco Ximénez, a Dominican who lived and worked in Chichicastenango, in Guatemala, from 1701 to 1703. Friar Ximénez copied the Indians' book word for word, and then

translated it into Spanish. Both his copy and the Spanish translation survive, but the Indian original has been lost.

According to the *Popol Vuh,* the great god K'ucumatz created humankind first from mud. But these 'earthlings' were weak and dissolved in water, so K'ucumatz tried again using wood. The wood people had no hearts or minds and could not praise their creator, so they were destroyed, all except the monkeys who lived in the forest, who are the descendants of the wood people. The creator tried once again, this time successfully, using substances recommended by four animals – the gray fox, the coyote, the parrot and the crow. White and yellow corn was ground into meal to form the flesh, and stirred into water to make the blood.

The *Popol Vuh* legends include some elements that made it easier for the Maya to understand certain aspects of Christian belief, including virgin birth and sacrificial death followed by a return to life.

Animism & Catholicism The ceiba tree's cruciform shape was not the only correspondence the Maya found between their animist beliefs and Christianity. Both traditional Mayan animism and Catholicism have rites of baptism and confession, days of fasting and other forms of abstinence, religious partaking of alcoholic beverages, burning of incense and the use of altars.

Contemporary Yucatecans

Today's Maya identify themselves as Catholic but they practice a Catholicism that is a fusion of shamanist-animist and Christian ritual. The traditional religious ways are so important that often a Maya will try to recover from a malady by seeking the advice of a religious shaman rather than a medical doctor. Use of folk remedies linked with animist tradition is widespread in Mayan areas.

Roman Catholicism accounts for the religious orientation of 85% of contemporary Yucatecans, while 12% of the Yucatán's population identify themselves as Protestants or evangelicals. Congregations affiliated with churches such as the Assemblies of God, the Seventh Day Adventists, the Church of Jesus Christ of Latter Day Saints, and Jehovah's Witnesses can also be found in the Yucatán.

Facts for the Visitor

HIGHLIGHTS
Ancient Mayan Cities

Mayan architecture was spectacular, containing thousands upon thousands of fanciful glyphs carved into altars, stelae and temples that narrated tales of the ruling dynasties. The Maya constructed with clarity of purpose, and the exact positioning of each major building served a specific function. For example, El Palacio del Gobernador (The Governor's Palace) at Uxmal, in central Yucatán state, was oriented in such a way that from the central doorway astronomers could observe Venus on the horizon as it rose across the sky to the tip of a pyramid situated several kilometers away. In another example, at the Yucatán's most famous and best-restored site, Chichén Itzá, the finely worked El Castillo pyramid features four stairways, each consisting of 91 steps. The sum of all four stairways, plus the continuous step around the top of each pyramid, totals 365 – the number of days in the solar calendar.

Anyone who leaves the Yucatán without seeing at least one ancient Mayan city is making a mistake. Among the most spectacular Mayan ruins on the peninsula are the abandoned cities of Chichén Itzá and Uxmal in Yucatán state; Cobá, Kohunlich and Dzibanché in the state of Quintana Roo; and Edzná and Calakmul in Campeche state. Most visitors hit Tulum in Quintana Roo as well, for its unique seaside setting. If time permits, visiting the lesser ancient sites along the Ruta Puuc in Yucatán state and the numerous sites along Hwy 186 between Escárcega and Xpujil in Campeche state will greatly add to your appreciation of the great Mayan people of time past.

Natural Attractions

The Yucatán's landscape, though much of it is flat, holds wonders at every turn. Just passing through in a vehicle you can see all sorts of exotica. Trees bear nests ranging from the huge mud constructions of termites to the delicate, dangling homes of orioles and oropendolas (similar to those of African weaver birds), as well as a host of epiphytic and parasitic plants (orchids, cacti and bromeliads). Any number of creatures

fly across the road, including the aforementioned orioles with their stunning yellow-and-black plumage, as well as gnatcatchers, flycatchers, hummingbirds, kingfishers and butterflies. Or they run across, like the basilisk lizard, which when hurried stands upright and sprints on its back legs. It can run across water this way also, earning it the nickname 'the Jesus Christ lizard.'

You're not likely to see a jaguar or other big cat from the bus, unless it's been run over, but it's nice to know they're out there. The comical long-nosed coati is a frequent, if hurried, road-crosser.

Getting out of the car and into a boat you can see a lot more, both above and below the surface. Many of the more than 530 bird species found on the peninsula are migratory waterfowl. Others stay put, such as the red flamingos in the Celestún and Río Lagartos biosphere reserves, both in Yucatán state. These reserves hold vast quantities of other avian fauna as well, and you can find flamingos in other spots along the peninsula's northern coast.

The Yucatán's Caribbean coast is flanked by the longest barrier reef in the Western Hemisphere. It starts near Honduras, and its corals shelter marine life of every size, shape and color. The snorkeling and diving are top-notch here.

Colonial Cities

Valladolid, Izamal and the many small towns with huge old monasteries scattered around Yucatán state deserve a mention here, but let's focus on the big ones; the top two.

Mérida This is a fascinating city to visit for a variety of reasons. Its cathedral is the oldest mainland cathedral in North America (only Santo Domingo's, in the Dominican Republic, is older). The cathedral faces Mérida's main square, around which are situated several splendid buildings, including the 1549 Casa de Montejo (House of Montejo) famous for its plateresque facade. Both colonial and grand 19th-century homes, and remnants of the city's original walls and gates, distinguish the capital of Yucatán state as well.

Mérida is also the peninsula's cultural center, priding itself on its traditions, such as the dances the city's residents have performed for generations, many of which are still done by men and women dressed in traditional Yucatecan attire. There's something on every night of the week – theater, concerts, film, music and more – and much of it doesn't cost a centavo.

Campeche The lovely walled city of Campeche, like Mérida a Unesco World Heritage site, has a long and sometimes violent history of conquistadors, pirates and viceroys. It too has a lovely cathedral, and the beautifully preserved and restored colonial center is a joy to stroll, as is the wide waterfront sidewalk. Sunsets in the center and on the waterfront are heartbreakingly beautiful.

The city has been putting on ever more performances for tourists and residents, as if in competition with Mérida; concerts, dance performances and other events are held most nights of the week.

Campeche is flanked at north and south by two perfectly preserved colonial forts. The southern one contains a museum with some fantastic Mayan pieces, including ceramics and the star attractions, jade burial masks excavated from the ruins of Calakmul.

Beach Resorts
Cancún Not to mention Cancún as a highlight of the Yucatán – granted, a very commercial one – would be to do it an injustice. Cancún is one of the world's top tropical playpens, and serves some as a good base from which to make day trips to the peninsula's top tourist attractions – of the natural and ancient-city varieties. The most expensive city in Mexico, Cancún offers lots of meal options and a rowdy nightlife thronging with teens and twentysomethings. Its exclusive resorts offer the older crowd some lovely sand, sun and surf, and the option of never going beyond the hotel's confines.

Playa del Carmen & Cozumel The majority of visitors to the Yucatán who aren't hanging out in Cancún are hanging out in Playa del Carmen or Cozumel – much smaller and less commercial versions of Cancún – soaking up the sun, sipping piña coladas and listening to beach music.

The beach–bar–disco scenes of Playa del Carmen and Cozumel aren't nearly as wild as the beach–bar–disco scenes of Cancún's Zona Hotelera, and that's one of the main reasons these two destinations appeal to so many people. Visitors here have many of the same options that they have in Cancún, the same luxury and excess, without feeling like they're part of a herd. (Few of Playa's hotels, for example, have more than 50 guest rooms.)

The island of Cozumel, separated only by a brief ferry ride from Playa del Carmen, also offers some world-class snorkeling and diving options.

PLANNING
When to Go
This depends in part on what you're going for. The dry season (November through April) is generally preferred for travel in the Yucatán, with November and early December perhaps the best times, as there are fewer tourists and prices are relatively low then. The busy winter tourism season runs from mid-December through March, and it's then that most room rates are at their highest; on and near Christmas, New Year's and Easter, expect to pay substantially more for rooms at many places.

May and June are the hottest and muggiest months. July and August are hot, not too rainy and busy with the US and European summer travel crowd. September and October are pretty good for travel, as the traffic decreases markedly and so do the rains. They're prime hurricane months, but don't let that keep you away.

The occasional spells of cool weather brought by the *nortes* (relatively cold storms bringing wind and rain from the north) in November through February or March make for the most pleasant ruins exploration, and go a long way toward making the city of Mérida more enjoyable as well. At the same time, the *nortes* decrease the number of good beach, snorkeling and flamingo-watching days.

Lonely Planet's *Read This First: Central & South America* is an invaluable predeparture guide that will help travelers new to the region hit the road with confidence.

Maps
A host of free city and regional maps are given away by tourist offices and contained

in promotional publications. Some are quite well done, some deplorable.

High-quality Yucatán Peninsula maps include the **ITMB** (W *www.itmb.com*) 1:1,000,000-scale *Yucatán Peninsula Travel Map*, in its 7th edition in 2003. It's easy to read and very detailed. The **Guía Roji** (W *www.guiaroji.com.mx*) 1:1,000,000-scale *Maya World* shows all of the peninsula and parts of Tabasco and Chiapas but isn't nearly as detailed as the ITMB map. Both maps are updated every couple of years.

Guia Roji also publishes an annual national road atlas called *Carreteras de México* that's widely available in Mexico, very detailed and in some ways easier to use (though considerably more expensive) than the ITMB map because it opens like a magazine.

Riviera Maya, *Cancún*, *Cozumel* and *Playa del Carmen*, four foldout maps published by the American couple behind **Can-Do Maps** (W *www.cancunmap.com*), are extremely well done and are updated annually. In addition to containing multiple insert maps, they also have dozens of color photos, many site-specific reviews and a very useful index for restaurants, hotels and attractions.

What to Bring

Anything you are likely to need on the Yucatán Peninsula you can probably buy there, some of it even more cheaply than you can back home. Toiletries such as shampoo, shaving cream, razors, soap and toothpaste are readily available throughout the Yucatán in all but the smallest villages.

You should bring your own contact lens solution, tampons, contraceptives, sunscreen and insect repellent – they are available in Mexico, but not always readily so, or in the brands you know, and sunscreen

tends to be pricey. Most of the 'ecoparks' on the Mayan Riviera don't allow visitors to bring in nonbiodegradable sunscreen, so if you're planning to visit one, bring your own or be prepared to buy some from them.

Other items you might find useful are a flashlight (torch) for exploring caves, pyramids and your hotel room when the electricity fails, a pocket knife, snorkeling or diving equipment, fishing equipment, a small sewing kit, a money belt or pouch that you can wear under your clothes, a small padlock and lip balm. If your Spanish is minimal, a small bilingual Spanish and whatever-you-speak dictionary isn't a bad idea.

Lightweight clothing made from synthetic fiber that dries quickly is best in the hot, humid Yucatán. You'll need a light sweater or heavy shirt to keep warm during air-conditioned bus rides or on cool, windy evenings in the *norte* season. A light rain jacket can sometimes come in handy from October to May and is a necessity from May to October. Sport sandals of the type developed for river rafting are an excellent item to bring; they can be worn at the beach, and while climbing pyramids or snorkeling cenotes.

For carrying it all, a backpack is most convenient if you'll be doing much traveling on foot. You can make it reasonably theft-proof with small padlocks. A light day-pack, too, is useful, as is something that can hold a water bottle.

RESPONSIBLE TOURISM

Many souvenirs sold in the region are made from endangered plants and animals that have been acquired illegally. By purchasing these items you aid in their extinction. Avoid purchasing any items made from turtle shell or coral. The sale and purchase of jaguar teeth and pelts is not only illegal, it's ethically criminal. Same goes for crocodile, ocelot and margay skins. Orchids are endemic and are also protected by domestic and international law; view but don't pick.

Don't carry off anything that you pick up at the site of an ancient city or out on a coral reef. And please be careful what you touch and where you place your feet when you're snorkeling and scuba diving; not only can coral cut you, but it's extremely fragile and takes years to grow even a finger's length. See the boxed text 'Considerations for Responsible Diving' later in this chapter.

Finding Your Way

Mexican street naming and numbering can be confusing. Many addresses do not have a street number; this is indicated by 's/n' (*sin número*, meaning 'without number'). When asking directions, it's better to ask for a specific place, such as the Hotel Central or the Museo Regional, than for the street it's on. To achieve a degree of certainty, ask three people.

Most of the Yucatán Peninsula has limited water reserves, and in times of drought the situation can become grave. Additionally, wastewater-treatment facilities (where they exist) can't always keep up with the strain placed on them by local residents, let alone tourists. Contamination of groundwater is becoming a serious problem.

Please do your part by keeping water use down, especially in areas that have signs requesting you to do so. Limit the length of your showers and the number of toilet flushes. And as mom always said, don't run the water while you're brushing your teeth or shaving!

TOURIST OFFICES
Local Tourist Offices
There are tourist offices in many of the Yucatán's cities, and many are staffed by friendly people, some of whom speak English or other foreign languages, but the information they provide is not always accurate. Schedules, prices, addresses and telephone numbers change so frequently in Mexico that even the most conscientious tourist office has trouble keeping up. Maps and brochures are sometimes the best you can hope for, and even they are in short supply at times.

You can call the Mexico City office of the national tourism ministry **Sectur** (☎ 800-903-9200) at any time – 24 hours a day, seven days a week – for information or help in English or Spanish.

Tourist Offices Abroad
In the USA and Canada you can call ☎ 800-482-9832 for Mexican tourist information. You can also contact a Mexican Government Tourism Office at the following locations worldwide:

Canada
Montreal: (☎ 514-871-1052) 1 Place Ville Marie, Suite 1931, QC H3B 2C3
Toronto: (☎ 416-925-0704, ext 22 or 23) 2 Bloor St West, Suite 1502, ON M4W 3E2
Vancouver: (☎ 604-669-2845) 999 West Hastings St, Suite 1110, BC V6C 2W2
France (☎ 01-42-86-96-12) 4 rue Notre Dame des Victoires, 75002 Paris
Germany (☎ 069-253-509) Taunusanlage 21, 60325 Frankfurt-am-Main
Italy (☎ 06-487-4698) Via Barberini 3, 00187 Rome
Spain (☎ 91-561-18-27) Calle Velázquez 126, Madrid 28006

UK (☎ 020-7488-9392) 41 Trinity Square, Wakefield House, London EC3N 4DJ
USA
Chicago: (☎ 312-606-9252) 300 North Michigan Ave, 4th Floor, IL 60601
Houston: (☎ 713-772-2581) 4507 San Jacinto, Suite 308, TX 77004
Los Angeles: (☎ 213-351-2075) 2401 W 6th St, 5th Floor, CA 90057
Miami: (☎ 305-718-4095) 1200 NW 78th Ave, No 203, FL 33126
New York: (☎ 212-821-0314) 21 East 63rd St, NY 10021

VISAS & DOCUMENTS
Visitors to Mexico should have a valid passport. Visitors of some nationalities have to obtain visas, but others (when visiting as tourists) require only the easily obtained Mexican government tourist card. Because the regulations sometimes change, it's wise to confirm them at a Mexican Government Tourism Office or Mexican embassy or consulate before you go. Several Mexican embassies and consulates, and foreign embassies in Mexico, have websites with useful information on tourist permits, visas and so on (see Embassies & Consulates later in this chapter), but they don't all agree with each other, so you should back up any Internet findings with some phone calls.

Travelers under 18 who are not accompanied by both parents may need special documentation (see Minors later in this section).

Passport
Though it's not recommended, US tourists can enter Mexico without a passport if they have official photo identification, such as a driver's license, plus some proof of their citizenship, such as a birth certificate certified by the issuing agency or a naturalization certificate (not a copy). Citizens of other countries who are permanent residents in the USA need their passports and permanent resident alien cards.

Canadian tourists may enter Mexico with official photo identification plus proof of citizenship, such as a birth certificate or notarized affidavit of it. Naturalized Canadian citizens, however, require a valid passport.

It is much better to have a passport, because officials are used to passports and may delay people who have other documents. This applies to officials at reentry points to the USA or Canada as well as to Mexico. In Mexico you will often need your passport when you change money.

Citizens of other countries should have a passport valid for at least six months after they arrive in Mexico.

Visas

Citizens of the USA, Canada, the EU countries, Australia, New Zealand, Argentina, Brazil, Chile, the Czech Republic, Hungary, Iceland, Israel, Japan, Norway, Poland, Singapore, Switzerland and Uruguay are among those who do not require visas to enter Mexico as tourists. The list changes from time to time; check well ahead of travel with your local Mexican embassy or consulate. Visa procedures, for those who need them, can sometimes take several weeks.

All tourists must obtain a Mexican government tourist card (see Travel Permits). Non-US citizens passing through the USA on the way to or from Mexico, or visiting Mexico from the USA, should check their US visa requirements.

Travel Permits

The Mexican tourist card – officially the Forma Migratoria para Turista (FMT) – is a brief card document that you must fill out and get stamped by Mexican immigration when you enter Mexico and must keep till you leave. It's available free of charge at official border crossings, international airports and ports, and often from airlines, travel agencies, Mexican consulates and Mexican government tourism offices. At the US–Mexico border you won't usually be given one automatically; you have to ask for it.

At many US–Mexico border crossings you don't *have* to get the card stamped at the border itself, as the Instituto Nacional de Migración (INM; National Immigration Institute) has control points on the highways into the interior where it's also possible to do it; but it's preferable to get it done at the border in case there are difficulties elsewhere.

One section of the card deals with the length of your stay in Mexico, and this section is filled out by the immigration officer. The maximum is 180 days but immigration officers will often put a much lower number (as little as 15 or 30 days in some cases) unless you tell them specifically that you need, say, 90 or 180 days. It's always advisable to ask for more days than you think you'll need, in case you are delayed or change your plans. Ultimately it's down to the whim of the individual immigration officer.

Travelers entering Mexico in Chiapas (from Guatemala) are never given more than 30 days initially, and those coming from Belize may not get more than 15 or 30 days on their tourist cards. You should be able to get an extension once you are deeper inside Mexico (see Extensions & Lost Cards later in this section).

Look after your tourist card, as Mexican law requires you to carry it with you at all times while you're in Mexico and you're asked to hand it in when you leave the country. If you overstay the limit on your card, you may be subject to a fine (normally around US$50 for up to one month).

Persons leaving Mexico need to stop and get their passports stamped at the Mexican Immigration Office just before the bridge. If you don't plan on returning soon, you'll need to turn in your tourist card. If you don't do so, and the immigration system should ever implement the computerization it's been striving for, the Mexican government may conclude later that you've stayed on in the country illegally, and this can cause problems if you return to Mexico, even years later.

If you *are* coming back within the period of time your tourist card gives you to remain in Mexico, tell the immigration officials and hold on to the card. This will save you from having to pay the tourist fee a second time. If the officials bridle, tell them you are traveling the Ruta Maya (Maya Route). Lonely Planet has received reports from travelers who say they were charged M$100 by Mexican immigration authorities for the privilege of keeping their tourist cards. They also reported being told that if they kept their cards and didn't pay, they'd have to pay a new DNI fee on return. There should be no charge to keep your tourist card.

Tourist Fee Foreign tourists and business travelers visiting Mexico are all charged a fee of about US$20 called the Derecho para No Inmigrante (DNI; Nonimmigrant Fee). The exact amount changes each year.

If you enter Mexico by air, the fee is included in the price of your air ticket. If you enter by land you must pay it at a branch of any of the Mexican banks listed on the back of your tourist card, at any time before you reenter the frontier zone on your way out of Mexico (or before you check in at an airport to fly out of Mexico). It makes sense to get the job done as soon as possible, and at least some Mexican border posts have bank offices where you can do so.

When you pay at a bank, your tourist card or business visitor card will be stamped to prove that you have paid.

Tourists only have to pay the fee once in any 180-day period. You are entitled to leave and reenter Mexico as many times as you like within 180 days without paying again. A similar multientry rule applies to business travelers, but their limit is 30 days. If you are going to return within the stipulated period, retain your card when you leave Mexico, though this may be difficult when you're flying out.

Extensions & Lost Cards If the number of days given on your tourist card is for some reason less than the 180-day maximum, its validity may be extended one or more times, at no cost, up to the maximum. To get a card extended you have to apply to the INM, which has offices in many towns and cities. The procedure costs around US$20 and should take between half an hour and three hours, depending on the cooperation of each particular immigration office. You'll need your passport, your tourist card, photocopies of the important pages of these documents, and, at some offices, evidence of 'sufficient funds.' A major credit card is usually OK for the latter, or an amount in traveler's checks anywhere from US$100 to US$1000 depending on the office.

Most INM offices will not extend a card until a few days before it is due to expire; don't bother trying earlier.

If you lose your card or need further information, contact the Mexico City office of the national tourism ministry, **Sectur** (☎ 55-5250-0123, 800-903-9200) or your embassy or consulate. Your embassy or consulate may be able to give you a letter enabling you to leave Mexico without your card, or at least an official note to take to your local INM office, which will have to issue a duplicate.

Minors

To prevent international child abduction, minors (people under 18) entering Mexico without both of their parents may be, and often are, required to show a notarized consent form, signed by the absent parent or parents, giving permission for the young traveler to enter Mexico. A form for this purpose is available from Mexican consulates. In the case of divorced parents, a custody document may be acceptable instead. If one or both parents are dead, or the traveler has only one legal parent, a notarized statement saying so may be required.

These rules are aimed primarily at visitors from the USA and Canada but may also apply to people from elsewhere. Procedures vary from country to country; contact a Mexican consulate to find out exactly what you need to do.

Travel Insurance

A travel insurance policy to cover theft, loss and medical problems is a good idea. It's also a good idea to buy insurance as early as possible. If you buy it the week before you fly, you may find, for example, that you're not covered for delays to your flight caused by strikes.

Mexican medical treatment is generally inexpensive for common diseases and minor treatment, but if you suffer some serious medical problem, you may want to find a private hospital or fly out for treatment. Travel insurance can typically cover the costs. Some US health insurance policies stay in effect (at least for a limited time) if you travel abroad, but it's worth checking exactly what you'll be covered for in Mexico. For people whose medical insurance or national health systems don't extend to Mexico – which includes most non-Americans – a travel policy is advisable.

You may prefer a policy that pays doctors or hospitals directly rather than requiring you to pay on the spot and claim later. If you have to claim later, make sure you keep all documentation. Some policies ask you to call collect to a center in your home country, where an immediate assessment of your problem is made. Check that the policy covers ambulances or an emergency flight home.

Some policies offer lower and higher medical-expense options; the higher ones are chiefly for countries such as the USA, which have extremely high medical costs. There is a wide variety of policies available, so check the small print.

Some policies specifically exclude 'dangerous activities,' which can include scuba diving, motorcycling and even trekking. A locally acquired motorcycle license is not valid under some policies.

Driver's License & Permits

If you're thinking of driving in Mexico, take your driver's license and a major credit card with you. For more information on car rentals, see the Getting Around chapter. For information on the paperwork involved in taking your own vehicle into Mexico, see the Getting There & Away chapter.

Note that international driving permits generally are not considered valid driver's licenses by Mexican authorities.

Hostel, Student & Teacher Cards

The International Student Identification Card (ISIC), the GO25 card for any traveler aged 12 to 25, and the international student travel confederation (ITIC) card for teachers can help you obtain reduced-price air tickets to or from Mexico at student- and youth-oriented travel agencies. In Mexico, reduced prices for students at museums, archaeological sites and so on are usually only for those with Mexican education credentials, but in practice the ISIC card will sometimes get you a reduction. It may also get you discounts on some bus tickets, and it, or the Hostelling International (HI) card will save you M$10 or so (about US$1) in some hostels in the Yucatán. The ITIC can get you the same discount; it and the GO25 are less recognized generally, but worth taking along if you have one already.

Copies

All important documents (passport data pages and visa pages, birth certificate, vehicle papers, credit or bank cards, travel insurance papers, air tickets, driver's license, traveler's check receipts or serial numbers etc) should be copied before you leave home. Leave one copy with someone at home and keep another copy with you, separate from the originals. When you get to Mexico, be sure to add a photocopy of your tourist permit and, if you're driving, vehicle import papers.

EMBASSIES & CONSULATES
Mexican Embassies & Consulates

Unless otherwise noted, details are for embassies or their consular sections. Updated details can be found at W www.sre.gob.mx, which also has links to the embassies' and consulates' own websites. Some of these sites, such as those of the Mexican consulates in New York and San Diego and the Mexican embassy in London, are useful sources of information on visas and related matters.

Mexico has consulates in many US cities, particularly in the border states. The webpage W www.mexonline.com/consulate .htm has links to some of the following, and lists many more.

Countries with Mexican embassies and consulates include:

Argentina (☎ 4789-8800, W www.embamex .int.ar) Arcos 1650, Belgrano, 1426 Buenos Aires

Australia (☎ 02-6273-3963, W www.embassyof mexicoinaustralia.org) 14 Perth Ave, Yarralumla, Canberra, ACT 2600

Belize (☎ 223-0193, W www.embamexbelize .gob.mx) 18 North Park St, Fort George Area, Belize City

Brazil (☎ 061-244-1011, W www.mexico.org .br) SES Av das Nacoes Lote 18, 70412-900 Brasilia

Canada (☎ 613-233-9917/9272, W www.em bamexcan.com) 45 O'Connor St, Suite 1500, Ottawa, ON K1P 1A4

France (☎ 01-53-70-27-70, W www.sre.gob.mx /francia) 9 rue de Longchamp, 75116 Paris *Consulate:* (☎ 01-42-86-56-20) 4 rue Notre Dame des Victoires, 75002 Paris

Germany (☎ 030-269-3230, W www.emba mex.de) Klingelhoferstrasse 3, 10785 Berlin

Guatemala (☎ 333-7254, W www.sre.gob.mx /guatemala) Edificio Centro Ejecutivo, 15a Calle No 3–20, Nivel 7, Zona 10, Guatemala City *Consulate:* (☎ 339-1009) Edificio Plaza Corporativa Reforma, Av Reforma 6–64, Zona 9, Torre Jardín 3rd Floor, Oficinas J-300 y J-2, Guatemala City

Ireland (☎ 01-260-0699) 43 Ailesbury Rd, Ballsbridge, Dublin 4

Italy (☎ 06-441151, W www.target.it/messico) Via Lazzaro Spallanzani 16, 00161 Rome

Japan (☎ 03-3580-2962, W www.embassy -avenue.jp/mexico) 2-15-1 Nagata-Cho, Chiyoda-Ku, Tokyo 100-0014

Netherlands (☎ 070-360-2900, W www.emba mex-nl.com) Burgemeester Patijnlaan 1930, 2585CB The Hague

New Zealand (☎ 04-472-0555, W www.mexico
.org.nz) 111–115 Customhouse Quay, 8th
Floor, Wellington
Spain (☎ 91-369-2814, W www.sre.gob.mx
/espana) Carrera de San Jerónimo 46, 28014
Madrid
UK (☎ 020-7235-6393, W www.mexicancon
sulate.org.uk) 8 Halkin St, London SW1X 7DW
USA (☎ 202-728-1600, W www.sre.gob.mx/eua)
1911 Pennsylvania Ave NW, Washington,
DC 20006
Consulate in Washington DC: (☎ 202-736-
1000) 2827 16th St NW, Washington,
DC 20009
Consulate in Atlanta: (☎ 404-266-2233)
Consulate in Boston: (☎ 617-426-4181)
Consulate in Chicago: (☎ 312-855-1380)
Consulate in Dallas: (☎ 214-252-9250)
Consulate in Los Angeles: (☎ 213-351-6800)
Consulate in Miami: (☎ 786-268-4900)
Consulate in New York: (☎ 212-217-6400)
Consulate in Philadelphia: (☎ 215-922-3834)
Consulate in Phoenix: (☎ 602-242-7398)
Consulate in San Francisco: (☎ 415-782-9555)
Consulate in Seattle: (☎ 206-448-3526)

Embassies & Consulates in Mexico

All embassies are in Mexico City, but many
countries also have consulates in other
cities around Mexico, including a number
on the Yucatán Peninsula. Cancún is home
to numerous foreign consulates, and several countries have diplomatic outposts in
Mérida as well. Embassies and consulates
often keep limited business hours (typically
from around 9am or 10am to 1pm or 2pm
Monday to Friday) and usually close on
both Mexican and their own national holidays. But many embassies provide 24-hour
emergency telephone contact.

Many Mexican and foreign embassies
and consulates have websites. Links to
many of them can be found on the Emba-
jadas page at W www.mexico.web.com. For
a comprehensive list of foreign embassies in
Mexico City visit W www.allaboutmexico
city.com/embassies.htm.

It's important to realize what your own
embassy – the embassy of the country of
which you are a citizen – can and can't do
to help you if you get into trouble. Generally speaking, it won't be much help in
emergencies if the trouble you're in is re-
motely your own fault. Remember that you
are bound by the laws of the country you
are in. Your embassy will not be sympa-

thetic if you end up in jail after committing
a crime locally, even if such actions are
legal in your own country.

In genuine emergencies, you might get
some assistance, but only if other channels
have been exhausted. If you need to get
home urgently, a free ticket home is ex-
ceedingly unlikely – the embassy would expect you to have insurance. If all of your
money and documents are stolen, the embassy might assist you with getting a new
passport, but a loan for onward travel is out
of the question.

Embassy addresses in the selective list
that follows include the *colonias* (neighborhoods) of Mexico City in which they are located and any metro stations convenient to
them. If you're visiting your embassy, it's
best to call ahead to check hours and confirm that the address you're heading for is
the right one for the service you want. All
telephone numbers given include area
codes.

Australia
Embassy: (☎ 55-5531-5225, W www.mexico
.embassy.gov.au) Rubén Darío 55, Polanco;
metro Polanco or Auditorio
Belize
Embassy: (☎ 55-5520-1274) Bernardo de
Gálvez 215, Lomas de Chapultepec
Consulate in Cancún: (☎ 998-887-8631) Av
Náder 34, 1st floor (enter via Lima)
Consulate in Chetumal: (☎ 983-832-1803)
Armada de México 91
Canada
Embassy: (☎ 55-5724-7900, W www.dfait
-maeci.gc.ca/mexico-city) Schiller 529,
Polanco; 400m north of the Museo Nacional
de Antropología; metro Polanco
Consulate in Cancún: (☎ 998-883-3360) Plaza
Caracol II No 330, Zona Hotelera
France
Embassy: (☎ 55-5280-9700, W www.francia
.org.mx) Campos Elíseos 339, Polanco; metro
Auditorio
Consulate-General: (☎ 55-9171-9840, W www
.consul-fr.org.mx) Lafontaine 32, Polanco;
open 9am to 1pm Monday to Friday; metro
Auditorio
Consulate in Cancún: (☎ 998-884-7022) Playa
Larga 11, Supermanzana 29, Manzana 10
Consulate in Mérida: (☎ 999-925-2291) Calle
33B No 528
Germany
Embassy: (☎ 55-5283-2200, W www.emba
jada-alemana.org.mx) Lord Byron 737,
Polanco; open 9am to noon Monday to

Friday; metro Polanco
Consulate in Cancún: (☎ 998-884-1898)
Punta Conoco No 36
Guatemala
Embassy: (☎ 55-5540-7520) Av Explanada
1025, Lomas de Chapultepec
Consulate in Cancún: (☎ 998-883-8296) Av
Náder 148
Italy
Embassy: (☎ 55-5596-3655, W www.emb
italia.org.mx) Paseo de las Palmas 1994,
Lomas de Chapultepec
Consulate in Cancún: (☎ 998-884-1261)
Alcatraces No 39
Netherlands
Embassy: (☎ 55-5258-9921) Av Vasco de
Quiroga 3000, 7th floor, Santa Fe
Consulate in Cancún: (☎ 998-886-0134)
Martinair office, international airport
Consulate in Mérida: (☎ 999-924-3122) Calle
64 No 418
New Zealand
Embassy: (☎ 55-5283-9460) Lagrange 103,
10th floor, Los Morales
Spain
Embassy: (☎ 55-5282-2271) Galileo 114,
Polanco; metro Auditorio
Consulate in Cancún: (☎ 998-848-9900)
Edificio Oásis, Blvd Kukulcán (Km 6.5), Zona
Hotelera
Consulate in Mérida: (☎ 999-927-1520, fax
923-0055) Calle 3 No 237, Fraccionamiento
Campestre
UK
Embassy: (☎ 55-5207-8500, W www.emba
jadabritanica.com.mx) Río Lerma 71, Colonia
Cuauhtémoc; north of the Monumento a la
Independencia; open 8:30am to 3:30pm
Monday to Friday; metro Insurgentes
Consular section: (☎ 55-5242-8500) Río
Usumacinta 30, at rear of embassy; open 9am
to 2pm Monday to Friday; metro Insurgentes
Consulate in Cancún: (☎ 998-881-0100) The
Royal Sands, Blvd Kukulcán (Km 13.5), Zona
Hotelera
USA
Embassy: (☎ 55-5080-2000, W www.us
embassy-mexico.gov) Paseo de la Reforma
305 at Río Danubio, Colonia Cuauhtémoc;
open 9am to 2pm and 3pm to 5pm Monday
to Friday; metro Insurgentes
Consulate in Cancún: (☎ 998-883-0272) Plaza
Caracol II, 2nd Floor, No 320-323, Blvd
Kukulcán (Km. 8.5), Zona Hotelera
Consulate in Cozumel: (☎ 987-872-4574),
2nd floor, Villa Mar Mall, Plaza Mayor be-
tween Avs 5 and Melgar
Consulate in Mérida: (☎ 999-925-5011) Paseo
de Montejo 453, at Av Colón

CUSTOMS

The normal routine when you enter Mexico
is to complete a customs declaration form
(which lists duty-free allowances), then
place it in a machine. If the machine shows
a green light, you pass without inspection.
If a red light shows, your baggage will be
searched.

MONEY
Currency

Mexico's currency is the peso, which is divided into 100 centavos. Coins come in denominations of five, 10, 20 and 50 centavos
and one, two, five, 10, 20 and 50 pesos, and
there are notes of 10, 20, 50, 100, 200 and
500 pesos. In a brilliant move, the government has begun producing 20-peso notes
made of polymer plastic.

In Mexico the '$' sign is used to refer to
pesos. Any prices quoted in US dollars will
normally be written as 'US$5,' '$5 Dlls' or
'5 USD' to avoid misunderstanding.

Coins and notes minted between 1993
and 1995 bear the wording 'nuevos pesos'
(new pesos), or the abbreviation 'N$.' They
are worth exactly the same as more recent
coins and notes which simply say 'pesos'
or '$.'

The bulk of prices in this book are given
in pesos, written as M$, but where US dol-
lar amounts are given (some hotels only
quote prices in dollars, as a hedge against
currency fluctuations), US$ is used.

Exchange Rates

At the time this book went to press, the following exchange rates applied:

country	unit		pesos
Australia	A$1	=	M$6.49
Belize	BZ$1	=	M$5.21
Canada	C$1	=	M$7.24
Euro zone	€1	=	M$11.54
Guatemala	Q10	=	M$13.38
Japan	¥100	=	M$8.63
New Zealand	NZ$1	=	M$5.78
UK	£1	=	M$16.52
USA	US$1	=	M$10.27

Exchanging Money

Many travelers find that carrying a combination of credit card, debit card or ATM card
and US dollars (each in a separate place)
works well.

Credit & Debit Cards Major international credit or debit cards, such as Visa, American Express and MasterCard, are accepted for payment by virtually all airlines, car-rental companies and travel agents in Mexico, and by many (but by no means all) hotels, restaurants and shops. You can also use them to obtain cash from ATMs or over the counter at banks. Some credit card providers charge fees on all foreign transactions, usually between 1% and 3%; check your card agreement. Cash advances nearly always incur fees, of course, so withdrawing funds directly from your checking or savings account is more economical.

Traveler's Checks & Cash If you don't have a credit or bank card, you can get by on major-brand traveler's checks in US dollars backed up by some cash dollars, though many find recording the details every time you cash a check (and carrying documentation separately from checks) to be a major hassle. Even if you do have a card, traveler's checks can make a good backup. American Express is a good brand to carry because it's recognized everywhere, which can prevent delays. In Mexico, you can call American Express toll-free at ☎ 800-828-0366.

You should be able to change Canadian dollars and British pounds, in cash or as checks, in main cities, but it might be time-consuming. Cash euros are changeable at a fair number of banks and currency exchanges in tourist centers, and most banks that change them give good rates.

Banks & Casas de Cambio You can exchange money in banks or at *casas de cambio* (exchange houses, often single-window kiosks). Banks go through a more time-consuming procedure than *casas de cambio* and usually have shorter exchange hours (typically 9am to 3pm or 4pm Monday to Friday, but sometimes stopping as early as noon). *Casas de cambio* can easily be found in just about every large or medium-size town and in many smaller ones. They're quick and often open evenings or weekends, but some don't accept traveler's checks.

Exchange rates vary from one bank or *casa de cambio* to another; banks are more likely to offer better rates. Different rates are often posted for *efectivo* (cash) and *documento* or *cheques de viajero* (traveler's checks).

If you have trouble finding a place to change money, particularly on a weekend, you can always try a hotel, though the exchange rate won't be the best.

ATMs You can use major credit cards and some bank cards, such as those on the Cirrus and Plus systems, to withdraw cash pesos from ATMs, which are very common in the Yucatán, and generally the best source of cash. Using a bank card (rather than a credit card) at them can be the most economical means of staying in the money in Mexico. ATMs give you a good exchange rate and you avoid the commission you would pay when changing cash or traveler's checks. Though the number of banks charging fees for foreign withdrawals is increasing, if you shop around at home you'll be able to find one that offers low or no fees.

Mexican banks call their ATMs by a variety of names – usually something like *caja permanente* or *cajero automático*. Each machine displays the cards it will accept. If an ATM refuses to give you money, try another one nearby.

International Transfers Should you need money wired to you in Mexico, an easy and quick, though not cheap, method is the Western Union Dinero en Minutos (Money in Minutes) service. It's offered by Elektra electronics and domestic goods stores (most are open 9am to 9pm daily), by the *telégrafos* (telegraph) offices in many cities, and by some other shops – all are identified by black-and-yellow signs bearing the words 'Western Union' and 'Dinero en Minutos.' Your sender pays the money over at a Western Union branch, along with a fee, and gives the details on who is to receive it and where. When you pick it up, take along photo identification. You can expect the exchange rate used to be well in Western Union's favor. **Western Union** *(in Mexico ☎ 800-12-1313, in USA ☎ 800-325-6000;* Ⓦ *www.western union.com)* has offices worldwide.

Security

Whenever you exchange money, always take the time to count it – and count it right there at the counter. In any transaction it's good to keep a running total in your head. When paying for something, wait until all of the change has been counted out before picking it up or heading off. A favorite ruse of dishonest clerks (in particular ticket-sellers) is to hand over the change *very* slowly, a note or coin at a time, in the hope that you'll pick it up and go before you have it all.

You can spread your risk around by carrying some of your funds on your person during the day (keeping the portion you're not likely to use in a separate spot under your clothing), leaving some in your room in *locked* baggage, and some in the hotel's *caja fuerte* (safe), preferably after counting it in front of the clerk when you hand it in. Some travelers like to divide their funds into several stashes in bags and around the room; be sure your memory is sharp if you use this technique!

To guard against robbery when using ATMs, try to use them during working hours and choose ones that are securely inside a bank building, rather than ones open to the street or enclosed only by glass.

Be wary of attempts at credit card fraud. A cashier may swipe your card twice (once for the transaction and once for nefarious purposes). Keep your card in sight at all times; do not let waiters or others take it away. If you sign an older-style receipt with carbon-paper inserts, ask for the inserts and destroy them after use.

For more tips on safeguarding your money, see Dangers & Annoyances later in this chapter.

Costs

In spite of some price drops in the face of lower occupancy rates, Cancún is the most expensive town in Mexico – far more than Mexico City or even Acapulco. Cozumel comes in at number two, and Playa del Carmen is not far behind; a few exclusive spots along the Caribbean coast (not towns) are even more expensive than Cancún. Small towns such as Ticul and Felipe Carrillo Puerto are much cheaper, and some old, established cities such as Mérida offer a good range of prices and many good values.

In Cancún and Cozumel, a single traveler staying in budget accommodations and eating two meals a day in restaurants should plan to spend between M$200 (staying in a dorm room) and M$500 per day during the low tourist season (April to mid-December). In good economic times, expect to pay up to 30% more during the high season, unless you're hostelling. Playa del Carmen is a bit less.

At most other places on the peninsula a budget traveler can figure on M$150 to M$300 a day for two restaurant meals and a room (the lower end applies if there are hostels and you use them). Add in the other costs of travel (snacks, purified water, soft drinks, admission to archaeological sites, local transportation etc), and you may find yourself spending an additional M$90 to M$130 or so per day.

If there are two or more of you sharing accommodations, costs per person come down considerably. Double rooms are often only a few dollars more than singles, and triples or quadruples are usually only slightly more expensive than doubles.

In the middle range, one person can live well on most of the peninsula for M$450 to M$750 per day in low season. Two people can usually find a clean, modern room with private bathroom and air-con for M$300 to M$450 and have the rest to pay for food, admission fees, transport and incidentals. Lodging costs are more likely to rise in high season in this range than in the budget category, in some instances by as much as 100%.

High-end hotels and resorts run a wide spectrum of prices (and most of them quote them in US dollars), from classy smaller hotels (away from Cancún and the other pricey spots) charging US$70 to US$100 a double to ultraluxe beachside palaces charging upwards of US$400 for a room. The cost of high-end dining ranges in a similar fashion, from two people being able to eat very well on M$400 a day to close to twice that for one person to have one dinner with all the frills.

Possible extra expenses include car rentals and souvenirs; see the Getting Around chapter for information on the cost of car hire.

Tipping & Bargaining

Tipping in the resorts frequented by foreigners (such as Cancún and Cozumel) has risen to US levels of 15%, though in less-expensive restaurants you can still get by with 10%, which is the norm in other areas. If you stay a few days in one place, you should leave up to 10% of your room costs for the people who have kept your room clean (assuming they have), at least M$10 a day. A porter in a mid-range hotel would be happy with M$10 for carrying two bags. Taxi drivers don't expect tips unless they provide some special service, but gas station attendants do (M$2 or so just for pumping gas, up to M$5 if they wash windows and do any checking). Baggers in supermarkets are usually tipped a peso or two.

In markets bargaining is the rule, and you may pay much more than the going rate if you accept the first price quoted. You should also bargain with drivers of unmetered taxis. Hotel room rates are often open to negotiation, especially in the off-season (but don't push it). If you are going to stay more than a night or two, always ask if this gets you a discount.

Taxes

Mexico's Impuesto de Valor Agregado (Value-Added Tax), abbreviated IVA (**ee**-bah), is levied at 15%. By law the tax must be included in most prices quoted to you and should not be added afterward. Signs in shops and notices on restaurant menus often state *'IVA incluido.'* Look carefully before ordering; occasionally they state instead that IVA must be added to the quoted prices; this is more common in pricier places.

Impuesto Sobre Hospedaje (Lodging Tax), abbreviated ISAH (ee-**ess**-e-**ah**-che), is levied on the price of hotel rooms. Each Mexican state sets its own rate, but in most it's 2%.

Some accommodations, especially in the budget range, will not charge you the taxes unless you want a receipt. Generally, though, IVA and ISH are included in quoted prices. In top-end hotels a price may often be given as, say, US$100 *más impuestos* (plus taxes), in which case you must add about 17% to the figure. When in doubt, ask, *'¿Están incluidos los impuestos?'* ('Are taxes included?')

Prices in this book all, to the best of our knowledge, include IVA and ISH, where payable.

Domestic and international airline tickets are subject to departure taxes; see the Getting There & Away and Getting Around chapters. For details of the DNI tourist fee of around US$20, payable by all tourists, see Travel Permits under Visas & Documents earlier in this chapter.

POST & COMMUNICATIONS
Sending Mail

Almost every town in the Yucatán has an *oficina de correos* (post office, also called simply *correo* or *correos*) where you can buy stamps and send or receive mail. Hours have gotten shorter in recent years, but some offices are still open Saturday mornings for stamp sales, and almost all are open from at least 9am to 3pm Monday to Friday.

A reduced-priority airmail letter or postcard weighing up to 20g costs M$8 to the US or Canada, M$8.50 to Europe or South America, and M$9 to Australasia (regular airmail is M$8.50, M$10.50 and M$11.50, respectively). Items weighing between 20g and 50g cost M$12.50, M$13.50 and M$15 reduced, and M$14, M$16.50 and M$19.50 regular.

Delivery times are elastic, and packages in particular sometimes go missing. If you are sending something by airmail, be sure to clearly mark it 'Correo Aéreo.' *Certificado* (certified) service helps ensure delivery and costs an extra M$16. An airmail letter from Mexico to the USA or Canada can take four to 14 days to arrive but often takes longer. Mail to Europe may take between one and three weeks, to Australasia a month or more.

If you're sending a package internationally from Mexico, be prepared to open it for customs inspection; take packing materials with you to the post office.

For assured and speedy delivery, you can use one of the expensive international courier services, such as United Parcel Service (UPS), Federal Express or DHL. Packages up to 1kg cost about US$25 to the US or Canada, and US$36 to Europe.

Receiving Mail

You can receive letters and packages care of a post office if they're addressed as follows (for example):

Jane SMITH (last name in capitals)
Lista de Correos
Cozumel
Quintana Roo 77609 (post code)
MEXICO

When the letter reaches the post office, the name of the addressee is placed on an alphabetical list, which is updated daily. If you can, check the list yourself – it's often pinned on the wall – because the item may be listed under your first name instead of your last. To claim your mail, present your passport or other identification. There's no charge, but many post offices only hold 'Lista' mail for 10 days before returning it to the sender. If you think you're going to pick mail up more than 10 days after it has arrived, have it sent to:

Albert JONES (last name in capitals)
Poste Restante
Correo Central
Campeche
Campeche 24079 (post code)
MEXICO

Poste restante may hold mail for up to a month, but there is no posted list of what has been received. Again, there's no charge for collection.

If you have an American Express card or American Express traveler's checks, you can have mail sent to you care of any of the 50-plus American Express offices located in Mexico. Take along your card or a traveler's check for identification when you collect the mail.

Inbound mail usually takes as long to arrive as outbound mail does, and international packages coming into Mexico may go missing, just like outbound ones.

Telephone

Local calls are cheap, but domestic long-distance and international calls can be very expensive.

There are three main types of places you can place a call from. Cheapest is a public pay phone. A bit more expensive is a *caseta de teléfono* or *caseta telefónica* – a call station, maybe in a shop or restaurant, where an operator connects the call for you and you take it in a booth. The third option is to make the call from your hotel, but many hotels can – and do – charge what they like for this service; it's nearly always cheaper to go elsewhere.

Public Pay Phones These are common in towns and cities: you'll usually find some at airports, bus stations and around the main square. Easily the most common, and most reliable on costs, are those marked with the name of the country's biggest phone company, Telmex. To use a Telmex pay phone

you need a *tarjeta telefónica* or *tarjeta Ladatel* (phone card). These come in denominations of M$30, M$50 or M$100 and they are sold at many kiosks and shops – look for the blue-and-yellow signs reading *'De venta aquí Ladatel.'* As you talk, the display shows you how much credit you have left on the card. Only a few pay phones are still coin-operated.

Beware the misleadingly named 'Savings' service advertised on many Telmex phones. Available for collect calls, credit-card calls and calls with some US calling cards, this service is actually a lot more expensive than a normal call; for example costs can be US$3.50 a minute to the USA, Canada or Europe.

In Cancún, Cozumel, Mérida and a few other cities you'll find phones with signs urging you to charge calls to MasterCard, Visa or American Express. Many of these charge very high rates – as high as US$30 for the first minute, US$8 per minute thereafter.

Casetas de Teléfono *Casetas* cost almost the same as Telmex pay phones, but you don't need a phone card to use them and they eliminate street noise. Many offer the same off-peak discounts as pay phones and private phones. *Casetas* usually have a telephone symbol outside, or signs saying *'teléfono,'* 'Lada' or 'Larga Distancia.'

Prefixes & Codes When dialing a call in Mexico, you need to know what *prefijo* (prefix) and *claves* (country or area codes) to dial before the number.

If you're calling a number in the town or city you're in, simply dial the seven-digit local number (eight digits in Mexico City, Guadalajara and Monterrey).

To call another town or city in Mexico, dial the long-distance prefix ☎ 01, followed by the three-digit area code (two digits for Mexico City, Guadalajara and Monterrey) and then the local number. You'll find area codes listed immediately underneath city and town headings in this book, except in some cases where we've included the area code in front of each number. If calling from one town to another in the same area code, try dialing just the seven-digit number first. If this doesn't work, try dialing ☎ 01 plus the number, or ☎ 01 and the area code and number; the system has a few bugs as of yet.

For international calls, dial the international prefix ☎ 00, followed by the country code, area code and local number. For example, to call the New York City number ☎ 212-987-6543 from Mexico, dial ☎ 00, then the US country code (☎ 1), then the Manhattan area code (☎ 212), then ☎ 987-6543.

Mexicans may present their phone numbers and area codes in all sorts of bizarre arrangements of digits (a consequence of having all their numbers changed once, and all their area codes twice, in the three years from 1999 to 2001); but if you just remember that the area code and the local number always total 10 digits, you shouldn't go far wrong.

To call a number in Mexico from another country, dial your international access code, then the Mexico country code (☎ 52), then the area code and number.

Toll-Free & Operator Numbers   Mexican toll-free numbers – all ☎ 800, usually followed by seven digits – always require the ☎ 01 prefix. You can call them from Telmex pay phones without inserting a telephone card.

Most US and Canadian toll-free numbers are ☎ 800 or ☎ 888 followed by seven digits. Some of these can be reached from Mexico (dial ☎ 00-1 before the ☎ 800), but you may have to pay a charge for the call.

For a Mexican domestic operator, call ☎ 020; for an international operator, call ☎ 090. For Mexican directory information, call ☎ 040.

Costs   The costs per minute from a Telmex pay phone or typical telephone *caseta* are approximately M$0.50 for local calls, M$5 for calls to other places in Mexico or to cellular (mobile) phones, M$10 to the USA, Canada or Central America, and M$22 to the rest of the world. *Caseta* charges are similar except that you'll more likely pay M$0.25 a minute for local calls. Most Telmex calls are cheaper on nights and weekends than the rates given here; see the information stickers in phone booths.

Collect Calls   A *llamada por cobrar* (collect call) can cost the receiving party much more than if *they* call *you,* so it's cheaper for them if you find a phone where you can receive an incoming call, then pay for a quick

call to the other party to ask them to call you back. Be forewarned, collect calls from Mexico can be outrageously expensive. It's a good idea to ask the operator for the per-minute rate before you place your collect call.

If you need to make a collect call, you can do so from pay phones without a card. Call an operator on ☎ 020 for domestic calls, or ☎ 090 for international calls, or use a Home Country Direct service. Mexican international operators can usually speak English.

Some telephone *casetas* and hotels will make collect calls for you, but they usually charge for the service. Others proudly announce that you can place collect calls for free, but then charge exorbitant rates to the receiving party. So take care.

Home Country Direct service, by which you make an international collect call via an operator in the country you're calling, is available to many countries. You can make these calls from pay phones without any card. Mexican international operators may know access numbers for some countries, but it's best to get information from your phone company before you leave for Mexico. The Mexican term for Home Country Direct is País Directo.

Telephone Cards   Lonely Planet's ekno global communication service provides low-cost international calls – for local calls, you're usually better off with a local phone card. Ekno also offers free messaging services, email, travel information and an online travel vault, where you can securely store all your important documents. You can join online at ⓦ www.ekno.lonelyplanet.com, where you will find the local-access numbers for the 24-hour customer-service center. Once you have joined, check the ekno website for the latest access numbers for each country and for updates on new features.

Many North American calling cards can be used for calls from Mexico to the USA or Canada by dialing special access numbers (ask the phone company about these before you leave for Mexico).

If you get an operator who asks for your Visa or MasterCard number instead of your calling card number, or says the service is unavailable, hang up. There have been scams in which calls are rerouted to super-expensive credit-card phone services.

Cellular Phones When calling Mexican cellular (mobile) phones whose numbers start with ☎ 044, you must always dial the area code after the ☎ 044, even if it is a local call. If you're calling from outside the area code and can't connect, try dropping the ☎ 044. Most Mexican cell phones work on the basis of *el que llama paga* (caller pays).

Few cellular phones from the US, Canada, Europe or Australasia will work in Mexico; and if they do, they're likely to be expensive (contact your service provider for coverage information, or visit Ⓦ www.gsmcover age.co.uk). But you can rent Mexican cell phones in the international area at Mexico City airport and at some other large airports.

Fax, Email & Internet Access
Public fax service is offered in many towns in the Yucatán by the public *telégrafos* (telegraph) office or offices of the companies Telecomm and Computel. Also look for *'Fax'* or *'Fax Público'* signs on shops, businesses telephone *casetas*, Internet cafés and in bus stations and airports. Expect to pay around M$10 to M$20 a page to the US or Canada.

Most towns of any size in the Yucatán have Internet cafés. The going rate for an hour of access is around M$15 at most places. To make the @ symbol (*arroba* in Spanish) in an email address, hold down the 'Alt' key and hit the '6' key then the '4' key on the number pad (not at the top of the keyboard; and be sure 'Num Lock' is on). If this doesn't work, ask someone *'¿Cómo se hace arroba?'*

DIGITAL RESOURCES
The World Wide Web is a rich resource for travelers. You can research your trip, hunt down bargain airfares, book hotels, check on weather conditions or chat with locals and other travelers about the best places to visit (or avoid!).

There's no better place to start your web explorations than the **Lonely Planet website** (Ⓦ *www.lonelyplanet.com*). Here you'll find travel news, succinct summaries on traveling to most places on earth, postcards from other travelers and the Thorn Tree bulletin board, where you can ask questions before you go or dispense advice when you get back. The subwwway section links you to the most useful travel resources elsewhere on the web.

There are dozens of websites touting accommodations and tourist-related services in and to the Yucatán. All, of course, were created to sell something, but some have useful information along with their eternally rosy descriptions of destinations.

Ⓦ **www.yucatantoday.com** An online version of *Yucatán Today*, the free monthly magazine covering Yucatán and Campeche states. It has plenty of informative updates and great links, as well as hotel, restaurant and reservation information, and maps.

Ⓦ **www.mexonline.com** Combines news, message/chat centers and a huge variety of other content and links; it covers the whole country but has a Yucatán section

Ⓦ **www.bill-in-tulsa.com** Covers lodging, food, and attractions on the Caribbean coast south of Cancún, from Akumal to Xcalak

Ⓦ **www.campeche.gob.mx** Site of Campeche state; scads of statistical and other sorts of information (almost entirely in Spanish)

Ⓦ **www.quintanaroo.gob.mx** Comparable to Campeche state site

Ⓦ **www.yucatan.gob.mx** Comparable to Campeche state site

Ⓦ **www.travel.state.gov/travel_warnings.html** Travel advisory page of the US State Department; occasionally provides useful information concerning crime issues in various parts of Mexico

See Newspapers & Magazines later in this chapter for more online possibilities.

BOOKS
Most books are published in different editions by different publishers in different countries. As a result, a book might be a hardcover rarity in one country while readily available in paperback in another. Fortunately, bookstores and libraries can search by title or author, so your local bookstore or library is the best place to find out about the availability of the following recommendations.

That said, the titles that are mentioned below can often be found in bookstores in Cancún, Mérida and Cozumel. However, they generally cost substantially more in Mexico than they do in the US, Canada or the UK.

Lonely Planet
Lonely Planet also publishes *Belize, Guatemala & Yucatán,* as well as the standalones *Belize* and *Guatemala*, which are

well worth the cover price if you intend to visit Mayan sites outside the Yucatán Peninsula. In addition to the three Yucatán states covered in this book, *BGY*, also covers the Mexican states of Tabasco and Chiapas. If you intend to travel in Mexico outside the five states covered in *BGY*, you might consider purchasing *Mexico*, which is *the* travel guide to the country. Handy companions for anyone traveling in Mexico are Lonely Planet's *Healthy Travel Central & South America* and *Latin American Spanish phrasebook*. The latter contains practical, up-to-date words and expressions in Latin American Spanish. Lonely Planet's *World Food Mexico* is an intimate, full-color guide to exploring Mexico and its cuisine. It covers every food or drink situation the traveler could encounter and plots the evolution of Mexican cuisine.

Lonely Planet's *Read This First: Central & South America* offers more tips on preparing for a trip to Mexico.

If you are going to be doing some diving and snorkeling, get Lonely Planet's *Diving & Snorkeling: Cozumel* – it has beautiful, full-color underwater shots and detailed accounts of the possible dives and dive outfitters in Cozumel.

Guidebooks & Travelogues

Those with a keen interest in pre-Hispanic sites should acquire *A Guide to Ancient Mexican Ruins* and *A Guide to Ancient Maya Ruins*, both by C Bruce Hunter. Between them, the two books provide maps and details on more than 40 sites.

Incidents of Travel in Central America, Chiapas & Yucatan and *Incidents of Travel in Yucatan*, by John L Stephens, are fascinating accounts of adventure and discovery by the enthusiastic 19th-century amateur archaeologist. The latter book is most always available in Cancún and Mérida bookstores. Both books contain superb illustrations by architect Frederick Catherwood, who accompanied Stephens in 1839 and 1841 as he explored a large part of the Mayan region. The two works have become classics in the literature on ancient Mayan cities.

Aldous Huxley traveled through Mexico, too; *Beyond the Mexique Bay*, first published in 1934, has interesting observations on the Maya. Also interesting, if extremely negative and skewed entirely by the au-

thor's feelings about the anticlerical violence occurring at the time, is Graham Greene's *The Lawless Roads*, chronicling the writer's travels through Chiapas and Tabasco in 1938.

Travelers' Tales Mexico, edited by James O'Reilly & Larry Habegger, is a very readable anthology containing about 50 articles and essays on all sorts of Mexican places and experiences, and it includes a number of compelling articles about Yucatecan adventures. The book makes for excellent in-country reading.

Time Among the Maya: Travels in Belize, Guatemala, and Mexico, by Ronald Wright, is a thoughtful account of numerous journeys made among the descendants of the ancient Maya and will certainly help you to 'feel' Mayan culture as you travel the region.

History & Society

Michael D Coe's *The Maya* traces the history, art and culture of the ancient civilization in a learned and well-illustrated but not overly lengthy text.

Richard & Rosalind Perry present Yucatán history fans with a special treat with their 1988 paperback *Maya Missions: Exploring the Spanish Colonial Churches of Yucatán*. This is one book that's difficult to put down. It tells the spectacular histories of the peninsula's monasteries, many of which were built atop ancient Mayan pyramids. Over the years, the churches came under attack by pirates, by Mayan rebels and by zealous revolutionaries, and the Perrys do a superlative job of recounting these attacks, as well as describing the architectural features unique to each of the missions.

Friar Diego de Landa's book *Yucatán Before and After the Conquest* can be bought in a number of bookstores and shops at archaeological sites in the Yucatán. Landa played a major role in wiping out Mayan culture and civilization, including the burning of Mayan texts. But he also wrote a superb book describing Mayan ceremonial festivals, daily life, history, clothing, human sacrifices, the Spanish conquest and more.

Yet another detailed, first-hand account of Mexico's colonization may be found in the *True History of the Conquest of New Spain*, by one of the conquistadors, Bernal Díaz del Castillo.

Art, Architecture & Crafts

Mask Arts of Mexico, by Ruth D Lechuga & Chloe Sayer, is a finely illustrated work by two experts. Sayer has also written two fascinating books tracing the evolution of crafts from pre-Hispanic times to the present, with dozens of beautiful photos: *Arts & Crafts of Mexico* is a wide-ranging overview, while *Mexican Textiles* is a comprehensive treatment of its absorbing topic, with a wealth of detail about Mexican life.

The Art of Mesoamerica, by Mary Ellen Miller, in the Thames & Hudson World of Art series, is a good survey of pre-Hispanic art and architecture. The most important single book on colonial architecture is George Kubler's *Mexican Architecture of the Sixteenth Century* (1948).

Wildlife & Environment

Tropical Mexico: The Ecotravellers' Wildlife Guide by Les Beletsky is a field guide to wildlife from Oaxaca to the Yucatán Peninsula, with color illustrations of more than 500 creatures.

Defending the Land of the Jaguar (1995), by Lane Simonian, is the detailed but absorbing story of Mexico's long, if weak, tradition of conservation, from pre-Hispanic forest laws to the modern environmental movement.

Dedicated bird-watchers should seek out the Spanish-language *Aves de México,* by Roger Tory Peterson & Edward L Chalif, published by Mexico's Editorial Diana. The English-language version of this book, *A Field Guide to Mexican Birds,* omits pictures of birds that also appear in Peterson's guides to US birds. An alternative is *A Guide to the Birds of Mexico & Northern Central America,* by Steve NG Howell & Sophie Webb.

In 1999, Howell came out with an excellent book, *A Bird-Finding Guide to Mexico,* which breaks down the country by regions and then provides maps and instructions on how to see the most interesting birds within each region. The last chapter, for example, which is devoted to the Yucatán Peninsula, provides readers with 10 superior birding sites on the peninsula, with easy-to-follow directions, user-friendly maps and a list of species to look for at each site.

In her 2002 *Check-List of the Birds of the Yucatán Peninsula,* Barbara MacKinnon identifies some 537 known species of bird on the peninsula and nearby islands. It's pretty much a must-have for serious bird-watchers.

NEWSPAPERS & MAGAZINES
English Language

The respected US newspapers the *Miami Herald* and the *New York Times,* along with *Time* and *Newsweek* magazines, are available in bookstores in Cancún, Cozumel, Playa del Carmen and Mérida; elsewhere in the Yucatán they're difficult or impossible to acquire.

Spanish Language

Mexico's local Spanish-language press is thriving. Even small cities often have two or three newspapers of their own, each with its own political agenda. Many are controlled by political parties and the quality of their reporting cannot be trusted. In addition, many won't report on allegations of corruption or drug trafficking, due to very real threats such stories pose to the journalists who write them.

However, Mérida's *El Diario de Yucatán* (ⓦ http://edicion.yucatan.com.mx) is an excellent newspaper that frequently reports on allegations of drug trafficking and governmental improprieties, despite expensive lawsuits, anonymous death threats and other pressures.

RADIO & TV

There's a broad range of radio programming available in Cancún and a fairly wide selection in Mérida and Campeche. In Chetumal it's possible to pick up several of the English radio stations broadcasting in Belize. Outside these areas there's scarcely a thing on the dial. If you'll be traveling around the peninsula in a rental car, you might want to consider bringing a portable tape/CD/MP3 player with you.

In the cities, better hotels will provide in-room cable TV or satellite TV with a host of Mexican and American programming. Outside of the cities, expect no more than three local stations on your in-room TV. Tube addicts needn't fret; most towns and all of the cities on the peninsula have bars, and they typically are rigged to receive satellite TV. Don't, however, expect the shows to be set to English-language programming unless you're in a very touristy locale.

PHOTOGRAPHY & VIDEO
Film & Equipment
Camera and film processing shops, pharmacies and hotels all sell film. Most types of film are available in larger cities and resorts, though slide film tends to be more rare outside Cancún (where several varieties of Fuji slide film are sold downtown at decent prices), and usually limited to Agfachrome and Kodak's Ektachrome.

Film on sale at low prices may be outdated. If the date on the box is obscured by a price sticker, look under the sticker. Avoid film from sun-exposed shop windows. Print processing *(revelando)* costs under M$2 per photo; it's almost always done in one hour and quality is usually good.

Video cameras and tapes are widely available at photo supply stores in the largest cities and in towns that receive many foreign visitors. Prices are significantly higher than you may be used to in North America or Europe. Videotapes on sale in Mexico (like the rest of the Americas and Japan) nearly all use the NTSC image registration system. This is incompatible with the PAL system common to most of Western Europe and Australia, and the SECAM system used in France.

If your camera breaks down, you'll be able to find a repair shop in most sizable towns, and prices will be agreeably low.

For more information on taking travel photographs, check out Lonely Planet's *Travel Photography*.

Restrictions & Photographing People
It is illegal to take pictures in Mexican airports and of police stations and penal institutions. Use of a tripod at most ruins sites requires a special (expensive) permit obtainable only in Mexico City.

Be forewarned that a fee for use of video cameras is charged at many ruins and other attractions. At most Mayan sites charging an entry fee, you need to pay an extra M$30 at the first site visited, which gives you a slip you can use all day, at as many sites as you can reach.

In general, Yucatecans enjoy having their pictures taken and will be happy to pose for your camera – if you ask. Increasingly, you may be asked to pay for the photo. This is especially true in areas that see heavy tourist traffic.

If local people make any sign of being offended by your desire to photograph them, you should put your camera away and apologize immediately, both out of decency and for your own safety. Also, many police officers and soldiers do not like having their pictures taken.

Airport Security
Avoid sending your film through airport x-ray machines, many of which are much stronger in these days of heightened security. Most security personnel will hand-inspect your film if you ask them to, removing the necessity of having it x-rayed. Don't forget to ask for your camera to be hand-inspected if it has film inside.

TIME
The entire Yucatán Peninsula observes the Hora del Centro, which is the same as US Central Time – GMT minus six hours in winter, and GMT minus five hours during daylight saving. Daylight saving time runs from the first Sunday in April to the last Sunday in October.

For the exact time, dial ☎ 030.

ELECTRICITY
Electrical current in Mexico is the same as in the USA and Canada: 110V, 60Hz. Though most plugs and sockets are the same as in the USA, Mexico actually has three different types of electrical sockets: older ones with two equally sized flat slots, newer ones with two flat slots of differing sizes, and a few with a round hole for a grounding (earth) pin. If your plug doesn't fit the Mexican socket, the best thing to do is get an adapter or change the plug. Mexican electronics stores and many supermarkets have a variety of adapters and extensions that should solve the problem.

WEIGHTS & MEASURES
Mexico uses the metric system. For conversion between metric and US or imperial measures, see the inside back cover of this book.

LAUNDRY
Laundry service is widely available throughout the Yucatán, but it never hurts to pack a small bottle or pouch of detergent so you don't waste time looking for a *lavandería*

(laundry). A 3kg load costs from M$30 to M$45, which typically includes drying and folding.

TOILETS

Public toilets are rare, so take advantage of facilities in places such as hotels, restaurants, bus terminals and museums; a fee of about M$2 is often charged in terminals and sometimes at archaeological sites. It's fairly common for toilets in budget hotels and restaurants to lack seats. If there's a bin near the toilet, put all toilet paper and other refuse in it or risk clogging the drain.

HEALTH
Predeparture Planning
Health Insurance Make sure that you have adequate health insurance. See Travel Insurance under Visas & Documents earlier in this chapter for details.

Immunizations Plan ahead for vaccinations: some of them require more than one injection, while some should not be given together. It's recommended that you seek medical advice at least six weeks before travel.

It's a good idea to be up-to-date on your tetanus, typhoid, polio and diphtheria shots and to check your immunity to measles (catching measles is not a pleasant prospect for an adult; those who had it as children are immune). You should also get vaccinated against hepatitis A (you can combine this with a vaccination against hepatitis B). You'll need a yellow fever certificate to enter Mexico only if you'll be arriving from an infected country.

Medical Information Services For advice on immunizations or other matters, talk to your doctor or an appropriate information service. In the USA, call the **Centers for Disease Control & Prevention's** international travelers' hot line (CDC; ☎ 877-394-8747; Ⓦ www.cdc.gov). In Canada, contact **Health Canada** (☎ 613-957-2991; Ⓦ www.hc-sc.gc.ca). In the UK, you can obtain a printed health brief for any country by calling **Medical Advisory Services for Travellers Abroad** (☎ 0906-8-224100; Ⓦ www.masta.org), whose website is also quite informative. In Australia, contact the **Australian Department of Health & Ageing** (☎ 1800-020-103; Ⓦ www.health.gov.au) or consult a clinic such as the **Travel Doctor TVMC** (Ⓦ www.traveldoctor.com.au), which has locations throughout Australia. The website of the **World Health Organization** (Ⓦ www.who.int) has late-breaking bulletins on health problems around the world and a searchable database of articles on many health topics.

Basic Rules
Food Hygiene and water quality have improved a lot in Mexico in recent years, but if you want to be ultrasafe, follow the advice here. Food can be contaminated with any one of a number of bacteria when it is harvested, shipped, handled, washed or prepared. Make sure the food you eat is freshly cooked and still hot. Steer clear of salads and uncooked vegetables; raw or rare meat, fish and shellfish; and unpasteurized milk and milk products (including cheese). Squeezing lime on salads may help reduce your danger from bacterial dysentery, as may eating lots of raw garlic, but these habits are far from foolproof.

If a place looks clean and well run and the vendor looks clean and healthy, then the food is probably safe. The food in busy restaurants is cooked and eaten quite quickly and is probably not reheated.

Water The number one rule is *be careful* of water, especially of ice. If you don't know for certain that the water is safe, assume the worst. Reputable brands of bottled water or soft drinks are generally fine. Only use water from containers with a serrated seal – not tops or corks. Many Mexican hotels have large bottles of purified water from which you can fill a water bottle or canteen. Unfortunately, the coolers holding these bottles are sometimes never cleaned, and some dispense water laden with green specks. Take care with fruit juice, particularly if water may have been added. Milk should be treated with suspicion, as it might be unpasteurized, though boiled milk is fine if it is kept hygienically. Coffee and tea should also be OK, since the water should have been boiled.

If you plan to travel off the beaten track, consider purchasing a water filter or solution. Tincture of iodine (2%), or water-purification drops or tablets containing tetraglycine hydroperiodide are sold in many pharmacies and sporting-goods stores (which also sell filters) in the US and elsewhere. Follow the directions carefully and remember that too much iodine can be harmful.

In Mexico ask for *gotas* (drops) or *pastillas* (tablets) *para purificar agua* (for purifying water) in pharmacies and supermarkets. For tincture of iodine, four drops per liter or quart of clear water is the recommended dosage; let the treated water stand for 20 to 30 minutes before drinking. Vigorously boiling water for five minutes is another way to purify the water, but at high altitudes water boils at a lower temperature, so germs are less likely to be killed. Boil it for longer in those environments.

Heat You can avoid heat-related problems by drinking lots of fluids and generally not overdoing things. Take time to acclimatize: avoid excessive alcohol intake or strenuous activity when you first arrive. See Heat Exhaustion & Heatstroke later in this section.

Protection against Mosquitoes Some serious tropical diseases are spread by infected mosquitoes. In general, mosquitoes are most bothersome between dusk and dawn and most prevalent in lowland and coastal regions and during the rainy season (May to October). You can discourage them by:

- wearing light-colored clothing, long pants and long-sleeved shirts
- using mosquito repellents containing the com pound DEET (N,N-diethylmetatoluamide) on exposed areas
- avoiding highly scented perfume or aftershave
- making sure your room has properly fitting mosquito screens over the windows
- using a mosquito net (it may be worth taking your own)

Medical Problems & Treatment

As you read the following catalog of potential illnesses, bear in mind that many people have traveled throughout the region staying in the cheapest accommodations and eating every manner of food without getting anything more serious than traveler's diarrhea.

If you come down with a serious illness, be careful to find a competent doctor and don't be afraid to get second opinions. Your embassy or consulate is a good place to turn for referrals. You may want to telephone

your doctor at home for consultation as well. In some cases it may be best to end your trip and fly home for treatment, difficult as this may be.

Heat Exhaustion & Heatstroke In hot regions, exercising excessively or failing to replace lost fluids and electrolytes can result in heat exhaustion, characterized by dizziness, weakness, headaches, nausea and profuse sweating. Salt tablets or rehydration formulas may help, but rest and shade are essential.

Heatstroke is more serious and can be fatal. It results from prolonged, continuous exposure to high temperatures. In this condition the victim sweats very little or not at all and has a high body temperature (39°C to 41°C, or 102°F to 106°F). Where sweating has ceased, the skin becomes flushed and red. Severe, throbbing headaches and lack of coordination will occur. The victim will become delirious or convulse. Hospitalization is essential, but meanwhile get victims out of the sun, remove their clothing, cover them with a wet sheet or towel and fan them continually.

Protect yourself against heat-related diseases by taking special care to drink lots of fluids. If you urinate infrequently and in small amounts, you're not drinking enough fluids. If you feel tired and have a headache, you're not drinking enough fluids. Don't just drink when you're thirsty; make it a habit to drink frequently, whether you're thirsty or not.

Sunburn In the tropics or deserts or at high altitude, you can get sunburned surprisingly quickly, even through cloud cover. Use a sunscreen, a hat, and barrier cream for your nose and lips. Calamine lotion or a commercial after-sun preparation are good for mild sunburn. Protect your eyes with good-quality sunglasses, particularly if you will be near water.

Diarrhea A change of water, food or climate can all cause the runs, but diarrhea caused by contaminated food or water is more serious. Despite precautions, you may still have a mild bout of traveler's diarrhea (TD, known informally among travelers as Montezuma's revenge or *turista*), but a few rushed toilet trips with no other symptoms are not indicative of a serious problem.

Beach life and water sports, Cancún

Night view, Cancún

SCOTT DOGGETT

Dady'O nightclub, Cancún

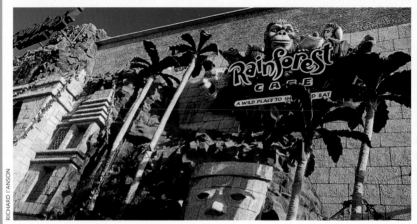

RICHARD I'ANSON

Along Boulevard Kukulcán, Cancún

Moderate diarrhea, involving half a dozen loose movements in a day, is more of a nuisance. Dehydration is the main danger with any diarrhea, particularly for children, in whom it can occur quite quickly, and fluid replacement is the mainstay of management. Good choices include soda water; weak black tea with a little sugar; or soft drinks allowed to go flat and diluted 50% with water.

With severe diarrhea, a rehydrating solution is necessary to replace lost minerals and salts. Commercially available oral rehydration salts are useful; add the contents of one packet to a liter of boiled or bottled water. In an emergency, you can make up a solution of six teaspoons of sugar and a half teaspoon of salt to a liter of boiled or bottled water. Stick to a bland diet as you recover.

Lomotil or Imodium can be used to bring relief from the symptoms, though they do not cure the problem. Use these drugs only if absolutely necessary – for example, if you *must* travel. Do not use them if you have a high fever or are severely dehydrated.

Avoid gut-paralyzing drugs such as Lomotil or Imodium if you have:

- watery diarrhea with blood and mucus
- watery diarrhea with fever and lethargy
- persistent diarrhea for more than five days
- severe diarrhea, if it is logistically difficult to stay in one place

In these situations, antibiotics may be necessary.

You can walk into a pharmacy in Mexico and buy medicines – often without a prescription – that might be banned for good reason in your home country. Well-meaning but ill-informed doctors or pharmacists might recommend certain medicines for gastrointestinal ailments, but such medicines may be worse than no medicine at all. It's best not to take these medicines without consulting a trusted physician, preferably your regular doctor at home.

Diarrhea can also be a sign of giardiasis, dysentery, cholera or typhoid.

Giardiasis The parasite causing this intestinal disorder is present in contaminated water. The symptoms are stomach cramps, nausea, a bloated stomach, frequent gas and watery, foul-smelling diarrhea. Giardiasis can appear several weeks after you have been exposed to the parasite. The symptoms may disappear for a few days and then return; this can go on for several weeks. Tinidazole, known as Fasigyn, or metronidazole (Flagyl) are the recommended treatments.

Dysentery This serious illness is caused by contaminated food or water and is characterized by severe diarrhea, often with blood or mucus in the stool.

Bacillary dysentery is characterized by a high fever and rapid onset of illness; headache, vomiting and stomach pains are also symptoms. It doesn't generally last longer than a week, but is highly contagious.

Amoebic dysentery ('amoebas') is often more gradual in onset, with cramping abdominal pain and vomiting less likely; fever may not be present. It will persist until treated and can recur and cause long-term health problems.

A stool test is necessary to diagnose which kind of dysentery you have, so you should seek medical help urgently. In an emergency, norfloxacin 400mg twice daily for three days or ciprofloxacin 500mg twice daily for five days can be used as presumptive treatment for bacillary dysentery.

For amoebic dysentery, metronidazole (Flagyl) can be used as presumptive treatment in an emergency. An alternative is Fasigyn. Avoid alcohol during treatment and for 48 hours afterward.

Typhoid This fever is a dangerous gut infection caused by contaminated water and food. Medical help must be sought.

In its early stages, sufferers may feel they have a bad cold or flu on the way, as early symptoms are headache, body aches and a fever that rises a little each day until it is around 40°C (104°F) or more. The pulse is often slow relative to the degree of fever present – unlike a normal fever, where the pulse increases. There may also be vomiting, abdominal pain, diarrhea or constipation.

In the second week, the high fever and slow pulse continue and a few pink spots may appear on the body; trembling, delirium, weakness, weight loss and dehydration may occur. Complications such as pneumonia, perforated bowel or meningitis may occur.

The drug of choice is ciprofloxacin at 750mg twice a day for 10 days; it's affordable in Mexico and sold over the counter. Alternatives are chloramphenicol and Ampicillin. Ampicillin has fewer side effects, but people who are allergic to penicillin should not be given it.

Cholera Though not common, this is the worst of the watery diarrheas and medical help should be sought. Outbreaks of cholera are generally widely reported, so you can often avoid problem areas. Fluid replacement is the most vital treatment; the risk of dehydration is severe as you may lose up to 20L a day. If there is a delay in getting to the hospital, then begin taking tetracycline. The adult dose is 250mg four times daily. It is not recommended for children under nine years nor for pregnant women. Tetracycline may help shorten the illness, but adequate fluids are required to save lives.

Hepatitis This is a general term for inflammation of the liver. It is common worldwide. Several different viruses can cause hepatitis, and they differ in the ways they are transmitted. The symptoms are similar in all forms of the illness, and include fever, chills, headache, fatigue, feelings of weakness and aches and pains, followed by loss of appetite, nausea, vomiting, abdominal pain, light-colored feces, dark urine, jaundiced (yellow) skin and yellowing of the whites of the eyes. People who have had hepatitis should avoid alcohol for some time after the illness, as the liver needs time to recover.

Hepatitis A is transmitted by contaminated food and drinking water. You should seek medical advice, but there is not much you can do apart from rest, drink lots of fluids, eat lightly and avoid fatty foods. Hepatitis E is transmitted in the same way as hepatitis A; it can be particularly serious in pregnant women.

Incidence of Hepatitis B is low in Mexico, although it's classed as intermediate in neighboring Guatemala. Hepatitis B is spread through contact with infected blood, blood products or body fluids (for example through sexual contact, unsterilized needles, blood transfusions or contact with blood via small breaks in the skin). Other risk situations include getting a shave, tattoo or body piercing with contaminated equipment. The symptoms of hepatitis B may be more severe than type A and the disease can lead to long-term problems such as chronic liver damage, liver cancer or a long-term carrier state. Hepatitis C and D are spread in the same ways as hepatitis B and can also lead to long-term complications.

There are vaccines against hepatitis A and B, but there are currently no vaccines against the other types of hepatitis. Following the basic rules about food and water (hepatitis A and E) and avoiding risk situations (hepatitis B, C and D) are important preventative measures.

HIV & AIDS Infection with the human immunodeficiency virus (HIV) may lead to acquired immune deficiency syndrome (AIDS), which is a fatal disease. In early 2003 government estimates put the number of AIDS cases in Mexico at around 60,000, and the rate of HIV infection at 0.3% of the general population (or around 300,000, a much lower percentage of the population than in any of Mexico's three neighbors: the USA, Guatemala and Belize).

Any exposure to blood, blood products or body fluids may put the individual at risk. The disease is often transmitted through sexual contact or dirty needles – vaccinations, acupuncture, tattooing and body piercing can be potentially as dangerous as intravenous drug use. HIV/AIDS can also be spread through infected blood transfusions; in developing countries such as Mexico it is possible that blood for a transfusion will not have been screened for HIV. If you do need an injection, ask to see the syringe unwrapped in front of you, or take a needle and syringe pack with you.

Insect-Borne Diseases

Both malaria and dengue are spread by mosquito bites. You can greatly reduce your risk of contracting them by following the antimosquito measures outlined in Protection against Mosquitoes under Basic Rules earlier in this section.

Malaria Most visitors to Mexico do not take antimalarial medicine, and do not get malaria, but there's a small risk of contracting the serious disease in rural areas of Quintana Roo and Campeche (neighboring

Chiapas and Tabasco are among seven other Mexican states where malaria exists).

Symptoms of malaria range from fever, chills and sweating, headache and abdominal pains to a vague feeling of ill-health, so seek examination immediately if there is any suggestion of the disease. It can be diagnosed by a simple blood test and is curable, as long as you seek medical help when symptoms occur. Without treatment malaria can develop more serious, potentially fatal effects.

The CDC lists chloroquine as the drug of choice for travelers in risk areas of the Yucatán and the rest of Mexico. You will usually be told to start taking the medicine one or two weeks *before* you arrive in a malarial area and continue taking it while you're there and for a month after you've left.

Dengue Fever This viral disease is fast becoming one of the top public health problems in the tropical world. An outbreak in the 2002 rainy season hit several coastal Mexican states, with Veracruz reporting more than 1000 cases. All three Yucatán Peninsula states had incidences, the most occurring in Quintana Roo, with close to 300 cases. The highest concentrations were in the southern portion of the state, from Chetumal north to Felipe Carrillo Puerto, though close to 20 cases were in Cancún. About a quarter of the infections were identified as the potentially fatal dengue hemorrhagic fever (DHF), which first appeared in the region in 2001.

Unlike the malaria mosquito, the *Aedes aegypti* mosquito which transmits the dengue virus is most active during the day, and is found mainly in urban areas, in and around human dwellings.

Signs and symptoms of dengue fever include a sudden onset of high fever, headache, joint and muscle pains and nausea and vomiting. A rash of small red spots sometimes appears three to four days after the onset of fever. In the early phase of illness, dengue may be mistaken for other infectious diseases, including malaria and influenza. Minor bleeding such as nose bleeds may occur in the course of the illness, but this does not necessarily mean that you have progressed to DHF, which is characterized by heavy bleeding. Recovery even from simple dengue fever may be prolonged, with tiredness lasting several weeks.

Seek medical attention as soon as possible if you think you may be infected. A blood test can exclude malaria and indicate the possibility of dengue fever. There is no specific treatment for dengue. Aspirin should be avoided, as it increases the risk of hemorrhaging; acetaminophen (paracetamol) can provide some relief. At the time of research, a vaccine against dengue fever was undergoing trials.

Less Common Diseases
The following diseases pose a small risk to travelers, and so are only mentioned in passing. Seek medical advice if you think you may have any of them.

Leishmaniasis This is a group of parasitic diseases transmitted by sand flies – tiny, almost invisible bloodsuckers known in Mexico as *jejenes* or *chaquistes*. Cutaneous leishmaniasis, types of which occur in the Yucatán Peninsula, Belize and Guatemala, affects the skin tissue causing ulceration and disfigurement. Visceral leishmaniasis, which is rare, affects the internal organs. Seek medical advice, as laboratory testing is required for diagnosis and correct treatment. The best precaution is to avoid sand fly bites by covering up, applying repellent and staying indoors during the early-evening biting hours.

Rabies This fatal viral infection occurs throughout Latin America. Many animals can be infected (such as dogs, cats, bats and monkeys). The disease is transmitted through the infected animal's saliva and any bite, scratch or even lick from an animal should be cleaned immediately and thoroughly. Scrub with soap and running water, and then apply alcohol or iodine solution. Medical help should be sought promptly to receive a course of injections to prevent the onset of symptoms and death.

Tetanus This disease is caused by a germ that lives in the soil and in the feces of horses and other animals. It enters the body via breaks in the skin. The first symptom may be discomfort in swallowing, or stiffening of the jaw and neck; this is followed by painful convulsions of the jaw and whole body. The disease can be fatal, but it can be prevented by vaccination.

Cuts, Bites & Stings

Skin punctures can easily become infected in hot climates. Treat any cut with an antiseptic such as Betadine. Avoid bandages and Band-Aids, which can keep wounds wet. If you're stung by a jellyfish, dousing the area in vinegar will deactivate any stingers that have not 'fired'; if you have no vinegar, immediate application of fresh urine can help. Calamine lotion, antihistamines and analgesics may reduce the reaction and relieve the pain.

Africanized ('killer') bees have reached the Yucatán Peninsula from Brazil. It's believed that crushing one releases a scent that sends the rest into a frenzy. If you're stung, don't hit back, but get away as quickly and as far as possible. Bees like to nest inside ruins; have a good look inside before entering any.

Scorpion stings are notoriously painful and can even be fatal. Scorpions may hide in shoes or clothing, so in rural areas shake these out before you put them on. When walking through undergrowth where snakes may be present, wear boots, socks and long trousers. Snake bites do not cause instantaneous death, and antivenins are usually available.

Hospitals & Clinics

Almost every town and city on the peninsula has either a hospital or a clinic, as well as Cruz Roja (Red Cross) emergency facilities (all of which are indicated by road signs showing a red cross). Most major hotels have a doctor available. Hospitals are generally inexpensive for common ailments (dysentery) and minor treatments (cuts and sprains).

Most hospitals have to be paid at the time of service, and doctors usually require immediate cash payment. Some facilities may accept credit cards. It's always a good idea to ask before service is rendered.

SOCIAL GRACES

The people of the Yucatán Peninsula are, by and large, being conquered again. Right and left the best land in the southeast of Mexico is being purchased by foreigners – either people from abroad or people from Mexico City (who are foreigners as far as most Yucatecans are concerned). With few exceptions, the people filling the desirable jobs are not Mayan. The people making infrastructure decisions, generally, are not Mayan. In many ways, the Maya are second-class citizens in their own land.

Yet the Maya remain generally friendly to outsiders. And whereas machismo (exaggerated masculinity) is a problem elsewhere in Mexico, on the Yucatán Peninsula it isn't much of a problem. In general, you'll find that the Yucatecans will treat you as you treat them. If you're friendly, you can expect friendliness in return.

Many Mayan women prefer to avoid contact with foreign men; in their culture, talking with strange men is not something that a virtuous woman does. With this in mind, male travelers in need of directions or information should try to find another man or a child to approach.

As mentioned earlier, photographers should not assume that people like having their picture taken. Before snapping away, seek permission.

Making Contact

No Yucatecan expects an outsider to speak Yucatec (the Mayan language spoken on the peninsula), though attempting a few words can be a real ice-breaker. Spanish *is* the official language of the region, so don't expect Yucatecans to speak English – outside the tourist areas of Cancún, Isla Mujeres, Cozumel and Playa del Carmen, anyway.

Just a few basic Spanish phrases will often do the trick, and all of the important ones can be found in the Language chapter at the end of this book. Please take the time to at least learn how to say 'hello' and 'thank you' in Spanish. You'll find the phrases in the Greetings & Civilities section in the Language chapter particularly useful, and they take only a few minutes to learn.

Even if you can speak Spanish quite well, you're bound to run into (Spanish-speaking) locals who are convinced they can't understand you.

Dress

Pay attention to your appearance when in the Yucatán. Mexicans, on the whole, are very conscious of appearance, grooming and dress; it's difficult for them to understand why a foreign traveler, who is assumed to be wealthy, would go around looking scruffy when even poor Mexicans do their best to look neat. Try to present as clean an appearance as possible, especially if you're dealing with officialdom (police, immigration officers etc); in such cases it's a good idea to look not only clean, but also as conservative and respectable as possible. Except in beach resorts and fishing villages, shorts are the marks of the tourist; this comment is intended for those of you who don't like to stand out in crowds.

Though standards of attire have relaxed somewhat in the Yucatán, in general it's better for women to dress conservatively in towns (except seaside resorts) and in off-the-beaten-track villages unaccustomed to tourists – no short shorts, no halter tops etc. All visitors should dress modestly when entering churches (and not chat inside them), as this shows respect for local people and their culture. Some churches in heavily touristed areas will post signs at the door asking that shorts and tank tops (singlets) not be worn in church, but in most places such knowledge is assumed.

Time
The fabled Mexican attitude toward time – 'mañana, mañana...' – has probably become legendary simply from comparison with the USA. But it's still true, especially outside the big cities, that the urgency Europeans and North Americans are used to is often lacking. Most Mexicans value *simpatía* (congeniality) over promptness. If something is really worth doing, it gets done. If not, it can wait. Life should not be a succession of pressures and deadlines. According to many Mexicans, life in the 'businesslike' cultures has been desympathized.

The foreign managers of maquiladoras typically contend with the mañana syndrome by closing the doors to their factories 15 minutes after the work day begins, thus preventing employees from straggling in whenever it suits them.

Given the Mexican attitude toward time, you often need to be specific when making an appointment with a local and it's important to you that they be prompt. Tell the Yucatecan to arrive at a specified time and not later. If you're arranging to go fishing and want to leave at 6 o'clock, for example, say 'six, not six-fifteen, not six-thirty – six *on the dot*.' If you speak Spanish, *'en punto'* is the Spanish equivalent for 'on the dot.' *'A la hora del norte'* is another way people

sometimes express not being on tropical time. The clarification can reduce frustration and prevent hard feelings.

Treatment of Animals
In general, domestic animals are no worse off on the Yucatán Peninsula than they are in most countries where humans may not have enough to eat. There is certainly no shortage of stray cats or horridly mangy, starving dogs. Mexicans may not be as sensitive to animal welfare as some other cultures but they don't in general wantonly mistreat animals. Bullfighting and cock-fighting, it may be argued, are evidence to the contrary. But Mexicans regard them as sport or art, and many traditions and rituals are associated with them.

WOMEN TRAVELERS
In the land that invented machismo, women have to make some concessions to local custom – but don't let that put you off. In general, Mexicans are great believers in the difference (rather than the equality) between the sexes. Lone women will probably experience some catcalls and attempts to chat them up. Normally these men only want to talk to you, but it can get tiresome. The best way to discourage unwanted attention is to avoid eye contact (sunglasses can help here) and, if possible, ignore the attention altogether. Otherwise, use a cool but polite initial response and a consistent, firm 'No.' It is possible to turn uninvited attention into a worthwhile conversation by making clear that you *are* willing to talk, but no more.

To avoid any unwanted situations, it may be useful to consider what the norm is for many Mexican women and to avoid doing anything that would be considered unusual. For example, a Mexican woman generally wouldn't challenge a man's masculinity, drink in a cantina, hitchhike, or go alone to isolated places. Some Mexican women swim in shorts and T-shirts, and except in beach resorts, it's advisable to wear shorts only when at a swimming pool.

GAY & LESBIAN TRAVELERS
Though gays and lesbians have made great social and legal strides in Mexico in recent years, they tend to keep a low profile, as they are still targets of discrimination and

sometimes violence – especially gay men. Cancún has a fairly active gay scene.

The **Gay Mexico Network** (W *www .gaymexico.net)* has information on gay-friendly hotels and tours in Mexico, as well as some interesting links and articles. The book *Gay Mexico: The Men of Mexico,* by Eduardo David (1998), has social analyses and practical information. Covering much more of the world (North America, Mexico, the Caribbean and European capitals), but with comprehensive listings of gay-friendly accommodations, restaurants and much more, are *Damron Women's Traveller,* and *Damron Men's Travel Guide,* both published annually by **Damron Company** (W *www.damron.com)* of San Francisco.

DISABLED TRAVELERS

The Yucatán Peninsula is not yet very disabled-friendly, though some hotels and restaurants (mostly towards the top end of the market) and some public buildings now provide wheelchair access. Worthy of special mention is Posada Margherita, a fully accessible and lovely small resort on the beach in Tulum's Zona Hotelera (see Zona Hotelera under Tulum in the Quintana Roo chapter) that offers scuba diving for travelers with limited mobility.

Mobility is easiest in the major tourist resorts and the more expensive hotels. Bus transportation can be difficult; flying or taking a taxi is easier.

Mobility International USA (☎ *541-343-1284;* W *www.miusa.org; PO Box 10767, Eugene, OR 97440)* advises disabled travelers on mobility issues, runs exchange programs (including in Mexico), and publishes *A World of Options: A Guide to International Educational Exchange, Community Service, and Travel for People with Disabilities.*

In the UK, **RADAR** (☎ *020-7250-3222;* W *www.radar.org.uk; 250 City Rd, London EC1V 8AF)* is run by and for disabled people. Its excellent website has links to good travel-specific sites.

Another excellent information source is **Access-able Travel Source** (W *www.access -able.com).*

SENIOR TRAVELERS

AARP (☎ *800-424-3410;* W *www.aarp.org; 601 E St NW, Washington, DC 20049, USA)* is an advocacy group for Americans 50 years and older and a good resource for travel bargains. Annual membership costs US$12.50.

Membership in the **National Council of Senior Citizens** (☎ *301-578-8800; 8403 Colesville Rd, Silver Spring, MD 20910, USA)* gives access to discount information and travel-related advice.

Elderhostel (☎ *877-426-8056;* W *www.el derhostel.org; 11 Ave de Lafayette, Boston, MA 02111, USA)* is a nonprofit organization providing educational travel programs to people over age 55. Its many fascinating programs in Mexico include birding and ruins trips to the Yucatán.

TRAVEL WITH CHILDREN

Mexicans as a rule like children. Any child whose hair is lighter than jet black will get called *güera* (blond) if she's a girl, *güero* if he's a boy. Though there are exceptions, children are welcome at all kinds of hotels and in virtually every café and restaurant.

Diapers (nappies) are widely available, but you may not easily find creams, lotions, baby foods or familiar medicines outside larger cities and tourist towns. Bring at least some of those that you need. It's usually not hard to find an inexpensive baby-sitter if the grown-ups want to go out on their own; just ask at your hotel.

On flights to and within Mexico, children under two generally travel for 10% of the adult fare, as long as they do not occupy a seat, and those aged two to 11 normally pay 67%. On many Mexican long-distance buses, children under 13 pay half-price and if they're under three, and small enough to sit on your lap, they will usually go free.

Lonely Planet's *Travel with Children* has lots of practical advice on the subject, as well as firsthand stories from many Lonely Planet authors, and others, who have done it.

DANGERS & ANNOYANCES

The US Department of State's consular information sheet on Mexico warns of a significant increase in the number of rapes, pick-pocketing incidents, purse snatchings and hotel-room thefts reported in Cancún and at other beach resorts in the country. In spite of this, the Yucatán Peninsula remains relatively safe, and with a few precautions, you can minimize danger to your physical safety. More at risk are your possessions, but again, a few sensible steps reduce the risk.

Official information can make Mexico sound more alarming than it really is, but foreign affairs departments can supply a variety of useful data about travel to Mexico: **Australia** (☎ 1300-555-135; W www.dfat .gov.au); **Canada** (☎ 800-267-6788; W www .dfait-maeci.gc.ca); **UK** (☎ 0870-606-0290; W www.fco.gov.uk); **USA** (☎ 202-647-5225; W www.travel.state.gov).

One thing to stress is that lone women, and even pairs of women, should always be very cautious about going to remote beach spots. Be careful going out at night as well.

Theft & Robbery

Theft, particularly pocket-picking and pilfering of unsecured items left in hotel rooms, is common in Mexico. Tourists are singled out, as they are presumed to be wealthy and carrying valuables. Crowded buses, bus stops, bus stations, airports, markets, streets and plazas, remote beach spots and anywhere frequented by large numbers of tourists are all prime locations for theft.

Precautions To avoid being robbed, do not go where there are few other people; this includes camping in secluded places, unless you are absolutely sure they're safe. Don't leave any valuables unattended while you swim, on crowded or empty beaches. Run-and-grab thefts by lurkers in the woods are a common occurrence on the Caribbean coast. Other suggestions include:

- Leave unnecessary valuable items at home. That includes all jewelry and watches that sparkle (real gold, real silver or otherwise).
- Photographers: a cheap or well-worn camera bag is a lot less eye-catching than a fancy one
- Never leave valuables in your hotel room in an unlocked bag, even if you're only leaving it for a short while. Always lock your bag.
- Keep some ready money in a pocket or two (buttoned or zipped if possible). Wear a money belt, shoulder wallet or a pouch on a string around your neck, underneath your clothing. Round-the-waist packs are an invitation to thieves.
- Don't keep money, credit or debit cards, wallets or bags in open view any longer than you have to. At ticket counters, keep a hand or foot on your bag at all times.
- Use ATMs only in secure locations, not those open to the street

- Take 1st-class buses whenever possible, especially on long trips and night rides
- Do not leave anything valuable-looking in a parked vehicle. Trunk theft is common in Mérida, Valladolid and Campeche.

One strategy for dividing risk is to keep an ATM card in a locked bag in your room and carry a credit card on your person (in one of the aforementioned under-your-clothing locations).

Highway Robbery Though it's rare on the Yucatán Peninsula itself, bandits occasionally hold up buses and other vehicles on intercity routes, especially at night, taking luggage or valuables. Sometimes buses are robbed by people who board as passengers. The best way to avoid highway robbery is not to travel at night. Roads linking the peninsula with Tabasco and Chiapas states are sometimes the scene of such robberies. These routes are also notorious for frequent thefts from luggage on 2nd-class buses, whose many stops and sometimes-crowded conditions (and sleepy passengers) afford miscreants the opportunity to unzip or slash open bags.

Short-Changing As is the case in many parts of the world, you should try to keep a running total of your restaurant, bar, or other bill in your head, and always count your change. The practice of short-changing or overcharging is becoming more prevalent throughout the Yucatán, mostly in establishments catering to tourists.

There are a couple of common ruses to watch out for. First, the addition of a tax or service charge to your bill (ignore that the bill is an official-looking receipt or says 'tip not included'). These charges are usually included in menu prices, but if they're not, it will be clearly stated somewhere on the menu. Second, being given change for a smaller note than you present. You can politely avoid this by making a comment about the amount of money that you are handing over, for example, asking 'Can you change a hundred pesos?' (¿Me puede cambiar cien pesos?)

Don't get paranoid; it will ruin your trip and can lead to ugly (sometimes unjustified) scenes. Just be on your guard, no matter how romantic or expensive or friendly a place is or how good the service is. Especially if you've had drinks. The best swindlers are those who, when caught out on a ruse, still have the *huevos* to stiff you another way.

Bad Cops Corrupt police (and security guards) can sometimes be a problem in the Yucatán. They've been known to accost tourist couples kissing passionately and threaten to haul them in for offending public morals, in hopes of extracting a bribe. This occurs mostly in touristed areas such as Isla Mujeres and Playa del Carmen, and is even more likely to happen (and to be more expensive) if the couple is, well, *coupling*. Don't get carried away by steamy tropical lust; get a room! Real or invented traffic offenses are another means used by some police officers to extract money. See Legal Matters below and Rules of the Road in the Getting Around chapter for more information.

LEGAL MATTERS

Mexican law is based on the Napoleonic code, presuming an accused person is guilty until proven innocent. Whatever you do, *don't* get involved in any way with illegal drugs: don't buy or sell, use or carry, or associate with people who do – even if the locals seem to do so freely. As a foreigner, you are at a distinct disadvantage, and you may be set up by others. Drug laws in Mexico are strict, and though enforcement may be uneven, penalties are severe. (The legal drinking age in Mexico is 18.)

If arrested, you have the right to notify your embassy or consulate. Consular officials can tell you your rights and provide lists of local lawyers. They can also monitor your case, make sure you are treated humanely, and notify your relatives or friends; but they can't get you out of jail. By Mexican law the longest a person can be detained by police without a specific accusation is 72 hours.

The national tourism ministry, **Sectur** *(☎ 800-903-9200)*, offers 24-hour telephone advice on tourist protection laws and where to obtain help.

If Mexican police wrongfully accuse you of an infraction, you can ask for the officer's identification or to speak to a superior or to be shown documentation about the law you have supposedly broken. You can also note the officer's name, badge number, vehicle number and department (federal, state or municipal). Pay any traffic fines at a police station and get a receipt. Then make your complaint to Sectur or local tourist police.

Alternatively, you can contribute to the problem of police corruption by offering a bribe.

BUSINESS HOURS

Stores are generally open from 9am to 2pm, closed for siesta, then reopened from 4pm to 7pm Monday to Saturday. In particularly hot locales such as Mérida and Chetumal, stores sometimes take a longer siesta but stay open later in the evening. Some may not be open on Saturday afternoon.

Offices have similar Monday to Friday hours; those with tourist-related business might be open for a few hours on Saturday as well.

Some Mexican churches, particularly those that contain valuable works of art, are locked when not in use, but most churches are in frequent use. Be careful not to disturb services when you visit them.

Archaeological sites are usually open 8am to 5pm daily. Most museums have one closing day a week, typically Monday. On Sunday, nearly all archaeological sites and museums are free for Mexican nationals, and the major ones can get very crowded.

PUBLIC HOLIDAYS & SPECIAL EVENTS

Mexico's frequent fiestas are highly colorful affairs that often go on for several days and add a great deal of spice to everyday life. There's a major national holiday or celebration almost every month, to which each town adds nearly as many local saints' days, fairs, arts festivals and so on. Christmas through New Year's Day and Semana Santa – the week leading up to Easter – are the chief Mexican holiday periods. If you're traveling at either time, try to book transport and accommodations well in advance.

National Holidays

Banks, post offices, government offices and many shops throughout Mexico are closed on the following days:

Año Nuevo January 1; New Year's Day
Día de la Constitución February 5; Constitution Day

Día de la Bandera February 24; Day of the National Flag

Día de Nacimiento de Benito Juárez March 21; anniversary of Benito Juárez's birth

Día del Trabajo May 1; Labor Day

Cinco de Mayo May 5; anniversary of Mexico's 1862 victory over the French at Puebla

Día de la Independencia September 16; commemorates the start of Mexico's war for independence from Spain

Día de la Raza October 12; commemorates Columbus' discovery of the New World and the founding of the mestizo (mixed-ancestry) Mexican people

Día de la Revolución November 20; anniversary of the 1910 Mexican Revolution

Día de Navidad December 25; Christmas Day is traditionally celebrated with a feast in the early hours of December 25 after midnight mass

Other National Celebrations

Though not official holidays, some of these are among the most important festivals on the Mexican calendar. Many offices and businesses close, and many federal government offices are closed for the entire stretch from Christmas through January 6.

Día de los Reyes Magos January 6; Three Kings' Day or Epiphany is the day that Mexican children traditionally receive gifts, rather than at Christmas (but some get two loads of presents!)

Día de la Candelaria February 2; Candlemas commemorates the presentation of Jesus in the temple 40 days after his birth. It is celebrated in Mexico with processions, bullfights and dancing in many towns.

Carnaval Late February or early March; Carnaval takes place the week or so before Ash Wednesday (which falls 46 days before Easter Sunday) and is a big bash preceding the 40-day penance of Lent. It's celebrated most festively on the peninsula in Mérida, with parades, music, food, drink, dancing, fireworks and fun.

Semana Santa March or April; Holy Week starts on Palm Sunday (Domingo de Ramos) and businesses close usually from Good Friday (Viernes Santo) to Easter Sunday (Domingo de Resurrección). Most of Mexico seems to be on the move at this time.

Informe Presidencial September 1; the president's state of the nation address to the legislature

Día de Todos los Santos November 1; All Saints' Day

Día de Muertos November 2; Day of the Dead or All Souls' Day is Mexico's most characteristic fiesta – the souls of the dead are believed to return to earth this day. Families build altars in their homes and visit graveyards to commune with their dead on the preceding night and the day itself, taking garlands and gifts of, for example, the dead one's favorite foods. A happy atmosphere prevails.

Día de Nuestra Señora de Guadalupe December 12; Day of Our Lady of Guadalupe honors Mexico's national patron, the manifestation of the Virgin Mary who appeared to an indigenous Mexican, Juan Diego, in 1531. A week or more of celebrations throughout Mexico leads up to the big day, the Day of our Lady, with children taken to church dressed as little Juan Diegos or indigenous girls. Runners carry torches along the roads.

Posadas December 16–24; candlelit parades of children and adults reenacting the journey of Mary and Joseph to Bethlehem are held for nine nights (the tradition is more alive in small towns than in cities)

Pastorelas December 25–January 5; dramas enacting the journey of the shepherds to see the infant Jesus are staged

Yucatecan Celebrations

In addition to the national holidays and celebrations mentioned above, every town and city on the Yucatán Peninsula holds its own fiestas, often in honor of its patron saint. Street parades of holy images, special costumes, fireworks, dancing, lots of music and plenty of drinking are all part of the colorful scene. Sometimes bloodless bullfights are on the program as well, or the Danza de la Cabeza de Cochino. This is a dance rooted in Mayan tradition that takes place around an altar holding a pig's head decorated with offerings of flowers, ribbons, bread, liquor and cigarettes. A likely time to catch it is at the Fiesta de la Inmaculada Concepción (Festival of the Immaculate Conception). Though Yucatecans also celebrate the Immaculate Conception on December 8, with the rest of the Catholic world, many towns on the peninsula hold nine days of devotions leading up to the last Sunday in January. Early the morning of that day the pig is ritually slaughtered and put to cooking.

Other lively patron saint festivals and town- or Yucatán-specific celebrations are mentioned in more detail in the destination chapters.

ACTIVITIES

There's absolutely no shortage of things to do on the Yucatán Peninsula: some of the best scuba diving and snorkeling in the world is available here, beach lovers will find plenty of powdery white sand on which to sunbathe and the ancient Mayan cities that dot the landscape of the Yucatán are a thrill to explore. And, of course, there's Cancún – the nightlife epicenter for all of Mexico – and the similar but quieter destinations of Playa del Carmen, Isla Mujeres and Cozumel.

The activities available to you on the peninsula are discussed in detail in the destination chapters. Here is a sampling of the popular options.

Diving & Snorkeling

The color and variety of marine life along much of the Riviera Maya, especially off the coast of Cozumel, is absolutely as-tounding. And Isla Holbox, on the northern tip of the Yucatán Peninsula, offers the chance to see whale sharks in unheard-of numbers.

Most of the dive operators on the peninsula – and there are literally hundreds of them – offer scuba instruction. Some offer a one-day 'resort dive,' in which students are taught the fundamentals and are then taken to a reef where they make one or two shallow dives. The degree of safety of these dives depends on the level of instruction. Only reputable dive operators are mentioned in this guide.

Resort dives are generally inexpensive, costing US$65 or less for two dives and some degree of instruction. Obtaining open-water certification typically costs US$350

Considerations for Responsible Diving

The popularity of diving is placing immense pressure on many sites. Please consider the following tips when diving, and help to preserve the ecology and beauty of reefs:

- Do not use anchors on the reef, and take care not to ground boats on coral. Encourage dive operators and regulatory bodies to establish permanent moorings at popular dive sites.
- Avoid touching living marine organisms with your body or dragging equipment across the reef. Polyps can be damaged by even the gentlest contact. Never stand on corals, even if they look solid and robust. If you must hold onto the reef, only touch exposed rock or dead coral.
- Be conscious of your fins. Even without contact, the surge from heavy fin strokes near the reef can damage delicate organisms. When treading water in shallow reef areas, take care not to kick up clouds of sand. Settling sand can easily smother the delicate organisms of the reef.
- Practice and maintain proper buoyancy control. Major damage can be done by divers descending too fast and colliding with the reef. Make sure you are correctly weighted and that your weight belt is positioned so that you stay horizontal. If you have not dived for a while, have a practice dive in a pool before taking to the reef. Be aware that buoyancy can change over the period of an extended trip. Initially you may breathe harder and need more weight; a few days later you may breathe more easily and need less weight.
- Take great care in underwater caves. Spend as little time as possible within them, as your air bubbles may be caught within the roof and thereby leave previously submerged organisms high and dry. Taking turns to inspect the interior of a small cave will lessen the chances of damaging contact.
- Resist the temptation to collect or buy corals or shells. Aside from the ecological damage, taking home marine souvenirs depletes the beauty of a site and spoils others' enjoyment. The same goes for marine archaeological sites (mainly shipwrecks). Respect their integrity; some sites are even protected from looting by law.
- Ensure that you take home all your trash and any litter you may find as well. Plastics in particular are a serious threat to marine life. Turtles can mistake plastic for jellyfish and eat it.
- Resist the temptation to feed fish. You may disturb their normal eating habits, encourage aggressive behavior or feed them food that is detrimental to their health.
- Minimize your disturbance of marine animals. In particular, do not ride on the backs of turtles, as this causes them great anxiety.

or more and takes several days. If you haven't dived before and want to test the waters, consider a resort dive with a reputable dive outfit before spending six times as much money getting certified.

Many dive outfits will take snorkelers out to the more easily swum sites for a smaller fee, and there is no shortage of places tube-breathers can put in straight off the beach. Many are covered in the destination chapters.

Snorkelers can do nearly as much damage to the marine environment as divers; please read and abide by the guidelines in the 'Considerations for Responsible Diving' boxed text.

Other Water Sports & Fishing

Many hotels and resorts offer kayaks (usually the simple sit-atop variety) for the use of their guests. Though it's not always an option, paddling takes on a completely new aspect when you explore mangrove thickets.

While wind- and kite-surfing have gained popularity in the region, there is virtually no place to do regular surfing.

The Caribbean coast has some good sport fishing. In addition to deep-sea fish such as marlin, swordfish, sailfish and tuna, anglers go after shallower species such as tarpon, permit and bonefish. The area around Punta Allen is famous for its catch-and-release fly fishing for these three (see Punta Allen in the Quintana Roo chapter).

COURSES

Taking classes in Mexico can be a great way to meet people and get an inside angle on local life as well as study the language or culture. Mexican universities and colleges often offer tuition to complement courses you may be taking back home. For long-term study in Mexico you'll need a student visa; contact a Mexican consulate. The website W www.edumexico.org has a comprehensive directory of higher education opportunities in the country.

There's a plethora of Spanish-language schools on the Yucatán Peninsula, and their prices vary substantially. Mérida, with its abundance of cultural activities, central location and colonial core, makes a great place to study Spanish. Among the schools there, **Centro de Idiomas del Sureste** (CIS; ☎ 999-923-0954; W www.cisyucatan.com .mx) stands out. It has three locations in

Mérida and offers small total-immersion classes (ie, taught entirely in Spanish). Thirty hours of instruction costs about US$790, but this includes a two-week homestay in a local household (with your own room) and three meals a day. Other plans are available.

Also in Mérida is the **Institute of Modern Spanish** (IMS; ☎ 877-463-7432; W www .modernspanish.com), which also offers year-round instruction and a host of instruction and housing options. At the time this book went to press, IMS was offering a week of 20 hours of instruction for US$170, and several homestay options, including shared and private rooms.

Albergue La Candelaria (☎/fax 856-2267; e fidery@chichen.com.mx; Calle 35 No 201F), Valladolid's youth hostel, offers Spanish- and Mayan-language classes with one-on-one instruction.

WORK
Paid Work

People who enter Mexico as tourists are not legally allowed to take employment. Mexicans themselves need jobs, especially with the economy what it is, and foreigners technically are only allowed to take positions that couldn't be filled by a national. The many expats working in Mexico have usually been posted there by their companies with all the necessary papers.

English speakers (and, though much less likely, German or French speakers) may find teaching jobs in language schools, *preparatorias* (high schools) or universities. The pay is low, but you can live on it.

A foreigner working in Mexico normally needs a permit or government license, but a school will often pay a foreign teacher in the form of a *beca* (scholarship), and thus circumvent the law, or the school's administration will procure the appropriate papers. It's helpful to know at least a little Spanish, even though some institutes insist that only English be spoken in class.

Volunteer Work

The University of Minnesota's **International Service and Travel Center** (ISTC; ☎ 612-626-4782; W www.istc.umn.edu) has a website with a database listing many volunteer possibilities, and the **Council on International Educational Exchange** (CIEE;

☎ 800-407-8839; Ⓦ www.ciee.org; 633 Third Avenue, 20th Floor, New York, NY 10017-6706) also has information on volunteer programs in Mexico.

Check out the **Alliance of European Voluntary Service Organisations** (Ⓦ www.alliance-network.org) or Unesco's **Coordinating Committee for International Voluntary Service** (Ⓦ www.unesco.org/ccivs) for information on opportunities for non-US residents.

Volunteer Vacations by Bill McMillon and *International Directory of Voluntary Work* by Louise Whetter & Victoria Pybus list lots of volunteer organizations and information sources.

Amigos de las Americas (☎ 800-231-7796; Ⓦ www.amigoslink.org; 5618 Star Lane, Houston, TX 77057, USA) trains and sends paying volunteers to work on public-health projects in Latin America. For work focused on the environment, **Earthwatch Institute** (Ⓦ www.earthwatch.org), with offices in the USA, Britain, Australia and Japan, also runs environmental projects in Mexico that you pay to take part in (usually around US$1000 per week).

ACCOMMODATIONS

Accommodations in the Yucatán range from beachside cabanas just south of the Tulum ruins to five-star resorts in Cancún's hotel zone. Note that in the destination chapters all room prices include taxes; rooms have private bathrooms unless otherwise noted; and 'singles' refers to rooms for one person, 'doubles' are for two people etc.

In Mexico, *cuarto sencillo* usually means a room with one bed, which is often a *cama matrimonial* (double bed). One person can often occupy such a room for a lower price than two people. A *cuarto doble* is usually a room with two beds, often both 'matrimonial.' To request a room for one say *'para una persona'* or for two, *'para dos personas'*.

Even in some nicer hotels, foul smells may emanate from the shower drain due to Mexican plumbing practices. Keeping the drain covered with a weighted-down plastic bag or other odor barrier while it's not in use makes for a more pleasant stay.

Reservations

The tourism high seasons in most places are Semana Santa (the week before Easter and a couple of days after it), most of July and August, and the Christmas–New Year holiday period of about two weeks. In popular destinations at these times it's best to go early in the day to the place of your choice to try to secure a room. Even in more out-of-the-way spots it's best to find lodging before the sun goes down.

You can try to reserve in advance, by telephone, email or fax, asking whether a deposit is required and how to send it, and requesting confirmation. Some places now take bookings on their websites. Others are reluctant to take bookings at all: if you telephone they might say they're full or that they can't hold a room after 7pm. Don't worry: you'll always end up with a room somewhere.

During these peak seasons, many mid-range and top-end establishments in tourist destinations raise their room prices, by anything from 10% to 50% over low-season rates. Budget places are more likely to keep the same rates all year. Annual price hikes usually happen in December or January.

In the recent hard times, however, hoteliers have been very reluctant to see a room go empty. At the time of research, many hotels had frozen their rates or lowered them to pre-2001 levels, and some were offering a free breakfast, to counteract the drop in tourism engendered by the sagging global economy and fear of terrorist attacks. Still others had begun offering hostel accommodation along with their regular rooms (some doing a better job of it than others).

Camping

Most organized campgrounds are also trailer parks, set up for RVs (camper vans) and trailers (caravans). Some are very basic, others quite luxurious. Expect to pay from about M$30 to M$60 to pitch a tent for two. Some restaurants or guesthouses in small beach spots will let you pitch a tent on their patch for M$25 or so per person.

All Mexican beaches are considered public property. You can camp for nothing on some of them, but security is nonexistent.

Hammocks & Cabanas

You can rent a hammock and a place to hang it – usually under a palm roof outside a small *casa de huéspedes* or beach restaurant – for M$60 on some parts of the peninsula. If you have your own hammock the cost comes down a bit. It's easy enough to buy hammocks in the Yucatán; Mérida specializes in them, and you'll find hammocks offered for sale in beach spots all along the Maya Riviera.

Cabanas are palm-thatched huts – some have dirt floors and nothing inside but a bed; others are deluxe, with electric light, mosquito nets, fans, fridge, bar and tasteful decor. Generally, prices for simple cabanas range from M$120 to M$350, though some of the fancy ones along the Caribbean go for far more.

Hostels

Several good hostels for international budget travelers have opened in the Yucatán in recent years. They provide dormitory accommodation for M$60 to M$100 or so per person, and communal kitchens, bathrooms and lounging space. Aside from being cheap, they're generally relaxed, and good places to meet other travelers. Most have a few private double rooms for rent as well.

Some are affiliated with Hostelling International (HI; the former International Youth Hostel Federation). Hostel cards are not generally required, though they will get you a discount of about M$10 in some hostels.

Hotels

Cheap hotels exist in every Mexican town, though on the Yucatán Peninsula there are substantially fewer than most other regions of Mexico. Expect to pay between M$100 and M$300 for a decent double room with private shower and hot water, more in Cancún, Cozumel or Playa del Carmen, and perhaps if you arrive during a popular time or an event. Many hotels in this range and the mid-range have rooms for three, four or five people that cost little more than a double. Many also provide purified drinking water at no extra charge; sometimes the bottles are not readily evident, so ask for *agua purificada*.

At a good mid-range hotel, two people can usually get a room with a private bathroom, TV and perhaps air-con for M$300 to M$600. The hotel will often have an elevator, restaurant and bar. These places are generally pleasant, respectable, safe and comfortable without being luxurious, though some can be quite nice.

The peninsula is home to many large, modern resort hotels. They offer the expected levels of luxury at expectedly lofty prices.

FOOD

It's tantalizing to consider that some of the dishes prepared in the Yucatán's kitchens today may be very similar to ones served in ancient times to Mayan royalty. Many often-used ingredients such as *pavo* (turkey), *venado* (venison) and *pescado* (fish) were available in ancient times, as they are today. In the Language chapter at the end of this book is a Food section specifically devoted to food, beverages and food-related words; it lists many Mexican and Yucatecan dishes.

Mexicans eat three meals a day: *desayuno* (breakfast), *comida* (lunch) and *cena* (supper). Each includes one or more of three national staples: tortillas, frijoles and chilies. Most mains are served with at least some sort of *guarnición* (accompaniment), often rice and beans.

Tortillas are thin round patties of dough made from ground corn *(maíz)* or wheat flour *(harina)* and cooked on griddles. Both kinds can be wrapped around or served under any type of food.

Frijoles are beans, served boiled, fried, refried, in soups, spread on tortillas or with eggs. If you simply order frijoles they may come in a bowl swimming in their own dark sauce, as a runny mass on a plate, or as a thick and almost black paste. No matter how they come, they're usually delicious and nutritious. The only bad ones are refried beans that have been fried using too much or low-quality fat.

Chilies (peppers) come in many varieties and are consumed in hundreds of ways. Some chilies such as the habanero and serrano are always spicy-hot, while others such as the *poblano* vary in spiciness according to when they were picked. If you are unsure about your tolerance for hot chilies, ask if the chili is *picante* (spicy-hot) or *muy picante* (very spicy-hot). The habanero is an important ingredient in *achiote,* the popular Yucatecan sauce that also includes chopped onions, the juice of sour oranges, cilantro (coriander leaves) and salt. You'll see a bowl of *achiote* on most restaurant tables in the Yucatán.

Breakfast

The simplest breakfast is coffee or tea and *pan dulce* (sweet rolls), a basket of which is set on the table; you pay for the number consumed. Many restaurants offer combination breakfasts for about M$22 to M$45, typically composed of *jugo de fruta* (fruit juice), *café* (coffee), *bolillo* or *pan tostado* with *mantequilla* and *mermelada* (roll or toast with butter and jam), and *huevos* (eggs), which are served in a variety of ways. In many places frequented by travelers, granola, *ensalada de frutas* (fruit salad), *avena* (oatmeal porridge) and corn flakes are available.

A hearty local breakfast favorite is *huevos motuleños,* eggs Motul-style (Motul is a town east of Mérida). Fresh tortillas are spread with refried beans, then topped with an egg or two, chopped ham, green peas and shredded cheese, with a few slices of fried banana on the side. It can be slightly *picante* or *muy picante*, depending on the cook.

Lunch

La comida, the biggest meal of the day, is usually served between 1pm and 3pm or 4pm. Many restaurants offer not only à la carte fare but also special fixed-price menus called *comida corrida, menú del día* or simply *menú,* though in some tourist-oriented restaurants, using this word may get you the written list of offerings (usually known as *la carta*).

Prices typically range from M$15 and up at a market *comedor* for a simple meal of soup, a meat dish, rice and coffee, to M$80 or more for elaborate repasts beginning with oyster stew and finishing with profiteroles – but typically you'll get three or four courses for about M$35. Drinks usually cost extra.

Dinner/Supper

La cena, the evening meal, is usually lighter than the *comida.* Fixed-price meals are rarely offered.

Snacks

Antojitos, or 'little whims,' are traditional Mexican snacks or light dishes. Some are actually small meals in themselves. They can be eaten at any time, on their own or as part of a larger meal. There are many, many varieties, some peculiar to local areas.

DRINKS

A variety of *bebidas* (drinks), alcoholic and nonalcoholic, are available in the Yucatán – as befits a region with such a warm climate. Don't drink any water unless you know it has been purified or boiled (see Basic Rules under Health earlier in this chapter). You can buy bottles of inexpensive purified or mineral water everywhere on the peninsula, and they are must-carry items on day trips to the Mayan ruins. Better yet, buy one and refill it from your hotel's supply.

If drink prices are not given on a menu, always ask before ordering.

Nonalcoholic Drinks

Coffee & Tea Ordinary Mexican *café,* grown mostly near Córdoba and Orizaba and in Chiapas, is flavorful but often served weak. Many coffeehouses serving stronger stuff (including espresso drinks) have opened in recent years in touristed towns. Some of these serve Mexican organic coffee, from Oaxaca or Chiapas. Tea, invariably in bags, is usually a disappointment for real tea-drinkers, though fancier varieties can now be found in some areas.

Fruit & Vegetable Drinks *Jugos* (pure fresh juices) are popular in Mexico and readily available from streetside stalls and juice bars, where the fruit normally is squeezed before your eyes. Every fruit and a few of the squeezable vegetables are used. Ever tried pure beet juice?

Licuados are blends of fruit or juice with water and sugar. *Licuados con leche* use milk instead of water. Possible additions include raw egg, ice and flavorings such as vanilla or nutmeg. The delicious combinations are practically limitless. In Mexico's many juice bars, you can expect the water used to be purified – but don't assume the same for streetside juice stalls.

Aguas frescas or *aguas de fruta* are made by mixing fruit juice or a syrup made from mashed grains or seeds with sugar and water. You will usually see them in big glass jars on the counters of juice stands. *Agua fresca de arroz* (literally, 'rice water') has a sweet, nutty taste.

Soft Drinks *Refrescos* are bottled or canned soft drinks, and there are some interesting and tasty local varieties. Sidral and

Manzanita are reasonable apple-flavored fizzy drinks. There's also a nonalcoholic variety of sangria.

There are many brands of *agua mineral* (mineral water) from Mexican springs – Tehuacán and Garci Crespo are two of the best and can sometimes be obtained with refreshing flavors, as well as plain.

Alcoholic Drinks

Breweries were established in Mexico by German immigrants in the late 19th century. Mexico's several large brewing companies now produce more than 25 brands of *cerveza* (beer), some of which are quite good (depending on your tastes). Each major company has a premium beer, such as Bohemia (the author's favorite) and Corona de Barril (usually served in bottles); several standard beers, such as Carta Blanca, Superior and Dos Equis; and 'popular' beers, such as Corona, Tecate and Modelo. All are blond lagers meant to be served chilled – it's a good idea to ask for *una cerveza fría* (a cold beer). Each of the large companies also produces a *negra* (or *oscura,* dark) beer, such as Negra Modelo and Noche Buena. Local Yucatán beers include the lagers Carta Clara and Montejo, and the tasty dark León Negra.

Mexico also produces a fascinating variety of intoxicating drinks made from grapes, grains and cacti. The traditional Mayan spirit in the Yucatán is *xtabentún* (shtah-behn-**toon**), an anise-flavored liqueur that, when authentic, is made by fermenting honey. Most modern versions of it have a goodly proportion of grain neutral spirits, and some are very thick. Argáez is quite a good brand. Foreign liquors are widely available, too.

ENTERTAINMENT

There are more entertainment options on the Yucatán Peninsula than you can shake a stick at. Nearly every week there's a major fiesta somewhere on the peninsula (see Public Holidays & Special Events earlier in this chapter).

In the larger cities and resort towns, the range of entertainment is broad, with music clubs (jazz, salsa, reggae, mariachi, rock), discos, bars and lounges abounding. Cancún's Zona Hotelera abounds with discos aimed at young drinkers. Mérida puts on free *vaquerías* – outdoor concerts featuring traditional Yucatecan dancing and dress. Every large city also has at least one cinema, where you'll usually find first-run Hollywood films in English with Spanish subtitles (children's films are legally allowed to be dubbed into Spanish) as well as other foreign films.

SPECTATOR SPORTS

Béisbol (baseball) is quite popular in Mexico, and the Yucatán is no exception. The level of professional play is quite high, equivalent at least to AAA ball in the US. The Mexican League season runs from April to early September, and among its teams are the Campeche Piratas, Cancún Langosteros (Lobstermen) and Yucatán Leones (Lions, of Mérida).

If you're around between October and January you can try to catch a Pacific League (PL) game on TV. The vocabulary of the game in Spanish is fascinating (for a fan), and the PL has the two best team names: the Guasave Algodoneros (Cotton-Pickers) and the Culiacán Tomateros (Tomato-Growers).

SHOPPING

Good buys in the Yucatán include guayaberas (light, elegant shirts with four square pockets), which are standard businesswear for men in southeast Mexico. Guayaberas originally hail from Yucatán, where they are slowly being replaced by the button-down, single-pocketed Oxford-style shirt so popular with American businessmen. Still, they remain the uniform of local politicians. The best guayaberas can be purchased in Mérida; see the Yucatán State chapter for further details.

Another clothing item is the *huipil,* a white dress with a wide band of brightly colored flower embroidery around the yoke and another one near the bottom of the dress. *Huipiles* are light, loose-fitting and traditionally made of cotton (synthetics are occasionally used today). They're ideally suited for the tropics and are worn by women of all ages. For more information about *huipiles*, see Textiles under Arts in the Facts about the Yucatán chapter, which also describes other handicrafts available on the peninsula, such as high-quality panama hats and lovely carved-wood objects.

Earthenware pots of widely varying quality can be found across the peninsula (potheads will want to visit Ticul, where shops near the city center sell the most interesting ceramics available in the Yucatán; the techniques used in Ticul predate the Spanish Conquest by hundreds of years).

Also widely available are handmade blankets, leather goods, decorative cloth, wicker baskets, brilliantly painted gourds and lots of amber jewelry. Silverwork, including jewelry, is often a good buy in the Yucatán as well.

Yucatecan hammocks are renowned for their quality and durability, so visit one of the hammock stores in Mérida or bargain with sellers in other places, particularly along the Mayan Riviera and Isla Holbox, where many residents weave and sell them. (For advice on what to look for in a hammock, see the boxed text 'Yucatecan Hammocks: The Only Way to Sleep' in the Yucatán State chapter.)

Getting There & Away

AIR

Most visitors to the Yucatán arrive by air. International air routes are structured so that virtually all flights into the region from the rest of the world pass through a handful of 'hub' cities: Dallas/Fort Worth, Houston, Los Angeles, Mexico City, Miami or San Salvador.

The majority of flights into the peninsula arrive at busy Aeropuerto Internacional de Cancún (call sign CUN). The region's other four international airports are Cozumel (CZM); Chetumal (CTM); Manuel Crescencio Rejón (MID), in Mérida; and Alberto Acuña Ongay (CPE), in Campeche.

Tickets

The cost of flying to the Yucatán depends on what time of year and day of the week you fly (you usually pay more around the summer and Christmas–New Year holidays, and on weekends), how long you're traveling (you'll usually pay less on a round-trip ticket if you come back within 90 days) and whether you can find a discount or advance-purchase fare or promotional offer. During spring break (roughly mid-March to mid-April) Cancún attracts swarms of college students and inexpensive fares vanish months in advance, as they do with other popular flights.

So start shopping for airfares as soon as you can. Airlines release discounted tickets to selected travel agents and specialist discount agencies, and these are usually the cheapest deals going. From time to time, airlines do have promotional fares and special offers, but generally they only sell fares at the official listed price. An exception to this is booking on the Internet. Some airlines offer excellent fares to Web surfers. They may sell seats by auction or simply cut prices to reflect the reduced cost of electronic selling.

Many travel agents have websites too, which can make the Internet an easy way to compare prices. An increasing number of online agents operate only on the Internet. Online ticket sales work well for a simple one-way or return trip on specified dates. But they're no substitute for a travel agent who knows about special deals and can offer advice on many other aspects of your flight and trip.

You may find the cheapest flights are advertised by obscure agencies. Most such firms are honest and solvent, but there are some rogue outfits around. Paying by credit card generally offers protection, as most card-issuers provide refunds if you can prove you didn't get what you paid for. Similar protection can be obtained by buying a ticket from a bonded agent, such as one covered by the Air Travel Organisers' Licensing (ATOL) scheme in the UK (more details available at ⓦ www.atol.org.uk). Agents who accept only cash should hand over the tickets straight away. After you've made a booking or paid your deposit, call the airline and confirm that the booking was made. Some travelers have reported being ripped off by fly-by-night mail-order ticket agents.

If you purchase a ticket and later want to make changes to your route or get a refund, you need to contact the original travel agent. Airlines only issue refunds to the purchaser of a ticket, usually the travel agent who bought the ticket on your behalf. Many travelers change their routes halfway through their trips, so think carefully before buying a ticket that is not easily refunded.

Sample fares are given in the regional sections later in this chapter, but they will be greatly affected by the amount of fluctuation in prices and exchange rates, and the solvency of some airlines following the war against Iraq.

One Internet site worth investigating for good fares is W www.ebookers.com.

Student & Youth Fares Full-time students and people under 26 have access to better deals than other travelers (cheaper fares and more flexibility to change flights or routes). You have to show a document proving your date of birth or a valid International Student Identity Card (ISIC) when buying your ticket and boarding the plane.

Departure Tax A departure tax equivalent to about US$25 is levied on international flights from Mexico. It's usually included in your ticket cost, but if it isn't, you must pay with cash during airport check-in. Ask your travel agent in advance.

The USA & Canada At the time of writing, Aeroméxico, Air Canada, America West, American, Continental, Mexicana, Northwest and United Airlines (among others) served Cancún, Cozumel and Mérida from the US and Canada, many with nonstop flights. Direct flights depart from the cities of Atlanta, Boston, Charlotte, Chicago, Cincinnati, Dallas/Fort Worth, Houston, Los Angeles, Memphis, Miami, Minneapolis, Montreal, New York, Philadelphia, Phoenix, Pittsburgh, St Louis and Toronto.

At the time of research the cheapest nonsale round-trip coach tickets from the US to Cancún cost US$348 (traveling from Phoenix in June on America West). From Canada to Cancún, round-trip flights started at US$509 (traveling from Toronto in March on Air Canada). At peak times such as Christmas, expect prices to rise by $200 or more. Costs from other US and Canadian cities vary, with some flights exceeding US$2000.

Discount travel agents in the USA and Canada are known as consolidators (although you won't see a sign on the door saying 'Consolidator'). You can locate them through the Yellow Pages and they also advertise in newspapers and magazines, listing tables of destinations and fares, and toll-free numbers to call. San Francisco is the ticket consolidator capital of the USA, although good deals can also be found in Los Angeles, New York and other big cities.

The *New York Times, Los Angeles Times, Chicago Tribune* and *San Francisco Chronicle* all produce weekly travel sections in which you'll find a number of travel agency ads. In Canada, the *Globe & Mail, Toronto Star, Montreal Gazette* and *Vancouver Sun* are good places to look for cheap fares.

Council Travel (☎ 800-226-8624; W www.counciltravel.com), America's largest student travel organization, has around 60 offices in the USA. Call for the office nearest you or visit its website. **STA Travel** (☎ 800-777-0112; W www.statravel.com) has offices in Boston, Chicago, Miami, New York, Philadelphia, San Francisco and other major cities.

Travel Cuts (☎ 800-667-2887; W www.travelcuts.com) is Canada's national student travel agency and has offices in all major cities.

Other Internet sites worth looking at include W www.orbitz.com and W www.smarterliving.com.

The UK There were no direct flights from the UK to the Yucatán at the time of research, and round-trip flights from London were running UK£500 plus taxes.

Discount air travel is big business in London. Advertisements for many travel agencies appear in the travel pages of weekend broadsheet newspapers (such as the *Sunday Times,* the *Independent* and the *Daily Telegraph*), *Time Out,* the *Evening Standard* and the free magazine *TNT.*

An excellent place to start your fare inquiries for Mexico is **Journey Latin America** (☎ 020-8747-3108; W www.journeylatinamerica.co.uk), with offices in London and Manchester.

For students or travelers under 26 years, a popular travel agency is **STA Travel** (☎ 0870-1600-599; W www.statravel.co.uk), which has branches across the country. It sells tickets to all travelers but caters especially to young people and students.

Continental Europe The number of airlines flying nonstop to Cancún and Mérida from Europe was decreasing at the time of research, leaving Lufthansa, LTU and Martinair among the few still offering such service. A few sample round-trip fares (excluding taxes) included €600 from Amsterdam, €670 from Munich and €818 from Paris.

Agencies specializing in cheap tickets and student and youth travel include the following:

France
Nouvelles Frontières (☎ 08-25-00-07-47, W www.nouvelles-frontieres.fr) Dozens of offices around the country
OTU Voyages (☎ 08-20-81-78-17, W www.otu.fr) Branches across the country

Germany
STA Travel (☎ 01805-456-422, W www.sta travel.de) Branches in major cities across the country

Italy
CTS Viaggi (☎ 06-462-0431, W www.cts.it) Branches all over Italy
Passagi (☎ 06-474-0923) Stazione Termini FS, Galleria Di Tesla, Rome

Scandinavia
Kilroy Travels (W www.kilroytravels.com) Branches in many cities

Spain
Halcón Viajes (☎ 902-300-600, W www.hal conviajes.com) Over 500 branches
Viajes Zeppelin (☎ 902-384-253, W www.v-zeppelin.es) Plaza Santo Domingo 2, 28013 Madrid

Central & South America Most flights originating in Latin America for Yucatán stop in Miami or Mexico City first. At the time of research, some round-trip fares to Cancún included US$660 from Caracas, US$705 from Lima, US$1250 from São Paulo and an amazing US$443 from Buenos Aires. Student and youth fares are available from agencies such as **IVI Tours** (☎ 02-993-6082; W www.ividiomas.com; Residencia La Hacienda, Piso Bajo, Local 1-4T, Final Av Principal de las Mercedes, Caracas, Venezuela); **Asatej** (in Argentina ☎ 011-4114-7595; W www.asatej.org), which has more than a dozen offices in Argentina, as well as branches in Uruguay, Chile and Mexico; and the **Student Travel Bureau** (☎ 55-21-2512-8577; W www.stb.com.br; Rua Visconde de Pirajá 550, Ipanema, Rio de Janeiro), with 30 branches around Brazil.

For online airfares from Argentina, Brazil, Chile, Uruguay or Venezuela, try W www.viajo.com.

At the time of writing, the consortium of Central American airlines with main offices in El Salvador, **TACA** (☎ 503-267-8222; W www.taca.com; 71 Av Norte, Centro Comercial Galerías, Local 21, San Salvador), was offering round-trip fares to Cancún of US$269 from Flores, Guatemala; US$406 from Guatemala City; US$313 from Panama; and US$408 from San Salvador.

Australia & New Zealand There are no direct flights from Australia or New Zealand to Mexico. The cheapest way to get there is usually via the USA (normally Los Angeles). From Sydney or Melbourne to Cancún, round-trip fares were running around A$3000 to A$3300 at the time of research. From Auckland to Cancún was NZ$3200 to NZ$3300. Check US visa requirements if you're traveling via the USA.

Two well-known agents for cheap airfares are STA Travel and Flight Centre. **STA Travel** (in Australia ☎ 1300-733-035; W www.statravel.com.au; in New Zealand ☎ 0508-782-872; W www.statravel.co.nz) has offices in all major cities and on many university campuses. **Flight Centre** (in Australia ☎ 13-31-33, in New Zealand ☎ 0800-24-35-44; W www.flightcentre.com.au) has branches throughout Australia and New Zealand.

Some discount ticket agencies, particularly smaller ones, advertise cheap airfares in the weekend newspapers, such as the Age in Melbourne and the Sydney Morning Herald. The New Zealand Herald has a travel section in which travel agents advertise fares.

Good websites for fares are W www.travel.com.au and W www.travel.co.nz.

Travelers with Special Needs

If you have special needs of any sort – you have a broken leg, you're a vegetarian, you're traveling in a wheelchair, you're traveling with a baby, you're terrified of flying etc – you should let the airline know as soon as possible so that it can make arrangements accordingly. You should remind the airline when you reconfirm your booking (at least 72 hours before departure) and again when you check in at the airport. The disability-friendly website W www.all gohere.com has a directory that provides information on the facilities offered by various airlines.

LAND

The few tourists who reach the Yucatán Peninsula by land do so either by entering Campeche state from Tabasco or Chiapas or by entering Quintana Roo from Belize. Short of crossing illegally from Guatemala into Campeche or Quintana Roo – an effort that would require transiting many kilometers of roadless jungle – there's simply no other way to reach the Yucatán by land. (Mexico can be entered from the USA at around 40 official road crossing points; for details on these and the handful of crossings from Guatemala, see Lonely Planet's *Mexico*.)

Crossing the Mexico–Belize border at the southern tip of Quintana Roo is a rather easy affair for most tourists. An old bridge on the Río Hondo at the town of Subteniente López, 8km southwest of Chetumal, marks the official crossing point.

At the time of writing, each person leaving Belize for Mexico needed to pay at the border a departure tax of US$10 and an 'environment tax' of US$3.75. An additional US$4.25 is charged for fumigation of private vehicles. All fees must be paid in cash (in Belizean or US currency; US$1 = BZ$2), and officials usually won't make change for US currency. For Mexican entry requirements, see Visas & Documents in the Facts for the Visitor chapter.

Bus

Buses run between Chetumal in Quintana Roo and the Belizean cities of Corozal, Orange Walk and Belize City. There's also bus service between Chetumal and Flores (Guatemala), near Tikal; this requires passing through Belize. See Chetumal in the Quintana Roo chapter for details.

Car & Motorcycle

For US and Canadian visitors, taking your own vehicle across the USA–Mexico border is a practical and convenient option. Coming from overseas, you may want to buy a used car or van in the USA, where they're relatively cheap, and drive through the USA to Mexico. Buying a car in Mexico is not a practical option because of the amount of time and bureaucracy involved.

Good makes of car to take to Mexico are Volkswagen, Nissan, General Motors, Ford and Chrysler, which have manufacturing or assembly plants in Mexico and dealers in most big Mexican towns. Big cars are unwieldy on narrow roads and use a lot of gasoline. A sedan with a trunk (boot) provides safer storage than a station wagon or hatchback. Volkswagen camper vans are economical, and parts and service are easy to find.

Mexican mechanics are resourceful, and most repairs can be done quickly and inexpensively, but it still pays to take as many spare parts as you can manage and know what to do with (spare fuel filters are very useful). Tires (including spare), shock absorbers and suspension should be in good condition. For security, have something to immobilize the steering wheel, such as 'the Club'; you should also consider getting a kill switch installed.

See the Getting Around chapter for information on driving and motorcycling once you're in Mexico, and details on renting vehicles.

Motor Vehicle Insurance It is very foolish to drive in Mexico without Mexican liability insurance. If you are involved in an accident, you can be jailed and have your vehicle impounded while responsibility is assessed, or, if you are to blame for an accident causing injury or death, until you guarantee restitution to the victims and payment of any fines. This could take weeks or months. A valid Mexican insurance policy is regarded as a guarantee that restitution will be paid, and it will also expedite release of the driver. Mexican law recognizes only Mexican motor *seguro* (insurance), so a US or Canadian policy is of no use.

Mexican motor vehicle insurance is sold in US border towns; as you approach the border from the USA you will see billboards advertising offices selling Mexican policies. At the busiest border crossings (to Tijuana, Mexicali, Nogales, Agua Prieta, Ciudad Juárez, Nuevo Laredo, Reynosa and Matamoros), there are insurance offices open 24 hours a day. Some deals are better than others.

Two organizations worth looking into, both of which also offer lots of useful travel information, are **Sanborn's** (☎ 800-222-0158; ⓦ *www.sanbornsinsurance.com)* and the **American Automobile Association** *(AAA;* ⓦ *www.aaa.com).* Short-term insurance is about US$15 a day for full coverage on a car worth under US$10,000; for periods of more than two weeks it's often cheaper to get an annual policy. Liability-only insurance costs around half what full coverage costs. The AAA can provide its members with Mexican insurance and the forms needed for taking a vehicle into Mexico.

Driver's License To drive a motor vehicle in Mexico, you need a valid driver's license from your home country. Mexican police are familiar with US and Canadian licenses. Those from other countries may be scrutinized more closely, but they are still legal. International driver's licenses, provided by auto clubs, generally are not considered valid driver's licenses by local authorities.

Importing Motor Vehicles The rules for taking a vehicle into Mexico have in the past changed from time to time. You can check current laws with the AAA, a Mexican consulate or a Mexican government tourist office, or call the **Mexican Tourism Board** (in USA ☎ 800-446-3942).

You will need a temporary import permit if you want to take a vehicle more than 25km into Mexico. The permits are available at the *aduana* (customs) office near border crossings; you can register for one in advance by visiting ⓦ www.banjercito.com.mx and going to the IITV (Importación Temporal de Vehículos vía Internet) section where you'll find registration forms in both Spanish and English. You need to do this at least 24 hours (no more than 15 days) before you show up at the border.

In addition to a passport and tourist card, you'll need the following documents, which must be in your own name: a certificate of title or ownership for the vehicle; a current registration card; a driver's license; and a valid Visa, MasterCard or American Express credit card, issued by a non-Mexican institution. If you don't have an international credit card you must pay a very large cash bond. Have at least one photocopy of each of these documents as well as the original.

One person cannot bring in two vehicles. If, for example, you have a motorcycle attached to your car, you'll need another adult traveling with you to obtain a permit for the motorcycle, and that person will need to have all of the right papers for it. If the motorcycle is registered in your name,

you'll need a notarized affidavit authorizing the other person to take it into Mexico.

If you don't have an international credit card, you will have to pay a large refundable cash deposit or bond to the Banco del Ejército or an authorized Mexican *afianzadora* (bonding company) at the border. The required amounts are determined by official tables of vehicle values and range from US$200 to US$400 depending on the age and type of the vehicle. The bond (minus administrative charges) or the deposit should be refunded when the vehicle finally leaves Mexico and the temporary import permit is canceled. If you plan to leave Mexico at a different border crossing, make sure you will be able to obtain a refund there. There are offices for Banco del Ejército and authorized Mexican bonding companies at or near all the major border points.

Your vehicle permit entitles you to take the vehicle in and out of Mexico for the period shown on your tourist card. If the car is still in Mexico after that time, the *aduana* may start charging fines to your credit card and the car can be confiscated. The permit allows the vehicle to be driven by other people if the owner is in the vehicle.

When you leave Mexico for the last time, you must have the permit canceled by the Mexican authorities. An official may do this as you enter the border zone, usually 20km to 30km before the border itself. If not, you'll have to find the right official at the border crossing. If you leave Mexico without having the permit canceled, once the permit expires the authorities may assume you've left the vehicle in the country illegally and start charging fines to your credit card.

Only the owner may take the vehicle out of Mexico. If the vehicle is wrecked completely, you must contact your embassy or consulate or a Mexican customs office to make arrangements to leave without it.

SEA

In fall of 2002, **Yucatán Express** (in USA ☎ 866-353-3779, in Mexico ☎ 800-514-8497; ⓦ www.yucatanexpress.com) began sailings of a cruise ship–vehicle ferry between Tampa (Florida) and Progreso, in Yucatán state. The sailings take place between November and April; each crossing takes a day and a half. At the time of writing there were weekly Friday-evening departures from Tampa and Sunday-evening departures from Progreso. Another sailing, between Tampa and Puerto Morelos, was canceled for an indefinite period.

This isn't the first time a company has offered such service between the US and Mexico; previous attempts have been unsuccessful. Fares for passage-only start at US$102/157 one-way/round-trip per person, based on double occupancy and including all taxes and port fees. This price is for two- to six-person cabins with separate toilets and showers. Buffet meals for the duration of the journey are an additional US$62.50/125 one-way/round-trip, or you can brown-bag it or order à la carte in an expensive restaurant.

One-way/round-trip vehicle fees (including port taxes) are US$104/208 for motorcycles and US$162/323 for vehicles less than 2m high. Larger vehicles are charged by length. See the company's website and Car & Motorcycle earlier in this chapter for details on bringing a vehicle into Mexico.

Getting Around

The Mexican holiday periods of Semana Santa (the week before Easter and a couple of days after it), mid-July to mid-August, and the Christmas–New Year period of about two weeks are hectic and heavily booked throughout the country. Try to book transportation well in advance for those periods.

AIR

Flights from other parts of Mexico arrive at the airports of Campeche, Mérida, Cancún, Cozumel and Chetumal. For details, see the Getting There & Away sections of those cities in the following chapters.

Except for a few charter services, and small airlines that crop up from time to time, intrapeninsular air travel is limited to Aerocaribe flights between Cancún, Mérida and Cozumel, and twice-weekly flights between Cozumel and Chichén Itzá. Various airlines have made a go of flying between Cancún and Chetumal, in southern Quintana Roo; check with a travel agent to see if any are doing so at your time of travel. When you factor in the time and expense of getting to and from the airports, it's nearly as fast to take a 1st-class bus between Cancún and Mérida as it is to fly, and the bus is a quarter the price.

Aerocaribe (in Cancún ☎ 998-884-2000; W www.mexicana.com) is a subsidiary of Mexicana, and if no one's staffing the Aerocaribe counter, Mexicana personnel can often answer questions.

Taxes

There are two taxes on domestic flights: IVA, the consumer tax (15%), and TUA, an airport tax of about US$8.50. In Mexico, the taxes are normally included in quoted fares and paid when you buy the ticket. If you bought the ticket outside of Mexico, TUA will not have been included – you will have to pay it when you check in.

BUS

The bus system on the peninsula is generally user-friendly, especially in Cancún and Ciudad Cancún. Intercity buses are fairly frequent and go most everywhere, typically for between M$40 and M$60 an hour

(60km to 80km) on 1st-class buses. For trips of up to three or four hours on busy routes, you can usually just go to the bus terminal, buy a ticket and head out within a couple of hours. For longer trips, or trips on routes with infrequent service, it's best to book a ticket at least a day in advance.

Seats on UNO, ADO, Maya de Oro, Plus, Cristóbal Colón, Altos, and several other lines serving the peninsula can be booked through **Ticket Bus** (☎ 800-702-8000; W www.ticketbus.com.mx), a reservations service with offices in Mérida, Cancún, Cozumel and Campeche.

Immediate cash refunds of 80% to 100% are often available if you cancel your ticket more than three hours before the listed departure time. To check whether refunds apply, ask '¿Se reembolsan cancelaciones?' ('Do you refund cancellations?')

All deluxe buses, most 1st-class buses and some 2nd-class buses are air-conditioned, so bring a sweater or jacket with you. Most have computerized ticket systems that allow you to select your seat from an on-screen diagram when you buy your ticket. Try to avoid the back of the bus, which is where the toilets are and tends to give a bumpier ride. On 2nd-class buses without air-con, it is a good idea to get a window seat so that you have some control over the window (other travelers may have different ideas about what's too warm or too cool).

Baggage is generally safe in the bus's baggage hold, but always get a receipt when you hand it over. This is usually a numbered ticket matching a receipt that an attendant attaches to the bag. As always, keep your most valuable items (passport, money etc) with you in the cabin *on your person.*

Food and drinks in bus stations are overpriced; bringing your own is cheaper. Drinks and snacks are provided on some of the deluxe services. The better buses have toilets, but it's a good idea to carry some toilet paper.

Highway robbery happens very occasionally. The risk is higher at night, on isolated stretches of highway far from cities, and in 2nd-class buses. See Dangers & Annoyances in the Facts for the Visitor chapter for more information. Many travelers have had valuables stolen from their bags, which thieves have cut or simply opened while the owner was asleep or otherwise occupied. This is common on overnight 2nd-class buses coming into the peninsula from Tuxtla Gutiérrez, Palenque and other towns. The frequent stops and quantity of people getting on and off make such buses (including those on the Altos line) easy pickings for thieves.

Terminals & Schedules

Many cities and towns have a main bus station where all long-distance buses arrive and depart, or separate 1st-class and 2nd-class stations. They're usually called Terminal de Autobuses, Central Camionera, Central de Autobuses, Central de Camiones or simply La Central. Note the crucial difference between the *Central* (the bus station) and the *Centro* (the city center), which are usually a long way apart! (It helps reduce heavy traffic in downtown areas.) Frequent local buses link bus stations with city centers.

If there is no single main terminal, different bus companies will have their own terminals scattered around town. Mérida is a good example; most of its several stations each have a variety of bus lines operating out of them.

Most bus lines have schedules posted at their ticket desks in the bus station, but they aren't always comprehensive. If your destination isn't listed, ask: it may be en route to one that is. From big towns, many different bus companies may run on the same routes, so compare fares and classes of service.

Classes of Service

Long-distance buses range in quality from comfortable, nonstop air-con vehicles to decaying, suspensionless ex-city buses grinding out their dying years on dirt roads to remote settlements. The differences between the deluxe and 1st-class bus lines are not clear-cut. All of these bus lines offer a combination of features, such as extra legroom, reclining seats, drinks, snacks or videos. But broadly, buses fall into three categories.

De Lujo Deluxe services run mainly on the busy routes. They bear names such as Plus, GL or Ejecutivo. The buses are swift, new, comfortable and air-conditioned. Fares may cost just 10% or 20% more than 1st-class, or as much as 60% more for the most luxurious lines, such as ETN and UNO, which have few or no stops and offer reclining seats, plenty of legroom, snacks, hot and cold drinks, videos and toilets on board.

Primera (1a) Clase First-class buses have a comfortable, numbered seat for each passenger and often show videos. Their standards of comfort are perfectly adequate, and they usually have air-con and a toilet. They stop infrequently and serve all the sizable towns. As with deluxe buses, you must buy your ticket in the bus station before boarding.

Segunda (2a) Clase Some lines have begun using the term *servicio intermedio* rather than *segunda clase.* Second-class buses serve small towns and villages, and also offer cheaper, slower travel on some intercity routes. A few are almost as quick and comfortable as 1st-class, with new, air-con vehicles, some of which show videos. Others are old, tatty, uncomfortable and liable to break down, and will stop anywhere for someone to get on or off. Except on some major runs, there's usually no set limit on capacity, which means that if you board midroute you might make the trip *parado* (standing) rather than *sentado* (seated). If you board midroute, you pay your fare to the conductor. Fares are anywhere from 15% to 40% lower than for 1st-class. Microbuses or 'micros' are small, usually fairly new, 2nd-class buses with around 25 seats, and usually run short routes between nearby towns.

Types of Service

It's a good idea to become acquainted with the following terms if you will be using buses to get around the peninsula.

Sin escalas Nonstop
Directo Very few stops
Semi-directo A few more stops than *directo*
Ordinario Stops wherever passengers want to get on or off; deluxe and 1st-class buses are never *ordinario*
Express Nonstop on short to medium trips, very few stops on long trips
Local Bus that starts its journey at the bus station you're in and usually leaves on time; preferable to *de paso*
De paso Bus that starts its journey somewhere else but is stopping to let off and take on passengers.

A *de paso* bus may be late and may or may not have seats available; you may have to wait until it arrives before any tickets are sold. If the bus is full, you may have to wait for the next one.
Viaje redondo/sencillo Round/one-way trip

COMBIS, TRUCKS & PICKUPS
In much of the peninsula, a variety of other vehicles perform the service of transporting people from A to B, especially on short haul routes and those linking rural settlements with one another or with larger communities. Volkswagen combis and more comfortable passenger-carrying Ford or Chevrolet vans operate shuttle services between some towns, usually leaving whenever they have a full load of passengers. Fares are typically a little less than 1st-class buses. *Combi* is often used as a catch-all term for these services regardless of van type, as is *taxi colectivo* (shared taxi) or simply *colectivo.* This text uses all interchangeably.

More primitive are passenger-carrying *camiones* (trucks) and *camionetas* (pickups). Standing in the back of a lurching truck with a couple of dozen *campesinos* (farm workers) and their machetes and animals is at least an experience to remember. Fares are similar to 2nd-class bus fares.

CAR & MOTORCYCLE
Driving anywhere in Mexico can be risky, but you can minimize those risks a great deal by driving only during daylight hours and by driving only on paved roads. That said, having your own wheels is often the only way to reach many destinations in a timely and convenient manner.

Rules of the Road
Traffic laws and speed limits rarely seem to be enforced on the highways. In the cities, obey the rules so you don't give the police an excuse to demand a 'fine' payable on the spot. Some foreign drivers escape through total ignorance (real or feigned) of Spanish (and English, at times) in dealing with the police. The standard bribe for minor traffic infringements is M$20 for locals; anywhere from M$20 to M$50 usually suffices for those foreigners who don't mind perpetuating police corruption.

Most Mexican drivers follow generally accepted (if not always 100% legal) road rules. You can save yourself a lot of stress by observing how they drive and either imitating it or at least just going with it (in the case of the more dangerous maneuvers). When drivers pull out to pass (overtake) a vehicle, they often flash their headlights at oncoming traffic. It's considered courteous for said traffic to flash in return and make room for the passer to get by. Many passing drivers also put on their left turn indicator while passing, and the right one when returning to their lane.

But as in some other countries, the left flasher is also sometimes used by a slower-moving vehicle to indicate it's safe to pass. Or it could mean the driver is going to turn left. Which explains the Mexican custom of pulling off to the right side of the road and waiting until traffic is clear in both directions before making a left turn (unless there's a special lane for turning left).

Fuel & Service
All *gasolina* (gasoline) and diesel fuel in Mexico is sold by the government's monopoly, Pemex (Petróleos Mexicanos). Most towns of any size have a Pemex station, and the stations are pretty common on major roads. Nevertheless, in remote areas it's better to fill up when you can; this book contains warnings about a few of the long gasless stretches. Some stations take credit cards, but you should count on having to use cash.

The gasoline on sale is all *sin plomo* (unleaded). There are two varieties: Magna, equivalent to US regular unleaded, and Premium, equivalent to US super unleaded. At the time of research, Magna cost a bit less than M$6 a liter (about US$2 a US gallon), and Premium was about M$7 a liter. Diesel fuel is widely available at just under M$5 a liter, though it sometimes contains water or particulates. Installing a pre-filter can help; fuel–water separators (widely available in Mexico) give protection as well. If diesel drivers change their oil and filter about every 3500km, they should have no problems.

All stations have pump attendants, and though most of them are honest, some employ a number of methods to cheat customers. Check that the pump registers zero pesos to start with (sometimes attendants leave them on, with the nozzle not replaced properly, between customers). Be quick to

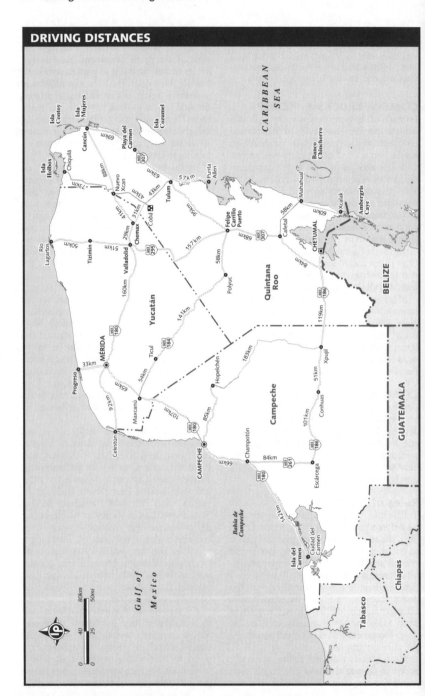

check afterward that you have been given the amount you requested – the attendants often reset the pump immediately and start to serve another customer. Having a passenger (if you're not traveling alone) watch the pump from start to finish can avoid problems. It's customary to tip two or three pesos when buying gas; more if you have the windows washed.

Road Conditions

The Yucatán has a wide network of roads ranging from excellent to excrement. Many highways are nearly up to European and North American standards, although some secondary highways (those serving remote communities) have a lot of potholes and are very slow going. Driving at night is especially dangerous – common hazards are unlit roads and vehicles, as well as rocks, livestock and wildlife on the roads. Other nocturnal dangers include the occasional intoxicated pedestrian or three-wheeled bicycle rider. Hijacks and robberies, though rare, occur usually at night. You can expect fairly frequent drug and weapon searches by the army and police, especially at state borders and on rural roads near the Caribbean.

Town and country roads are often poorly or idiosyncratically signposted, especially in the wake of a hurricane.

In towns and cities, be especially wary of *Alto* (Stop) signs, *topes* (speed bumps) and holes in the road. They are often not where you'd expect, and missing one can cost you in traffic fines or car damage. Speed bumps are also used to slow traffic on highways that pass through built-up areas: they are usually signed, but not always, and some of them are severe.

Toll Roads The few toll *(cuota)* roads on the peninsula are quicker and safer than the free alternatives, as they are well maintained, lack speed bumps, and have a higher speed limit. But they can be expensive. The worst is the road that runs from Cancún nearly to Mérida. It has only two exits in its entire length and costs an outrageous M$285 to go the distance in either direction.

Motorcycle Hazards Certain aspects of Mexican roads make them particularly hazardous for bikers, including poor signage of road or lane closures, lots of dogs and other animals on the roads, a lack of hotels and motels on some stretches of highway, debris and deep potholes. In addition, it rains a lot on the peninsula, and many roads get extremely slick when wet. Sunburn is another hazard.

Parking

It's inadvisable to park on the street overnight, and many cheap city hotels don't provide parking. Sometimes you can leave a car out front and the night porter will keep an eye on it. You may have to use a commercial *estacionamiento* (parking lot), which might cost M$50 to M$70 overnight and M$3 to M$7 per hour during the day. When parking on the street, look carefully for signs prohibiting it; sometimes they are posted flat against walls and at a height that makes them impossible to see from inside the car.

Other signs to watch for are *'se usará grúa*' which means cars will be towed, and *'se ponchan llantes gratis,'* 'tires punctured for free' – private citizens put the latter sign up in their driveways. In some towns, a yellow-painted curb means parking is allowed, while white means no parking. Other towns reverse this; observe the general trend.

Breakdown Assistance

The Mexican tourism ministry, Secretária de Turismo (Sectur), maintains a network of Ángeles Verdes (Green Angels) – bilingual mechanics in green trucks who patrol each major stretch of highway in Mexico at least twice daily during daylight hours searching for stranded motorists. They make minor repairs, replace small parts, provide fuel and oil, and arrange towing and other assistance by radio if necessary. Service is free; parts, gasoline and oil are provided at cost.

Most mechanical problems can be fixed efficiently and inexpensively by mechanics in towns and cities as long as the parts are available. Volkswagen, Ford, Nissan/Datsun, Chrysler and General Motors parts are the easiest to obtain; others may have to be ordered from the USA.

Accidents

Under Mexico's legal system, all drivers involved in a road accident are detained and their vehicles impounded while responsibility is assessed. For minor accidents, drivers will probably be released if they have insurance to cover any damage they may have caused. But the culpable driver's vehicle may remain impounded until damages are paid. If the accident causes injury or death, the responsible driver will be jailed until he or she guarantees restitution to the victims and payment of any fines. Determining responsibility *could* take weeks or even months. (Mexican drivers often *don't* stop after accidents.)

Your embassy can give you only limited help, and adequate Mexican insurance coverage is the only real protection. For detailed information, see Motor Vehicle Insurance in the Getting There & Away chapter.

Rental

Auto rental in Mexico is expensive by US or European standards, but it can be worthwhile if you want to visit several places in a short time and have three or four people to share the cost. It can also be useful for getting off the beaten track, where public transport is slow or scarce.

It's very easy to rent a vehicle in the Yucatán if you meet certain requirements. Renters must have a valid driver's license from their home country and a passport, and are usually required to be at least 25 years old. Sometimes 21 years of age is acceptable, but you may have to pay more. A major credit card or a large cash deposit is needed. Be sure to get a signed rental agreement and read the small print, and to check carefully the condition of the car, including the fuel level, against the diagram that usually accompanies the contract, before signing anything.

In addition to the basic daily or weekly rental rate, you pay for insurance, tax and fuel. Ask exactly what the insurance covers; at a legal minimum you need third-party insurance (liability, or *daños a terceros*). Damage and loss policies sometimes cover only 90% of the car's value in case of theft and don't cover 'partial theft,' such as theft of wiper blades or tires.

Most rental agencies offer a choice between a per-kilometer deal and unlimited kilometers. The latter is usually preferable if you intend to do some hard driving. Local firms are often cheaper than the international ones. During the low tourist season, you can usually find a Volkswagen Beetle – often the cheapest car available – for M$300 to M$400 a day with unlimited kilometers and insurance and tax included; add M$150 to M$250 if renting the vehicle during high tourist season – you'll need to book ahead to get this rate then. The charge for drop-off in another city is usually about M$3 per kilometer.

You can book vehicles through the various agencies listed in the individual state chapters, or through the foreign offices of the big-name international agencies. Doing the latter can sometimes get you lower rates, but be aware that some of these offices are only affiliated with the companies whose names they bear. In the event of a dispute, the big-name agency may bow out and leave you to try to settle with the Mexican firm. See the boxed table 'Car Rental Companies' for contact details of international firms that have offices located in the Yucatán.

Small (50cc–125cc) motorcycles and scooters are rented in a few tourist centers. You're usually required to have a driver's license and credit card. Even when new these bikes don't have great suspension, and can be difficult to control with more than one person aboard – don't double up. If you have no experience riding, don't rent a motorcycle at all. Mexico is not the place to

Car Rental Companies

company	in the USA	in Mexico	website
Alamo	☎ 800-462-5266	☎ 800-849-8001	W www.goalamo.com
Avis	☎ 800-230-4898	☎ 998-886-0221	W www.avis.com
Budget	☎ 800-472-3325	☎ 800-712-0324	W www.drivebudget.com
Europcar	☎ 877-940-6900	☎ 998-887-3272	W www.europcar.com
Hertz	☎ 800-654-3001	☎ 800-709-5000	W www.hertz.com.mx
Thrifty	☎ 800-847-4389	☎ 998-886-0333	W www.thrifty.com

learn; speed bumps, unfamiliar traffic patterns and driving habits, speeding autos and drunken fellow travelers combine to assure a steady stream of accidents and injuries, as well as the occasional fatality.

Mexico has a helmet law, which the police strictly enforce. If you rent a bike, be sure to request a helmet.

BICYCLE
Cycling on the peninsula's highways can be hair-raising because of the narrow shoulders and speeding traffic. Many routes see a lot of local bicycle traffic, but on some of them you'll often see cyclists, pedestrians and even dogs step off the pavement and wait by the side of the road until traffic passes. The tropical sun can be brutal, but at least the roads are mostly flat. If you're bringing your own bike to tour, be prepared to handle your own repairs.

Rental
Some touristed areas that offer relatively sedate conditions for biking, as well as inexpensive rentals (often of one-speed bikes), include Valladolid, Isla Mujeres and Cozumel.

Purchase
Of course it's possible to purchase a bicycle in the Yucatán. Indeed, if you plan on staying on the peninsula for months and want to get around by bike or at least exercise on one, purchasing isn't a bad option, as there are many inexpensive models available in the big cities. A good place to pick up a cheap bike is the duty-free Zona Libre between Belize and Mexico; see Zona Libre near the end of the Quintana Roo chapter.

HITCHHIKING
Hitchhiking is never entirely safe in any country in the world, and is not recommended. Travelers who decide to hitch should understand that they are taking a small but potentially serious risk. People who do choose to hitch will be safer if they travel in pairs and let someone know where they are planning to go. A woman traveling alone certainly should not hitchhike in Mexico, and even two women together is not advisable.

However, some people do choose to hitchhike, and it's not an uncommon way of getting to some of the off-the-beaten-track archaeological sites and other places that tend to be poorly served by bus. Always be alert to possible dangers wherever you are.

In Mexico, it's customary for the hitchhiker to offer to pay for the ride, especially if the ride is in a work or commercial vehicle. As a general rule, offer about M$15 per person for every 30 minutes of the ride but not less than M$20 total and never more than M$100.

LOCAL TRANSPORTATION
Generally known as *camiones,* local buses are the cheapest way of getting around cities and to nearby villages. They run everywhere, frequently, and are dirt cheap (fares in cities are rarely more than M$4).

Colectivos and *combis* run in towns as well as between towns, and are cheaper than taxis, quicker and less crowded than buses. They run along set routes, which are usually displayed on the windshield, and will pick you up or drop you off on any corner along that route. Tell the driver where you want to go; you normally pay at the end of the trip, and the fare usually depends on how far you go.

Taxis are common in towns and cities. They're often surprisingly economical, and they're useful if you have a lot of baggage, need to get from point A to point B quickly, or are worried about theft on public transport. If a taxi has a meter, ask the driver, *'¿Funciona el taxímetro?'* ('Does the meter work?') If it doesn't, or if the taxi doesn't have a meter, or you're taking a long ride, establish the price of the ride *before* getting in.

Quintana Roo

The state of Quintana Roo (kin-tah-nah **roh**), Mexico's only Caribbean property, stretches north from the border with Belize to the extreme northeastern tip of the Yucatán Peninsula. The coastline is blessed with numerous white-sand beaches custom-made for lazing on, and the longest barrier reef in the Western Hemisphere runs not far offshore almost its entire distance to Isla Mujeres. The crystal-clear Caribbean waters of the reefs here teem with tropical fish, and provide a profusion of excellent diving and snorkeling sites ranked among the world's best. The state also holds the three longest underwater cave systems in the world, their colossal connecting hallways filled with speleological wonders and water as clear as thin air. Quintana Roo is home to several impressive Mayan ruins and to resorts of every size and flavor.

Owing in part to its geographic isolation and the effects of the War of the Castes, the region did not have an official name until 1902, when it was given the status of territory and named after Andrés Quintana Roo, the poet-warrior-statesman who presided over the drafting of Mexico's constitution. In 1974, largely as a result of the development of Cancún, 'QR' achieved statehood.

Cancún

☎ 998 • pop 457,000

For many travelers, Cancún is merely a port of entry, a gateway into the Yucatán Peninsula to be passed through as quickly as possible. For millions of others, however, it is a full-blown destination in itself.

In the 1970s Mexico's ambitious tourism planners decided to outdo Acapulco with a brand-new, world-class resort located on the Yucatán Peninsula. The place they chose was a deserted sand spit located offshore from the little fishing village of Puerto Juárez, on the peninsula's eastern shore. The name of the place was Cancún. Vast sums were sunk into landscaping and infrastructure, yielding straight, well-paved roads, potable tap water and great swaths of sandy beach. Cancún's raison d'être is to shelter planeloads of tourists who fly in to spend

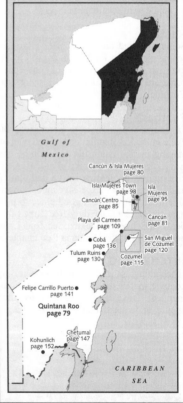

Gulf of Mexico

Cancún & Isla Mujeres page 80

Isla Mujeres Town page 98

Cancún Centro page 85

Isla Mujeres page 95

Playa del Carmen page 109

Cancún page 81

Cobá page 136

San Miguel de Cozumel page 120

Tulum Ruins page 130

Cozumel page 115

Felipe Carrillo Puerto page 141

Quintana Roo page 79

Chetumal page 147

Kohunlich page 152

CARIBBEAN SEA

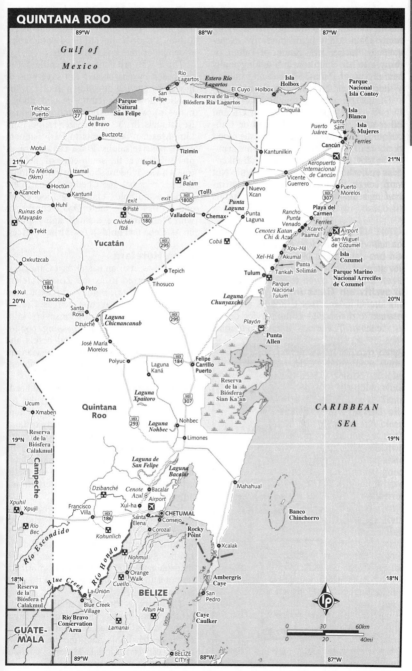

QUINTANA ROO

Gulf of Mexico

Río Lagartos
Estero Río Lagartos
El Cuyo
Holbox
San Felipe
Reserva de la Biósfera Ría Lagartos
Chiquilá
Telchac Puerto
Parque Natural San Felipe
MEX 27
Dzilam de Bravo
Buctzotz
Isla Holbox
Parque Nacional Isla Contoy
Puerto Juárez
Punta Sam
Isla Blanca
Isla Mujeres
Ferries
Cancún

Motul
Tizimín
Kantunilkin
Espita
To Mérida (9km)
Izamal
Ek' Balam
21°N
Aeropuerto Internacional de Cancún
Acanceh
Hoctún
Kantunil
Huhí
exit
exit
(Toll)
MEX 180D
Nuevo Xcan
Vicente Guerrero
Puerto Morelos
MEX 307
Ruinas de Mayapán
Pisté
MEX 180
Valladolid
Chemax
Punta Laguna
Punta Laguna
Playa del Carmen
Tekit
Chichén Itzá
Rancho Punta Venado
Ferries
Airport
San Miguel de Cozumel
Xcaret
Xpu-Há
Paamul
Cenotes Katan Chi & Azul
Yucatán
MEX 295
Cobá
Xel-Há
Akumal
Isla Cozumel
Oxkutzcab
Tepich
Punta Solimán
Parque Marino Nacional Arrecifes de Cozumel
Xul
MEX 184
Peto
Tihosuco
Tulum
Tankah
20°N
Tzucacab
Parque Nacional Tulum
Santa Rosa
Dzuiché
Laguna Chicnancanab
Laguna Chunyaxché
MEX 295
José María Morelos
Playón
Punta Allen
Polyuc
MEX 184
Felipe Carrillo Puerto
Laguna Kaná
Laguna Xpaitoro
Reserva de la Biósfera Sian Ka'an
MEX 307
CARIBBEAN SEA
Ucum
Xmaben
Quintana Roo
MEX 293
Laguna Nohbec
Nohbec
19°N
Reserva de la Biósfera Calakmul
Limones
Campeche
Laguna de San Felipe
Laguna Bacalar
Dzibanché
Cenote Azul
Bacalar
Airport
Mahahual
Xpuhil
Xpujil
Francisco Villa
Xul-ha
MEX 186
CHETUMAL
Sánta Elena
Banco Chinchorro
Río Bec
Kohunlich
Consejo
Corozal
Rocky Point
Nohmul
Xcalak
18°N
Reserva de la Biósfera Calakmul
Blue Creek
Orange Walk
Cuello
Río Hondo
Ambergris Caye
La Unión
Blue Creek Village
BELIZE
San Pedro
GUATE-MALA
Río Bravo Conservation Area
Lamanai
Altun Ha
Caye Caulker

0   30   60km
0   20   40mi

Río Escondido

BELIZE CITY

89°W   88°W   87°W

one or two weeks in a resort hotel, throng the beaches and pack the clubs before flying home again. Many board buses for excursions to Chichén Itzá, Xcaret or Tulum, or browse in air-conditioned shopping malls straight out of Dallas. More than 2 million visitors descend on Cancún each year.

During spring break (roughly mid-March to mid-April), hordes of partying US and other university students descend on Cancún, driving up lodging prices and the blood pressure of locals, many of whom are scandalized by the public displays of drunkenness and other debauchery that ensue. Not surprisingly, accident and crime rates (including sexual assaults) tend to go up at this time also.

ORIENTATION

Cancún consists of two very distinct areas – Ciudad Cancún and Isla Cancún (the Zona Hotelera).

Downtown Cancún

On the mainland lies Ciudad Cancún, a planned city founded as the service center of the resort. The area of interest to tourists is referred to as *'el centro'* (downtown). The main north–south thoroughfare is Av Tulum, a wide boulevard lined with banks, shopping centers and restaurants.

Those who are content to trundle out to the beach by bus or taxi can save pots of money by staying downtown in one of the smaller, low- to medium-priced hotels, many of which have swimming pools. Restaurants in the city center range from ultra-Mexican taco joints to fairly smooth and expensive salons. Plaza Las Américas, on Av Tulum at the south edge of the centro, is a vast modern shopping mall holding Sears, Liverpool and Chedraui department stores; a multiplex cinema; a food court; and a salsa dance club. Don't confuse it with Plaza América, a small, aging arcade on Av Cobá that holds a few airline offices.

Zona Hotelera

The sandy spit of an island, Isla Cancún, is usually referred to as the Zona Hotelera (so-na oh-te-le-ra). Boulevard Kukulcán, a four-lane divided avenue, leaves Ciudad Cancún and heads eastward for several kilometers along the island passing condominium developments, several hotels and shopping complexes, to Punta Cancún (Cancún Point) and the Centro de Convenciones (Convention Center).

From Punta Cancún, the boulevard heads south for 13km, flanked on both sides for much of the way by mammoth hotels, shopping centers, dance clubs and many restaurants and bars, to Punta Nizuc (Nizuc Point). Here it turns westward and then rejoins the mainland, cutting through light tropical forest for a few more kilometers to its southern terminus at Cancun's international airport.

Few of the buildings in the Zona Hotelera have numbered addresses. Instead, because the vast majority of them are on Blvd Kukulcán, their location is described in relation to their distance from the 'Km 0' roadside marker at the boulevard's northern terminus in Ciudad Cancún. Each kilometer is similarly marked.

The airport is about 8km south of the city center. Puerto Juárez, the port for passenger ferries to Isla Mujeres, is about 3km north of the center. Punta Sam, the dock for the slower car ferries to Isla Mujeres, is about 7km north of the center.

CANCÚN & ISLA MUJERES

CANCÚN

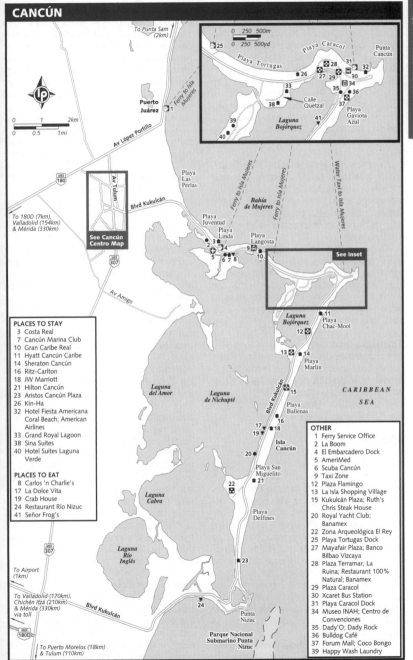

To Punta Sam (2km)

Ferry to Isla Mujeres

Puerto Juárez

Av López Portillo

To 180D (7km), Valladolid (154km) & Mérida (330km)

Blvd Kukulcán

Av Tulum

See Cancún Centro Map

Av Amigo

0   250   500m
0   250   500yd

Playa Caracol
Playa Tortugas
Punta Cancún
Playa Gaviota Azul
Calle Quetzal
Laguna Bojórquez

Playa Las Perlas

Bahía de Mujeres

Ferry to Isla Mujeres

Water Taxi to Isla Mujeres

Playa Juventud
Playa Linda
Playa Langosta

Laguna Bojórquez
Playa Chac-Mool

Laguna del Amor

Laguna de Nichupté

See Inset

Playa Marlin

Blvd Kukulcán

CARIBBEAN SEA

Playa Ballenas

Isla Cancún

Playa San Miguelito

Laguna Cabra

Playa Delfines

Laguna Río Inglés

To Airport (1km)

To Valladolid (170km), Chichén Itzá (210km) & Mérida (330km) via toll

Blvd Kukulcán

To Puerto Morelos (18km) & Tulum (110km)

Punta Nizuc

Parque Nacional Submarino Punta Nizuc

PLACES TO STAY
3 Costa Real
7 Cancún Marina Club
10 Gran Caribe Real
11 Hyatt Cancún Caribe
14 Sheraton Cancún
16 Ritz-Carlton
18 JW Marriott
21 Hilton Cancún
23 Aristos Cancún Plaza
26 Kin-Ha
32 Hotel Fiesta Americana Coral Beach; American Airlines
33 Grand Royal Lagoon
38 Sina Suites
40 Hotel Suites Laguna Verde

PLACES TO EAT
8 Carlos 'n Charlie's
17 La Dolce Vita
19 Crab House
24 Restaurant Río Nizuc
41 Señor Frog's

OTHER
1 Ferry Service Office
2 La Boom
4 El Embarcadero Dock
5 AmeriMed
6 Scuba Cancún
9 Taxi Zone
12 Plaza Flamingo
13 La Isla Shopping Village
15 Kukulcán Plaza; Ruth's Chris Steak House
20 Royal Yacht Club; Banamex
22 Zona Arqueológica El Rey
25 Playa Tortugas Dock
27 Mayafair Plaza; Banco Bilbao Vizcaya
28 Plaza Terramar; La Ruina; Restaurant 100% Natural; Banamex
29 Plaza Caracol
30 Xcaret Bus Station
31 Playa Caracol Dock
34 Museo INAH; Centro de Convenciones
35 Dady'O; Dady Rock
36 Bulldog Café
37 Forum Mall; Coco Bongo
39 Happy Wash Laundry

INFORMATION

Tourist Offices

There is a sporadically staffed **tourist information booth** in the international arrivals section of the airport. Downtown, the **Cancún Convention & Visitors Bureau** (☎ 884-6531; Av Cobá near Av Tulum; open 9am-2pm & 4pm-7pm Mon-Fri) has ample supplies of printed material and usually a fairly knowledgeable English-speaker in attendance. Its primary focus is Cancún, but the bureau has information on the state of Quintana Roo as well.

Its parent, the **state tourism office** (Sedetur; ☎ 881-9000; Pecari 23; open 9am-9pm Mon-Fri), is mysteriously tucked away without a sign a fair walk south of the centro, but its information is good and there's usually someone in attendance who speaks English well.

The magazine *Cancún Tips*, available at some tourist offices and many hotels, has good maps and somewhat current information. The fat stack of coupons inside are good for everything from a free glass of wine with a meal to large discounts on the rack rates of some hotels.

Immigration

For visa and tourist-card extensions (usually same-day service), visit the **Instituto Nacional de Migración** (☎ 884-1404; Av Náder 1 at Av Uxmal; open 9am-1pm Mon-Fri), immigration office, downtown. Enter the lefthand, southernmost of the two offices.

Money

Among the banks in the Zona Hotelera are **Banco Bilbao Vizcaya** (Mayafair Plaza), across from the Fiesta América Cancún hotel; two branches of **Banamex** (Plaza Terramar; Royal Yacht Club) with currency exchanges and ATMs; and **Bital** (Centro de Convenciones), a full-service bank. There are ATMs and *casas de cambio* (open long hours) at Punta Cancún and inside practically all the malls. Most of the resorts on the island will change money, but they offer poor exchange rates and sometimes limit transactions to guests only. Exchange rates on the island are generally less favorable than those downtown, but not enough to warrant a special trip.

ATMs are common downtown, and there are several banks on Av Tulum between Avs

Cobá and Uxmal, including **Bancomer** and **Banamex**. Most banks are open 9am to 4pm Monday to Friday, and 10am to 2pm Saturday, but foreign-exchange transactions are sometimes limited to between 10am and noon. More convenient are the many currency-exchange booths on the east side of Av Tulum, halfway between Avs Cobá and Uxmal (and scattered elsewhere throughout the city); most are open 8am to 8pm daily.

ATMs are also located at Cancún's international airport; for more details see under Air in the Getting There & Away section later.

Post & Communications

There is no post office in the Zona Hotelera, but most hotels' reception desks sell stamps and will mail letters. The **main post office** (cnr Avs Xel-Há & Sunyaxchén; open 9am-4pm Mon-Fri, for stamps only 9am-1pm Sat) is downtown at the edge of Mercado 28.

There are numerous Telmex pay phones throughout Cancún that accept prepaid phone cards. Beware of phones accepting credit cards; charges can be very high. The **call center** at Soberanis Hostal (Av Cobá 5) offers good rates on international calls and calls to other parts of Mexico, as well as decent Internet connections at reasonable rates.

At the time of research, Internet access in the Zona Hotelera was scarce, expensive and sketchy. An unnamed place on the 2nd-floor of **Kukulcán Plaza** charges M$10 for five minutes or M$70 per hour. Other malls, including **Plaza Caracol**, have terminals charging similar prices.

Public Internet facilities in Cancún centro come and go, but there is usually a cluster along Av Uxmal in the block north of the bus terminal. Many of these facilities also offer telephone and fax services. At the time of research **Vikings del Caribe** (Av Uxmal at Pino; open 8am-midnight daily) offered lightning-fast connections at bargain rates (M$12 per hour), as well as a variety of phone services.

Travel Agencies

In the Zona Hotelera, most big hotels have travel agencies. Downtown, next to the Soberanis Hostal, **Nómadas Travel** (☎ 892-2320; W www.nomadastravel.com.mx; Av Cobá 5) is a student-oriented agency that books and makes changes to air tickets, makes some accommodation reservations on the Yucatán Peninsula, and offers packages to Cuba, among other services.

Bookstores

Fama (Av Tulum 105), downtown near the southern end of Tulipanes, has a large variety of domestic and international magazines, and a fair selection of Mexican road atlases and books in various languages. There are some guidebooks and many texts dealing with Cancún, the Yucatán Peninsula and the ancient Mayan civilization.

Laundry

All the resorts in the Zona offer laundry service, but if you want to save some money try **Happy Wash Laundry** (☎ 044-999-884-49960; Paseo Pok-Ta-Pok; open 9am-9pm Mon-Sat), near the Hotel Suites Laguna Verde. It charges M$15 per kilogram and takes two hours for the service.

Lava y Seca (☎ 892-4789; Crisantemos 20; open 9am-6pm Mon-Sat), downtown, charges M$30 to wash, dry and fold up to 3kg.

Medical Services

AmeriMed (☎ 849-4911, 24hr emergency ☎ 881-3434; Blvd Kukulcán Km 4; open 8am-9pm daily), just west of the Playa Linda bridge, has bilingual (Spanish and English) doctors and a complete emergency room, and accepts many insurance plans from around the world.

Dangers & Annoyances

Cancún has a reputation for being safe, and the Zona Hotelera is certainly well policed. However, as the city's mainland component grows ever larger (in part because of an influx of people fleeing the crime and pollution of Mexico City), it is seeing an increase in street crime. If you stick to the touristed areas you should have few problems. As elsewhere, avoid leaving valuables unattended in your hotel room or beside your beach towel.

Vehicular traffic on Blvd Kukulcán, particularly as it passes between the malls, bars and discotheques at Punta Cancún, is a serious concern. Pedestrians (many of them drunk) are regularly hit by cars (some of whose drivers are drunk). The stationing of traffic cops throughout the Zona Hotelera has finally resulted in limiting the speed at which buses fly through the area. The buses still tailgate, however; you're best off pulling into the left lane (yes, the passing lane) to let them overtake you.

See Beach Safety under Beaches later for information on water hazards.

MAYAN RUINS

There are two sets ·of Mayan ruins in the Zona Hotelera, and though neither is particularly impressive, both are worth a look if time permits. In the **Zona Arqueológica El Rey** (admission M$29; open 8am-5pm daily), on the west side of Blvd Kukulcán between Km 17 and Km 18, there's a small temple and several ceremonial platforms. The other, much smaller, site is **Yamil Lu'um** (admission free), atop a beachside knoll on the parklike grounds separating the Sheraton Cancún and Park Royal Pirámides hotels. Only the outward-sloping remains of the weathered temple's walls still stand, but the ruin makes for a pleasant venture, as much for its lovely setting as anything else. To reach the site visitors must pass through either of the hotels flanking it or approach it from the beach – there is no direct access from the boulevard.

The tiny Mayan structure and chac-mool statue on the beautifully kept grounds of the Sheraton Hotel are authentic and were found on the spot.

MUSEO INAH

This archaeological museum (☎ 883-0305; admission M$32; open 9am-8pm Tues-Fri, 10am-7pm Sat & Sun), operated by the National Institute of Anthropology and History (INAH), is on the south side of the Centro de Convenciones in the Zona Hotelera. Most of the items – including jewelry, masks and skulls exhibiting the deformities caused intentionally by Mayan parents to beautify their children – are from the post-Classic period (AD 1200–1500). Also here are part of a Classic-period hieroglyphic staircase (inscribed with dates from the 6th century) and the stucco head that gave the local archaeological zone its name of El Rey (The King).

Most of the informative signs are in Spanish only, but at the ticket counter you can get a fractured-English information sheet detailing the contents of the museum's 47 showcases. The museum also has a small but good selection of books on Mayan-related subjects, and a tiny gift counter.

BEACHES
Access

Under Mexican law you have the right to walk and swim on every beach in the country except those within military compounds. In practice, it is difficult to approach many stretches of beach without walking through the lobby of a hotel, particularly in the Zona Hotelera. However, as long as you look like a tourist (this shouldn't be hard, right?), you'll usually be permitted to cross the lobby and proceed to the beach.

Starting from Ciudad Cancún in the northwest, all of Isla Cancún's beaches are on the left-hand side of the road (the lagoon is on your right). The first beaches are Playa Las Perlas, Playa Linda, Playa Langosta, Playa Tortugas and Playa Caracol; after you round Punta Cancún, the beaches to the south are Playa Gaviota Azul, Playa Chac-Mool, Playa Marlin, the long stretch of Playa Ballenas, Playa San Miguelito and finally, at Km 17, Playa Delfines.

Delfines is about the only beach with a public parking lot big enough to be useful; unfortunately, its sand is coarser and darker than the exquisite fine, white sand of the more northerly beaches.

Beach Safety

Cancún's ambulance crews respond to as many as a dozen near-drownings per week. The most dangerous beaches seem to be Playa Delfines and Playa Chac-Mool.

As experienced swimmers know, a beach fronting onto open sea can be deadly dangerous, and Cancún's eastern beaches are no exception. Though the surf is usually gentle, undertow is a possibility, and sudden storms (called *nortes*) can blacken the sky and sweep in at any time without warning. A system of colored pennants warns beachgoers of potential dangers:

Blue	Normal, safe conditions
Yellow	Use caution, changeable conditions
Red	Unsafe conditions; use a swimming pool instead

WATER SPORTS

For decent **snorkeling**, you need to travel to one of the nearby reefs. Resort hotels, travel agencies and various tour operators in the area can book you on day-cruise boats that take snorkelers to the barrier reef, as well as to other good sites in the region. Scuba Cancún (see following) offers a Cancún snorkeling tour for US$27. To see the relatively sparse aquatic life off Cancún's beaches, you can rent equipment for about US$10 a day from most luxury hotels.

For **diving**, try **Scuba Cancún** (☎ 849-7508; W www.scubacancun.com.mx; Blvd Kukulcán Km 5), a family-owned and PADI-certified operation with many years of experience. It offers a variety of dive options (including cenote, night and nitrox dives), and snorkeling and fishing trips, at reasonable prices. The bilingual (English and Spanish) staff are safety oriented and environmentally aware; there's also a Japanese-speaking instructor.

Most of the major resorts rent **kayaks** and the usual water toys; a few make them available to guests free of charge.

ORGANIZED TOURS

Most hotels and travel agencies work with companies that offer tours to surrounding attractions. **Mundo Maya Travel** (☎ 884-4564 ext 403; W www.mayaworld.cc; Av Cobá 5), in the lobby of the Soberanis Hostal, offers good rates on tours to such places as: Chichén Itzá (M$400, including guide and buffet lunch), Tulum ruins and Xel-Há (M$440, including guide), and Xcaret (M$595). All prices are per person and include admission.

PLACES TO STAY

As happens in other popular Yucatán Peninsula destinations, the rates at some of Cancún's hotels change with the tourist seasons; every hotelier's idea of when these seasons change is slightly different. Some raise rates in July and August, when Europeans (and Mexican students) take their vacations. Rate changes occur more at mid-range and top-end establishments, though during Semana Santa (Easter Week) rates can rise at budget hotels as well. Broadly, Cancún's high season is from mid-December through March, with peaks at Semana Santa and the week between Christmas and January 1. Lodging can get tight from mid-March to mid-April, when thousands of (mostly American) university students are in town for spring break festivities.

Wherever possible in the following listings, simple low- and high-season prices

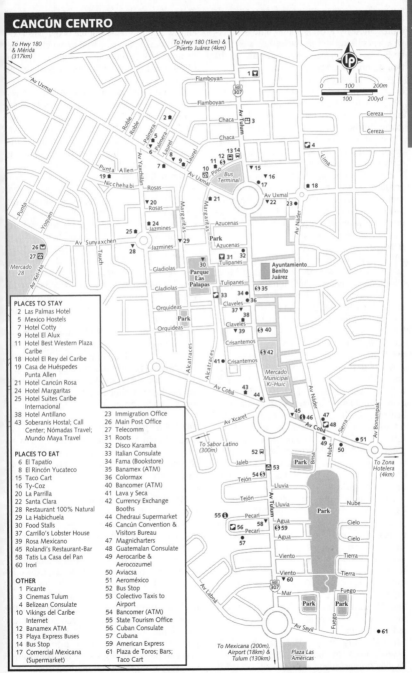

CANCÚN CENTRO

PLACES TO STAY
2 Las Palmas Hotel
5 Mexico Hostels
7 Hotel Cotty
9 Hotel El Alux
11 Hotel Best Western Plaza Caribe
18 Hotel El Rey del Caribe
19 Casa de Huéspedes Punta Allen
21 Hotel Cancún Rosa
24 Hotel Margaritas
25 Hotel Suites Caribe Internacional
38 Hotel Antillano
43 Soberanis Hostal; Call Center; Nómadas Travel; Mundo Maya Travel

PLACES TO EAT
6 El Tapatío
8 El Rincón Yucateco
15 Taco Cart
16 Ty-Coz
20 La Parrilla
22 Santa Clara
28 Restaurant 100% Natural
29 La Habichuela
30 Food Stalls
37 Carrillo's Lobster House
39 Rosa Mexicano
45 Rolandi's Restaurant-Bar
58 Tatis La Casa del Pan
60 Irori

OTHER
1 Picante
3 Cinemas Tulum
4 Belizean Consulate
10 Vikings del Caribe Internet
12 Banamex ATM
13 Playa Express Buses
14 Bus Stop
17 Comercial Mexicana (Supermarket)
23 Immigration Office
26 Main Post Office
27 Telecomm
31 Roots
32 Disco Karamba
33 Italian Consulate
34 Fama (Bookstore)
35 Banamex (ATM)
36 Colormax
40 Bancomer (ATM)
41 Lava y Seca
42 Currency Exchange Booths
44 Chedraui Supermarket
46 Cancún Convention & Visitors Bureau
47 Magnicharters
48 Guatemalan Consulate
49 Aerocaribe & Aerocozumel
50 Aviacsa
51 Aeroméxico
52 Bus Stop
53 Colectivo Taxis to Airport
54 Bancomer (ATM)
55 State Tourism Office
56 Cuban Consulate
57 Cubana
59 American Express
61 Plaza de Toros; Bars; Taco Cart

are detailed; more complex schemes are represented by a price range unless otherwise specified; and peak-season rates may be higher. All places listed have air-conditioning unless otherwise noted.

As in most of the Yucatán Peninsula, bookings in Cancún were off throughout 2002 due to the global economic downturn and fear of terrorist attacks, which led to many higher-end hotels offering much lower rates than in years past. Some hotels began offering discounts and some began offering extras such as free breakfasts.

Even in good economic times, and regardless of season, if your showing hesitation about a place doesn't bring the price down, it's worth testing the waters by asking for a *descuento* (discount).

Budget

All budget accommodations listed here are downtown and, with the exception of Mexico Hostels, have air-conditioning. 'Budget' is a relative term; prices in Cancún are higher for what you get than most anywhere else in Mexico. Much of Cancún's cheap lodging is within a few blocks of the bus terminal. Go northwest on Av Uxmal to reach the first four places described here.

Mexico Hostels (☎ 887-0191; W *www .mexicohostels.com; Palmera 30; dorm beds with/without HI card M$90/100*) has more than 70 bunks in fan-cooled four- and six-bed rooms (single-sex and co-ed), lockers, Internet access, cheap laundry service and a full rooftop kitchen. Rooms are clean, with good ventilation (the entire facility is non-smoking), though things can get a bit cramped when it's full. Rates include continental breakfast.

Las Palmas Hotel (☎ 884-2513; *Palmera 43; doubles M$280*) has a cage full of vocal parakeets in the lobby, and clean, cool rooms with comfy beds and TV. It's down a side street and readers give it good marks.

Hotel El Alux (☎ 884-6613, fax 884-3065; W *www.hotelalux.com; cnr Av Uxmal & Laurel; singles M$280, 1-/2-bed doubles M$310/370*), a reader-recommended place, has 35 ample, fairly quiet (if dimly lit) rooms, each with phone, TV and pleasant red-tile floors.

Hotel Cotty (☎ 884-0550, fax 884-1319; W *www.hotelcotty.com; Av Uxmal 44; singles/ doubles/triples/quads M$300/338/376/414*)

has 38 clean rooms, all with cable TV, phone and two comfortable double beds. The 2nd-floor rooms in the rear tend to get club noise from Av Yaxchilán. Rates include a selection of full breakfasts, and the hotel has off-street parking.

Casa de Huéspedes Punta Allen (☎ 884-0225; W *www.puntaallen.da.ru; Punta Allen 8; doubles M$320-360*) is a friendly, family-run guesthouse. The ample rooms have good bathrooms, and a light breakfast is included. From Av Uxmal, walk south along Av Yaxchilán and take the first right.

Hotel Cancún Rosa (☎ 884-0623; *Margaritas 2; singles/doubles M$336/392*) has an aquatic theme going, from the swimming pool to the aquarium in the lobby to the simple fountain upstairs. Its quiet rooms are done in pastels and have good beds.

Soberanis Hostal (☎ 884-4564, 800-101-0101, fax 887-5138; W *www.soberanis.com .mx; Av Cobá 5; dorm beds with/without HI card M$100/120, doubles M$395*) is a good value. All rooms have very comfortable beds, tile floors, cable TV and nicely appointed bathrooms. Though primarily a hotel, the Soberanis also has four-bed 'hostel' rooms with the same amenities as the regular rooms, including a free breakfast. The **cafeteria** serves affordable lunches and dinners and the hotel also has a bar, Internet facilities, a phone center, a tour agency and a student-oriented travel agency.

Mid-Range

Downtown Mid-range in Cancún is a two-tiered category; the downtown area is much cheaper than the Zona Hotelera and only a short bus ride away from the Zona's beaches.

Hotel El Rey del Caribe (☎ 884-2028, fax 884-9857; W *www.reycaribe.com; cnr Avs Uxmal & Náder; doubles US$44-66*) boasts a lush courtyard, a lovely small pool, a small Jacuzzi and off-street parking. Each of the 24 rooms has a fully equipped kitchenette, supercomfy bed, and safe (you can use your own lock). There is no extra charge for up to two children under 11. The rooms at the back are very nice lodgings indeed, with floors made of tropical hardwood. The other rooms are very well maintained and upgraded frequently. El Rey is a true eco-tel that composts, employs solar collectors and cisterns, uses gray water on the gardens and even has a few composting toilets. Its owners are also educating other hotels and businesses in the area about such methods. The price range reflects five different seasons.

Hotel Antillano (☎ 884-1132, 800-288-7000, fax 884-1878; Claveles 1; doubles M$500-695), just off Av Tulum, is a very pleasant and quiet place with a pool, good central air-con and cable TV. Rates include continental breakfast and the use of a beach club in the Zona Hotelera.

Hotel Suites Caribe Internacional (☎ 884-3999, fax 884-1993; W www.caribeinternacional.com; cnr Avs Sunyaxchén & Yaxchilán; doubles/triples/suites M$560/616/672) is a six-story hotel boasting 80 rooms with cable TV. The junior suites have two comfortable beds, a sofa and kitchenette. Amenities include secure parking, a small pool in an agreeable courtyard, and a restaurant and bar. Rates are often negotiable here; try asking for a discount.

Hotel Best Western Plaza Caribe (☎ 884-1377, fax 884-6352, in USA ☎ 800-528-1234; W www.hotelplazacaribe.com; Pino between Avs Tulum & Uxmal; doubles M$600-800), directly across from the bus terminal, is a franchise hotel offering 140 comfortable rooms with full amenities, including a pool and restaurant.

Hotel Margaritas (☎ 884-9333, 800-711-1531; fax 884-1324; e ventashic@sybcom.com; cnr Av Yaxchilán & Jazmines; doubles Sept-Nov M$840, Dec-Aug M$1120), across the street from the Suites Caribe, also sports six floors. It's a cheerful place with 100 guestrooms, a pool, restaurant, bar, and attentive service.

Zona Hotelera Hotels near Blvd Kukulcán in the Zona Hotelera are close to cheap, convenient transportation. Apart from the Aristos, all the following hotels are on Laguna Nichupté rather than the sea, but some have agreements with seaside beach clubs so guests can get their fill of the Caribbean.

Hotel Suites Laguna Verde (☎ 883-3414, fax 883-4897; e suitescancun@suitescancun.com.mx; Paseo Pok-ta-Pok Km 1; rooms from US$79) is separated from the lagoon by a golf course and offers good value, especially when promotions lower the price. All 48 kitchen-equipped suites have a dining table, couch and two good queen-size beds; most have garden views. The pool isn't

huge but it's nice, and there's a restaurant. Prices include use of the Fat Tuesday beach club. The hotel is off Blvd Kukulcán Km 7.

Grand Royal Lagoon (☎ 883-2749; W www.grlagoon.com; Quetzal 8-A; rooms/studios M$900/1000) has rooms with cable TV and safes; most have two double beds, while some have kings. Studios come with kitchenette and balcony. The hotel has a small pool, and guests have use of the Fat Tuesday beach club. The hotel is 100m off Blvd Kukulcán Km 7.7.

Sina Suites (☎ 883-1017, fax 883-2459; e suitessina@cancun.novenet.com.mx; Calle Quetzal 33; suites M$800-1400) is an older but comfortable and friendly lagoon-side establishment with 33 spacious suites. Each has two double beds, a separate living room (with a sofa bed) and satellite TV, a kitchen and 1½ bathrooms. Other amenities include a pool featuring great views across the lagoon (as do some of the rooms), a bar and a restaurant.

Aristos Cancún Plaza (☎ 885-3333, fax 885-0236; W www.aristoshotels.com; Blvd Kukulcán Km 20.5; rooms M$800), nearly out to Punta Nizuc, used to be a condominium complex but now offers one of the best values of the Zona's moderately priced digs, given its beachfront location and amenities. All of the 300 rooms have marble floors, balconies or terraces with sea or lagoon views (some have stainless steel sinks in the main room, reminders of the condo days) and cable TV. The hotel also has multiple bars (including one in the pool and one beachside) and a restaurant. Prices rise by M$200 from December 23 to January 15.

Cancún Marina Club (☎ 849-4999, 800-719-5523, fax 849-7071; e hmarinac@prodigy.net.mx; Blvd Kukulcán Km 5.5; rooms M$672-1000), a popular hotel, has a water-sports center, a very inviting pool and a pleasant restaurant–bar overlooking the lagoon. Among the 75 rooms (equipped with hairdryers and safes) are 10 penthouses.

Top End Double-room rates in this category start at US$160. All of these resorts are in the Zona Hotelera and border the Caribbean. Guestrooms come equipped with air-conditioning and satellite TV, and many have balconies with sea views. Often the best room rates available are contained in hotel-and-airfare packages; shop around. Because the rates offered by each resort vary greatly depending on when and where guests book reservations, and because all of the resorts are conveniently located along Blvd Kukulcán, these listings are arranged by location along the boulevard rather than by cost.

Costa Real (☎ 881-7340, in USA ☎ 800-543-7556; W www.realresorts.com.mx; Blvd Kukulcán Km 4; doubles May–mid-Dec US$112-200, mid-Dec–Apr US$168-300) is a large resort in attractive grounds. It has all-inclusive and room-only rate plans and a shared-facilities agreement with the much more spectacular Gran Caribe Real.

Gran Caribe Real (☎ 881-7340, fax 881-7399, in USA ☎ 800-543-7556; W www.real resorts.com.mx; Blvd Kukulcán Km 5.5; rooms US$123-272, suites US$157-306) has 500 rooms (all with ocean views), including 52 junior suites. All come with private terraces that overlook a dazzling swimming pool and 200m of beach.

Kin-Ha (☎ 883-2377, fax 883-2147; e kinha3@mail.caribe.net.mx; Blvd Kukulcán Km 8; rooms/suites US$200/250), a self-contained hotel, has 162 rooms and suites in four buildings. All rooms feature a balcony and two double beds or one king-size bed. A travel agency, car rental agency, minimarket, bars and a gym are on the premises.

Hyatt Cancún Caribe (☎ 848-7800, fax 883-1514, in USA ☎ 800-633-7313; W www .hyatt.com; Blvd Kukulcán Km 10.3; rooms from US$180) is a luxurious place, with a range of accommodations among its 226 lovely guestrooms and suites. It has multiple pools, restaurants and tennis courts, and a prime beachfront location.

Sheraton Cancún (☎ 883-1988, fax 885-0974, in USA ☎ 800-325-3535; Blvd Kukulcán Km 12.5; rooms from US$131) has tremendous appeal, from the elegant lobby to the immaculate gardens, and the gorgeous tiled art in the restaurant. The resort has more than 1km of beach, and 'shares' a real Mayan ruin with its neighbor to the north.

Ritz-Carlton (☎ 881-0808, fax 885-1048, in USA ☎ 800-241-3333; W www.ritzcarl ton.com; Blvd Kukulcán Km 13.9; rooms US$223-705) is quite a large resort. It ain't the Ritz, but…hey wait a sec, it IS the Ritz! And it lets you know with 369 ocean-view rooms, kilometers of marble, 400m of sugary beach, three lighted tennis courts, an ocean-

front whirlpool, two pools, a fitness center and a large variety of water sports options. This resort has won top hotel honors, among them *Travel and Leisure* magazine's 'best hotel in Latin America' award.

JW Marriott (☎ 848-9600, fax 848-9606, in USA ☎ 800-228-9290; W www.marriott .com; Blvd Kukulcán Km 14.5; rooms from US$212) is a recent construction with 449 very nicely appointed guestrooms with balconies and great sea views in a 14-story block. The hotel has two outdoor pools, a 7m dive pool with an artificial reef, an enormous spa with indoor pool, tennis courts, and multiple restaurants; you get the idea.

Hilton Cancún (☎ 881-8000, fax 881-8080, in USA ☎ 800-228-9290; W www .hiltoncancun.com; Blvd Kukulcán Km 17; rooms from US$147) has 426 ocean-view rooms in a massive pyramid. It has its own 18-hole golf course, tennis courts, a fitness center and a gigantic pool complex.

PLACES TO EAT
Budget

Though you can find a meal in any price range in the Zona Hotelera, the best selection of budget eats is available downtown, away from the big resorts.

Downtown The main market is set back from the street, west of the post office. Its official name is long; locals simply call it **Mercado Veintiocho** (Market 28). Most eateries are in the inner courtyard and open from about 7:30am to 6pm daily. Inexpensive Mexican food can also be found at the **booths** in the northeast corner of Parque Las Palapas, and at two good **taco carts** operating in the evening – one at the north edge of the Comercial Mexicana parking lot (across Av Tulum from the bus terminal) and the other at the southeast edge of the Plaza de Toros (Bullring) parking lot, at Avs Sayil and Bonampak.

El Rincón Yucateco (☎ 892-3225; Av Uxmal 24; dishes M$40-80, set meals M$35; open 7am-11:30pm Mon-Sat), across from the Hotel Cotty, serves excellent yet inexpensive Yucatecan food (try the delicious *salbutes de cochinita*, fried tortillas topped with succulent shredded pork and chopped onion), and good *comidas corridas* (set lunches).

Ty-Coz (☎ 884-6060; Av Tulum; sandwiches M$25-40; open 9am-11pm Mon-Sat) is a bakery–café just north of the Comercial Mexicana supermarket. It has granite table-tops and a pleasing ambience, and serves good espresso drinks, baguettes and crois-sants, as well as sandwiches made with a variety of meats and cheeses.

Tatis La Casa del Pan *(☎ 892-3877; cnr Pecari & Av Tulum; breakfasts M$25-35, sandwiches & light dishes M$28-37; open 7am-10pm Mon-Sat)* is another bakery–café, featuring whole-wheat bread, good espresso drinks, stuffed croissants, focaccia and in-expensive breakfasts.

El Tapatío *(☎ 887-8317; cnr Av Uxmal & Palmera; dishes M$30-90, set meals M$35)*, as the name implies, features cuisine from the state of Jalisco, but the varied menu has all kinds of good food. They also serve in-credible (and incredibly big) fruit and veg-gie juices, shakes and smoothies. Order from the list or concoct your own; anyone up for a blend of yogurt, granola, banana and beet? That combination will set you back all of M$19.

Santa Clara *(cnr Avs Uxmal & Tulum; open 10am-10:30pm daily)* specializes in ice cream, but also serves coffee drinks and various sweet dishes.

Comercial Mexicana *(cnr Avs Tulum & Uxmal)*, a centrally located supermarket, has a good selection of produce, meats, cheeses and cookies.

Zona Hotelera For budget eats in the Zona Hotelera, try the food courts, which can be found in every large mall.

La Ruina *(☎ 883-3848; Plaza Terramar; mains M$65-80; open 8am-2pm daily)* is pretty much a hole in the wall on the back (north) side of the shopping center, facing Blvd Kukulcán near Km 8.5. Its highlights are tasty Mexican traditionals, most of which come with guacamole, rice and beans.

Restaurant Río Nizuc *(mains M$60-75; open noon-5pm daily)*, at the end of a short, nameless road near Blvd Kukulcán Km 23, is an out-of-the-way outdoor restaurant at the edge of a mangrove-flanked channel. It's a local hangout, and a nice place to set-tle in a chair under a *palapa* (thatched, palm-leaf-roofed shelter with open sides) and watch convoys of snorkelers in sporty little boats pass by. Octopus, conch and fish are served in various ways (fried, with gar-lic, as ceviche), and the beer is cheap.

Mid-Range

Downtown As with budget restaurants, the downtown area has a wider variety of mid-priced places than the Zona Hotelera.

Rolandi's Restaurant-Bar *(☎ 884-4047; Av Cobá 12; 1-person pizzas M$57-81, mains M$69-109; open 1pm-12:30am daily)* is an Italian-Swiss eatery with a wood-fired pizza oven, between Avs Tulum and Náder just off the southern roundabout. It serves elab-orate pizzas, spaghetti plates and a range of northern Italian dishes.

Restaurant 100% Natural *(Cien por Ciento Natural; ☎ 884-3617; Av Sunyaxchén; mains M$35-90; open 7am-11pm daily)*, near Av Yaxchilán, is one of a chain of restaur-ants serving juice blends, a wide selection of yogurt-fruit-vegetable combinations, and brown rice, pasta, fish and chicken dishes. The on-site bakery turns out whole-wheat products, and the entire place is very nicely decorated and landscaped. Service is excel-lent – at times even too attentive.

Irori *(☎ 892-3072; Av Tulum 226; rolls M$26-55, nigiri M$24-60/pair, teppanyaki M$95-150; open 1pm-11pm Mon-Sat, 1pm-7pm Sun)* is actually on Calle Viento, in the southern part of town. It's a Japanese-run restaurant serving sushi and many other Japanese favorites in an intimate and nicely decorated setting.

La Parrilla *(☎ 887-6141; Av Yaxchilán 51; mains M$64-200)* is a traditional Mexican restaurant popular with locals and tourists alike. It serves a varied menu from all over Mexico, with Yucatecan specialties thrown in. Mains include tasty *calamares al mojo de ajo* (squid in garlic sauce, M$107), steaks and sautéed grouper. Mole enchiladas and delicious piña coladas both run about M$65.

Zona Hotelera The Zona Hotelera's mid-range choices are mostly franchise places serving upscale American fast food with some Mexican options. Some are of the kind where waitstaff pour liquor down pat-rons' throats straight out of the bottle, to chanting crowds – and sometimes shake the drinker's head violently and/or blow a whistle loudly. These include **Señor Frog's** *(Blvd Kukulcán Km 9.8; dishes M$100-170)* and **Carlos 'n Charlie's** *(Blvd Kukulcán Km 5.5; dishes M$100-170)*.

Restaurant 100% Natural *(☎ 883-1180; Plaza Terramar, Blvd Kukulcán Km 8.65; mains*

M$35-90; open 7am-11pm daily) is a smaller and less aesthetically pleasing branch of the downtown health-food restaurant.

La Isla Shopping Village, Plaza Flamingo and the Forum mall hold other options to get a bite.

Top End

Downtown Restaurants in this category offer better value than those in the Zona Hotelera.

Rosa Mexicano (☎ 884-6313; Claveles No 4; mains M$80-300; open 5pm-11pm daily), a long-standing favorite, serves unusual Mexican dishes in a pleasant hacienda decor. There are some concessions to Cancún, such as tortilla soup and filete tampiqueña, but also squid sautéed with three chilies, garlic and scallions, and shrimp in a *pipián* sauce (made of ground pumpkin seeds and spices).

Carrillo's Lobster House (☎ 884-1227; Claveles 35; shrimp & fish dishes M$110-180, lobster dishes around M$340), a somewhat formal restaurant, is the place to head for lobster. The restaurant has air-conditioning indoors and is fan-cooled outdoors, and entertainment is provided by mariachis.

La Habichuela (☎ 884-3158; Margaritas 25; mains M$127-300) is an elegant restaurant with a lovely courtyard dining area, just off Parque Las Palapas. The specialty is shrimp and lobster in curry sauce served inside a coconut with tropical fruit (M$297).

Zona Hotelera Though there are many establishments in this category in the Zona Hotelera, their prices sometimes reflect their location more than the quality of food.

The Crab House (☎ 885-3936; Blvd Kukulcán Km 14.8; dishes M$130-176; open 1pm-11:30pm daily) offers a lovely view of the lagoon that complements the seafood. The long menu includes many shrimp and fillet-of-fish dishes. Crab and lobster are priced by the pound (M$195-405).

La Dolce Vita (☎ 885-0161; Blvd Kukulcán Km 14.8; pizzas M$105-125, mains M$115-175; open noon-11:30pm daily), overlooking the lagoon, is one of Cancún's fanciest Italian restaurants.

Ruth's Chris Steak House (☎ 885-0500; Kukulcán Plaza; steaks M$202-349; open 1pm-11pm daily) is part of the Ruth's Chris chain which is known internationally for its

aged, corn-fed, USDA prime beef. Side dishes run high here; can you believe M$76 for creamed spinach?

ENTERTAINMENT
Clubs

Zona Hotelera The demise of the Ballet Folklórico has left the Zona Hotelera's nightlife to young crowds attracted to loud and booze-oriented clubs – the kind that often have an MC urging women to display body parts. See Places to Eat for more details on **Carlos 'n Charlie's** and **Señor Frog's**, both of which have dancing in the evenings. Most of the dance clubs charge around US$12 admission, which may include two or three drinks; admission with open-bar privileges (ie, drink all you want) runs US$20-25. These prices ebb and flow with the amount of business, and promotional coupons and flyers can bring them down by a few bucks. Though some clubs open as early as 5:30pm, most don't get hopping much before midnight. Many have theme nights: Ladies' Night (women get in and/or drink free), 'Male Hot Body Contest,' 'Bikini Contest' etc ad nauseam.

The first four listed here are clustered along the northwest-bound side of Blvd Kukulcán.

Coco Bongo (☎ 883-5061; The Forum Mall; open 10:30pm-5am daily) is often the venue for MTV's nighttime coverage of spring break. The club opens with celebrity impersonators, dancers and circus acts (clowns, acrobats and the like) for an hour or so, then the rock, pop and hip-hop start playing and most of the older audience members vacate the premises.

Dady'O (☎ 800-234-9797; Blvd Kukulcán Km 9; open 10pm-4:30am daily), opposite the Forum mall, is one of Cancún's more elaborate dance clubs. The setting is a five-level black-walled faux cave with a two-level dance floor and zillions of laser beams and strobes. The predominant beats are Latin, house, techno, trance and hip-hop, and the crowd is predominantly twenty-somethings.

Dady Rock (☎ 883-3333; Blvd Kukulcán Km 9; open 5:30pm-3:30am), a steamy rock and roll club with recorded techno and rock, and live music, is next door to Dady'O and attracts a slightly older crowd than its neighbor. Admission is free until 10pm.

Bulldog Café (☎ *883-1133 ext 544; Blvd Kukulcán Km 9; open 10pm-late*) bills itself as 'the home of rock and roll,' and features live bands and a jumbo Jacuzzi.

La Boom (☎ *849-7587; Blvd Kukulcán Km 3.8; open 10pm-late*) features trance, house and some techno on one side, and hip-hop and pop on the other, played at many decibels by guest DJs. The crowd ranges from around 18 to 30 years of age. La Boom claims to have the longest-running bikini contest in Cancún (Friday nights).

Downtown Clubs located downtown are generally mellower. Built into the **Plaza de Toros** (*Bullring; cnr Avs Bonampak & Sayil*) are several bars, some with music, that draw a largely local crowd.

Roots (☎ *884-2437; Tulipanes 26; cover M$30 Fri & Sat; open Mon-Sat 6pm-1am*) features jazz, reggae or rock bands and the occasional flamenco guitarist. Roots is a full-menu restaurant as well as a club, serving pasta, salads, seafood and meat dishes, with main dishes running M$66 to M$159.

Mambo Café (☎ *887-7891; Plaza Las Américas; admission men/women M$50/30; open 10pm-6am Thur-Sun*) is upstairs from the food court in the middle of the huge mall on the southern stretch of Av Tulum. It features live salsa, Cuban and other Caribbean music and is very popular with Cancún's young people. Women enter free on Thursday nights.

Sabor Latino (☎ *892-1916; cnr Avs Xcaret & Tankah; admission men/women M$60/40, free Wed; open 10:30am-6am daily, Wed-Sat only in low season*), on the 2nd floor of Chinatown Plaza, is another happening club. Its live acts feature Dominican salsa and other tropical styles.

There's a significant gay scene downtown, but it's not apparent until well after sunset. There are no lesbian clubs in town, though lesbian couples often frequent the predominantly male clubs mentioned here.

Disco Karamba (☎ *884-0032; cnr Azucenas & Av Tulum; open Thur-Sun 10pm-6am*), above the Ristorante Casa Italiana, has frequent drink specials. Cover ranges from free to M$70.

Picante (*Av Tulum 20; open 9pm-6am daily*), set back from Av Tulum, a few blocks north of Av Uxmal, isn't as hot as its name suggests, but it is the longtime neigh-

borhood gay bar. It often features movies shown at high volume until about 1am, when the music comes on.

Cinema
Cinemas Tulum (☎ *884-3451; Av Tulum 10; admission M$45*) is a five-plex showing first-run Hollywood films with subtitles, as well as other foreign films and Mexican releases. Matinees and all shows on Tuesday and Wednesday are M$25.

SHOPPING
Neither downtown nor the Zona Hotelera fits the bill as a bargain-hunter's paradise – the store coupons in *Cancún Tips* for 35% off any jewelry purchase should give you some idea of the mark-ups involved – but window-shoppers will have plenty to keep their eyes occupied in the Zona. It is packed with freestanding shops and others nestled in small clusters or wedged between restaurants, bars and dance clubs. Moreover, there are also four very large shopping malls and several smaller ones, all located along Blvd Kukulcán. You'll see stores selling Colombian emeralds, silverwork, Cuban cigars, goods by Bulgari, Lladró, Mont Blanc, Guess, Fendi, Swatch, Hugo Boss and many others, as well as shops offering lewd T-shirts, 'Cancún' ashtrays and keychains and the like.

The largest (and among the stuffiest, attitude-wise) of the indoor malls is chichi **Plaza Kukulcán** (*Blvd Kukulcán Km 13*). Of note here is the huge art gallery (taking up near half of the 2nd floor), the many stores selling silverwork, and **La Ruta de las Indias**, a shop featuring wooden models of Spanish galleons and replicas of conquistadors' weaponry and body armor. But all is not lost; the plaza has a bowling alley and a large food court.

The most fun of the island's malls is **La Isla Shopping Village** (*Blvd Kukulcán Km 12*), an indoor–outdoor place with canals, a somewhat bogus aquarium, giant, ultramodern parasol structures, and enough other visual distractions to keep even the most inveterate hater of shopping amused while his or her significant other browses the numerous stores. These include a large **Nike** clothing shop, a **Hippo** café offering a variety of CDs and magazines (as well as espresso beverages), and stores hawking

Swatch, Diesel, DKNY, Tommy Hilfiger and on and on. A multiplex cinema and varied food court round out La Isla's attractions.

For last-minute purchases before flying out of Cancún, try the **Mercado Municipal Ki-Huic** *(Av Tulum)*, north of Av Cobá downtown. It's a warren of stalls and shops carrying a wide variety of souvenirs and handicrafts. It's 100% tourist trap, so even hard bargaining may not avail. Across Av Tulum is the **Chedraui** supermarket, whose upstairs clothing department sometimes has souvenir-grade items, at very affordable prices.

For a wide assortment of Fuji film including Velvia, Provia and Reala, try **Colormax** *(Av Tulum)*, just north of Calle Claveles. They do developing as well.

GETTING THERE & AWAY
Air
Cancún's **international airport** *(☎ 886-0049)* is the busiest in southeastern Mexico. The airport has a few ATMs; the best place to change money is the **Banamex bank** along the back wall just outside the domestic baggage-claim area (behind the coffee shop); it has an ATM and offers good exchange rates. Opposite it are baggage lockers costing M$60 for 24 hours.

Cancún is served by many direct international flights (for more information see the Getting There & Away chapter).

Between Mexicana and its subsidiaries Aerocaribe and Aerocozumel, there is at least one and up to eight direct daily flights to each of the following destinations: Mexico City (one-way M$1135), Oaxaca (M$1800), Tuxtla Gutiérrez (M$2175) and Villahermosa (M$1750). Aerocaribe has two flights daily to Mérida (M$1125), and six to Cozumel (M$725). They also fly twice daily to Havana, Cuba (US$290 round-trip), but you can get better package deals through local travel agents. Cubana, the Cuban national airline, has daily flights as well.

Aviacsa, a regional carrier based in Tuxtla Gutiérrez, has direct flights from Cancún to Mexico City, with connections for Oaxaca, Tapachula, Tuxtla Gutiérrez and Villahermosa, as well as points in central and northern Mexico.

Magnicharters flies direct to Monterrey, Mexico City, Guadalajara and León.

Grupo Taca flies from Cancún to Flores via Guatemala City, connecting to points in Central America several times a week.

If you intend to fly from Cancún to other parts of Mexico, reserve your airline seat ahead of time to avoid any unpleasant surprises. The following airlines are represented in Cancún:

Aerocaribe & Aerocozumel (☎ 884-2000) Av Cobá 5, Plaza América
Aeroméxico (☎ 884-1097) Av Cobá 80; just west of Av Bonampak
American Airlines (☎ 800-904-6000) Hotel Fiesta Americana Coral Beach, Blvd Kukulcán Km 8.7; plus an airport counter
Aviacsa (☎ 887-4214, fax 884-6599) Av Cobá 37
Continental (☎ 886-0169, 800-900-5000, W www.continental.com) Airport counter
Copa (☎ 800-265-2672) Airport counter
Cubana (☎ 887-7210) Calle Pecari
Delta (☎ 800-123-4710, 886-0368) Airport counter
Grupo Taca (☎ 886-0008, W www.taca.com) Airport counter
Magnicharters (☎ 884-0600) Av Náder 93
Mexicana (☎ 881-9090, 24hr toll-free ☎ 800-502-2000) Av Cobá 39
Northwest (☎ 800-907-4700) Airport counter
US Airways (☎ 800-007-8800, W www.usairways.com) Airport counter

Bus
Cancún's modern, sparkling bus terminal occupies the wedge formed where Avs Uxmal and Tulum meet. Across Pino from the bus terminal, a few doors from Av Tulum, is the ticket office and miniterminal of Playa Express, which runs air-conditioned buses down the coast to Tulum approximately half-hourly until early evening, stopping at major towns and points of interest along the way. Riviera covers the same ground with 1st-class (though not necessarily better) service.

ADO sets the 1st-class standard, while UNO, ADO GL and Super Expresso provide luxury services. Mayab provides good 'intermediate class' (modern, air-con buses, tending to make more stops than 1st class) to many points. Oriente's 2nd-class air-con buses often depart and arrive late. Noreste buses vary in quality; some are pretty shabby indeed.

The staff at the ADO/Riviera information counter in the bus terminal gives good information on many of the bus services. Following are some of the major routes serviced daily:

Chetumal M$135 to M$162, 5½ to 6½ hours, 382km; many buses

Chichén Itzá M$71 to M$100, three to four hours, 205km; one Riviera bus at 9am, hourly 2nd-class Oriente buses from 5am to 5pm

Chiquilá (for Isla Holbox) M$55, 3½ hours, 161km; Mayab buses at 8am and 12:30pm, Noreste buses at 1:45pm

Felipe Carrillo Puerto M$80 to M$98, 3½ to four hours, 230km; eight 1st-class Riviera buses and hourly 2nd-class Mayab buses

Mérida M$114 to M$180, four to six hours, 318km; 15 UNO, ADO GL and Super Expresso buses, hourly 2nd-class Oriente buses (5am to 5pm)

Mexico City (Terminal Norte) M$786, 24 hours, 1821km; one ADO bus

Mexico City (TAPO) M$786 to M$876, 22 to 24 hours, 1821km; one ADO and two ADO GL buses

Palenque M$370 to M$410, 12 to 13 hours, 870km; three Altos and Colón buses

Playa del Carmen M$22 to M$32, one to 1¼ hours, 68km; Riviera every 15 minutes from 5am to midnight, many Playa Express and Mayab buses. See also To/From the Airport under Getting Around later in this section.

Puerto Morelos M$14 to M$16, 40 minutes, 36km; numerous buses

Ticul M$166, six hours, 395km; six Mayab buses

Tizimín M$69, three to four hours, 212km; nine 2nd-class Noreste and Mayab buses

Tulum M$40 to M$56, 2¼ to three hours, 134km; many Riviera, Playa Express and other buses

Valladolid M$57 to M$79, two to three hours, 158km; 26 buses

Villahermosa M$406, 12 hours, 947km; 11 buses

Car Rental-car agencies with facilities at the airport include: **Alamo** (☎ 886-0179), **Avis** (☎ 886-0222), **Budget** (☎ 886-0026), **Dollar** (☎ 886-0179) and **Hertz** (☎ 886-0150), among others. You can receive better rates if you reserve ahead of time, but it doesn't hurt to do comparison shopping after arriving and before signing your original agreement.

Downtown Cancún's streets are laid out in a way that forces you to go all the way round very long blocks to get to many places. Couple this with frequent heavy traffic and enormous roundabouts, and you have a hellish town to drive in. You're best off leaving the rental car parked, and walking or catching a bus to most places till you're ready to get out of town. Be warned also that Hwy 180D, the 238km toll *(cuota)* road running much of the way between Cancún and Mérida, costs M$285 for the distance and has only two exits before the end. The first, at Valladolid, costs M$195 to reach from Cancún and the second, at Pisté (for Chichén Itzá), is an additional M$40.

GETTING AROUND
To/From the Airport

White TTC buses to downtown Cancún (M$40) leave the airport about every 20 minutes between 5:30am and 11:30pm from a small parking lot between the Budget and Executive car rental agencies. A straight line drawn from the exit of the international arrivals terminal (past all the vans) would reach the small lot and its ticket booth decorated with a Coca-Cola sign. Once in town, the buses travel up Av Tulum and will stop most anywhere you ask. One central stop is across from the Chedraui supermarket on Av Cobá (not to be confused with the Chedraui farther south in Plaza Las Américas).

Comfortable shared vans depart from the curb in front of the international terminal about every 15 minutes for the Zona Hotelera and downtown; they charge M$90 per person. If volume allows, they will separate passengers into downtown and Zona groups. Otherwise, depending who's going exactly where, they may head downtown first and then to the Zona. Going the opposite way, via Punta Nizuc, can take up to 45 minutes from the airport to downtown.

Regular taxis into town or to the Zona Hotelera cost up to M$380. If you follow the access road out of the airport and past the traffic-monitoring booth (a total of about 300m), you can often flag down a taxi leaving the airport empty that will take you for much less (you can try for M$40) because the driver is no longer subject to the expensive regulated airport fares.

Going to the airport from downtown the same TTC airport buses ('Aeropuerto–Centro') head south on Av Tulum. You can flag them down anywhere it's feasible, from well north of the bus terminal to well south of Av Cobá; some official stops are shown on the Cancún Centro map.

Colectivo taxis head to the airport from a stand in front of the Hotel Cancún Handall on Av Tulum about a block south of Av Cobá. These operate between 6am and 9pm (but check beforehand), charge M$40 per person and leave when full. The official rate for private taxis from town is M$120.

Riviera runs nine express 1st-class buses from the airport to Playa del Carmen between 10:45am and 8:30pm (M$65, 45 minutes to one hour). The service is direct and tickets are sold at a counter in the international section of the airport.

Bus

To reach the Zona Hotelera from downtown, catch any bus with 'R1,' 'R2,' 'Hoteles' or 'Zona Hotelera' displayed on the windshield as it travels along Av Tulum toward Av Cobá, then eastward on Av Cobá. The one-way fare is M$6.

To reach Puerto Juárez and the Isla Mujeres ferries, catch a Ruta 13 ('Pto Juárez' or 'Punta Sam', M$4) bus heading north on Av Tulum. Some R1 buses make this trip as well; tickets cost M$6.

Taxi

Cancún's taxis do not have meters. Fares are set, but you should always agree on a price before getting in. From downtown to Punta Cancún is M$80, to Puerto Juárez M$30.

North of Cancún

Most of the land north and northwest of Cancún up to the mouth of the Gulf of Mexico is uninhabited and roadless. The main attractions in the northern corner of Quintana Roo are three islands: Isla Mujeres, Isla Contoy and Isla Holbox. Isla Mujeres is popular for its beaches and touristed-though-relaxed town; Contoy is a bird sanctuary; and Holbox is known for its seashells, diverse wildlife, and laid-back community of fisherfolk and hammock-weavers.

ISLA MUJERES

☎ 998 • pop 12,000

The chief attributes of Isla Mujeres (Island of Women) are its easygoing tropical social life and sandy beach fronting waters that are turquoise blue and bathtub warm. Though its proximity to Cancún is apparent each morning as boatloads of package tourists arrive for a day's excursion, the island has not given itself over entirely to tourism yet, and fishing is still a mainstay of the local economy. Yes, there are T-shirt shops and agencies renting mopeds and golf carts, but there's nothing near the number of touts you'll find in Cancún and Playa del Carmen, and Isla Mujeres continues to offer some good values in food and lodging, a popular sunbathing beach and access to dive and snorkel sites.

In recent years a large naval presence has appeared on the island, with the construction of a base south of the main town. The sailors mostly work at drug interdiction. All that naval gray is in sharp contrast to the bright Caribbean colors the town is being done up in. The *Pintando Isla Mujeres* program has invited 400 artists from all around the world to paint many of the town's buildings.

History

Although many locals believe Isla Mujeres got its name because Spanish buccaneers kept their lovers there while they plundered galleons and pillaged ports, a less romantic but still intriguing explanation is probably more accurate. In 1517 Francisco Hernández de Córdoba sailed from Cuba to procure slaves for the mines there. His expedition came upon Isla Mujeres, and in the course of searching it the conquistadors located a stone temple containing clay figurines of Mayan goddesses. Córdoba named the island after the icons.

Today some archaeologists believe that the island was a stopover for the Maya en route to worship their goddess of fertility, Ixchel, on the island of Cozumel. The clay idols are thought to have represented the goddess.

Orientation

The island is 8km long, 150m to 800m wide and 11km off the coast. The town of Isla Mujeres, with its ferry docks, is at the island's northern tip, and a lighthouse and vestiges of the Mayan temple are at the southern tip. The two are linked by Av Rueda Medina, a loop road that more or less follows the coast. Between them are a handful of small fishing villages, several saltwater lakes, a string of westward-facing beaches, a large lagoon and a small airstrip.

The eastern shore is washed by the open sea, and the surf there is dangerous. The most popular sand beach (Playa Norte) is at the northern tip of the island.

Information

The **tourist information office** (☎ 877-0767; Av Rueda Medina; open 8am-8pm Mon-Fri, 9am-2pm Sat & Sun) is between Madero and Morelos. It offers a number of brochures, and one member of its friendly staff speaks English; the rest speak Spanish only.

The **immigration office** (☎ 877-0189; Av Rueda Medina; open 9am-5pm Mon-Fri, 9am-noon Sat & Sun) is next door to the tourist information office, but frequently has a sign up that reads, 'Sorry, gone to Cancún.'

Within a couple of blocks of the ferry docks lie several banks, including **Bital** (Av Rueda Medina) directly across from the Zona Hotelera ferry dock. Most exchange currency, have ATMs and are open 8:30am to 5pm Monday to Friday and 9am to 2pm Saturday.

The island has a **post office** (Guerrero at López Mateos; open 9am-4pm Mon-Fri), and abundant Telmex card phones.

Among the several places offering Internet services are **Compulsla** (Abasolo; open 8am to 10pm daily), just south of Juárez, and the **Coral Scuba Dive Center** (Hidalgo between Abasolo & Madero; open 9am-10pm

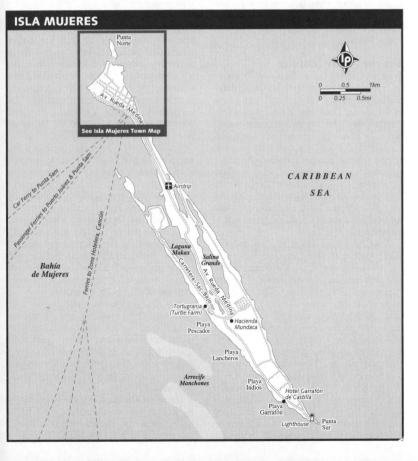

ISLA MUJERES

Punta Norte

Av Rueda Medina

See Isla Mujeres Town Map

Car Ferry to Punta Sam

Passenger Ferries to Puerto Juárez & Punta Sam

Ferries to Zona Hotelera Cancún

Bahía de Mujeres

Airstrip

CARIBBEAN SEA

Laguna Makax

Salina Grande

Carretera Sac-Bajo

Av Rueda Medina

Tortugranja (Turtle Farm)

Hacienda Mundaca

Playa Pescador

Playa Lancheros

Arrecife Manchones

Playa Indios

Playa Garrafón

Hotel Garrafón de Castilla

Lighthouse

Punta Sur

0   0.5   1km
0   0.25   0.5mi

daily), which charge M$15 and M$20 per hour, respectively.

Cosmic Cosas *(Matamoros 82; open 9am-10:30pm daily)*, just north of Hidalgo, has speedy wireless connections for M$15 per hour and is also a nifty bookstore that buys, sells and trades mostly English-language books (largely novels), some travel guides, history titles and books on the Maya. It has a comfortable living room where visitors are welcome to relax and play board games; the friendly owners enjoy offering tourist information as well. Cosmic Cosas is also a clearing house for people wanting to participate in volunteer activities such as medical clinics, trash cleanup and animal rescue.

Laundries in town will wash, dry and fold 4kg of clothes for M$30 to M$40. The cheapest among them (unless you want colors washed separately) is **Lavandería Ángel** *(Plaza Isla Mujeres; open 8am-9pm Mon-Sat)*, just off Hidalgo.

Beaches & Swimming

Walk west along Calle Hidalgo or Guerrero to reach the town's principal beach, **Playa Norte**, sometimes called Playa Los Cocos or Cocoteros. The slope of the beach is very gradual, and the transparent, calm waters are only chest-high even far from shore. Playa Norte is well supplied with bars and restaurants and can get crowded at times.

Five kilometers south of town is **Playa Lancheros**, the southernmost point served by local buses. The beach is less attractive than Playa Norte, but it sometimes has free musical festivities on Sunday. A taxi ride to Lancheros is M$22.

Another 1.5km south of Lancheros is **Playa Garrafón**, with translucent waters, colorful fish and no sand. Unfortunately the reef here has been heavily damaged by hurricanes and careless visitors. The water can be very choppy, sweeping you into jagged areas, so it's best to stay near shore. Avoid the overhyped and overpriced Parque Natural (which has constructed a horrendous eyesore of an observation tower that has you praying for a hurricane) and visit instead the **Hotel Garrafón de Castilla** *(☎ 877-0107; Carretera Punta Sur Km 6; admission M$20; open 9am-5pm daily)*, which provides chairs, umbrellas, showers and baths with the entrance fee. Snorkeling gear is M$60 extra. It has a roped-off swimming area (from which one could sneak-swim into the parque next door, were one so inclined) as well as a restaurant and snack bar. The hotel rents lockers and towels, and offers snorkeling tours to the offshore reef for M$180. Taxis from town cost M$44.

Hacienda Mundaca

The story behind the ruins of this estate *(Av Rueda Medina; admission M$10; open 9am-5pm daily)* is perhaps more intriguing than what remains of it. A 19th-century slave trader and reputed pirate, Fermín Antonio Mundaca de Marechaja, fell in love with a local woman known as La Trigueña (The Brunette). To win her, Mundaca built a two-story mansion complete with gardens and graceful archways, as well as a small fortification.

But while Mundaca built the house, La Trigueña married another islander. Brokenhearted, Mundaca died and his house, fortress and garden fell into disrepair. Some documents indicate that Mundaca died during a visit to Mérida and was buried there. Others say he died on the island, and indeed there's a grave in the town cemetery that supposedly contains his remains. Despite the skull and crossbones on his headstone (a common memento mori) there's no evidence in history books that Mundaca was ever a pirate. Instead, they tell that Mundaca accumulated his wealth by transporting slaves from Africa to Cuba, where they were forced to work mines and sugarcane fields.

Today, the mostly ruined complex holds some walls and foundations, a large central pond, some rusting cannons and a partially rebuilt house. At the southern end stands a gateway and a small garden. You can still make out the words *Entrada de La Trigueña* (La Trigueña's Entrance) etched into the impressive stone arch of the gate.

The shady grounds make for pleasant strolling (bring repellent), and a small zoo is scattered across them, holding local fauna, including a cage-crazed jaguar, some spider monkeys, crocodiles, *jabalíes* (peccaries), a boa constrictor, and the smallest species of deer on the North American continent.

Hacienda Mundaca is at the large bend in Av Rueda Medina, about 4km south of the town. It's easily reached by bus or bike; a taxi from town will cost M$22.

Temple of the Jaguars and Shields, Chichén Itzá

RICHARD I'ANSON

Palacio Municipal, Mérida

JOHN ELK III

Temple of the Warriors, Chichén Itzá

ROSS BARNETT

DAN HERRICK

Ballet Folklórico, Mérida

JOHN NEUBAUER

Traditional dance troupe, Cancún

JOHN ELK III

Mexican Night festivities, Mérida

Turtle Farm

Three species of sea turtle lay eggs in the sand along the island's calm western shore. Although they are endangered, sea turtles are still killed throughout Latin America for their eggs and meat, which is considered a delicacy. In the 1980s, efforts by a local fisherman led to the founding of the **Isla Mujeres Turtle Farm** *(Isla Mujeres Tortugranja; ☎ 877-0595; Carretera Sac Bajo Km 5; admission M$20; open 9am-5pm daily)*, which protects the turtles' breeding grounds and places wire cages around their eggs to protect against predators.

Hatchlings live in three large pools for up to a year, then are tagged for monitoring and released. Because most turtles in the wild die within their first few months, the practice of guarding them through their first year greatly increases their chances of survival. Moreover, the turtles that leave this protected beach return each year, which means their offspring receive the same protection.

The main draw here is several hundred sea turtles, ranging in weight from 150g to more than 300kg. The farm also has a small but good quality aquarium, displays on marine life and a gift shop. Tours are conducted in Spanish and English.

If you're driving, biking or walking from the bus stop, bear right at the 'Y' just beyond Hacienda Mundaca's parking lot (the turn is marked by a tiny sign). The facility is easily reached from town by taxi (M$22).

Punta Sur

At the south end of the island lies a lighthouse, a modern sculpture garden and the severely worn remains of a temple dedicated chiefly to Ixchel, Mayan goddess of the moon and fertility. (The conquistadors found various clay female figures here; whether they were all likenesses of Ixchel or represented several goddesses is unclear.) In 1988 Hurricane Gilbert nearly finished the ruins off, and there's now little to see other than the sculpture garden, the sea and, in the distance, Cancún. At the time of research some sort of tourist complex was being constructed, and the ruins and sculpture garden cost an absurd M$50 to visit. For the moment you can duck the fee by bearing left before the lighthouse and enjoying the view from the small dirt parking lot. From downtown, a taxi costs M$44.

Diving & Snorkeling

Within a short boat ride of the island are a handful of lovely reef dives, such as Barracuda, La Bandera, El Jigueo and Manchones. A popular nonreef dive is **Ultrafreeze** (or El Frío), the intact hull of a 60m-long cargo ship thought to have been deliberately sunk in 30 meters of water, 90 minutes by boat northeast of Isla Mujeres. The name of the site is due to the unusually cool water found there.

At all of the reputable dive centers you need to show your certification card, and you will be expected to have your own gear. Equipment rental adds M$100 to the prices listed here. One reliable place is friendly **Sea Hawk Divers** *(☎/fax 877-0296; ⓔ abarran@ prodigy.net.mx; Carlos Lazo)* which offers dives for US$35 to US$45, a resort course for US$75 and snorkeling tours from US$20. Kayaks and underwater cameras are available for rent and the staff speak English.

Among the bigger dive operations on the island is **Coral Scuba Dive Center** *(☎ 877-0763, fax 877-0371; ⓦ www.coralscubadivecenter.com; Hidalgo between Abasolo & Madero)*. It offers dives for US$29 to US$59, snorkel trips for US$15 and a variety of courses.

The fisherfolk of Isla Mujeres have formed a cooperative to offer snorkeling tours of various sites from M$140, including the reef off Playa Garrafón, and day trips to Isla Contoy. You can book through the **Fisherman's Cooperative Booth** *(☎ 877-0283; Av Rueda Medina)* in a *palapa* steps away from the dock.

Deep-Sea Fishing

The fishing cooperative (see Diving & Snorkeling above) offers trips fishing for marlin, swordfish and dorado from US$40/150 per hour/half day, including bait and tackle, soft drinks, snacks and beer.

Places to Stay

'High season' rates cover roughly mid-December through March. During this period you can expect many places to be booked solid by midday (earlier during Easter week).

Budget The **Poc-Na Hostel** *(☎/fax 877-0090; ⓦ www.pocna.com; cnr Matamoros & Carlos Lazo; campsites per person with/without* card M$50/55, dorm beds with/without card M$70/80, doubles low/high season M$200/250) is Mexico's oldest youth hostel, and now, having been entirely renovated by the new management and staffed by a multinational crew of friendly travelers, it ranks among the country's best. It has fan-cooled six-, eight- and 10-bed co-ed dormitories as well as women's dorms and a few air-con doubles. The large main common area has hammocks to chill in and an excellent sound system putting out tunes till the wee hours. Outside the surrounding walls, the property extends through 100m of sand and coco palms to the edge of the Caribbean and the hostel's own beach bar. Though there are no cooking facilities for guests, the kitchen serves good, inexpensive food (and beer and

wine). By the time you read this the Poc-Na should have a game room with billiard table, and tents to use in the campsites.

Hotel Las Palmas (☎ 877-0965; Guerrero 20; doubles M$160), across from the Mercado Municipal, has basic, deteriorating but clean rooms with fan.

Hotel Caribe Maya (☎ 877-0684; Madero 9; doubles with fan/air-con M$150/200) offers rooms which, though a bit musty, are a solid value.

Hotel El Caracol (☎ 877-0150, fax 877-0547; Matamoros between Hidalgo & Guerrero; doubles with fan/air-con low season M$150/250, high season M$200/300) offers 18 clean, well-furnished if worn rooms with insect screens and tiled bathrooms; many have two double beds and the air-con is good.

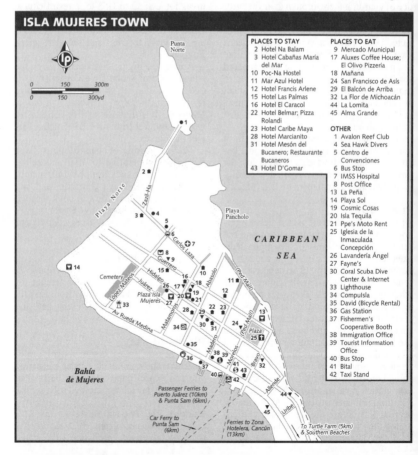

ISLA MUJERES TOWN

PLACES TO STAY
2 Hotel Na Balam
3 Hotel Cabañas María del Mar
10 Poc-Na Hostel
11 Mar Azul Hotel
12 Hotel Francis Arlene
15 Hotel Las Palmas
16 Hotel El Caracol
22 Hotel Belmar; Pizza Rolandi
23 Hotel Caribe Maya
28 Hotel Marcianito
31 Hotel Mesón del Bucanero; Restaurante Bucaneros
43 Hotel D'Gomar

PLACES TO EAT
9 Mercado Municipal
17 Aluxes Coffee House; El Olivo Pizzería
18 Mañana
24 San Francisco de Asís
29 El Balcón de Arriba
32 La Flor de Michoacán
44 La Lomita
45 Alma Grande

OTHER
1 Avalon Reef Club
4 Sea Hawk Divers
5 Centro de Convenciones
6 Bus Stop
7 IMSS Hospital
8 Post Office
13 La Peña
14 Playa Sol
19 Cosmic Cosas
20 Isla Tequila
21 Ppe's Moto Rent
25 Iglesia de la Inmaculada Concepción
26 Lavandería Ángel
27 Fayne's
30 Coral Scuba Dive Center & Internet
33 Lighthouse
34 Compulsla
35 David (Bicycle Rental)
36 Gas Station
37 Fishermen's Cooperative Booth
38 Immigration Office
39 Tourist Information Office
40 Bus Stop
41 Bital
42 Taxi Stand

Punta Norte

0   150   300m
0   150   300yd

Playa Norte
Zazil-Ha
Carlos Lazo
Guerrero
Hidalgo
Juárez
López Mateos
Plaza Isla Mujeres
Av Rueda Medina
Matamoros
Madero
Morelos
Abasolo
(Ped Mall)
(Ped Mall)
Bravo
Allende
Uribe
Cemetery
Plaza

Playa Pancholo

CARIBBEAN SEA

Bahía de Mujeres

Passenger Ferries to Puerto Juárez (10km) & Punta Sam (6km)

Car Ferry to Punta Sam (6km)

Ferries to Zona Hotelera, Cancún (13km)

To Turtle Farm (5km) & Southern Beaches

Hotel Marcianito (☎ 877-0111; Abasolo 10; rooms M$300-350), the 'Little Martian,' is a neat, tidy and recommended hotel with 13 fan-cooled rooms that are upgraded frequently. Upper-floor rooms are the more expensive ones.

Mid-Range The **Hotel D'Gomar** (☎ 877-0541; Av Rueda Medina; doubles with fan/air-con low season M$200/350, high season M$300/450), a friendly place facing the ferry dock between Morelos and Bravo, has four floors of attractive, ample and well-maintained rooms with double beds (air-con rooms have two) and large bathrooms. Most have hammocks as well.

Hotel Francis Arlene (☎/fax 877-0310; Guerrero 7; rooms with fan/air-con low season M$300/500, high season M$450/500) offers good-sized, comfortable rooms with fan and fridge. Most have a king bed or two doubles, and many have balconies and sea views.

Mar Azul Hotel (☎ 877-0120, fax 877-0011; Madero; doubles M$600), a block north of Guerrero right on the eastern beach, has a pool, restaurant and 91 nice, sizable rooms on three floors. All have balconies and many have wonderful sea views.

Hotel Belmar (☎ 877-0430, fax 877-0429; ⓦ www.rolandi.com; Hidalgo between Abasolo & Madero; air-con doubles US$28-90, suite with Jacuzzi US$95-134) is above the Pizza Rolandi restaurant and is run by the same friendly family. All rooms are comfy and well kept; price ranges span four distinct seasons.

Hotel Mesón del Bucanero (☎ 877-0210, 800-712-3510; ⓦ www.bucaneros.com; Hidalgo between Abasolo & Madero; doubles US$29-72) is above the Bucaneros restaurant. Its nicely decorated rooms (most with air-con) all have TVs and are priced according to their various combinations of beds, balcony, tub and fridge – one even has a blender and toaster.

Top End All rooms in this category have air-con.

Hotel Cabañas María del Mar (☎ 877-0179, fax 877-0213; ⓦ www.cabanasdelmar.com; cnr Carlos Lazo & Zazil-Ha; doubles low season M$550-880, high season M$770-1100), near Playa Norte, has 73 well-furnished rooms (all with balcony or terrace,

many with sea or pool views and lovely tiled bathrooms), a large, lush courtyard and a restaurant and swimming pool. Rates include continental breakfast, and at last pass were highly negotiable when paid in cash.

Hotel Na Balam (☎ 877-0279, fax 877-0446; ⓦ www.nabalam.com; Calle Zazil-Ha; low/high season rooms US$136/182, suites US$175-302) has 19 rooms and suites facing Playa Norte near the northern tip of the island, and another 12 in an annex across the road. All are decorated with simple elegance and numerous nice touches, and are equipped with safes, hammocks and private balconies or patios – many on the beach side have fabulous sea views. The hotel offers yoga and meditation classes as well as massage services, a pool and a recommended restaurant.

Avalon Reef Club (☎/fax 999-2050, 800-713-8170; ⓦ www.avalonvacations.com; Zazil-Ha at Islote Yunque; doubles M$1400-1848, suites M$2744-3304, studios & villas M$1624-2744) occupies its own islet off the northern tip of Isla Mujeres. The seven-story hotel building is built at the very edge of the rough, windward sea side of the island, but the islet has a sheltered beach and shallow lagoon on its southern side. The studios and villas are in two-story structures detached from the hotel tower, and are equipped with kitchenettes. All accommodations are comfortably appointed; many have superb views. The complex boasts multiple restaurants and bars, a pool and a spa–fitness center.

Places to Eat

Inside the remodeled **mercado municipal** (town market; Guerrero between Matamoros & López Mateos) are a couple of stalls selling hot food cheap – a plate of chicken mole and rice, or tuna with olives in a tortilla can go for as little as M$15. Other stalls sell a variety of produce, and a juice stand serves up liquid refreshments. Four open-air restaurants out the front serve simple but decent and filling meals at fair prices.

San Francisco de Asís, a chain supermarket on the plaza, has a solid selection of groceries, baked goods and snacks.

Aluxes Coffee House (Matamoros between Guerrero & Hidalgo; bagels M$20, sandwiches M$42-49; open 8am-10pm daily) serves bagels with cream cheese, sandwiches, muffins, and hot and iced espresso drinks.

El Olivo Pizzería (*Matamoros between Guerrero & Hidalgo; pizza slices M$10-15; open 1pm-10pm daily*) sells delicious slices of pizza, with plain mozzarella or various toppings.

Mañana (☎ 044-998-866-4347; cnr Matamoros & Guerrero; dishes M$20-40; open 10am-7pm daily) is a small, relaxing indoor–outdoor café that serves baguette sandwiches, coffee, *licuados* (blends of fruit or juice with water or milk, and sugar) and some Middle Eastern dishes.

La Lomita (*Juárez between Allende & Uribe; mains M$35-50; open 9am-10:30pm Mon-Sat*), 'The Little Hill,' serves good, inexpensive Mexican food in a small, colorful setting. Seafood and chicken dishes predominate.

Alma Grande (*Av Rueda Medina between Allende & Uribe; mains M$50-75; open 9am-9pm Mon-Sat*) is a tiny, colorfully painted shack dishing up cocktails of shrimp, conch and octopus, heaping plates of delicious ceviche, and seafood soups.

El Balcón de Arriba (☎ 877-0513; Hidalgo; mains M$50-100; open 3pm-10:30pm daily), just east of Abasolo, is an airy, casual 2nd-floor eatery popular with tourists. El Balcón serves good fruit drinks, some veggie dishes and a large selection of seafood. Try the rich *camarones a la Reina* if you have a friend who can help out.

Restaurante Bucaneros (☎ 877-0126; Hidalgo between Abasolo & Madero; mains M$26-113, set meals M$67; open 7:30am-11pm daily), below the Hotel Mesón del Bucanero, is a fan-cooled, mostly outdoor restaurant with a pleasing ambience and a variety of alcoholic and nonalcoholic tropical shakes and drinks. The best deal is the set *menú especial,* which gives you a choice of several mains accompanied by soup or salad and a dessert.

Pizza Rolandi (☎ 877-0430; Hidalgo between Abasolo & Madero; mains M$68-100, pizzas M$58-87; open 8am-11pm daily), below the Hotel Belmar, bakes very good thin-crust pizzas and calzones in a wood-fired oven. The menu also includes pasta, fresh salads, fish, good coffee and some Italian specialties.

La Flor de Michoacán (*cnr Hidalgo & Bravo; open 9am-9pm daily*), near the plaza, is the place to go for excellent and inexpensive milkshakes, fruit drinks and shaved ices.

Entertainment

Isla Mujeres' highest concentration of nightlife is along Hidalgo, and hot spots on or near the beach form an arc around the northern edge of town. Loud disco–bar–restaurants open and close seasonally on Hidalgo. **Fayne's** (*Hidalgo near Matamoros; open 6pm-midnight daily*) is one of the latest, often featuring live reggae, salsa and other Caribbean sounds.

Isla Tequila (*cnr Hidalgo & Matamoros*) is quieter than its neighbors. Some Tex-Mex food and snacks are available, but the emphasis is on reasonably priced beer and mixed drinks.

Playa Sol (*Playa Norte; open 9am-10pm or whenever*) is a happening spot day and night, with volleyball, a soccer area and good food and drinks at decent prices. It's a great spot to watch the sunset, and in high season bands play reggae, salsa, merengue or other danceable music.

Hotel Na-Balam (*Calle Zazil-Ha*) has a beach bar that's a popular spot on weekend afternoons (every other week in the off-season), with live music, dancing and a three-hour-long happy hour. A little way up the beach and across the bridge is the Avalon Reef Club's **Castaway Bar** (☎ 999-2050; Zazil-Ha at Islote Yunque; open 11am-late), which has regular promotions such as 'Ladies Drink Free' night and 'Viva México,' with mariachis and tequila specials.

La Peña (*Guerrero between Morelos & Bravo; open 7:30pm-3am'ish*), off the north side of the plaza, is an English-run club with a great atmosphere, a fabulous music mix and an excellent sea breeze coming off the north shore. Some say it's the best in town.

Getting There & Away

There are five main points of embarkation to reach Isla Mujeres. The following description starts from the northernmost port and progresses southeast. (See the Cancún map.) To reach Puerto Juárez or Punta Sam from downtown Cancún, catch any bus (M$4) displaying those destinations and/or 'Ruta 13' as it heads north on Av Tulum. Some R1 ('Zona Hotelera'; M$6) buses make the trip as well; ask before boarding.

Punta Sam Car ferries, which also take passengers, depart from Punta Sam, about 8km north of Cancún center, and take about an hour to reach the island. Departure times are 8am, 11am, 2:45pm, 5:30pm and 8:15pm from Punta Sam; and 6:30am, 9:30am, 12:45pm, 4:15pm and 7:15pm from Isla Mujeres. Walk-ons and vehicle passengers pay M$15; drivers are included in the fare for cars (M$185), vans (M$226), motorcycles (M$71) and bicycles (M$58). If you're taking a car in high season, it's good to get in line an hour or so before departure time. Tickets go on sale just before the ferry begins loading.

Puerto Juárez About 4km north of the Cancún city center (15 minutes by bus) is Puerto Juárez. Enclosed, air-con express boats depart for Isla Mujeres (M$35 one-way, 25 minutes) every 30 minutes from 6am to 8pm from here with a final departure at 9pm; they rarely leave on time. Slower, open boats (M$18 one-way, 45 minutes), which some people enjoy more than the express boats, run roughly every hour from 5am to 5:30pm.

Zona Hotelera Services from the following three spots in the Zona Hotelera change names and schedules frequently; ask your concierge to check for you before heading out to catch boats from any of the following places. All take about 25 minutes to reach Isla Mujeres.

El Embarcadero Shuttles depart from this dock at Playa Linda four times daily in low season, between 9:30am and 1:30pm, returning from Isla Mujeres at 10:30am, 1:30pm, 3:30pm and 5:15pm. The one-way fare is M$75 and includes soft drinks on board. High season sees up to seven departures each way. El Embarcadero is a beige building between the Costa Real Hotel and the channel, on the mainland side of the bridge (Blvd Kukulcán Km 4).

Playa Tortugas The Isla Shuttle (☎ 883-3448) leaves from the dock on Playa Tortugas (Blvd Kukulcán Km 6.35) at 9:15am, 11:30am, 1:45pm and 3:45pm, returning from Isla Mujeres at 10:15am, 12:30pm, 3:30pm and 6:30pm. The one-way fare is M$90.

Playa Caracol This dock shares a parking lot with the Xcaret bus terminal and is next

to the Fiesta Americana Coral Beach. From here the **Fast Cat** (☎ 849-7699) makes its first departure of the day at 9:45am; the one-way fare costs M$75. In high season only, **Asterix Water Taxi** (☎ 886-4847) also provides service.

Getting Around

With all rented transportation it's best to deal directly with the shop supplying it. They're happier if they don't have to pay commissions to touts, and the chances for misunderstandings are fewer. Rates are usually open to negotiation.

Bus & Taxi Local buses (M$3) depart about every 25 minutes from next to the Centro de Convenciones (near the back of the market) and head south along Av Rueda Medina, stopping along the way. You can get to the entrance of Hacienda Mundaca, within 300m of the Turtle Farm (Tortugranja) and as far south as Playa Lancheros (1.5km north of Playa Garrafón). Taxi rates are set by the municipal government and posted at the taxi stand just south of the passenger ferry dock. To get to both the Turtle Farm and Playa Lancheros by cab costs M$22, while Garrafón or Punta Sur, the furthest points on the island, cost M$44.

Motorcycle & Golf Cart Two-wheeled motorized transport can be dangerous; even on sedate Isla Mujeres people die in bike mishaps (see Car & Motorcycle in the Getting Around chapter). If you rent a scooter or 50cc–100cc 'moped,' shop around, compare prices and look for a newer machine in good condition with a full gas tank, and requiring a reasonable deposit. Costs vary, and are sometimes jacked up in high season, but generally start at about M$80 per hour, with a two-hour minimum, M$200 all day (9am to 5pm) and M$300 for 24 hours.

Many people find golf carts a good way to get around the island, and caravans of them can be seen tooling down the roads. They average M$120/350 per hour/day and M$450 for 24 hours. A good, no-nonsense place for both bikes and golf carts is **Ppe's Moto Rent** (☎ 877-0019; *Hidalgo between Matamoros & Abasolo*).

Bicycle Cycling is a great way to get around the island, provided you're reasonably fit and the weather's not too hot. Many bicycles are single-speed, with coaster (ie, push-back-on-the-pedal) brakes; these give you a good workout on the gradual hills. A number of shops rent bikes for about M$20/70 an hour/day. Before you rent, compare prices and the condition of the machines in a few shops, then arrive early in the day to get your pick of the better ones and take the time to have the seat adjusted properly. Some places ask for a deposit of about M$100. **David** (☎044-998-860-0075; Av Rueda Medina), near Abasolo, has a decent selection.

PARQUE NACIONAL ISLA CONTOY

From Isla Mujeres you can take an excursion by boat to Isla Contoy, a national park and bird sanctuary 30km to the north. The island is about 800m at its widest point and more than 7km long. Its dense foliage is home to more than 100 species, including brown pelicans, olive cormorants, turkey birds, brown boobies and red-pouched frigates, and the island is subject to frequent visits by red flamingos, snowy egrets and white herons.

There is good snorkeling both en route to and just off Contoy, which sees about 1500 visitors a month. Bring mosquito repellent.

Getting There & Away

Daily visits to Contoy are offered by the **fisherman's cooperative** (☎ 998-877-0283; Av Rueda Medina). The trip lasts from 9am to 5pm and includes a light breakfast; lunch (with fish caught en route); snorkeling (gear provided); park admission; scientific information on the island; and your choice of purified water or soft drinks, plus beer. It costs M$400 per person (sometimes discounted).

The trip gives you about two hours of free time to explore the island's two interpretive trails and to climb the 27m-high observation tower. For M$100 per person, a park biologist will take you on a tour of Laguna Puerto Viejo, a prime nesting site; funds go toward park upkeep and research projects. Contact the **park headquarters** (☎ 998-877-0118) on Isla Mujeres.

ISLA HOLBOX
☎ 984 • pop 1600

With its friendly fishing families and hammock-weaving cottage industry, Isla Holbox (hol-**bosh**) is a beach site not yet overwhelmed by gringos, though many foreigners (particularly Italians) are settling in and building guesthouses, attracted by the natural wonders and very laid-back lifestyle. The island is about 30km long and from 500m to 2km wide, with seemingly endless beaches, tranquil waters and a galaxy of shells in various shapes and colors. Lying within the 154,052-hectare Yum Balam reserve, Holbox is home to more than 150 species of birds, including roseate spoonbills, pelicans, herons, ibis and flamingos. The waters are abundant with fish, and dolphins can be seen year-round; in summer, whale sharks congregate relatively nearby in unheard-of quantities.

Where's the downside? The water is not the translucent turquoise common to Quintana Roo beach sites, because here the Caribbean mingles with the darker Gulf of Mexico. During the rainy season there are clouds of mosquitoes; bring repellent and be prepared to stay inside for a couple of hours each evening.

Orientation & Information

The town of Holbox, where you'll arrive by boat from Chiquilá, has the bulk of the island's lodgings and places to eat. Walking north from the ferry dock via Calle Juárez (though few town residents use or even know street names), it's only about nine blocks to the beach on the other side of island. Along the way, you'll pass the central plaza ('el parque'), which is ringed by some restaurants and a few inexpensive places to stay. It's also the site of the town's **Internet café** (open 9am-midnight daily), which offers both OK connections for M$15 per hour and a caseta telefónica for local and international calls. Note that the island has no bank or ATM, and many places to stay and eat do not accept credit cards.

Many hotels will book tours of the area's attractions. Posada Mawimbi offers canoe and kayak trips to the other side of island, as well as motorboat trips toward the middle of the island.

Places to Stay

Cabanas are sprouting everywhere in Holbox. High, low (and mid, where they exist) seasons vary from place to place. Some include the month of December and Easter week as their high season; others throw in

July and August, and some recognize a special low time that may include May, June, September and October. The following listings show only the range of prices from lowest to highest. The first three listings are utilitarian concrete constructions inland from the beach. The Mawimbi, Tortugas and Palapa are newer, Italian-run places at the edge of the beach, using lots of varnished hardwood, timbers and thatch.

Posada La Raza (☎ 875-2072; *Juárez; doubles M$100-120, in summer M$220-250*) is a modest, clean one-story place on the west side of the parque. Rooms have one double and one single bed, and ceiling and floor fans. Guests have use of a small kitchen and hand-laundry facilities, and can hang clothes or sunbathe on the roof.

Posada Los Arcos (☎ 875-2043; *Juárez; singles/doubles/triples/quads with fan M$100/ 150/200/250, with air-con M$200/250/300/ 350*), next door to Posada La Raza, is similar but a touch more upscale. Its rooms are located around a central courtyard and all have hot and cold water. Rates rise by 50% in summer.

Posada d'Ingrid (☎ 875-2070; *doubles with fan M$175-250, rooms with air-con M$350-400*) is a friendly place one block west and one block north of the northwest edge of the parque. All rooms have hot water and TV; the nice, modern air-con rooms sleep up to four people in two beds.

Posada Mawimbi (☎/fax 875-2003; W *www.mawimbi.com.mx; doubles with/ without kitchenette M$450/350*) is a pleasant, two-story place with some lovely decorative flourishes, located just off the beach and about three blocks east of Juárez. All of the rooms have a fan and comfortable beds; many rooms also have a balcony and hammock. Those with kitchenettes use both floors, with the beds and bathroom upstairs and the cooking and dining space downstairs. They were in the process of opening a dive shop at last pass, and are a good source of information on the area's natural attractions.

Hotel La Palapa (☎/fax 875-2121; W *www .hotellapalapa.com; singles/doubles/triples/ quads low season M$150/300/350/400, high season M$250/400/450/500*) is on the beach about a block west of Juárez. Its six colorful, innovatively built rooms ring a central core, the whole covered by a large thatched roof. Most have hammocks, and one has a kitchenette. Windsurfers and a sailboat are available for guest use.

Hotelito Casa Las Tortugas (☎/fax 875-2129; W *www.holboxcasalastortugas.com; rooms low season M$300-450, high season M$400-650*), has the same rustic but refined style as its neighbor, the Mawimbi, with an even greater abundance of charming touches, particularly in the bathrooms. Many rooms have kitchenettes and balconies, with hammocks to laze in outside, and there's a wonderful common area in the form of a hutlike lookout above the 2nd floor.

Faro Viejo (☎ 875-2217, fax 875-2186; W *www.faroviejoholbox.com.mx; Juárez at beach; doubles/triples M$500/600; 2-/4-/ 6-person suites M$800/1200/1400*), has a variety of rooms, including two- and three-bedroom suites (one with kitchenette) and some air-con doubles. Rooms are on two floors, all face the sea and some have lovely tiled bathrooms. 'The Old Lighthouse' is the most architecturally conventional of the beach accommodations; it's also on the only stretch of beach where golf cart traffic is banned (a big plus). The hotel is comfortable and very well maintained, has a good restaurant and bar, and rents bicycles to guests for $50 per day.

Villas Delfines (☎ 884-8606, fax 884-6342; W *www.holbox.com; bungalows US$60-110*) is an eco-tel on the beach about 1km east of town that composts waste, catches rainwater and uses solar power. Its large beach bungalows are built on stilts, fully screened and fan-cooled. The hotel has a restaurant and offers very reasonable meal plans, and rents bicycles, horses, windsurfers and kayaks.

Places to Eat

The island's specialty dish is lobster and eggs, and you'll see lobster and shrimp offered in many forms on most menus. The hotel restaurants at Faro Viejo and Villas Delfines offer good if a bit pricey food. Holbox's other culinary offerings include:

Edelín Pizzería & Restaurant (*pizzas M$45-110; mains M$40-80; open 11am-midnight daily*), on the southeast corner of the plaza, serves good, Sardegnian-style pizza, plus *tortas,* ceviches, fish fillets, shrimp and lobster; beer costs M$12.

La Isla del Colibrí *(breakfast M$25-30, mains M$40-60; open 8am-1pm & 7pm-10:30pm Thur-Tues)* is a small restaurant in a gaily painted, Caribbean-style wooden house on the southwest corner of the parque. It serves breakfasts (and espresso drinks), *licuados,* juices and a variety of meat and seafood dishes.

La Peña Colibrí *(mains M$55-70; open 5pm-11pm Thur-Tues),* next door to La Isla del Colibrí, is a romantic spot serving Mexican dishes with an international flair, as well as wine and mixed drinks. On Friday and Saturday from about 9pm to closing, musicians perform at the Peña. It's often a flamenco guitarist accompanied by a dancer, and by all accounts they get some pretty good talent coming through.

Getting There & Around

A *barco* (boat) ferries passengers (M$30, 25 minutes) to Holbox from the port village of Chiquilá eight times daily from 5am to 6pm in winter, 6am to 7pm in summer. Buses departing Chiquilá usually wait for the boat to arrive. Smaller, faster and wetter *lanchas* make the crossing whenever anyone's willing to pay M$180 for the entire boat (holding up to about six people with gear; the fare is higher after dark).

Two Mayab buses leave Cancún daily for Chiquilá (M$55, 3½ hours, 161km), at 8am and 12:30pm, as does one Noreste bus at 1:45pm. There are also Oriente buses from Valladolid (M$60, 2½ hours) at 1:30am; and Tizimín (M$44) at 4:30am, 11am, 12:15pm and 2:15pm. Alternatively, take a 2nd-class bus traveling between Valladolid (or Mérida) and Cancún to El Ideal, on Hwy 180 about 73km south of Chiquilá. From there you can take a cab (about M$200; be ready to bargain) or catch one of the Chiquilá-bound buses coming from Cancún, which pass through El Ideal around 10:30am and 3:30pm.

Cabbing it from Cancún is another possibility; you may be able to get a taxi for as little as $500.

Buses (all 2nd class) leave Chiquilá for Cancún (M$58) at 7:30am and 1:30pm; Tizimín (M$40) at 7:30am, 1:30pm and 4:30pm; Valladolid (M$57) at 5:30am; and Mérida (M$117) at 5:30am. All schedules are subject to change, so try to verify ahead of time.

If you're driving, you can either park your car in the Chiquilá parking lot for a usurious M$25 a day (8am to 6pm or any fraction thereof), take your chances parking it on the pier (crowded in high season) or try to catch the infrequent car ferry to Holbox. The ferry is actually a barge pulled by a tugboat and is often out of commission due to weather or mechanical problems, so you end up stranded for a few days. It doesn't run daily in any case, and you won't have much use for a car once you reach Holbox. The best news is that Chiquilá has a gas station.

Holbox's sand streets see few autos, but golf carts have become ubiquitous, and, for many residents, rather annoying. A movement is afoot to ban or at least limit their use. Unless you're mobility-impaired, do everyone a favor and refrain from contributing to noise pollution by renting one. **La Puesta del Sol**, near the northeast corner of the parque, rents bicycles for $70 a day. OK, if you must know, they also rent golf carts.

Tulum Corridor

The Tulum Corridor is the 135km stretch of Hwy 307 that runs from Cancún to the town of Tulum. It is flanked by light to west by light forest and to the east by turnoffs to beachside communities, Mayan ruins and 'ecoparks.' The corridor, which promoters often refer to as the Riviera Maya, has undergone intense development along much of its length. Hotels, megaresorts, time-share complexes and restaurants continue to be built at an alarming rate. Though the goose that laid the golden egg (or the hen, in the Spanish version of the tale) is close to being killed, there are still some relatively secluded spots to enjoy.

The three top tourist destinations along the corridor are Tulum, which is famous for its seaside Mayan ruins; Playa del Carmen, the corridor's chief party town; and Cozumel, world famous for its snorkeling and dive sites.

Secondary destinations include the private parks of Xcaret, Xel-Há and Tres Ríos, which offer such activities as snorkeling on nearby reefs and paddling through mangroves. Qualified divers will find the very best cavern-diving opportunities in this area as well.

This sections runs from north to south. Public buses travel along Hwy 307, but don't reach all the sights listed. If you're short on time and plan on making many stops, consider renting a car.

PUERTO MORELOS
☎ 998 • pop 2800

Puerto Morelos, about 33km south of Cancún, offers some splendid opportunities for dining, diving, snorkeling, shopping, spiritual pursuits and…reading. Once a quiet fishing village known principally for its vehicle ferry to Cozumel, the town has a growing number of seasonal foreign residents as well as a core of permanent expats – together they constitute about 50% of the population. Many of them are attracted by the possibility that Puerto Morelos will largely dodge the development ravaging much of the rest of the area.

In 1998 the Mexican government created the 90-sq-km Parque Marino Nacional Arrefices de Puerto Morelos, a marine park which extends northward paralleling the shore to the southern boundary of the Punta Nizuc NMP. In spite of this, a businessman from Sinaloa proposed bulldozing the mangroves lining the road into town to construct a megaproject entailing thousands of hotel rooms, a marina, condominiums and a shopping mall and golf course, among other delights. Local residents fought the project tooth and nail for years, finally managing to shrink its extent considerably. Much of the mangrove – which is vital to the health of the reef – will be spared, though at the time of research construction had begun on the marina.

Another project that could have a significant impact on the town's character – the car ferry/cruise ship from Tampa, Florida, to Progreso and Puerto Morelos – faces an uncertain future. In January 2003, after a month of runs to Puerto Morelos, the company announced it was suspending service until the town's port authority did an adequate job of dredging the channel leading to the pier.

Orientation & Information

Puerto Morelos' central plaza is 2km east of Hwy 307 nearly at the end of the main road into town (the main dock is the true end of the road). The town, all of three streets wide from east to west, stretches several blocks to the north of the plaza and about three long blocks south. A **Bital ATM** stands off the northeast corner of the plaza, and diagonally across the plaza is **Computips** (open 9am-8:30pm Mon-Fri, 3pm-8:30pm Sat-Sun), an air-con Internet place charging M$15 an hour.

Alma Libre (☎ 871-0713; www.almalibre books.com; open 10am-4pm & 6pm-9pm Tues-Sat, 4pm-9pm Sun; closed July-Sept) has more than 20,000 new and used books – from 'beach trash' to travel and wildlife guides, books on Mexican cooking and Mayan culture (including a Spanish/English/Mayan dictionary), as well as regional maps and much more. The friendly owners take trades (generally two-for-one) or sell most of their used books for half the cover price. They stock titles in French, German and other languages in addition to the English and Spanish works.

Diving & Snorkeling

Several excellent dive sites for a variety of skill levels are within a few kilometers of Puerto Morelos, including a 34m-long naval vessel (a minesweeper or destroyer, depending who you talk to) that was deliberately sunk. The ship has large holes cut into it for divers to enter, and lies in water ranging from 18m to 26m deep, stem to stern.

Both divers and snorkelers can see turtles, sharks, stingrays, eagle rays, moray eels, lobsters, staghorn and brain corals and of course loads of colorful tropical fish. The barrier reef is less than 600m offshore; snorkelers are required to wear a life jacket and pay a M$20 park admission fee to visit it. You're best off hiring a boat and guide for M$200 at the main dock to take you out. There's usually no shortage of either.

Mystic Diving (☎ 871-0634; W www.mys ticdiving.com), on the east (beach) side of the plaza, is one of several outfits in town offering dive and snorkel trips.

Organized Tours

Goyo's (☎ 871-0189; W www.mayajungle .com) is run by 'Goyo' Morgan, a longtime fixture in Puerto Morelos (transplanted from the US) and a great source of information and lore on the area. He offers a 'cenote jungle adventure' to a former *chiclero* (chicle-tappers) village. The medicinal uses of various plants are explained and a swim in a cenote and lunch with a local Mayan family are included. Goyo also does healings and has a line of natural products made from local ingredients.

Places to Stay

Posada Amor (☎ 871-0033, fax 871-0178; W www.posadaamor.com; singles with shared/ private bathroom from M$196/258, doubles from M$258/323) is 100m southwest of the plaza and has been in operation for many years. It has a wide variety of simple fancooled rooms with some creative touches, a shady back area with tables, *palapas* and plenty of plants, and offers meals as well. Prices drop by 15% from May to October.

Hotel Inglaterra (☎/fax 871-0418; e michael@hotelinglaterra.freeserve.co.uk; Av Niños Héroes 29; doubles/triples/quads M$300/400/500 Dec 20-April 20, M$200/ 300/400 April 21-Dec 19) is about half a block north and one block east of the plaza. It's one of the cheapest air-con places in town. Rooms are decent if not great, and the hotel provides free coffee and tea.

Hotel Ojo de Agua (☎ 871-0027, fax 871-0202; W www.ojo-de-agua.com; air-con 1-/2-bed rooms M$560/620; fan rooms with kitchenette M$670) offers 36 rooms in a fairly modern building on a nice stretch of beach. It's about three blocks north of the plaza and has its own restaurant.

Hotel Hacienda Morelos (☎/fax 871-0448; doubles M$670), on the waterfront about 150m south of the plaza, has 15 very appealing, breezy rooms with sea views, kitchenettes and air-con, as well as a small pool and a good restaurant. This is a great value.

Rancho Libertad (☎/fax 871-0181; W www.rancholibertad.com; downstairs/upstairs doubles mid-Apr–mid-Dec US$49/59, mid-Dec–mid-Apr US$69/79; air-con US$10 extra) is a mellow resort with its own secluded stretch of beach south of the ferry terminal, a few hundred meters south of the plaza. Its 15 guestrooms are in one- and two-story thatched bungalows with good ventilation and very comfy beds suspended from the ceiling by ropes; they rock you gently to sleep. The rooms could use some

sprucing up, and a few dogs wander the grounds and sleep on the bungalows' porches. Guests can use the fridge and kitchen in the main building to prepare meals; room rates include a good buffet breakfast and use of bikes and snorkel gear (as available). Singles cost US$10 less, triples US$10 more. The resort has drums for sale and offers several flavors of massage. A cab from the highway will run M$20 to M$25.

Places to Eat

Tío's (dishes M$15-30; open 6:30am-11pm daily) is a modest, friendly place directly across from the lighthouse, just off the northeast corner of the plaza. They serve great fish tacos in the morning (three for M$18), and good Yucatecan and Mexican dishes such as *panuchos, salbutes, sopa de pollo* and *tortas* the rest of the time.

La Nueva Luna (☎ 871-0513; Av Rojo Gómez; mains M$40-50; open 8am-1:30pm & 6pm-10pm Wed-Mon), the place to go for faux-meat dishes (think soy ham for starters), is less than a block north of the northwest corner of the plaza. It serves baguette sandwiches, smoked trout and other goodies in a soothing ambience. Along with Mama's Bakery, following, it's a good place to get information on the many yoga and spiritual-growth workshops given in town.

Mama's Bakery (☎ 845-6810; dishes M$30-45; open 7:30am-4pm) is a couple of blocks north of the previous listing. In addition to a variety of gourmet breads, they serve brownies, cakes by the slice, coffee, juice blends and several (mostly eggy, some fruity) breakfast dishes, available with fried potatoes. At M$30, the delicious sticky buns may seem steep, but how can you stint when it comes to comfort food?

Le Café d'Amancia (items M$15-40; open 8am-11pm daily) is a spotlessly clean place with pleasing ambience on the southwest corner of the plaza. It serves bagels, sandwiches, pies, espresso drinks and fruit and veggie *licuados*.

Hola Asia (☎ 871-0679), on the south side of the plaza, was closed for remodeling at last pass, but got rave reviews from all interviewed who'd dined there. It serves Thai, Chinese, Japanese and Indian dishes.

Seafari (☎ 044-998-259-6356; mains M$35-90, set meals M$35-45; open noon-

11pm daily) serves a variety of well-prepared Mexican and Yucatecan dishes, including a taco buffet, a hefty *comida corrida,* seafood selections and vegetarian options. It's on the northwest corner of the plaza.

John Gray's Kitchen *(☎ 871-0655; Av Niños Héroes; mains M$90-125; open 6pm-10pm Mon-Sat)*, one block west and two blocks north of the plaza, turns out some truly fabulous food. John, the personable owner-chef, seeks out only the freshest and best ingredients. Though he describes his cuisine as 'simple but not simplistic,' the preparation and presentation of each dish is done with painstaking care. An eclectic menu changes frequently, and may include Thai curried chicken, fresh fish with baked tomatoes and Kalamata olive sauce, grilled pork chop with chipotle butter, and an excellent Caesar salad, plus an array of scrumptious desserts.

Entertainment
Chip's Bar *(☎ 871-0673; open 5pm-midnight Mon-Fri, 6pm-midnight Sat)* is a clean, well-lit place (with air-con!) and is good for a quiet drink most nights.

La Caverna *(☎ 044-998-704-9644; open 9am-3pm Mon-Sat)*, popular with the town's younger set, is done up like a mellow, candlelit cave. Musicians occasionally play here; the rest of the time the mix is good and often at a fairly low volume.

Shopping
One block south of the plaza's west corner is the **artisans market**, with several stalls under one thatched roof. On offer are hammocks, clothing (including hats and *huipiles*), jewelry, lots of products made from seashells and more – much of it produced by locals. It's refreshingly low key, and you can often see the craftspeople at work.

Getting There & Away
Most Playa Express and Riviera buses traveling between Cancún and Playa del Carmen drop you on the highway. Some Mayab buses enter town; the Riviera bus running between Cancún airport and Playa del Carmen will sometimes enter the town on request.

Taxis are usually waiting at the turnoff to shuttle people into town, and there's often a taxi or two near the plaza to shuttle people back to the highway. Many drivers will tell you the fare is per person or overcharge in some other manner; strive for M$12 for the 2km ride, for as many people as you can stuff in.

You're better off leaving from Calica south of Playa del Carmen (see the Cozumel Getting There & Away section), but the **transbordador** *(vehicle ferry; ☎ 871-0008, in Cozumel ☎ 987-872-0950)* to Cozumel leaves Puerto Morelos most days at 4am or 5am. At last pass passenger vehicles weren't allowed Tuesday or Friday, and an additional departure left at 2pm or 4pm on some days. All times are subject to change according to season or the weather; during high seas, the ferry won't leave at all. You must get in line at least two hours (four is officially recommended) before departure and hope there's enough space. The voyage takes anywhere from 2½ to four hours and costs M$778 per car (driver included), M$58 per passenger. Departure from Cozumel is from the dock in front of the Hotel Sol Caribe, south of town along the shore road.

JARDÍN BOTÁNICO
Two kilometers south of the turnoff for Puerto Morelos is the **Jardín Botánico Dr Alfredo Barrera** *(admission M$70; open 9am-5pm daily Nov-April, 9am-5pm Mon-Sat May-Sept)*, a 60-hectare nature preserve with nearly 3km of trails through several native habitats. The garden has sections dedicated to epiphytes (orchids and bromeliads), palms, ferns, succulents (cacti and their relatives), ornamental plants and plants used in traditional Mayan medicine. The flora is identified in English, Spanish and Latin. The preserve also holds a large animal population, including the only coastal troops of spider monkeys left in the region. Birders come to observe the many migratory and resident bird species. A lookout tower affords views over the mangrove to Puerto Morelos and the sea.

For the anthropologically minded, the preserve has re-creations of a Mayan house and a *chiclero* camp, as well as some genuine Mayan ruins (circa AD 1400). Bring repellent. Buses may be hailed directly in front of the garden.

TRES RÍOS
Tres Ríos *(☎ 998-887-8077; W www.tres-rios.com; Km 54 Hwy 307; adults/children basic admission M$215/170, all-inclusive*

M$760/590; open 9am-5pm daily), 21km south of Puerto Morelos, is the first of three 'ecoparks' you'll encounter between Cancún and Tulum, and the least environmentally harmful one. It's actually a fairly cool place: a 1.5 sq km swath of coastal forest where – despite the name – four underground rivers surface a kilometer or so from the sea.

Paying the basic admission, visitors can explore the freshwater, jungle-flanked rivers in canoes or kayaks; ride mountain bikes along jungle paths; and just hang out on the white-sand beach. Also included in the basic price is use of showers, toilets, hammocks and a life jacket for swimming. Everything else is at an additional cost.

The all-inclusive package gets you towels, a locker, snorkeling gear (M$50 extra with the basic fee), speedboat rides, horseback riding and food and drink (including domestic alcohol, which you might want to save for last). Various combinations of activities are offered in promotional packages, most of which include transportation from Cancún.

The snorkeling is good, especially out at the reef, and you can ride horses along the beach. Note that only biodegradable sunscreen is allowed here.

A special Tres Ríos bus leaves Cancún's Plaza Mayafair (Blvd Kukulcán Km 8.5) at 8:30am and returns at 5pm daily. Most buses traveling Hwy 307 will drop you near the entrance.

KAILUUM II

This rather unique resort (in USA ☎ 800-538-6802; W www.mexicoholiday.com; singles/doubles/triples Dec-Feb US$120/140/175, Mar-Nov US$80/95/125) is 62km south of Cancún and about 2km east of Hwy 307. It's next to the more conventional Capitán Lafitte on a gorgeous stretch of beach, and features 31 'tentalapas,' ample canvas tents pitched under thatched shelters and equipped with excellent beds that provide great sea views. They're right on the beach and just above the level of the sea. Each has a porch with hammocks, and many have their own gardens.

Kailuum has no electricity and doesn't allow cell phones, children or even flashlights; it's very tranquil. The immaculate shared bathrooms and toilets are ecofriendly, and guests can play volleyball, paddle kayaks, read and pour themselves drinks at

the self-serve honor bar. Very good food (lots of fish, though they'll do vegetarian on request) is prepared fresh daily, and served under an enormous, sand-floor palapa, lit at night by nearly 200 candles. An agreement with Capitán Lafitte allows guests to take breakfast or dinner there if they wish. You're best off getting here by rental car or taxi; it's a hike from the bus stop.

PUNTA BETE

Punta Bete, a rocky, reef-hugged point 65km south of Cancún, is reached by a dirt road that runs past a large new housing development and weaves 2.5km from Hwy 307 (turn at the sign for Xcalacoco) before reaching the sea. North and south of the stubby point there are beautiful and occasionally wide stretches of beach upon which sit a few small, low-profile hotels with hot-water private bathrooms, a few restaurants and a super-pricey resort.

Los Piños (upstairs/downstairs rooms M$300/250) is a rustic but clean hotel with eight spacious guestrooms and a simple but likeable restaurant with a fine sea view.

Paradise Point Resort (W www.paradise-point-resort.com; singles/doubles/triples US$35/40/45; open Nov-May) features nine basic but clean beachfront cabanas with double or king beds and solar-powered lamps. There's an inexpensive restaurant for guests only.

Coco's Cabañas (☎/fax 998-887-9964; W www.cancun-reservations.com; rooms US$35-45) consists of five nicely decorated cabanas with electricity, fan, good beds and hammocks. It's a short walk from the beach and has a bar, a small pool, a pleasant garden area and a restaurant. The English-speaking German owner has done a very good job on the whole place.

All of the hotels and restaurants in Punta Bete are within walking distance of each other, but as with Kailuum, you're best off getting here by rental car or taxi.

PLAYA DEL CARMEN
☎ 984 • pop 49,000

Playa del Carmen's many attractions have made it one of the fastest-growing cities in Mexico in recent years. Pleasure-seekers can enjoy hopping nightlife, lovely beaches with good snorkeling, varied and delicious international cuisine, an array of good-value

PLAYA DEL CARMEN

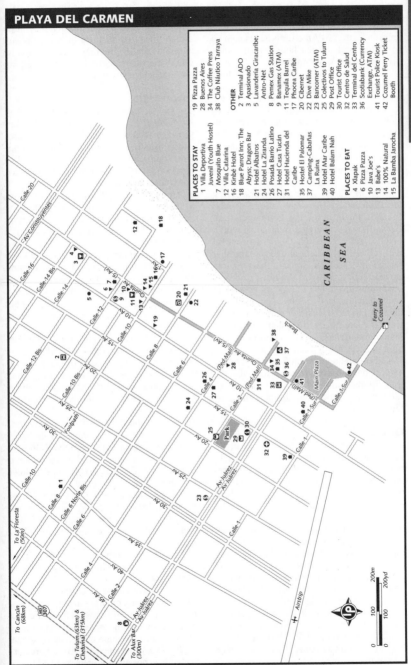

PLACES TO STAY

1 Villa Deportiva Juvenil (Youth Hostel)
7 Mosquito Blue
12 Villa Catarina
16 Kinbé Hotel
18 Blue Parrot Inn; The Abyss; Dragon Bar
21 Hotel Albatros
24 Hotel La Ziranda
26 Posada Barrio Latino
27 Hotel Casa Tucán
31 Hotel Hacienda del Caribe
35 Hostel El Palomar
37 Camping-Cabañas La Ruina
39 Hotel Mar Caribe
40 Hotel Balam Nah

PLACES TO EAT

4 Xlapak
6 Pizza Pazza
10 Java Joe's
13 Babe's
14 100% Natural
15 La Bamba Jarocha
19 Pizza Pazza
28 Buenos Aires
34 The Coffee Press
38 Club Náutico Tarraya

OTHER

2 Terminal ADO
3 Apasionado
5 Lavandería Giracaribe; Antro-Net
8 Pemex Gas Station
9 Banamex (ATM)
11 Tequila Barrel
17 Phocea Caribe
20 Cibernet
22 Dive Mike
23 Bancomer (ATM)
25 Colectivos to Tulum
29 Post Office
30 Tourist Office
32 Centro de Salud
33 Terminal del Centro
36 Scotiabank (Currency Exchange, ATM)
41 Tourist Police Kiosk
42 Cozumel Ferry Ticket Booth

hotels and, just a boat ride away, fantastic diving. Many Europeans (particularly Italians) and not a few Americans have taken up residence and opened hotels, restaurants, dive shops and other businesses.

For decades 'Playa' was a simple fishing village that foreigners only passed through on their way to a ferry that would take them to Cozumel and the reefs that Jacques Cousteau made famous with a documentary. But with the construction of Cancún, the number of travelers roaming this part of the Yucatán increased exponentially, as did the number of hotels and restaurants to serve them.

Most of Playa's foreign visitors during the 1980s and 1990s were Europeans who found Cancún a bit too commercial. In Playa, they discovered a small town with a lovely stretch of beach facing a beautiful reef, a few small hotels, and restaurants that served fresh seafood. Some of these visitors stayed. Today, many of the town's accommodations are stylish European-owned and -managed inns, and the city is gradually extending farther and farther north, south and west as more hotels, time-shares and other residential developments continue to be built.

The official population figure is given as 49,000, but some residents estimate that the true figure combined with the number of visitors in a good high season can be as high as 250,000.

Orientation

Playa is mostly laid out on an easy grid, but its northward expansion has resulted in many unsigned streets in that area, aggravated by a confusing series of *bis* streets (Calle 12 bis = Calle 12-A), some of which end after a few blocks. Quinta Av (**keen**-ta; 5th Avenue) is the most happening street in town, especially along its pedestrian stretch.

The Terminal del Centro – the older bus terminal receiving all 2nd-class services and Riviera's coastal buses – is opposite the main plaza at the intersection of Quinta Av and Av Juárez, while the new 1st-class terminal is several blocks north.

Though Quinta Av is a popular place to stroll and dine, or drink and people-watch, or any combination of the above, the number of restaurant and time-share touts can be dismaying at times.

Also be warned that the city sees large volumes of large people disgorged by large cruise ships that dock (or occasionally run aground) nearby. But they – and most of the touts – can generally be avoided by walking a few blocks away from the pier.

Information

The **tourist information office** (☎ 873-2804; Av Juárez at 15 Av; open 9am-9pm Mon-Sat, 9am-5pm Sun) is well stocked with brochures and is usually staffed by a speaker of English, Italian and German. A **tourist police kiosk** (☎ 873-0291; open 24 hours) guards the north corner of the main plaza.

Among the many banks around town are a **Scotiabank** (Quinta Av) with both ATM and a currency-exchange counter, across Quinta Av from the Terminal del Centro, a **Bancomer** (Av Juárez) with ATM four blocks west, and a **Banamex** (cnr Calle 12 & 10 Av).

For medical treatment, try the **Centro de Salud** (☎ 873-0493; 15 Av), near Av Juárez.

The **post office** (cnr 15 Av & Av Juárez; open 9am-5pm Mon-Fri, for stamps only Sat 9am-1pm) is a couple blocks inland from the main plaza.

One of Playa's longer-running Internet places is the air-con **Cibernet** (Calle 8; open 8am-11pm daily), just east of Quinta Av. It charges M$15 per hour for generally good connections. Two of the many other places are **Antro-Net** (10 Av between Calles 12 & 14; open 8am-midnight Mon-Sat, 10am-10pm Sun) and the café at the **Blue Parrot** (Calle 12 at the beach), which charge M$20 and M$30 per hour respectively. Both have speedy connections. The Blue Parrot's terminals have the best ergonomics in town (for those prices they ought to).

Friendly **Lavandería Giracaribe** (10 Av between Calles 12 & 14; open 8:30am-8:30pm Mon-Sat), located next to the Antro-Net, washes and dries clothes for $10 a kilogram.

The **Coffee Press** (Calle 2 at Quinta Av) sells used books and does two-for-one exchanges.

Never leave valuables unattended on the beach, especially on the isolated stretches to the north. Run-and-grab thefts while victims are swimming or sleeping on isolated beaches are a common occurrence (the jungle has eyes), and sneak thefts on more populated beaches are not unknown.

Diving & Snorkeling

Some recommended dive centers are:

The Abyss (☎ 873-2164, W www.abyssdive shop.com) Blue Parrot Inn, Calle 12
Dive Mike (☎ 803-1228, W www.divemike.com) Calle 8 between Quinta Av & the beach; English, Danish, Norwegian, Swedish, German, French, Italian, Spanish and Japanese spoken
Phocea Caribe (☎ 873-1210, fax 873-1024, W www.phoceacaribedive.com) 1 Av btw Calles 10 & 12; French, English and Spanish spoken

All offer cenote dives as well, and Dive Mike offers snorkel tours by boat to the reef and a secluded beach for US$30 including sandwich, soft drinks and all gear. To tag along on a dive boat and snorkel is US$10 (a steal). Ask about his cenote snorkel tours (US$45).

Beaches

You can swim on Playa's white-sand beaches nearly anywhere, but some folks like a bit more than sand and surf. **Playa Tukán Beach Club** (Calle 28 Norte at beach; open 8am-6pm) has a small pool, a bar and restaurant, and lots of thatch umbrellas with lounge chairs (M$25 per person). It's OK if you don't mind crowds. For more breathing room you can go a little farther north, to the defunct Coco Beach Club near the foot of Calle 38, where a few scrawny palms serve for shade (if you get thirsty you can hit the **Zubul Beach Reef Bar** just to the south). Going north from Coco the beach extends for uncrowded kilometers, but you need to be extra careful with your belongings, as thefts are common.

Places to Stay

Playa del Carmen has been developing rapidly for several years, and may have finally overbuilt – at least for as long as the global economy is in the doldrums. High season is generally from January 7 through March. In peak season (December 20 to January 6) many places raise rates up to 70% over high-season rates. Low season is the rest of the year. Note that hotel managers change their minds about these seasons constantly; most places varying from the norm have their dates listed. All rates given here include taxes.

Budget The **Villa Deportiva Juvenil** (☎/fax 873-1508; Calle 8; dorm beds M$40), at the end of 35 Av, offers cheap, reasonably clean lodging in single-sex, somewhat worn dorms with lockers. It's a trek to the beach, mattresses are grubby, and no towels are provided, but the place has table tennis, a TV area and a skateboard park.

Camping-Cabañas La Ruina (☎/fax 873-0405; e laruina@dicoz.com; Calle 2; tent or hammock space per person M$50; 1-bed/2-bed doubles with shared bathroom M$160/225; doubles with private bathroom M$275-357) lets you pitch your tent or hang your hammock (they're available for rent as well) in a large lot near the beach. Some rooms have ceiling fans, some have air-con – the cheapest are bare and bleak, and the most expensive front the beach.

Hostel El Palomar (☎ 803-2606; e hostel elpalomar@hotmail.com; Quinta Av between Av Juárez & Calle 2; low-/high-season dorm beds M$80/110, doubles M$250/300) is a friendly, nonsmoking place across from the Terminal del Centro. It has two 18-bed, single-sex dorms and, on the 3rd floor, a few modest shared-bathroom doubles (each with balcony, hammock and good sea views). A rooftop terrace with kitchen facilities has great views of the Caribbean. Rates include breakfast, sheets, towels, soap, BIG lockers and drinking water.

Hotel Mar Caribe (☎ 873-0207; cnr 15 Av & Calle 1; 1-/2-bed rooms in low season M$200/250, high season M$250/350), is a simple, secure and very clean nine-room place with fan-cooled rooms. The owners speak French, Spanish and some English.

Hotel Casa Tucán (☎/fax 873-0283; e casatucan@playadelcarmen.com; Calle 4 between 10 & 15 Avs; rooms M$150-450), a German/Texan-run hotel, is a warren of 29 rooms of several types. All are fan-cooled, a couple have kitchenettes, and the cheapest have shared bathrooms. Tucán has a swimming pool, a pleasant tropical garden and a café serving good, affordable food.

Hotel La Ziranda (☎ 873-3933; W www .hotellaziranda.com; Calle 4 between 15 & 20 Avs; rooms low/high season M$250/350) was constructed in late 2000. Its two buildings have 15 nice rooms, all with balconies or terraces and two double beds or one king. The grounds are agreeably landscaped and the staff are friendly.

Posada Barrio Latino (☎/fax 873-2384; W www.posadabarriolatino.com; Calle 4 between 10 & 15 Avs; single/double/triple low season M$220/270/320, high season M$290/370/420, air-con extra M$80), offers 16 clean rooms with good ventilation, ceiling fans, tiled floors, bathrooms and hammocks (in addition to beds). The friendly Italian owners speak English and Spanish, the place is often full and the front gate is always kept locked.

Mid-Range Expect these prices to jump when the economy gets back on track.

Kinbé Hotel (☎ 873-0441, fax 873-2215; W www.kinbe.com; Calle 10 near 1 Av; doubles with air-con May 1-July 20 & Sept 1-Dec 14 M$350-450, Dec 15-Apr 30 & July 21-Aug 31 M$450-550), an Italian-owned and -operated hotel, has 19 clean, simple but elegant rooms with lovely aesthetic touches, a gorgeous lush courtyard garden and a breezy rooftop terrace with fab views.

Hotel Balam Nah (☎ 873-2117, fax 873-2116; W www.hotelbalamnah.com; Calle 1 between Quinta & 10 Avs; doubles with fan/air-con M$390/490, with air-con and balcony M$590) has good beds and bathrooms, tile floors and, in most rooms, small fridges. Rooms are on three floors around a viney courtyard (the front, balcony rooms are not worth the extra cost). At last pass, management was maintaining the same prices year-round.

Villa Catarina (☎ 873-2098, fax 873-2097; e villacatarina@prodigy.net.mx; Calle Privada Norte between Calles 12 & 14; doubles Apr 16-Dec 14 US$40-55, Dec 15-Apr 15 US$60-80) nestles quietly near the beach amid a lush, flowery garden. Rooms vary from cabanas to palapa towers and beyond; some have air-con, others fan.

Top End Italian-run **Hotel Hacienda del Caribe** (☎ 873-3132, fax 873-1149; W www.haciendadelcaribe.com; Calle 2 between Quinta and 10 Avs; doubles US$65-123) was built in 2000. Its large, quiet, comfortable rooms have lovely decor, air-con and cable TV. The courtyard has a small pool with hydromassage, and parking in a nearby lot is free while you stay. The price range given here reflects five different times of year and includes peak season.

Hotel Albatros (☎/fax 873-0001; e albatros@playadelcarmen.com; Calle 8 between Quinta Av & beach; doubles with fan/air-con Dec 16-Apr 30 US$82/92, May 1-Dec 15 US$51/61), has 36 lovely rooms. The older section, close to the beach, is the nicer bit; its clusters of rooms are under thatched roofs and look brand new inside. Most have two beds and a terrace or balcony. Air-con rooms have a fridge, microwave and coffeemaker.

Mosquito Blue (☎ 873-1245, fax 873-1337; W www.mosquitoblue.com; Quinta Av between Calles 12 & 14; standard/deluxe doubles Dec 16-Apr 30 & Aug 1-Aug 30 US$130/140, May 1-July 31 & Sept 1-Dec 15 US$100/110) strives for – and at times achieves – ultrachicness. Its cloistered interior boasts two pools and courtyards, a bar and restaurant and very nicely decorated rooms furnished in Indonesian mahogany. Art and artistic touches abound throughout the hotel, which has junior and master suites as well as the standard and deluxe rooms.

Blue Parrot Inn (☎ 873-0083, fax 873-0049, in USA ☎ 800-854-4498; Calle 12 at beach; rooms US$51-303) is the place a lot of people wish they were staying when they wander up the beach and discover it. Many of the charming units (all air-con except for the beachfront palapas, which are the cheapest lodgings) have terraces, sea views, and full kitchens. The Inn has evolved with Playa over many years, and its bar is a local hot spot.

Places to Eat

As happens in other tourist-oriented places on the Yucatán Peninsula, some Playa restaurants (or their unscrupulous waitstaff) add a service charge to the bill.

La Floresta (Hwy 307; tacos M$9-10, ceviches & cocktails M$50-70; open 9am-5pm daily), on the west side of the highway opposite Calle 8, has shrimp tacos to die for. Don't even think about it, just sit down and order at least three right away. The shrimp are lightly battered, then fried and served in a soft corn tortilla with a dab of mayo and some chopped tomato and onions. Squeeze a lime wedge over it, add a touch of spicy green or red salsa and chow down. The ceviches and cocktails (octopus, conch, oyster, and shrimp) are good too, but who has room?

Java Joe's (Quinta Av between Calles 10 & 12; open 6:30am-9:45pm daily; breakfast M$20-30, sandwiches M$35-55) serves breakfast all day, as well as deli sandwiches, bagels and good espresso drinks.

The Coffee Press *(Calle 2 near Quinta Av; open 7:30am-10pm daily; breakfast M$27-33, lunch mains M$31-44)* makes some of the best breakfasts and coffee drinks in town, and serves a selection of gourmet teas.

Pizza Pazza *(☎ 803-0903; 10 Av between Calles 8 & 10 • Calle 12 between 10 & Quinta Avs; open 12:30pm-1am daily; slices M$16)* bakes some brilliant thin-crust Sardegnian pies, with various tasty toppings.

Xlapak *(Quinta Av between Calles 14 & 14 bis; open 8am-11pm daily; breakfast M$20, lunch & dinner M$49-160)* serves delicious food at unbelievably low prices. Lunch and dinner consists of a starter, a main dish (accompanied by rice, steamed veggies and garlic bread) and a dessert. Try the spaghetti with *calamares y chaya* (squid and a spinach-like green) and wash it down with one of a wide selection of juices and drinks. The restaurant is very nicely done up like a Mayan temple, with faithfully rendered reproductions of Mayan murals on the walls, and plants everywhere.

Club Náutico Tarraya *(☎ 873-2040; Calle 2 at the beach; open noon-10pm daily; mains M$38-70)* is one of the few restaurants in Playa del Carmen that dates from the 1960s. It continues to offer good seafood at decent prices.

100% Natural *(☎ 873-2242; cnr Quinta Av & Calle 10; mains M$35-90; open 7am-11pm daily)* may be a franchise, but the trademark fruit and vegetable juice blends, salads, various veggie and chicken dishes and other healthy foods are delicious and filling. The green courtyard is inviting and service is very good.

Babe's *(☎ 984-877-5494; Calle 10 between Quinta & 10 Avs; open noon-11pm Mon-Sat; mains M$43-78)* serves some excellent Thai food, including a yummy home-style *tom ka gai* (chicken and coconut-milk soup) brimming with veggies. Among other recommended choices is the excellent Vietnamese salad (with shrimp and mango). Most dishes can be done vegetarian, and to mix things up a bit the Swedish cook has some tasty Greek items on the menu as well.

Buenos Aires *(☎ 873-2751; Calle 6 between Quinta & 10 Avs; open 6pm-midnight daily; mains M$52-105)* is one of Playa's several versions of Argentine *parrillas* (grills), and is well known for its steaks, ribs, burgers and other meaty items, made only with Angus beef.

La Bamba Jarocha *(☎ 803-1549; Calle 10 between Quinta & 1 Avs; open noon-11pm daily; mains M$75-120)* is a good choice for seafood and Mexican dishes.

Entertainment

Tequila Barrel *(☎ 873-1061; Quinta Av between Calles 10 & 12; open 11am-1am)*, a sparkling clean bar and grill, pours a huge selection of tequila and other spirits, and spins old rock and Motown CDs. Live bands, such as local blues favorites Chiva Azul, play here from time to time.

Dragon Bar *(☎ 873-0083; Calle 12 at the beach; open 11am-4am)* is the Blue Parrot Inn's immensely popular open-sided *palapa* beachfront bar with swing chairs. The DJ is augmented by the occasional live band, including the peripatetic Chiva Azul. By the time you read this there should be an adjacent indoor disco with a state-of-the-art sound system, allowing the party to go on in bad weather and at higher volume.

Apasionado *(☎ 803-1101; cnr Quinta Av & Calle 14; open 8:30pm-2am daily)* is a jazz bar–restaurant with live music most nights, from Latin jazz to steel drums. The upstairs venue is beautiful – an enormous *palapa* is festooned with huge flat lampshades and tin globes emitting a soft yellow light. The phyllo-wrapped tuna tartare (M$98) is a real treat.

Xlapak *(Quinta Av between Calles 14 & 14 bis; open 8am-11pm daily)* offers various evening activities to go along with its great food (see under Places to Eat), including salsa dancing classes, Aztec dance exhibitions and slide shows on the Mayan world (with narration in German or English).

Alux *(☎ 803-0713; Av Juárez; snacks M$40-90, mains M$120-140; open 7pm-2am daily)*, about three blocks west of Hwy 307, is an amazing must-visit. It's a restaurant–lounge situated in a cavern: stalactites, stalagmites, pools and all. Candles and dim electric lights illuminate numerous nooks and crannies converted into sofalike seating. Wander through, have a bite to eat or a drink and revel in the atmosphere (which, by the way, is a bit short on oxygen, though not so much as to leave you gasping). Alux offers live music nightly at 10pm, and a party on Saturday night.

Getting There & Away

Bus Playa has two bus terminals; each sells tickets and provides information for at least some of the other's departures. The newer one, **Terminal ADO** (20 Av), just east of Calle 12, is where most 1st-class bus lines arrive and depart. Riviera's buses (which don't entirely deserve the designation '1st-class' anyhow) use the old terminal. A taxi from Terminal ADO to the main plaza will run about M$12.

The old station, **Terminal del Centro** (cnr Av Juárez & Quinta Av), gets all the 2nd-class (called 'intermedio' by such lines as Mayab) services. Riviera buses to Cancún and its airport have a separate ticket counter, on the Av Juárez side of the terminal. Services run as follows:

Cancún M$32, one hour, 68km; Riviera buses every 15 minutes from 5:30am to midnight
Cancún International Airport M$65, 45 minutes to one hour, 64km; nine direct Riviera buses between 7am and 7:30pm
Chetumal M$117 to M$158, five to 5½ hours, 315km; many 1st- and 2nd-class buses
Chichén Itzá M$140, three to four hours, 272km; one Riviera bus at 7:30am
Cobá M$41 to M$46, one to 1¾ hours, 113km; one Riviera bus at 7:30am, one 1st-class Super Expresso bus at 11:30am, two Mayab buses
Mérida M$196, five hours, 385km; nine 1st-class Super Expresso buses
Palenque M$314 to M$394, 12 to 13 hours, 800km; one bus each by Maya de Oro (deluxe), Colón (1st-class) and Altos (ostensibly 1st-class)
San Cristóbal de Las Casas M$397 to M$501, 16 to 18 hours, 940km; one bus each by Maya de Oro (deluxe), Colón (1st-class) and Altos (ostensibly 1st-class)
Tulum M$28, one hour, 63km; several Riviera and Mayab buses
Valladolid M$60 to M$97, 2½ to 3½ hours, 169km; various Riviera and Mayab buses

Colectivo Vans Shared vans head south to Tulum (M$20, 45 minutes) from Calle 2 near 20 Av as soon as they fill (about every 10 or 15 minutes) from 5am to 10pm. They will stop anywhere along the highway between Playa and Tulum, charging a minimum of M$10. Luggage space is somewhat limited, but they're a good alternative to the bus.

Boat Ferries to Cozumel (M$80, one-way) leave at 6am, 8am, 9am, 10am, 11am, 1pm,

3pm, 5pm, 6pm, 7pm, 9pm and 11pm. The air-conditioned catamaran takes about half an hour, depending on weather. An open-air boat (same ticket but running less regularly) takes 45 minutes to an hour; it operates mostly in the summer season.

COZUMEL
☎ 987 • pop 67,000

Cozumel, 71km south of Cancún, is a teardrop-shaped coral island ringed by crystalline waters. Measuring 53km by 14km, it is Mexico's largest island. Called Ah-Cuzamil-Peten (Island of Swallows) by its earliest inhabitants, Cozumel has been a favorite destination for divers since 1961, when a Jacques Cousteau documentary on its glorious reefs appeared on TV. Today, no fewer than 100 world-class dive sites have been identified within 5km of Cozumel, and no less than a dozen of them are shallow enough for snorkeling. The dominant non-native species on the island are divers and cruise-ship passengers; interbreeding yields the occasional cruising diver. Though many of Cozumel's native citizens (particularly the older ones) are friendly, and polite to the point of courtliness, these days a certain percentage of the populace seems determined to squeeze the last centavo out of the foreign visitor.

People here are so used to hearing butchered Spanish (or English, with no attempt made to even speak Spanish) that they are prepared to not understand you before you even open your mouth. And of course this leads to their not understanding you even if your Spanish is pretty good. Except for the diving and snorkeling, there's little reason to visit Cozumel.

History

Mayan settlement here dates from AD 300. During the post-Classic period, Cozumel flourished as a trade center and, more importantly, a ceremonial site. Every Maya woman on the Yucatán Peninsula and beyond was expected to make at least one pilgrimage here to pay tribute to Ixchel, the goddess of fertility and the moon, at a temple erected in her honor. Archaeologists believe this temple was at San Gervasio, a bit north of the island's geographical center.

At the time of the first Spanish contact with Cozumel (in 1518, by Juan de Grijalva and his men), there were at least 32 Mayan building groups on the island. According to Spanish chronicler Diego de Landa, Cortés a year later sacked one of the Mayan centers but left the others intact, apparently satisfied with converting the island's population to Christianity. Smallpox introduced by the Spanish wiped out half the 8000 Maya, and of the survivors, only about 200 escaped genocidal attacks by conquistadors in the late 1540s.

The island remained virtually deserted into the late 17th century, its coves providing sanctuary for several notorious pirates, including Jean Lafitte and Henry Morgan. In 1848, Indians fleeing the War of the Castes began to resettle Cozumel. At the beginning of the 20th century the island's by-then mostly mestizo population grew,

thanks to the craze for chewing gum. Cozumel was a port of call on the chicle export route, and locals harvested the gum base on the island. After the demise of chicle Cozumel's economy remained strong owing to the construction of a US air base here during WWII.

When the US military departed, the island fell into an economic slump, and many of its people moved away. Those who stayed fished for a living until 1961, when Cousteau's documentary broadcast Cozumel's glorious sea life to the world. The tourists began arriving almost overnight.

Orientation & Information

It's easy to make your way on foot around the island's only town, **San Miguel de**

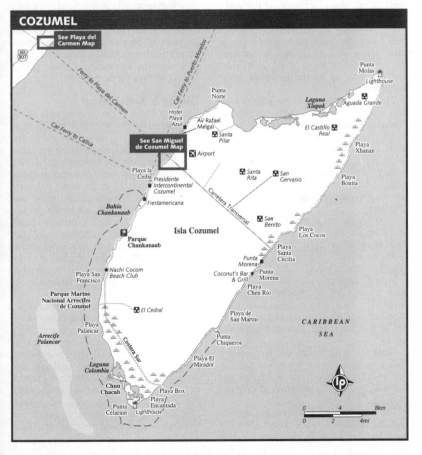

Cozumel. The waterfront boulevard is Av Rafael Melgar; along Melgar south of the main ferry dock (the 'Muelle Fiscal') is a narrow sand beach. The main plaza is just opposite the ferry dock. A convenience store at the landward end of the ferry dock stores luggage for M$20 per day, but the shelves used are not big enough for a full-sized backpack. The airport is 2km northeast of town.

Cozumel's **tourist information office** (☎/fax 869-0212; open 9am-5pm Mon-Fri, 9am-1pm Sat), is hidden upstairs in the Plaza del Sol, a shopping area on the southeast side of the main plaza. It operates a **branch** (open 8am-4pm Mon-Sat) at the foot of the ferry dock. The helpful **tourist police** (☎ 872-0092) patrol the island and staff a **kiosk** (open 8am-11pm daily) at the northeast edge of the plaza.

For currency exchange, try any of the banks near the main plaza shown on the map. Many have ATMs and all are open 8am or 9am to 4:30pm Monday to Friday and on Saturday morning; **Banca Serfin** keeps longer hours.

The many *casas de cambio* around town may charge as much as 3.5% commission (versus the bank rate of 1%) to cash a traveler's check, but they keep longer hours. Most of the major hotels, restaurants and stores will also change money or accept US dollars in payment – some at a fair rate. Many establishments charge a percentage when accepting credit cards; always ask beforehand.

Next door to the **post office** (Calle 7 Sur at Av Melgar open 9am-4pm Mon-Fri) is a **Telecomm office** handling faxes, money orders and such. Telmex card phones are abundant around town.

Most Internet places in town offer fairly slow access. Air-con **Rockafé** (Salas between Avs 15 & 20 Sur; open 9am-11pm Mon-Sat) is as good a place as any, charges M$20 per hour and serves snacks and drinks.

Fama (Av 5 Norte between Av Juárez & Calle 2 Norte; open 9am-10pm Mon-Sat) carries books and periodicals in English and Spanish, as well as a selection of CDs and clothing.

The large washers at **Margarita Laundromat** (☎ 872-2865; Av 20 Sur near Calle 3 Sur; open 7am-9pm Mon-Sat, 8am-5pm Sun) cost M$30 per load (soap costs M$4.50 extra); 15 minutes of dryer time is M$16. **Express Lavandería** (☎ 872-3655; Salas between Aves 5 & 10 Sur; open 8am-9pm Mon-Sat, 8:30am-4pm Sun) will wash and dry a small/medium/large load for M$60/90/120.

Museo de la Isla de Cozumel

Exhibits at this fine museum (☎ 872-1434; Av Melgar between Calles 4 & 6 Norte; admission M$30; open 9am-5pm daily) present a clear and detailed picture of the island's flora, fauna, geography, geology and ancient Mayan history. Thoughtful and detailed signs in English and Spanish accompany the exhibits. It's a good place to learn about coral before hitting the water, and it's one not to miss before you leave the island. Hours may vary seasonally. A courtyard in the back contains a Mayan *na* (traditional thatched house) with someone in attendance who will explain (in Spanish) the various elements that made up Mayan domestic life: the toys, utensils, foodstuffs, a raised garden bed for kitchen herbs and more.

Diving & Snorkeling

Cozumel is one of the most popular diving destinations in the world. It has fantastic year-round visibility (commonly 40m and greater) and a jaw-droppingly impressive variety of marine life that includes spotted eagle rays, moray eels, groupers, barracudas, turtles, sharks, brain coral and some huge sponges. The island has strong currents, making drift dives the standard. Even when diving or snorkeling from the beach you should evaluate conditions and plan your route, selecting an exit point downcurrent beforehand, then staying alert for shifts in current direction. Always keep an eye out (and your ears open) for boat traffic as well.

Prices vary, but in general, expect to pay about US$70 for a two-tank dive (less if you bring your own BCD and regulator), US$60 for an introductory 'resort' course and US$350 for PADI open-water-diver certification. Multiple-dive packages and discounts for groups or those paying in cash can bring these rates down significantly. For more information, pick up a copy of Lonely Planet's *Diving & Snorkeling Cozumel,* with detailed descriptions of local dive sites.

There are scores of dive operators on Cozumel. The following list contains details of some of some reputable ones that come recommended. All limit the size of their groups to six or eight divers, and take pains to match up divers of similar skill levels. Some offer snorkeling and deep-sea fishing trips as well as dives and diving instruction. Those out of the center will provide transport.

Victor Brito Barreiro (*☎/fax 872-3223,* **W** *www .angelfire.com/ga/cozumeldiving/MMT.htm*), based south of town. Victor is head of Cozumel's diving instructors association and has many years of experience.

Aquatic Sports (*☎ 872-0640,* **W** *www.scuba cozumel.com*) Av 15 Sur & Calle 21 Sur. Owner Sergio Sandoval has been diving for more than 30 years but is as enthusiastic as ever.

Deep Blue (*☎/fax 872-5653,* **W** *www.deepblue cozumel.com*) Av 10 Sur at Salas. This PADI,

Cozumel's Top Dive Sites

Ask any dive operator in Cozumel to name the best dive sites in the area and the following names will come up time and again:

Santa Rosa Wall
This is the biggest name of the name sites. The wall is so large most people are able to see only a third of it on one tank. Regardless of where you're dropped, expect to find enormous overhangs and tunnels covered with corals and sponges. Stoplight parrotfish, black grouper and barracuda hang out here. Average visibility is 30m and minimum depth 10m, with an average closer to 25m. Carry a flashlight with you, even if you're diving at noon, as it will help to bring out the color of coral at depth and illuminate the critters hiding in crevices.

Punta Sur Reef
This is also a deep wall dive, with a minimum depth of 20m, but it's unforgettable for its coral caverns, each of which is named. Before you dive be sure to ask your dive master to point out The Devil's Throat. This cave opens into a cathedral room with four tunnels, all of which make for some pretty hairy exploring. Only cave-certified divers should consider entering The Devil's Throat, but anyone who visits Punta Sur Reef will be impressed by the cave system and the butterfly fish, angelfish and whip corals that abound there.

Colombia Shallows
Also known as Colombia Gardens, Colombia Shallows lends itself equally well to snorkeling and scuba diving. Because it's a shallow dive (maximum depth 10m, average 2m to 4m), its massive coral buttresses covered with sponges and other resplendent lifeforms are well illuminated. The current at Colombia Gardens is generally light to moderate; the combination of shallow water and light current allows you to spend hours at the site if you want, and you'll never get bored spying all the elkhorn coral, pillar coral and anemones that live there.

Palancar Gardens
Also known as Palancar Shallows, this dive can also be appreciated by snorkelers due to the slight current usually found there and the low maximum depth of the site (20m). The Gardens consists of a strip reef about 25m wide and very long, riddled with fissures and tunnels. The major features here are enormous stovepipe sponges and vivid yellow tube sponges, and you can always find damselfish, parrot fish and angelfish around you. In the deeper parts of the reef, divers will want to keep an eye out for the lovely black corals.

Arrecife Cantarell
On this section of reef off the northwest side of the island, large numbers of eagle rays congregate from late November to the end of January. Many divers are happy to see just one of these large rays up close; watching squadrons of them is quite a sight.

NAUI, TDI and IANTD operation has very good gear and fast boats that give you a chance to get more dives out of a day. Among the dives they offer are trips to Arrecife Cantarell when the eagle rays are congregating.

There are at least two hyperbaric chambers in San Miguel: **Buceo Médico Mexicano** (☎ 872-1430, fax 872-1848; Calle 5 Sur between Avs Melgar & 5 Sur) and **Cozumel Hyperbaric Research** (☎ 872-0103; Calle 6 Norte between Avs 5 & 10 Norte), in the Médica San Miguel clinic.

All of the best snorkeling sites are reached by boat. A half-day tour will cost from US$30 to US$50. Most strictly snorkeling outfits operating in town go to one of three stretches of reef near town, all accessible from the beach. If you go with a dive outfit instead, you can often get to better spots, such as Palancar Reef or adjacent Colombia Shallows, near the island's south end. **Ramón Zapata** (☎ 044-987-100-2256) runs snorkeling trips leaving from Playa Palancar for about US$25 per person, but you'll need to make your own way to the beach (see Playa Palancar later in this section).

You can save on boat fares (and see fewer fish) by walking into the gentle surf north of town. One good spot is **Hotel Playa Azul**, 4km north of the turnoff to the airport; its *palapas* offer shade, and it has a swimming area with a sheltering wharf and a small artificial reef. If you'd like to sit at one of the *palapas* the waiters ask only that you buy a drink or a bite to eat. Next door to the south, the **Club Cozumel Caribe** has underwater cement statuary that makes for some interesting snorkeling. The club was undergoing renovation at the time of research and made a good free shady spot; when it reopens you should again be able to swim or walk to its waters via the Hotel Playa Azul.

Touring the Island

In order to see most of the island you will have to rent a vehicle or take a taxi. The following route will take you south from San Miguel, then counterclockwise around the island. There are some places along the way to stop for food and drink, but it's good to bring water all the same.

Sad to say, access to many of Cozumel's best stretches of beach has become limited.

Resorts and residential developments with gated roads make it the most difficult. Pay-for-use beach clubs occupy some other prime spots but you can park and walk through or around them and enjoy adjacent parts of the beach without obligation. Sitting under their umbrellas or otherwise using the facilities requires you to fork out some money, either a straight fee or a *consumo mínimo* (minimum consumption of food and drink), which can add up to a pretty ridiculous US$15 per person in some places. It's not always strictly applied, especially when business is slow.

Several sites along the island's west coast offer horseback riding (most of the horses look like they would keel over). The asking price is M$160 an hour; bargain hard.

Parque Chankanaab This park (admission US$10; open 6am-6pm daily) on the bay of the same name is a very popular snorkeling spot, especially when cruise ships are in port, though there's not a lot to see in the water beyond some brightly colored fish and deliberately sunken artificial objects. The beach is a nice one, though, and 50m inland is a limestone lagoon surrounded by iguanas and inhabited by turtles. You're not allowed to swim or snorkel there, but it's picturesque all the same. The beach is lined with *palapas* and fiberglass lounge chairs, and you can rent snorkel and dive equipment or try out 'snuba' (diving with a helmet that requires no special training).

Dolphin and sea lion shows are included in the admission price, as is the use of dressing rooms, lockers and showers. The grounds also hold a small archaeological park containing replica Olmec heads and Mayan artifacts, a small museum featuring objects imported from Chichén Itzá, and a botanical garden with 400 species of tropical plants. Other facilities include a restaurant, a bar and snack shops. A taxi from town costs M$90 one-way.

Playa San Francisco The lovely white sands of San Francisco run for more than 3km; its main access is via the beach club **Nachi-Cocom** (Km 16.5 Carretera Costa Sur; consumo mínimo M$100 per person; open 10am-5pm Mon-Sat, 11am-5pm Sun), just north of the Allegro Resort. The club offers better value than most, with a good swimming pool and Jacuzzi, a restaurant and bar, kayak and snorkeling equipment rental and a wharf. The facilities are in good shape, and the club offers various packages including buffet, open-bar, snorkeling and kayaking. (Sounds like a sure-fire puke!)

El Cedral This Mayan ruin is the oldest on the island. It's the size of a small house and has no ornamentation, but costs nothing to visit and is easy to reach, unlike San Gervasio and other ruins on Cozumel. It's 3.5km down a signed paved road that heads off to the left (east) a kilometer or two south of Nachi-Cocom's access road, hiding amid a forest of pole structures painted yellow and white and erected as souvenir stalls. El Cedral is thought to have been an important ceremonial site; the small church standing next to the tiny ruin today is evidence that the site still has religious significance for locals.

Playa Palancar About 17km south of town, Palancar is another great beach. It has a **beach club** renting hydro bikes, kayaks, snorkel gear and sailboats, plus a restaurant and a dive operation. Nearby Arrecife Palancar (Palancar Reef) has some very good diving, as well as snorkeling (see Diving & Snorkeling earlier).

Parque Punta Sur The southern tip of the island has been turned into a rather overpriced **'ecotouristic park'** (☎ 872-0914; admission M$100; open 9am-5pm daily). Visitors board an open vehicle for the 3km ride to visit picturesque Celarain lighthouse and the small nautical museum at its base. Another vehicle carries visitors to Laguna Colombia, part of a three-lagoon system that is the habitat of crocodiles and many resident and migratory waterfowl. A pontoon-boat ride on the lagoon costs M$30 extra; it gives you a chance to see more birds. Crocs can be seen (when they feel like it) from shore, via a trail through mangrove or a bridge over the lagoon.

Plans for future development of the park include 'ecological villas,' a zoo, horseback riding facilities and a family entertainment center. The planners would seem to be following the pattern of gaining a toehold in a protected area by starting as a nature park, then expanding.

East Coast The eastern shoreline is the wildest part of the island and presents some beautiful seascapes and many small blowholes. Swimming is dangerous on most of the east coast, because of riptides and undertows. With a bit of care you can sometimes swim at Punta Chiqueros, Playa Chen Río and Punta Morena. A few small restaurants along the coast road serve seafood and drinks; some are overpriced, but all have good views of the Caribbean.

Coconut's Bar & Grill (☎ 044-987-871-8845; mains M$45-80; open 10am-6pm daily) serves drinks and Tex-Mex food (including shrimp fajitas) on a promontory over the sea offering some of the best views on this side of the island.

Punta Morena (☎ 872-5831; doubles low/high season M$120/200; main dishes M$50-105) has a tin-roofed row of six very basic cement-block rooms facing the sea (and right above the beach). They don't have electricity but do come with towels and private bathrooms, and a stiff breeze often blows in off the sea. Morena is Cozumel's hot spot for surfing; 'hot' being a relative term. Note that the phone number is for the owners' home, and is only good from 8am to 9am and 7:30pm onwards.

Punta Molas Beyond where the east coast highway meets the Carretera Transversal, intrepid travelers may take a poorly maintained, infrequently traveled road toward Punta Molas, the island's northeast point, accessible only by 4WD or on foot. About 17km up the road are the Mayan ruins known as El Castillo Real, and a few kilometers farther is Aguada Grande. Both sites are quite far gone, their significance lost to time. In the vicinity of Punta Molas are some fairly good beaches and a few more minor ruins. If you head up this road be aware that you can't count on flagging down another motorist for help in the event of a breakdown or accident, and most rental agencies' insurance policies don't cover any mishaps taking place on unpaved roads.

San Gervasio This **Mayan complex** (admission M$52; open 7am-4pm daily) is Cozumel's only preserved ruins, and a prime example of the local government's efforts to milk dollars out of cruise-ship passengers. San Gervasio is thought to have been the site

QUINTANA ROO

SAN MIGUEL DE COZUMEL

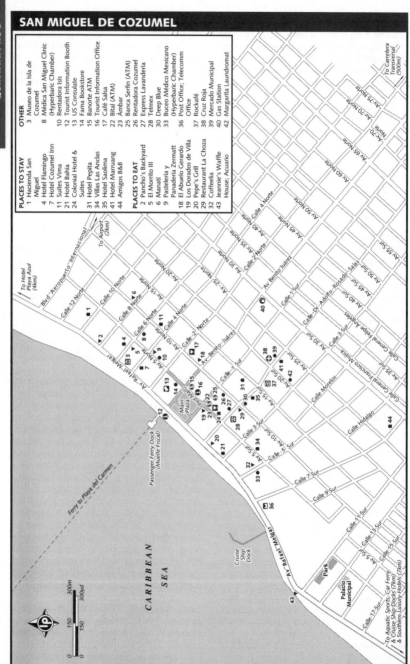

PLACES TO STAY
1   Hacienda San Miguel
4   Hotel Flamingo
7   Hotel Cozumel Inn
11 Suites Vima
21 Hotel Bahia
24 Colonial Hotel & Suites
31 Hotel Pepita
34 Villas Las Anclas
35 Hotel Saolima
41 Hotel Marruang
44 Amigos B&B

PLACES TO EAT
2   Pancho's Backyard
5   El Morrito III
6   Manatí
9   Pastelería y Panadería Zermatt
18 El Abuelo Gerardo
19 Los Dorados de Villa
20 Pepe's Grill
29 Restaurant La Choza
32 Coffeelia
43 Jeannie's Waffle House; Acuario

OTHER
3   Museo de la Isla de Cozumel
8   Médica San Miguel Clinic (Hyperbaric Chamber)
10 Rentadora Isis
12 Tourist Information Booth
13 US Consulate
14 Fama Bookstore
15 Banorte ATM
16 Tourist Information Office
17 Café Salsa
22 Bital (ATM)
23 Ambar
25 Banca Serfin (ATM)
26 Rentadora Cozumel
27 Express Lavandería
28 Telmex
30 Deep Blue
33 Buceo Médico Mexicano (Hyperbaric Chamber)
36 Post Office; Telecomm Office
37 Rockafé
38 Cruz Roja
39 Mercado Municipal
40 Gas Station
42 Margarita Laundromat

of the sanctuary of Ixchel, goddess of fertility, and thus an important pilgrimage site at which Mayan women – particularly prospective mothers – worshiped. But its structures are small and crude, and the clay idols of Ixchel were long ago destroyed by the Spaniards. Even so, the national government's INAH levies a hefty M$30 entrance fee. The island *ayuntamiento* tacks on another M$20, for maintenance of its ticket booth and the road in, which at last pass, hadn't been repaved in years.

Places to Stay

All hotel rooms come with private bathroom and fan, unless otherwise noted. Almost all places raise their rates at Christmas and Easter weeks. 'High season' is mid-December to mid-April, but whatever the season, if business is slow, most places are open to negotiation.

Budget See Punta Morena, in the earlier East Coast section.

Hotel Saolima (☎ 872-0886; Calle Rosado Salas between Avs 15 & 10 Sur; doubles with fan/air-con M$200/260) has simple, musty rooms opening onto a plant-filled patio strip. Upstairs rooms get more light.

Hotel Marruang (☎ 872-1678; Calle Rosado Salas between Avs 20 & 25 Sur; rooms M$200), entered via a passageway across from the municipal market, is simple and clean, with well-screened fan rooms.

Hotel Cozumel Inn (☎ 872-0314, fax 872-3156; Calle 4 Norte between Avs Melgar & 5 Norte; fan singles M$224; doubles with fan/air-con M$280/336) has 30 well-maintained rooms with good beds, and a small swimming pool. Watch out, though, their card says 'Bats with hot water'!

Hotel Pepita (☎/fax 872-0098; Av 15 Sur between Calle 1 Sur & Calle Rosado Salas; doubles M$310) is friendly with well-maintained rooms grouped around a garden. All have two double beds, refrigerators and aircon (many catch a good breeze), and there's free morning coffee. Once one of the best deals in town, the Pepita at last pass was maintaining its rates while many others were dropping theirs. It's still a great place to stay.

Mid-Range The colorful **Hotel Flamingo** (☎ 872-1264; W www.hotelflamingo.com; Calle 6 Norte between Avs 5 Norte & Melgar;

rooms low season M$290-490, high season M$390-590) is a nicely decorated place with a few fan rooms on the ground floor and spacious air-conditioned rooms (some with fridges) sporting direct-dial phones upstairs. The only flaw with the rooms are the super-low-flow showerheads – guests have been known to unscrew them. Common areas include a leafy courtyard where you can eat breakfast or have a drink, and a rooftop sundeck with good sea views. The Flamingo also offers a one-for-one book exchange and guests can rent bikes and snorkel equipment.

Suites Vima (☎/fax 872-5118; Av 10 Norte between Calles 4 & 6; singles/doubles M$350/400) has 12 spotless and spacious modern rooms with tile floors, good air-con and bathrooms, fridges, tables and chairs. A small swimming pool with a current to swim against lies in a green area in back.

Colonial Hotel & Suites (☎ 872-9090, 800-227-2639, fax 872-9073; W www.suites colonial.com; Av 5 Sur between Calles Rosado Salas & 1 Sur; studios/suites Apr 27-Dec 19 US$49/58, Jan 4-Apr 26 US$57/68, Dec 20-Jan 2 US$63/75) is down a passageway off Av 5 Sur. It features lovely studios and nice, spacious, one-bedroom 'suites' (beds are separated by low partitions) with kitchenettes. All rooms have cable TV, fridge and air-con, and lots of varnished wood touches. Rates include coffee and pastries; it's a very well-run place.

Hotel Bahía (☎ 872-9090, 800-227-2639, fax 872-9073; W www.suitesbahia.com; cnr Av Melgar & Calle 3 Sur; doubles from US$49-63) offers some rooms with sea views and balconies, and all have the same amenities and general setup as the Colonial (they're under the same management). The unmarked entrance is on Calle 3 Sur, just past the Pizza Hut.

Amigo's B&B (☎ 872-3868, fax 872-3528; W www.bacalar.net; Calle 7 Sur between Avs 25 & 30 Sur; doubles/triples/quads Jan 4-Apr 30 US$65/75/85, Sept & Oct US$30/40/50, May 1-Aug 31 & Nov 1-Dec 20 US$50/60/70) has a large garden, an inviting pool and a good lounging area stocked with reading material. It's worth the hike from the center to enjoy one of the three well-appointed, cottage-style rooms here. All have air-con and full kitchenettes and rates include a good breakfast. Book ahead.

Villas Las Anclas (☎ 872-6130, fax 872-5476; ⓦ www.lasanclas.com; Av 5 Sur between Calles 3 & 5 Sur; suites year-round US$50) has lovely, roomy two-story suites, with air-con and kitchenettes, clustered around a leafy garden. This is an excellent value (especially if they maintain their prices).

Hacienda San Miguel (☎ 872-1986, fax 872-7043; ⓦ www.haciendasanmiguel.com; Calle 10 Norte between Av 5 & Melgar; rooms Sept 1st-Dec 23 US$55-75, Jan 1-Aug 31 US$70-85) offers small and large studios and junior suites, all with air-con and fully equipped kitchenettes, around a parklike central courtyard. It's a quiet place built and furnished to resemble an old hacienda, and niceties such as bathrobes and continental breakfast served in your room make this a very good value. They do divers' packages, and long stays can bring rates down by amazing amounts.

Top End Several kilometers north and south of town are a few big luxury resort hotels. See the Cozumel map for locations. All rooms in this category have air-con.

The **Presidente Intercontinental Cozumel** (☎ 872-9500, fax 872-9501; ⓦ www.cozumel .interconti.com; Carretera a Chankanaab Km 6.5; rooms from US$190) is one of the island's oldest luxury hotels. It has a lovely beach and 253 posh guestrooms, many with sea views, set amid tropical gardens and swimming pools. Wild iguanas roam the grounds. Unlike the all-inclusives further south, the Presidente is sufficiently close in to town to allow you several dining options; truth be told, the city has grown south around the hotel. Unfortunately, it's also very close to one of the cruise-ship piers.

Fiestamericana (☎ 872-2622, fax 872-2666, in USA ☎ 800-343-7821; ⓦ www.fies tamericana.com; Carretera a Chankanaab Km 7.5; rooms from US$122) is a dive resort with plenty of gardens, a spectacular swimming pool, 172 mostly ocean-view rooms (with balconies, safes and full minibars) and 56 'Tropical Casitas' behind the main building. Lodging options include all-inclusive and room-only plans.

Hotel Playa Azul (☎ 872-0199, fax 872-0110; ⓦ www.playa-azul.com; Carretera a San Juan Km 4; doubles from US$146, suites from US$180) is in the sedate area north of town on its own pretty little stretch of beach (it's not deep but it's a gem). Rooms are spacious and comfortable, and all of them have a sea view, a balcony or terrace, a safe and one king or two queen beds. The hotel has a bar, restaurant and gorgeous pool, and guests can golf free at a nearby course.

Places to Eat

Budget Cheapest of all eating places, with tasty food, are the little market loncherías next to the Mercado Municipal on Rosado Salas between Avs 20 and 25 Sur. Most offer soup and a main course for around M$30, with a large selection of dishes available; ask about cheap comidas corridas not listed on the menu.

Pastelería y Panadería Zermatt (cnr Av 5 Norte & Calle 4 Norte; open 7am-9pm Mon-Sat, 7am-3pm Sun) bakes pastries, cakes and whole-wheat breads and serves espresso and cappuccino. Unlike many Mexican bakeries, they do their cooking in the early morning.

Coffeelia (☎ 872-8402; Calle 5 Sur between Avs Melgar & 5 Sur; breakfast M$30-50, set meals M$38; open 7:30am-11pm Mon-Sat) is a focal point for Cozumel's art community. The menu includes quiches, good salads and vegetarian dishes, and the premium, organic Chiapas coffee is roasted fresh locally. The atmosphere is relaxed and the ambience agreeable.

El Morrito III (☎ 876-8907; Calle 6 Norte between Avs Melgar and 5 Norte; mains M$30-70, sandwiches M$14-30) is a small, inexpensive mom 'n' pop eatery serving up good Mexican dishes, egg breakfasts and licuados.

Mid-Range Near the edge of the plaza, **Los Dorados de Villa** (☎ 872-0197; Calle 1 Sur near Av 5 Sur; mains M$40-100; open 8am-11:30pm daily) specializes in food from the Distrito Federal (Mexico City and surroundings), but has a wide variety of Mexican dishes including seafood and cuts of meat. The spinach crepes are great.

El Abuelo Gerardo (☎ 872-2102; Av 10 Norte between Av Juárez & Calle 2 Norte; mains M$40-100; open 8am-10:30pm daily) also has an extensive, mostly Mexican menu that includes seafood. Guacamole and chips are on the house.

Restaurant La Choza (☎ 872-0958; cnr Rosado Salas & Av 10 Sur; mains M$81-110;

open 7am-10:30pm daily) is an excellent and popular restaurant specializing in authentic regional cuisine. All mains come with soup. La Choza sometimes offers an inexpensive *comida corrida* in the afternoon.

Jeannie's Waffle House (☎ 872-6095; Av Melgar & Calle 11 Sur; breakfast dishes M$30-70, sandwiches M$50-60; open 6am-3pm daily) is on the seaward side of Av Melgar, and the views are great from the outdoor courtyard. They serve waffles, of course, plus hash brown potatoes, eggs, sandwiches and other tidbits.

Acuario (Av Melgar & Calle 11 Sur; mains M$40-150; open 3pm-11pm daily) is Jeannie's Waffle House by day, but transforms into a romantic and not unreasonably priced restaurant serving Mexican dishes, steaks and seafood in the evening.

Top End This category is a mixed bag on Cozumel.

Pancho's Backyard (☎ 872-2141; Av Melgar & Calle 8 Norte; lunch mains M$40-120, dinner mains M$100-160; open 10:30am-10:30pm Mon-Sat, 5pm-10:30pm Sun) is very atmospheric, set in a beautifully decorated inner courtyard. The food's not bad, either!

Manatí (☎ 044-987-1000-787; cnr Calle 8 Norte & Av 10 Norte; mains M$70-140) serves inventive cuisine in a pleasant, New Age ambience. There's usually a veggie dish on the menu, as well as pasta, chicken, meat and fish dishes, plus espresso drinks.

Pepe's Grill (☎ 872-0213; Av Melgar near Calle Rosado Salas; appetizers M$109-120, mains M$196-253; open 5pm-11pm daily) is Cozumel's traditional place to drop loads of cash in dining richly. Mains are mostly meat (steaks and prime rib), plus charcoal-broiled lobster (available at market price, typically around M$350). At least the prices include a salad bar (available separately at M$50). Flambé desserts are a house specialty.

Entertainment

Cozumel can't keep up with Playa del Carmen as a night spot, but it has its moments. **Ámbar** (Av 5 Sur between Calles 1 Sur & Rosado Salas; open Tues-Thur 9pm-3am) is an artfully decorated lounge and bar with a lovely garden area out back, board games and a DJ spinning lounge and house music inside, and, on Saturday nights from around 11pm, live music.

Café Salsa (☎ 044-9800-7800; Av 10 Norte between Calle 2 Norte & Av Juárez; open Thur-Sun 9pm-4am) gets very smoky – and we don't mean just the atmosphere. There is very little ventilation, and live Caribbean bands get the audience dancing and puffing away.

Getting There & Away

Air Some airlines fly direct from the US, but European flights are usually routed via the US or Mexico City. **Continental** (☎ 800-900-5000, in USA & Canada ☎ 800-231-0856; W www.continental.com) has direct flights from Newark and Houston.

Mexicana (☎ 872-0305) flies direct to Mexico City on Saturday and Sunday. **Aerocozumel** (☎ 872-0928), with offices at the airport, flies a few times daily between Cancún and Cozumel. At the time of research, Aerocaribe/Aerocozumel operated Tuesday and Thursday flights between Cozumel and Chichén Itzá, but their future was uncertain.

Ferry Passenger ferries run to Cozumel from Playa del Carmen, and vehicle ferries run from Puerto Morelos (see those sections for details). A more convenient vehicle ferry (taking only about one hour, as opposed to over two hours from Puerto Morelos) leaves the Calica facility (officially known as the Terminal Marítima Punta Venado) south of Playa del Carmen. Schedules are not set in stone, but there should at least be a 9am departure on Monday, Wednesday, Thursday, Saturday and Sunday, and usually an early afternoon and an early evening departure those days as well. Fares are M$778 for cars, M$989 for a suburban-sized vehicle (both including the driver) and M$58 per passenger. You need to line up at least two hours before departure (earlier is better, they say).

Getting Around

To/From the Airport The airport is about 2km north of town. You can take a van from the airport into town for about M$45 (slightly more to the hotels south of town), but you'll have to take a taxi (M$45 from town, M$90 to M$190 from southern hotels) to return to the airport.

Taxi Some locals refer to the 'taxi mafia'; as in some other towns in the Yucatán, the taxi syndicate in Cozumel wields a good bit of power. A movement is afoot to implement a bus service and get the syndicate to lower the fixed fares it charges. Fares in and around town are US$2 per ride; luggage may cost extra. Carry exact change; drivers often 'can't' provide change.

Car A car is the best and safest way to get to the island's farther reaches. All rental contracts should automatically include third-party insurance *(daños a terceros)*; check that taxes are included in the price you're quoted. Collision insurance usually runs about M$50 extra with a M$5000 deductible for the cheapest vehicles. Rates start at around M$350 (for a beat-up VW Beetle), all-inclusive, though you'll pay more during late December and January. There are plenty of agencies around the main plaza.

When renting, check with your hotel to see if they have an agreement with any agencies, as you can often get discounts. Note that some agencies will deduct tire damage (repair or replacement) from your deposit, even if tires are old and worn. Be particularly careful about this if you're renting a 4WD for use on unpaved roads; straighten out the details before you sign. And always check your car's brakes before driving off. Note that vehicles rust very quickly in Cozumel's salt air.

One fairly no-nonsense place, with cars in good shape, is **Rentadora Isis** (☎ 872-3367; *Av 5 Norte between Calles 2 & 4 Norte)*. VW Beetles rent for around M$450 for 24 hours, with little seasonal variation in prices.

If you rent, observe the law on vehicle occupancy. Usually only five people are allowed in a vehicle. If you carry more, the police will fine you. You'll need to return your vehicle with the amount of gas it had when you signed it out. This can be tricky as agencies usually don't rent out cars with full tanks. There's a gas station on Av Juárez five blocks east of the main square.

Motorcycle Solo touring of the island by motorbike is OK provided you have experience with them and with driving in Mexico. Two people on a bike is asking for trouble, though, as the machines' suspension is barely adequate for one. Many auto drivers speed and pass aggressively on Cozumel, and it has its share of *topes* (speed bumps).

Riders are injured in solo crashes nearly every day, and deaths, usually involving other vehicles, are not uncommon. That said, rental opportunities abound, with prices ranging from M$200 to M$400 a day (depending on the agency, the season, volume of business and whether Uranus is in retrograde), but you may be able to haggle down to less, with third-party insurance and tax included. Collision insurance is not usually available for bikes; you break, you pay.

To rent, you must have a valid driver's license, and you must leave a credit card slip or put down a deposit (usually M$1000). There is a helmet law and it is enforced (the fine for not wearing one is M$250), although most moped-rental people won't mention it. Before you sign a rental agreement, be sure to request a helmet.

The best time to rent is first thing in the morning, when all the machines are there. Choose one with working horn, brakes, lights, starter, rearview mirrors and a full tank of fuel; remember that the price asked will be the same whether you rent the newest machine or the oldest rattletrap.

Bring a towel to toss on the bike's seat when parked – the black plastic can get blisteringly hot in the sun. Keep in mind that you're not the only one unfamiliar with the road here, and some of your fellow travelers may be hitting the bottle. Drive carefully.

Rentadora Isis (see under Car earlier in this section) rents scooters for M$250 per day – you need to return them before dark.

Bicycle A full day's bicycle rental typically costs M$50 to M$100 (depending on season), and can be a great way to get to the northern and southern beaches on the west side of flat Cozumel. The completely separate bicycle/scooter lane on the Chankanaab highway sees a good deal of car traffic from confused tourists and impatient cabdrivers, so be careful.

Rentadora Cozumel (☎ 872-1120; *Av 10 Sur between Rosado Salas & Calle 1 Sur)* is one of a few shops offering bikes for rent; shop around. **Hotel Flamingo** (see Places to Stay earlier) rents bikes to guests.

XCARET

Once a precious spot open to all, **Xcaret** (☎ 984-871-5200; *adult/child 5-12 years old M$490/245; open 8:30am-10pm daily)*, pronounced shkar-**et**, is about 10km south of Playa del Carmen and has been turned into a heavily Disneyfied 'ecopark.' There are still Mayan ruins (and their re-creations) and a beautiful inlet on the site, but much of the rest has been created or altered using dynamite, jackhammers and other terraforming techniques, largely without permits. The park offers a cenote and 'underground river' for swimming, a restaurant, an evening show of 'ancient Mayan ceremonies' worthy of Las Vegas, a butterfly pavilion, a botanical garden and nursery, orchid and mushroom farms and a wild-bird breeding area.

Package tourists from Cancún and cruise passengers come daily, paying the admission fee, and additional fees for many of the attractions and activities, such as snorkeling (M$100 equipment rental, M$20 locker, M$30 towels) and swimming with captive dolphins. Many visitors swear by the place.

Carnival Cruise Lines is attempting to establish a 'home port' at the Calica facility just south of Xcaret, and the park itself, whose construction began after the government granted permission for a small private home to be built on the property, has now constructed its own megahotel.

RANCHO PUNTA VENADO

This delightful spot for **horseback riding** (☎ 984-877-9701; open 8am-5pm daily) is about 5km south of Xcaret and 2km farther east of the highway. The ranch sits on some 8 sq km of land, much of it virgin jungle, and has a cenote and a 3km-long stretch of isolated beach. In addition to guided horseback tours (US$50 per person, maximum group size 10 people) you can also make arrangements to snorkel and kayak. In the course of a ride you're likely to see monkeys, deer, coatis and various other mammals, as well as crocodiles, snakes and lots of birds, including the occasional toucan. The horses are well cared for and the owners are very hospitable.

PAAMUL

Paamul, 87km south of Cancún, is a de facto private beach on a sheltered bay. Like many other spots along the Caribbean coast, it has signs prohibiting entry to nonguests, and parking is limited.

The attractions here are great diving and a sandy, palm-fringed beach which, though lovely, holds many small rocks, shells and

spiked sea urchins in the shallows offshore; take appropriate measures. A large RV park here is greatly favored by snowbirds; the 'BC' license plates you see are from British Columbia, not Baja California. An attractive alabaster sand beach lies about 2km north.

Scuba-Mex (☎/fax 984-875-1066; W www .scubamex.com) offers diving trips to any of 30 superb sites at very reasonable prices (US$28/22 for the first/subsequent dives with your equipment; US$39/33 with their equipment). It also offers dive packages and certification courses.

Paamul Hotel (☎/fax 984-875-1051; W www.paamul.com.mx; tent sites per person M$70, RV sites M$200, double rooms and cabanas M$400-500, Dec-Feb & Aug M$700) has eight beachfront air-con rooms with good beds and 10 lovely, spacious cabanas built on stilts. Each cabana has two beds, a ceiling fan, hot-water bathroom and a veranda with awning. Gaps in the wooden floors provide additional ventilation, and a serene atmosphere prevails. Numerous spaces for recreational vehicles have full hookups (they're well removed from the cabana area).

Giant sea turtles come ashore here at night in July and August to lay their eggs. If you run across one during an evening stroll along the beach, keep a good distance away and keep your flashlight off or you may scare it away. Do your part to contribute to the survival of the turtles, which are endangered; let them lay their eggs in peace.

To reach Paamul by bus requires a 500m walk from the highway to the hotel and beach.

CENOTES

On the west side of the highway south of Playa del Carmen are a series of several cenotes (limestone sinkhole/caverns filled with water) that you can visit and usually swim in for a price. Among these is **Cristalino Cenote** (admission M$25/15 adults/ children; open 6am-5:30pm daily), just south of the Barceló Maya Resort. It's easily accessible, only about 70m from the entrance, which is just off the highway. The well-tended cenote has mangrove on one side and a large open section you can dive into by climbing a ladder up to a ledge above it. The water extends about 20m into an overhung, cavelike portion.

Two more sinkholes, Cenote Azul and El Jardín de Edén are just south of Cristalino along the highway.

XPU-HÁ

Xpu-há (shpoo-**ha**) is a beach area, about 95km south of Cancún, that extends for several kilometers. It's reached by numbered access roads (most of them private).

Hotel Villas del Caribe (☎/fax 984-873-2194, ☎ 044-984-876-9945; ⓦ www.hotel villasdelcaribe.com; cabanas US$35-45, rooms US$45-55), at the end of X-4 (Xpu-Há access road 4), is a laid-back place sitting on a handsome stretch of beach whose northern reaches are nearly empty. All rooms have a terrace or balcony and are very clean and quiet, with fans and good beds; most have hammocks as well. Guests can participate in yoga and meditation classes, and the hotel offers meal plans at its good onsite restaurant.

AKUMAL

Famous for its beautiful beach and large, swimmable lagoon, Akumal (Place of the Turtles) does indeed see some sea turtles come ashore to lay their eggs in the summer, although fewer and fewer arrive each year thanks to resort development. Akumal is one of the Yucatán Peninsula's oldest resort areas and consists primarily of pricey hotels, condominiums and residential developments (occupied mostly by Americans and Canadians) on nearly 5km of wide beach bordering four consecutive bays. With the exception of Villa Las Brisas, all sights and facilities are reached by taking the first turnoff, Playa Akumal, as you come south on the highway. Note that this turn is one of those Mexican oddities where you have to swing to the right off the highway, swing left and then head straight across both lanes of traffic. It's about 500m from the highway to the entrance.

Activities

Although increasing population is taking its toll on the reefs that parallel Akumal, **diving** remains the area's primary attraction. Dive trips and deep-sea **fishing** excursions are offered by **Akumal Dive Shop** (☎ 984-875-9032; ⓦ www.akumal.com). It also offers snorkeling trips to the reef and beaches unreachable by car for US$30, and an all-day swimming, snorkeling, fishing and beach tour on a catamaran sailboat for US$60, including food and drinks.

At the northern end of Akumal, **Laguna Yal-Kú** (adults/children M$60/30; open 8am-5:30pm daily) is a beautiful lagoon 2km from the entrance and over about a zillion topes. The rocky lagoon runs about 500m from its beginning to the sea and is home to many brightly colored fish, and the occasional visiting turtle and manta ray. Showers, parking and bathrooms are included in the admission price, lockers are an extra M$10, and snorkel gear and lifejackets each cost M$50 to rent. Cabs from the Playa Akumal entrance charge about M$30 to the lagoon.

Places to Stay & Eat

Que Onda (☎ 984-875-9101; ⓦ www.queon daakumal.com; rooms Dec 16-Jan 15 & Easter week US$85, Jan 16-Apr 15 US$65, Apr 16-Dec 15 US$50) is an Italian-run hotel and restaurant, with all the marvelous decorative touches that so often entails. It's set amid an expanse of greenery in a fairly residential area only 50m from Laguna Yal-Kú. The six fan-cooled rooms have white-tile floors and great beds; some have sofas, and the upstairs ones have terraces. A large and lovely upstairs suite runs US$110 to US$150 depending on the season. The hotel also offers a gorgeous pool, free Internet access, bicycles and snorkeling gear, and half-price admission to the lagoon. The **restaurant** serves delicious pasta, handmade daily, at prices reasonable for the area.

Villa Las Brisas (☎/fax 984-875-2963; ⓦ www.aventuras-akumal.com; lodging US$51-258), on the beach in Aventuras Akumal, is an attractive, modern place with two hotel-type rooms, some one- and two-bedroom condos and a studio apartment – all under two roofs. The friendly owners speak English, Spanish, German, Italian and some Portuguese. The turnoff is 2.5km south of the turnoff for Playa Akumal.

Just outside the entrance to Playa Akumal are two **minimarkets** that stock a good selection of inexpensive food. **La Cueva del Pescador** restaurant, inside and just north of the entrance, serves three meals daily.

XEL-HÁ
Information

Once a pristine natural lagoon brimming with iridescent tropical fish and ringed on three sides by untouched mangroves, **Xel-Há** *(shell-hah;* ☎ *984-875-6000; adults/children 5-11 years Mon-Fri M$250/130, Sat & Sun M$190/ 100; open 9am-6pm daily)* is now a private park with landscaped grounds, developed cenotes, caves, nature paths, underwater walks with oxygen helmet (at an extra price), several restaurant/bars and more. It's very touristy, but the lagoon is still beautiful – the fish have stuck around (they get fed) and the place can be fun when it's not too crowded. The basic admission includes use of showers, bathrooms, inner tubes, life jackets, deck chairs and hammocks, and use of a bag to carry your belongings in.

You get all of the above plus a towel, snorkel gear, locker, food and beverages (including all accompanying tips and taxes) for M$520/260 per adult/child. There's an ATM at the park entrance. Note that you must wear only biodegradable sunscreen when swimming; it's on sale here.

Most buses traveling between Playa and Tulum will drop you at the Xel-Há ticket booth (about 45km south of Playa del Carmen); on the way out you need to either hire a cab or walk (under 1km) to the highway to flag a bus.

There is a small **archaeological site** *(admission Mon-Sat M$27, free Sun; open 8am-5pm daily)* on the west side of the highway 500m south of the park's turnoff. The ruins, which are not all that impressive, date from the Classic and post-Classic periods.

Underwater Cave Tours

About 1km south of Xel-Há is the turnoff for Cenote Dos Ojos, which provides access to the enormous Dos Ojos cave system. You can take guided snorkel and dive tours of some amazing underwater caverns, floating past illuminated stalactites and stalagmites in an eerie wonderland. With an aggregate length of nearly 57km, it's the third largest underwater cave system in the world. Numbers 1 and 2, Ox Bel Ha and Nohoch Nah Chich (about 97km and 61km total length, respectively), are relatively nearby. Divers have tried for years to find a passage linking Dos Ojos and Nohoch Nah Chich to prove them to be one humongous system. They succeeded in linking Nohoch with one of its outlets to the sea (at Cenote Manatí in Tankah). While that was going on, new kid on the block Ox Bel Ha was found to be really big.

Hidden Worlds *(☎ 984-877-8535;* Ⓦ *www .hiddenworlds.com.mx)* is an American-run outfit offering three-hour guided snorkeling tours for US$40, and one-/two-tank dive tours for US$50/80. The snorkeling price includes a flashlight, wet suit, equipment and transportation to the cenotes on a unique 'jungle mobile.' The drive through the jungle is an experience in itself, and the guides are very knowledgeable and informative. Lights have been strung in some sections of cave, affording magnificent views of the formations. In other sections you rely on handheld lights. The diving tours are at 9am, 11am and 1pm daily; equipment rental costs extra. You don't need to make a reservation, but it never hurts to call.

These are cavern (as opposed to cave) dives and require only standard open-water certification. No certification is needed for the snorkeling tours; they do involve swimming a fair distance with fins and a lifejacket.

Another way to see part of the system is through the **Dos Ojos** *(open 8am-4:30pm)* operation, a short distance north of Hidden Worlds. It's run by the Mayan community who own the land. The entrance fee is M$80, snorkeling gear is M$70 more. With sunlight only you can see about half of what's on offer. For M$400 per person (minimum two people; M$350 in groups of four or more) you get admission, gear, flashlights and a guide. Either way you'll have to walk or drive your own vehicle the 2.5km to the cave entrance. Even with the guides you're not likely to be told much, though you will see twice as much. You can dive here as well, if accompanied by a certified cave diver.

BAHÍAS DE PUNTA SOLIMÁN

These two beautiful, protected bays are separated by a narrow point, 123km south of Cancún and 11km north of Tulum. The area offers good wildlife watching, kayaking, snorkeling and dining opportunities. A few hundred meters in after the signed turnoff from Hwy 307, you can bear left (north) to reach **Oscar y Lalo's** *(☎ 984-804-6973; mains M$60-140; open 10am-8pm daily; campsites M$25 per person)*, a picturesque restaurant that has the entire Bahía Solimán to itself.

The kitchen puts out heaping plates of food, including fish fillets (M$100) and barracuda steaks (M$60), both of which come with french fries, fried banana, rice, beans and a plate of tortillas with green and red salsa. Chicken fajitas also run M$60, and couples can order elaborate specials such as king crab stuffed with lobster and shrimp (M$650). Tourists tend to photograph the food here, which gives you an idea of the presentation, and the restaurant's beachside hammocks are ideal for an after-meal snooze.

Oscar rents kayaks for M$80 an hour; you can paddle out to the reef that shelters the entire mouth of the bay and snorkel or bird-watch. The dense mangrove around the 150m stretch of (somewhat spiky) white beach breeds quite a few mosquitoes and sand flies; you'll want a tent with very good screens if you're camping.

Back on the main access road, heading straight a short distance beyond the turnoff for Oscar's brings you to an intersection. Continuing straight here leads to the end of the point via a road that splits and rejoins itself a few times. The little-traveled track makes a great nature walk: you can see both bays, and birding in the perennially dry mangrove area is terrific. Birds of interest here include the Yucatán vireo, Yucatán woodpecker, rose-throated tanager, black catbird and orange oriole. If you're very lucky you may spot one of the pumas seen in the area from time to time.

Turning right (south) at the intersection rather than going straight takes you along the edge of the bay on the other side of the point, also named Bahía Solimán (though some call it Bahía de San Francisco). It has terrific coral heads, tons of colorful fish, plenty of grouper and reef sharks, and the occasional sea turtle and even tuna. A number of beach houses, some quite luxurious, line the road. Most of them rent by the week, at well over US$1000. A good website for house rentals in the area is Ⓦ www.locogringo.com.

One happy exception to the rent-the-whole-house-for-a-bundle rule is German-owned **Casa Seis Machos** *(☎ 984-804-3345; double rooms May-Nov M$450, Dec-April M$600)*, which has six fan-cooled bedrooms all with tile floors, private bathrooms and sliding glass doors opening onto a balcony or terrace overlooking the bay.

The road continues south beyond another point and through what, at last pass, looked to be a large residential development in the making – lot after lot, each with its electric meter waiting out the front for connection. It continues into the Tankah area and loops back northwest to rejoin the highway. Most people get to Punta Solimán by car, or by taking a bus to Tulum and a taxi from there.

TANKAH

A few kilometers south of the Hwy 307 turnoff for Punta Solimán is the turnoff for Tankah, which also has a picturesque stretch of beach and accommodations that have the sea for a front yard and mangrove out the back.

Besides the attractions of beach and reef, Tankah offers **Cenote Manatí**, named for the gentle 'sea cows' that used to frequent it. It's actually a series of seven cenotes connected by a channel that winds through the mangrove a short distance before heading back underground briefly to reach the sea. The snorkeling's great, as is the birding; and both are free.

To reach the places described here, turn east at the 'Casa Cenote' sign, go 700m, then turn left and head north up the coast. They're listed from south to north, and the farthest one is less than 2km from the highway. Room rates vary seasonally and the ranges given here don't include the Christmas (and for some, Easter and Thanksgiving) peaks. High season is roughly mid-December to late April.

Tankah Inn *(in Canada ☎ 250-342-2834, in USA ☎ 936-636-7721; Ⓦ www.tankah.com; doubles US$77-100)* has five comfortable rooms with tile floors; their beds, bathrooms and cross-ventilation are all good. A large upstairs kitchen–dining room and common area has splendid views. At last pass the inn's dive operation was still getting back on its feet, but they were at least ready to offer snorkel tours by boat to the reef for US$20, and rent out snorkel gear (US$6/day) and kayaks (US$5/hour, free for guests).

Casa Cenote *(☎ 998-874-5170, fax 984-871-2092; Ⓦ www.casacenote.com; double suites with breakfast & dinner US$123-168)* is just across the road from Cenote Manatí, leading many people to apply the hotel's name to the water feature. Its seven beachside 'casitas' are lovingly done up with Mayan touches, and each has a screened sliding glass door leading to its own little terrace

Flamingos, Río Lagartos

Howler monkey, Punta Laguna

Crocodile, Laguna Cobá

Sand sculpture, Playa del Carmen

Cenote Dzitnup, near Valladolid

Ruins, Uxmal

with hammock. By the time you read this, all rooms should have air-con. The *palapa*-style restaurant serves fresh seafood, with a Texas-style barbecue on Sundays. Room-only rates are offered in addition to the meal plan (which lets you order anything on the menu, including shrimp and lobster).

TULUM
☎ 984 • pop 6900

Tulum's coastline has kilometers of beautiful beaches, a dramatically situated Mayan ruin, excellent diving and snorkeling and a variety of lodgings and restaurants to fit every budget. While the town itself remains singularly unattractive (possibly even buttugly), it does offer good options for dining, sleeping and having fun, and can be a viable base for those wanting to explore the greater surrounding area, including Cobá and the massive Reserva de la Biósfera Sian Ka'an to the south.

Orientation & Information
Tulum lies some 130km south of Cancún and is spread out over quite a large area. Approaching from the north on Hwy 307 the first thing you reach is Crucero Ruinas, where the old access road (closed to vehicle traffic about 100m in from the highway) heads in a straight line about 800m to the ruins' ticket booth. About 400m farther south on 307 (past the gas station) is the new entrance for vehicles going to the ruins; it leads to a parking lot. Another 1.5km south on the highway brings you to the Cobá junction; turning right (west) takes you to Cobá, and turning east leads about 3km to the north–south road servicing the Zona Hotelera, the string of waterfront lodgings extending for more than 10km south from the ruins. This road eventually enters the Reserva de la Biósfera Sian Ka'an, continuing some 50km past Boca Paila to Punta Allen.

The town, sometimes referred to as Tulum Pueblo, flanks the highway (called Av Tulum through town) south of the Cobá junction. It has Telmex pay phones, numerous currency-exchange booths (one with an ATM) and a **Bital bank** *(open 8am-5pm Mon-Sat)* offering good exchange rates and a 24-hour ATM.

Tulum's **post office** *(Av Tulum; open 9am-4pm Mon-Fri)* is about five blocks north of the bus terminal.

The **Weary Traveler hostel** *(☎ 871-2389; W www.intulum.com; Av Tulum; open 24 hrs)*, near the south end of town, has several terminals with fast Internet access (M$15 per hour). John, the friendly operator, also offers travelers' information, free valuables storage (recommended if you're staying out at the beach cabanas), a big two-for-one book exchange and coffee and juice drinks.

Savana's *(☎ 871-2081; Av Tulum; open 8am-9pm Mon-Fri, 8am-2pm & 5pm-9pm Sat, 8am-2pm Sun)* also offers Internet access (at a similar price), along with copier, fax and telephone services and a book exchange. It's about four blocks north of the Weary Traveler and across the street.

Diving & Snorkeling
Cenote Dive Center *(☎ 871-2232; W www.cenotedive.com; Av Tulum)* is a recommended outfit specializing in guided cavern and also offering cave dives. The staff speak English, Spanish, German and Scandinavian languages, and do cenote and cavern snorkeling trips.

Acuatic Tulum, the dive shop at Don Armando's (see Places to Stay) is a PADI, NACD and TDI operation offering low-cost reef dives and renting snorkel gear for M$50 pesos day, or you can try a two-stop snorkeling tour to the reef by boat for M$120, including gear and water.

Tulum Ruins
The ruins of Tulum *(admission M$37; open 7am-5pm daily in winter, 8am-6pm in summer)* can be easily summed up in three words: location, location, location. The grayish-tan buildings occupy a cliff-top site overlooking the Caribbean, with a small stretch of pristine beach lapped by turquoise waters. Even on dark, stormy days, the ruins with their imposing ramparts look fit for the cover of a magazine. It's true the extents and structures are of a modest scale, the late post-Classic design, workmanship and ornamentation inferior to those of earlier, more grandiose projects. But the layout is neat, compact and easily taken in, and you can't fault the planners' choice of building sites.

Tulum is a prime destination for tour groups from Cancún and off the cruise ships docked in the area. To best enjoy the ruins, you should visit them either early in the

QUINTANA ROO

TULUM RUINS

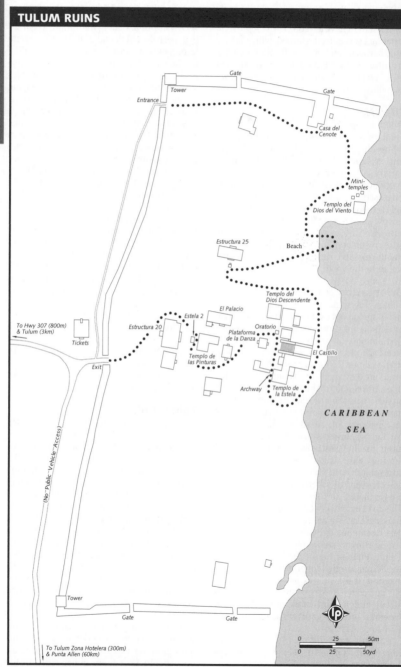

morning or late in the afternoon, when you don't have to dodge the mobs. Parking costs M$30 for cars, M$50 for vans and pickups, and the optional shuttle from the lot to the ticket booth (about a seven-minute walk) is M$15 round-trip. Cabs from town charge M$20 and can drop you off at the old entrance road, about an 800m walk from the ticket booth.

Interestingly, a group of *voladores* has set up shop in the ruins parking lot, regularly performing their ceremony for tips. These are Totonac Indians from the north of Veracruz state who whirl dangling upside-down from ropes attached to a tall steel pole. They seem oddly out of place here, as though they've taken a wrong turn somewhere.

History Most archaeologists believe that Tulum was occupied during the late post-Classic period (AD 1200–1521) and that it was an important port town during its heyday. When Juan de Grijalva sailed past in 1518, he was amazed by the sight of the walled city, its buildings painted a gleaming red, blue and yellow and a ceremonial fire flaming atop its seaside watchtower.

The ramparts that surround three sides of Tulum (the fourth side being the sea) leave little question as to its strategic function as a fortress. Several meters thick and standing 3m to 5m high, the walls protected the city during a period of considerable strife between Mayan city-states. Not all of Tulum was situated within the walls. The vast majority of the city's residents lived outside them; the civic-ceremonial buildings and palaces likely housed Tulum's ruling class.

The city was abandoned about 75 years after the Spanish conquest. It was one of the last ancient cities to be abandoned; most others had been given back to nature long before the arrival of the Spanish. Maya pilgrims continued to visit over the years, and Indian refugees from the War of the Castes took shelter here from time to time.

The name 'Tulum' is Mayan for 'wall,' though that was not how its residents knew it. They called it Zama, or 'Dawn.' 'Tulum' was apparently applied by explorers during the early 20th century.

Walking Tour From the ticket booth, head along nearly half the length of Tulum's enormous **wall**, which measures approximately 380m south to north and 170m on its sides. Just before reaching the northwest corner, you enter the site through a breach in the wall. The **tower** at the corner, once thought to be a guardpost, is now believed by some to have been a type of shrine.

Heading east you'll reach the **Casa del Cenote**, named for the small pool at its southern base, where you can sometimes see the glitter of little silvery fish as they turn sideways in the murky water. A small tomb was found in the casa. Walk south toward the bluff holding the **Templo del Dios del Viento** (Temple of the Wind God). It was roped off at the time of research, which is a shame, as it provides the best views of El Castillo juxtaposed with the sea below. Now you'll have to be content with burning up rolls of film on the iguanas draped all over the place.

Below the Wind God's hang-out is a lovely little stretch of **beach**. It's quite swimmable when conditions are good, but take note of the lifeguards and the warning flags. After your dip, head west to **Estructura 25**, with some interesting columns on its raised platform, and, above the main doorway (on the south side), a beautiful stucco frieze of the Descending God. Also known as the Diving God, this upside-down, part-human figure appears elsewhere at Tulum, as well as at several other east coast sites and Cobá. It may be related to the Maya's reverence for bees (and honey), perhaps a stylized representation of a bee sipping nectar from a flower.

South of Estructura 25 is **El Palacio**, notable for its X-figure ornamentation. From here, head east back toward the water and skirt the outside edge of the central temple complex (keeping it to your right). Along the back are some good views of the sea, and heading inland again on the south side, you can enter the complex through a corbeled archway past the restored **Templo de la Estela** (Temple of the Stela), also known as the Temple of the Initial Series. Stela 1, now in the British Museum, was found here. It was inscribed with the Mayan date corresponding to AD 564 (the 'initial series' of Mayan hieroglyphs in an inscription gives its date). At first this confused archaeologists, who believed Tulum had been settled several hundred years later than this date. It's now thought that Stela 1 was brought to Tulum from Tankah, a settlement 4km to the north dating from the Classic period.

At the heart of the complex you can admire Tulum's tallest building, a watchtower appropriately named **El Castillo** (The Castle) by the Spaniards. Note the Descending God in the middle of its facade, and the Toltec-style 'Kukulcanes' (plumed serpents) at the corners, echoing those at Chichén Itzá. To the Castillo's north is the small, lopsided **Templo del Dios Descendente**, named for the relief figure above the door.

Walking west toward the exit will take you to the two-story **Templo de Las Pinturas**, constructed in several stages around AD 1400–1450. Its decoration was among the most elaborate at Tulum and included relief masks and colored murals on an inner wall. The murals have been partially restored but are nearly impossible to make out. This monument might have been the last built by the Maya before the Spanish conquest, and with its columns, carvings and two-story construction, it's probably the most interesting structure at the site.

Have a last look over the whole ruins before heading out the exit (which was until very recently the entrance; INAH seems to delight in changing these things around from time to time).

Places to Stay

Most of the places here showing a range of prices have several different low and 'shoulder' periods, and a peak season that can consist of merely Christmas week, or last from December through February.

Tulum Pueblo & North Hotels in town and at Crucero Ruinas are easier to reach and generally more secure than the seaside lodgings. Though the Crucero spots are more than 2km from town, they can be reached by bus or shared van (as opposed to taxi for the beach). If you crave sand and surf, see the Zona Hotelera section after this.

The Weary Traveler (☎ 871-2389; ⓦ www .intulum.com; Av Tulum; singles/doubles M$75/130; private rooms M$200) is across the main street from the bus terminal and one block south. Rooms have two bunk beds – one with single mattresses and one with double – and a fan, toilet, shower and sink. The Traveler provides free shuttle service to the beach, a full breakfast and use of kitchen facilities. It's a great place to meet fellow travelers.

Hotel El Crucero (☎ 871-2610; ⓦ www .el-crucero.com; Crucero Ruinas; bed in 4-bed dorm M$80; 1-/2-bed fan rooms M$200/300; 2-bed air-con rooms M$500) reopened in late 2002 under youthful US management. Dorm rooms have bathrooms and lockers, while air-con rooms are done up in themes, such as the Power Puff Playroom and the Lizard Lounge. The hotel has a garden area plus a bar and restaurant (they're proud of the shark tacos), and Internet access. You can rent bicycles and store bags as well. It's a 10-minute walk to the ruins, and 15 to the beach.

L'Hotelito (☎ 871-2061; Av Tulum; air-con doubles/triples/quads low season M$300/ 400/450, high season M$650/800/900; fan triples low/high season M$250/550) is a decent Italian-run place on the west side of the highway three blocks north of the bus terminal. Air-con rooms are downstairs and well-screened (with wooden-slat windows). Fan rooms are upstairs (so they catch the breeze better) and have mosquito nets over the beds. The bathrooms are OK, and the **restaurant** serves homemade pastas.

Hotel Acuario (☎ 871-2195, fax 871-2194; Crucero Ruinas; doubles/triples/quads M$336/448/560), one of Tulum's longer-running places, is very close to a fast stretch of highway, making the front rooms noisy. Rooms vary – the front ones are better appointed generally, but the quieter back rooms are perfectly acceptable; some have great bathrooms and all have air-con. The hotel is about a 10-minute walk from the ruins and has a **restaurant**, Internet access, an often-empty pool and a lookout high above the 4th floor with views of the ruins.

Kin-Ha Suites (☎/fax 871-2321; ⓔ hotel kinha@tulum.cc; Orión between Sol & Venus; doubles with fan/air-con M$350/400) is about seven blocks northeast of the bus terminal. Italian-run, it has pleasant rooms surrounding a small courtyard garden, each with a hammock out front.

Zona Hotelera At the ticket booth for the ruins, the old access road curves south and becomes the Carretera Tulum Ruinas – Boca Paila, eventually reaching Punta Allen. A locked gate just south of the edge of the ruins keeps cars away from the site. Less than 300m south of this gate is the entrance to the first in a string of seaside hotels that extends for more than 12km – Tulum's Zona Hotelera. Accommodations range from rustic cabanas with sand floors to pricey bungalows with pricier restaurants. Some places have no electricity, or shut their generators off at 9pm or 10pm; many have no phone.

The cheapest way to sleep here is to have your own hammock and mosquito net; if you don't, several of the inexpensive places rent them for about M$35 a night. In the cheapest places you'll have to supply your own towel and soap. Most places (even the expensive ones, though they have nets over beds) aren't well screened against bugs; bring repellent. See the 'Tips for Tulum's Cabanas' boxed text for warnings and more information.

The following places are ordered north to south; not all establishments are listed.

Cabañas El Mirador (*cabana with hammock/bed M$80/150*) is the closest place to the ruins. It has 28 cabanas (half with sand floors), most with beds (otherwise bare), all a long walk from the shared bathrooms. The beach is wide here, and a decent restaurant with great views sits back and above the cabanas.

Cabañas Don Armando (*single/double/triple/quad cabanas with shared bathroom M$140/160/180/220; with private bathroom M$260-350*), the next spot down and only a 10-minute walk from the ruins, is a popular place. It has a good dive center, a basketball court, a restaurant–bar–disco and a nice stretch of beach. All structures are very tidy and nicely painted. The cabanas' poles have been filled in with concrete, which makes them more secure (bring your own lock) but hinders ventilation. The driveway is marked mainly by a Corona beer sign. Be warned that the disco plays music at very high volumes sometimes until 1am or 2am.

El Paraíso (*fax 871-2007; fan rooms M$450-750*) has 14 rooms in a one-story hotel-type block, each with two good beds, private hot-water bathroom, fine cross-ventilation and 24-hour electricity. The restaurant is very presentable, with decent prices, and the level beach, with its palm trees, *palapa* parasols, swing-chaired bar and soft white sand, is among the nicest you'll find on the Mayan Riviera.

La Vita è Bella (☎ 806-4628; ⓦ *www.lavitaebella-tulum.com; bungalows M$800-1000*), a few hundred meters south of El Paraíso, offers lovely bungalows with tile floors, big comfy beds, well-screened sliding doors, good bathrooms with colorful sinks, and wide verandas with hammocks. All overlook a narrow but nice beach that holds beach umbrellas and chairs. It's Italian-run (surprise!), so the restaurant serves authentic pizza from its wood-fired oven. The lights go out at 11pm, but these hours may be extended.

Hotel Diamante K (ⓦ *www.diamantek.com; cabanas with shared bathroom M$250-550, with private bathroom M$600-2000*) is about 2.5km south of the ruins and 500m north of the road to Cobá (and to Tulum

Tips for Tulum's Cabanas

The waterfront cabanas south of the Tulum ruins are world famous among backpackers. The first four sit nearly side by side within 1km of the ruins. Thereafter, they are mixed in with more expensive places and spread out over the next 11km or so. Here are a few tips to keep in mind if you intend to stay at one of them:

- Cabanas closest to the ruins are usually fully occupied by 10am or 11am every day from mid-December through March and in July and August. Arrive early, or make a reservation the night before.
- Taxis or bicycles are recommended to cover the distance between the cabanas and the bus terminal or the bus stops at Crucero Ruinas and the Zona Arqueológica; it's 3km from the highway to the coast road alone. Many people hitch the distance.
- The cheapest cabanas are made of sticks and built on sand (some have concrete floors). Bring a mosquito net to hang over yourself at night.
- Few of the flimsy, primitive cabanas can be reliably secured. Thieves lift the poles in the walls to gain entrance, burrow beneath through the sand or pile it up to reach windows, or jimmy the locks. Thefts are common. Never leave valuables unattended in a cabana.
- Bring a pair of sandals or flip-flops. Most of the cabanas, even at the pricier places, have shared bathrooms. Shoes help you keep sand out of your bed and reduce the chance of catching athlete's foot.

Pueblo). It has a range of imaginatively constructed and decorated cabanas, from small and simple to large and luxurious. Many have suspended beds with mosquito nets. The tiny beach area with hammocks and palms is surrounded by a rocky cove, giving it plenty of privacy. Diamante K has a fine restaurant–bar and a very good vibe.

The following listings are all south of where the road from town (and Cobá) meets the Tulum to Punta Allen road, forming a T intersection (referred to hereafter as 'the T').

Cabañas La Conchita (fax 871-2092; double rooms M$850-1350), about 2km south of the T, has eight units: three freestanding and five in two-story structures. They're well built, all have safes, 24-hour hot water, and electricity from 6pm to 10pm (candles after 10pm); most have cool, concrete walls, standard windows with some degree of sea view and lockable doors (good security). The beach and landscaping here are lovely. Rates include a big breakfast, and the range represents several different times of year. When sending a fax to Cabañas La Conchita make sure to mark it 'Attn: La Conchita.'

Restaurant y Cabañas Nohoch Tunich (☎ 871-2271, fax 871-2092; cabanas with shared bathroom M$300-350, with private bathroom M$350-450, rooms M$450-650) offers both tidy, appealing hotel-type rooms with porches and electricity (until 11pm), and thatch-and-board cabanas – the nicest of which are very near the beach and have an abundance of dark hardwood, including the floors. Rooms and cabanas are fan-cooled.

Piedra Escondida (☎/fax 871-2217; e pie draescondida@tulum.com; rooms US$85-120) offers very good service in its eight large rooms (four upstairs and four at ground level). All have private bathrooms and balconies or porches and are nicely decorated; some have excellent views. La Piedra also has a pleasing *palapa*-style restaurant–bar, and shares a small beach with neighboring Nohoch Tunich and another hotel.

Posada Margherita (W www.posadamar gherita.com; doubles US$70-140) has something virtually unheard of in the Yucatán: wheelchair access. The four ground-floor rooms have ramps, wide doorways and wide bathrooms with grab rails – the restaurant and other public areas have ramps or paths; even the dive shop offers scuba for those with limited mobility.

The whole place is very nicely done, with numerous decorative touches, and it's extremely ecofriendly. All six rooms have tile floors, very good bug screening, 24-hour lights and a terrace or balcony with hammock. One room sleeps up to five people; the others can hold three. The beach here is wide and lovely. Overlooking it is the restaurant, which turns out some great food. Although a bit pricey, it's all made fresh daily, including the pastas. Breakfast is included in room rates.

Cabañas La Zebra (W www.zebratulum .net; cabanas M$350-550) is 8.5km south of the T, the last 2km or so of which is a bit bumpy. At the time of research, the US owners said they were upgrading the 10 cement-floored cabanas to tile-floored villas. Stay tuned for price and facility changes; all the old units had hot-water, private bathrooms, fans, 24-hour electricity, one single and one double bed, and ocean views. The property is more forested than many others listed here, and has a restaurant–bar.

Places to Eat
Tulum Pueblo All of the following places are on Av Tulum (Hwy 307).

Hell's Kitchen (☎ 871-2389; mains M$30-50; open 8am-10pm daily) is the Weary Traveler's adjacent restaurant. It serves mostly good traditional Mexican dishes, with vegetarian options. The Traveler itself holds a weekly Sunday barbecue – M$40 for veggie, M$45 to M$60 depending how much meat and fish you want. Featuring live music and dancing (flamenco, belly and fire), it's quite the event, drawing people from as far away as Playa del Carmen.

Don Cafeto (breakfasts M$28-55, lunch & dinner mains M$60-100; open 7am-11pm daily) offers good breakfasts and Mexican food (including seafood dishes), as well as espresso drinks. Most orders are accompanied by a great assortment of pickled vegetables (including pickled garlic; give us a kiss, then!).

Charlie's (☎ 871-2573; mains M$50-90; open 11am-11pm Tues-Sun), opposite the bus station, boasts a terrific ambience, a lovely garden and your choice of indoor or courtyard dining. The food is largely Mexican, with a selection of M$35 salads thrown in.

París de Noche (☎ 871-2532; mains M$50-120, set meals M$90-120; open noon-

2am Tues-Sun) serves some big portions, so bring an appetite or a friend. The French chef won a *Time Out* award at the restaurant he ran in London. He serves a mix of French and Mexican dishes (as well as steaks and seafood) that includes escargots, ceviche, and a delicious green salad with chèvre that's a full meal in itself.

Two small supermarkets provide an alternative to eating out: the **Stop 'n Go**, 100m east of Hwy 307 on the road to Cobá, and the **Super Mar Caribe**, about four blocks north of the bus terminal.

Zona Hotelera The Zona has a very appealing option in addition to the hotel restaurants (most of which welcome non-guests).

Gringo Dave's *(☎ 984-100-5067; lunch mains M$75, dinner mains M$65-90; open 9am-10pm daily)*, north of the junction, has tables on a rocky bluff above the water, offering some fabulous views. The service and food are first-rate, and include some vegetarian options among the seafood and meat dishes (occasionally they have steak and lobster dinners for M$110). After your meal, you can sack out in a hammock and rock to sleep, or swim at the small beach just south (wait an hour first!). One very nice cabana is available for rent, as are three ho-hum cement rooms.

Getting There & Away

The bus terminal (a waiting room, really) is toward the southern end of town. When leaving Tulum, you can also wait at Crucero Ruinas for intercity buses and the shared vans to Playa del Carmen. Following are some distances, travel times and prices for buses leaving Tulum:

Cancún M$46 to M$56, two hours, 132km
Chetumal M$89 to M$107, 3½ to four hours, 251km
Chichén Itzá M$70, 3½ hours, 190km
Cobá M$16 to M$22, 45 minutes, 45km
Felipe Carrillo Puerto M$36 to M$42, 1½ hours, 95km
Mérida M$126, four hours, 320km (avoid 2nd-class buses, which take much longer)
Playa del Carmen M$23 to M$28, one hour, 63km
Valladolid M$40 to M$45, two hours, 106km

If you're headed for Valladolid, be sure your bus is traveling the short route through Chemax, not via Cancún. Shared vans leave for Playa del Carmen (M$20, 45 minutes) from opposite the Weary Traveler hostel, and for Felipe Carrillo Puerto (M$35, one hour) from just south of the hostel.

Getting Around

Taxi fares are fixed and pretty cheap; from either of the two taxi stands in Tulum Pueblo (one south of the bus terminal, which has fares posted, the other four blocks north on the opposite side of the street) to the ruins it's M$20, fares to most cabanas mentioned here are M$30 to M$35.

Bicycles can be a good way to get around. A few places rent them, mostly at M$60 a day, including the Weary Traveler hostel, Acuatic Tulum (the dive shop at Don Armando's, which will throw in a mask and snorkel for an extra M$20), and the Punta Piedra dive shop, 1km north of Cabañas Nohoch Tunich.

GRAND CENOTE

A little over 3km from Tulum on the road to Cobá is Grand Cenote, a worthwhile stop on your way between Tulum and the Cobá ruins, especially if it's a hot day. You can snorkel (M$50) among small fish and see underwater formations in the caverns here if you bring your own gear. A cab from downtown Tulum costs M$35 one-way, and it's an easy bike ride.

COBÁ

Among the largest of Mayan cities in its time, Cobá, 50km northwest of Tulum, offers the chance to explore mostly unrestored antiquities set deep in tropical jungle.

History

Cobá was settled earlier than Chichén Itzá or Tulum, and construction reached its peak between AD 800 and 1100. Archaeologists believe that this city once covered 50 sq km and held 40,000 Maya.

Cobá's architecture is a mystery; its towering pyramids and stelae resemble the architecture of Tikal, which is several hundred kilometers away, rather than the much nearer sites of Chichén Itzá and the northern Yucatán Peninsula.

Some archaeologists theorize that an alliance with Tikal was made through marriage to facilitate trade between the Guatemalan and Yucatecan Maya. Stelae appear to depict female rulers from Tikal holding ceremonial bars and flaunting their power by standing on captives. These Tikal royal females, when married to Cobá's royalty, may have brought architects and artisans with them.

Archaeologists are also baffled by the extensive network of *sacbés* (stone-paved avenues; *sacbeob* is the plural in Maya) in this region, with Cobá as the hub. The longest runs nearly 100km from the base of Cobá's great pyramid Nohoch Mul to the Mayan settlement of Yaxuna. In all, some 40 *sacbés* passed through Cobá, parts of the huge astronomical 'time machine' that was evident in every Mayan city.

The first excavation was by the Austrian archaeologist Teobert Maler in 1891. There

COBÁ

1 Villas Arqueológicas Cobá
2 Las Pirámides
3 Hotel y Restaurant El Bocadito; Bus Tickets
4 Entrance/Tickets

To Punta Laguna (17km) & Nuevo Xcan (43km)

To Chemax (29km) & Valladolid (57km)

0   250   500m
0   250   500yd

To Tulum (40km)

Nohoch Mul
Templo 10
Xaibé
Ballcourt
Grupo Cobá
Grupo de las Pinturas
Grupo Macanxoc

Laguna Cobá
Laguna Macanxoc
Laguna Xkanha
Laguna Zacalpuc
Laguna Sina A Kal

was little subsequent investigation until 1926, when the Carnegie Institute financed the first of two expeditions led by Sir J Eric S Thompson and Harry Pollock. After their 1930 expedition, not much happened until 1973, when the Mexican government began to finance excavation. Archaeologists now estimate that Cobá contains some 6500 structures, of which just a few have been excavated and restored, though work is ongoing.

Orientation & Information

The small, tranquil village of Cobá, 2.5km west of the Tulum–Chemax road, has a small cheap hotel, several small, simple and low-cost restaurants and the upscale Villas Arqueológicas Cobá hotel.

The **archaeological site** *(admission M$37; open 7am-6pm daily)* has a parking lot charging M$15 per passenger car.

Be prepared to walk several kilometers on paths, depending on how much you want to see. Bring insect repellent and water; the shop next to the ticket booth sells both at reasonable prices, though at the time of research there was a temporary-looking drinks stands within the site near the Nohoch Mul pyramid. Avoid the midday heat if possible; it gets extremely humid here. Most people spend around two hours at the site.

A short distance inside, at the Grupo Cobá, is a concession renting bicycles at M$25 per day. These can only be ridden within the site, and are useful if you really want to get around the farther reaches; also they're a great way to catch a breeze and cool off. If the site is crowded, however, it's probably best to walk.

You may want to buy a book on Cobá before coming. On-site signage and maps are minimal and cryptic. Guides near the entrance size you up and ask whatever they think you're worth, anywhere from M$80 to over M$660, depending on the length of the tour. They can be worth it (well, not M$660!), as they are up on the latest restoration work. At last pass, the Nohoch Mul pyramid was the only structure the public was allowed to climb.

Grupo Cobá

Walking just under 100m along the main path from the entrance and turning right brings you to the **La Iglesia** (The Church), the most prominent structure in the Cobá Group. It's an enormous pyramid; if you were allowed to climb it, you could see the surrounding lakes (lovely from above on a clear day) and the Nohoch Mul pyramid.

Take the time to explore Grupo Cobá; it has a couple of corbeled-vault passages you can walk through. Near its northern edge, on the way back to the main path and the bicycle concession, is a very well-restored **juego de pelota** (ball court).

Grupo Macanxoc

About 500m beyond the juego de pelota, the path forks. Going straight gets you to the Grupo Macanxoc, a group of stelae that bore reliefs of royal women who are thought to have come from Tikal. They are badly eroded, and it's a 1km walk; the flora along the way is interesting, however.

Grupo de las Pinturas

You can reach the Grupo de las Pinturas (Paintings Group) by heading 200m toward the Grupo Macanxoc and turning left. If you're on a bike, you'll have to park it here and return to it (this is the case at a few other spots as well). The temple here bears traces of glyphs and frescoes above its door and remnants of richly colored plaster inside.

You approach the temple from the southeast. Leave by the trail to the northwest (opposite the temple steps) to see two stelae. The first of these is 20m along, beneath a *palapa*. Here, a regal figure stands over two others, one of them kneeling with his hands bound behind him. Sacrificial captives lie beneath the feet of a ruler at the base. You'll need to use your imagination, as this and most of the other stelae here are quite worn. Continue along the path past another badly weathered stela and a small temple to rejoin the Nohoch Mul path and turn right (or, if you rented a bike, turn around or go left to retrieve it).

Grupo Nohoch Mul

Continuing northeast you will reach, on the right side of the path, another ball court (half-restored at last pass). Look at the ground in the center of the court to spot a carved stone skull (the winner or the loser of the ballgame?) and the carved relief of a jaguar. More weathered stelae lie at the north end. After the ball court, the track bends between piles of stones – a ruined

temple – and you reach a junction of sorts. Turn right (east) and head to the structure called **Xaibé**. This is a tidy, semicircular stepped building, almost fully restored. Its name means 'the Crossroads,' as it marks the juncture of four separate *sacbés*.

Going north from here takes you past Templo 10 and Stela 20. The exquisitely carved stela – worn, but not nearly so badly as the others – bears the date AD 730 and a familiar theme: a ruler standing imperiously over two captives. In front of it is a modern line drawing depicting the original details.

By this time you will have noticed **Nohoch Mul** (Big Mound) just to the north. Also known as the Great Pyramid, which sounds a lot better than Big Mound, Nohoch Mul reaches a height of 42m, making it the second tallest Mayan structure on the Yucatán Peninsula. Calakmul's Estructura II, at 45m, is the tallest. Climbing the old steps can be scary for some; see the 'Pyramid Scheme' boxed text for tips.

Two diving gods are carved over the doorway of the temple at the top (built in the post-Classic period, AD 1100–1450), similar to the sculptures at Tulum. The view from up top is over many square kilometers of flat scrubby forest, with peeks of lake, and Xaibé as the sole visible Mayan structure. Still, it's inspiring.

Pyramid Scheme

Every year people lose their footing on the steps of ancient pyramids in Mexico and tumble to their deaths. You should always wear snug footwear with good traction (or go barefoot) when you climb.

Give this sure-fire technique a try: zigzag up the steps, making diagonal passes to either side of the stairway. This is an especially useful method if your feet are too large for the shallow steps. It works well on the descent, also, as it prevents you from looking straight down (a view that can be quite vertiginous and unnerving). Use the entire width of the stairway, and to keep your stride smooth, try to ascend or descend a stair with each step you take if you feel comfortable doing so.

Once you master this style, you'll never descend again using the embarrassing sit-and-bump-down-on-your-butt method.

After descending, walk past Templo 10 and turn right to make a loop back to the ruined-temple junction. In all it's a 1.4km, half-hour walk back to the site entrance.

Places to Stay & Eat

There's no organized campsite, but you can try finding a place along the shore of the lake, which is inhabited by crocodiles (local children can show you a safe swimming spot).

Hotel y Restaurant El Bocadito (☎ 985-852-0052; rooms M$80-100) has very basic, fan-cooled rooms with private bathrooms. The **restaurant** (mains M$45-75) is well run and serves decent food. They'll store luggage while you visit the ruins. El Bocadito also serves as Cobá's bus terminal.

Villas Arqueológicas Cobá (☎/fax 985-858-1527, in USA ☎ 800-258-2633; doubles/triples M$656/806) is a Club Med hotel next to the lake. It was built to resemble an old hacienda, with red-tile floors and rooms grouped around a large inner courtyard with a swimming pool. It's one of three on the Peninsula, all with nearly the exact same plan. The restaurant is expensive but serves good Yucatecan cuisine, and the rooms are pretty decent, with good air-con. All in all it's a nice place to relax.

Restaurant Las Pirámides (mains M$50), a few doors down from the Club Med, has good lake views and friendly service.

Several small restaurants by the site parking lot serve inexpensive meals.

Getting There & Away

Most buses serving Cobá swing down almost to the lake to drop off passengers before turning around. Buses run six to eight times daily between Tulum and Cobá (M$16 to M$22); six of these also serve Playa del Carmen (M$41 to M$46, one to 1¾ hours). Buses also run to Valladolid (M$19 to M$25, 45 minutes), Chichén Itzá (M$48 to M$50, 1½ hours) and Mérida (M$106, 3½ hours).

For day-trippers from Tulum, one way to reach Cobá at a decent hour is by forming a group to split the cost of a taxi, about M$400 round-trip, including two hours at the site.

The 31km road from Cobá to Chemax is arrow-straight and in good shape. If you're driving to Valladolid or Chichén Itzá this is the way to go.

PUNTA LAGUNA

Punta Laguna is a fair-sized lake with a small Mayan community nearby, 20km northeast of Cobá on the road to Nuevo Xcan. The forest around the lake supports populations of spider and howler monkeys, as well as a variety of birds, and contains small, unexcavated ruins.

Villagers charge M$30 for entrance to the lake area, and about M$150 for a guided visit, which is your best chance of spotting simians. Some of the locals have been making observations for biologists, watching the monkeys' every move and writing them down; they can tell you a lot about them, in Spanish and English.

You can also rent canoes to paddle on the lake, an eerily beautiful sight when shrouded in morning mist. The best time to arrive is early morning – around sunup, before the monkeys are in full swing – or late afternoon, when the spider monkeys come to the water to drink.

Public transport is so sparse as to be nonexistent. In a car, you can reach Punta Laguna by turning southwest off Hwy 180 at Nuevo Xcan and driving 26km, or by heading 18km northeast from the Cobá junction. The Weary Traveler hostel (see Tulum Places to Stay) does tours that include the ruins of Cobá, a visit to Punta Laguna and snorkeling in a cenote. The tours are M$400 (general public) or M$350 (hostel guests), and include a guide, transport, a picnic lunch and all entrance fees.

The South

The southern half of Quintana Roo from approximately Tulum to the Belizean border is very different from the state's northern half. Although the state capital (Chetumal) is here, the south is much less developed than the north. The highway linking Tulum and Chetumal passes through tropical forest most of the way, with few breaks in the scenery. Felipe Carrillo Puerto, the main city between Tulum and Chetumal, offers the tourist little in the way of attractions, although it does offer good and inexpensive accommodations.

There are some pleasant and tranquil seaside destinations along the coast at Punta Allen, Mahahual and Xcalak. Several good-value places overlook the beautiful Laguna Bacalar, offering fine escapes for people who are really looking to get away from it all.

The southern half of Quintana Roo will mostly appeal to people who want to see a section of Caribbean Mexico before it gets developed, but they'd best hurry, as big plans are in motion for parts of the region. As for the capital city, it offers tourists a fine museum featuring the ancient Maya, but little else. The ruins of Dzibanché and Kohunlich are definitely worth a stop if you happen to be in the vicinity.

TULUM TO PUNTA ALLEN

Punta Allen is the end of a narrow spit of land that stretches south nearly 40km from its start below Tulum. There are some charming beaches along the way, with plenty of privacy, and most of the spit is within the protected, wildlife-rich Reserva de la Biósfera Sian Ka'an.

The road can be a real muffler-buster between gradings, especially when holes are filled with water from recent rains, making it impossible to gauge their depth. The southern half, south of the bridge at Boca Paila, is the worst stretch (and the bridge itself is pretty shaky). At the time of research, the road was so bad that no public conveyances used it (a van used to make the trip daily from Tulum Pueblo to Punta Allen). No one knows when or if the government will come up with funds for road repair; a motorcycle might be the ideal means of getting to the lower reaches. But there are a couple of options for those without their own amphibious vehicle. Read on.

Reserva de la Biósfera Sian Ka'an

Over 5000 sq km of tropical jungle, marsh, mangroves and islands on Quintana Roo's coast have been set aside by the Mexican government as a large biosphere reserve. In 1987 the UN classified it as a World Heritage site – an irreplaceable natural treasure.

Sian Ka'an (Where the Sky Begins) is home to howler monkeys, anteaters, foxes, ocelots, pumas, crocodiles, eagles, raccoons, tapirs, peccaries, giant land crabs, jaguars and hundreds of bird species, including *chocolateras* (roseate spoonbills) and some flamingos. There are no hiking

trails through the reserve; it's best explored with a professional guide.

Sian Ka'an Ecoturismo (☎ 984-871-2363; e siankaan_tours@hotmail.com; Av Tulum between Satélite & Géminis, Tulum) runs tours out of Tulum that include pickup in the Zona Hotelera. They include a guided walk of the interpretive trail at the Muyil archaeological site south of Tulum, and a boat trip through Lagunas Muyil, Chunyaxché, and Boca Paila via an ancient Mayan trade route along a natural channel. Or so says the guide; the local Mayas maintain that their ancestors carved it out. On the way you can see abundant birdlife and visit little-known Mayan temples. The tour ends with beach time and a picnic, followed by a van ride up the coast on the notorious road (the good half). It costs M$680 per person (M$544 per child aged five to seven years), including food and drinks.

If you can get to Punta Allen, three locals with training in English, natural history, interpretation and birding conduct bird-watching, snorkeling and nature tours, mostly by boat, for about US$110 for five to six people: **Baltazar Madera** (☎ 984-871-2001, in Tulum ☎ 984-879-8234), **Marcos Nery** (reachable through the local phone exchange: ☎ 984-871-2424), and **Chary Salazar** (enquire in town). The latter two are experts on endemic and migratory bird species, and Chary also does walking tours when she's available.

Punta Allen

The town of Javier Rojo Gómez is more commonly called by the name of the point 2km south. Nearly destroyed by Hurricane Gilbert in 1988, Punta Allen has a population of fewer than 400, many of whom fish for lobster, and sports a laid-back ambience reminiscent of the Belizean cayes. There's also a healthy reef 400m from shore that offers snorkelers and divers wonderful sights.

The area is known primarily for its catch-and-release bonefishing, and for that many people come a long way; tarpon and snook are very popular sportfish as well. The guides listed in the Sian Ka'an section, as well as cooperatives in town, do fishing trips for about US$200, including lunch. A few places such as **Cuzan Guest House** (☎ 983-834-0358; w www.flyfishmx.com) offer all-in packages of accommodations, guides, boats and meals for up to US$3600 per person per week.

Places to Stay & Eat You don't *have* to be a millionaire to stay in Punta Allen.

Tres Marías *(doubles M$250)* is a locally run set of simple cabanas in the middle of town.

Posada Sirena *(☎ 984-878-7795, fax 984-871-2092; ⓦ www.casasirena.com; doubles US$30-40)* offers fully furnished cabanas with kitchens and hot-water showers.

The restaurant **Vigía Grande** and the **Cuzan Guest House** are among the town's dining choices. They serve Mexican dishes and seafood, naturally including lobster.

Getting There & Away At the time of research, the only way to reach Punta Allen on scheduled public transport was to take a shared-taxi van from Felipe Carrillo Puerto to Playón (M$80, 2½-three hours, 69km) and a water taxi from there. The price of a boat ride (M$10 to M$50 per person, 2km) varies with the number of passengers (four or fewer pay the highest price). Boats run between 9am and 5pm, weather permitting; call ☎ 984-877-8017 between 8am and 5pm for information. One van daily leaves Carrillo Puerto between 10:30am and 11am, from Calle 71 east of Hwy 307. Call ☎ 983-809-2773 or ☎ 983-834-1048 to check, or to arrange a private trip. As the travel time indicates, much of the road is in very rough shape. If you have a car, you can reach Playón via a shorter, less bumpy route by turning east off Hwy 307 about 42km south of Tulum (the turnoff is signed 'Vigía Chico') and driving another 42km on the unpaved road (1½ to two hours). About 1km in you'll need to stop at a gate and register to enter the biosphere reserve.

The road is in fair shape and passes many freshwater ponds – some quite large – through forest, vast wetlands and eventually mangrove, with bird-watching opportunities galore along the way. Bear left at both intersections to reach Playón, which is nothing more than a boat landing.

FELIPE CARRILLO PUERTO
☎ 983 • pop 21,000

Now named for a progressive governor of Yucatán, this crossroads town 95km south of Tulum was once known as Chan Santa Cruz, the rebel headquarters during the War of the Castes. Besides its historical and cul-

tural significance, Carrillo Puerto has a couple of modest attractions and the only gas station, bank and hotels for some distance around. Though not a place most travelers would want to spend a lot of time in, the town has a slower pace (and lower prices) than more-touristed parts of the peninsula. It seems to continually be sprucing itself up and takes pride in its civic projects.

History

In 1849, when the War of the Castes turned against them, the Maya of the northern Yucatán Peninsula made their way to this town seeking refuge. Regrouping, they were ready to sally forth again in 1850 when a 'miracle' occurred. A wooden cross erected at a cenote on the western edge of the town began to 'talk,' telling the Maya they were the chosen people, exhorting them to continue the struggle against the whites, and promising victory. The talking was actually done by a ventriloquist who used sound chambers, but the people looked upon it as the authentic voice of their aspirations.

The oracular cross guided the Maya in battle for more than eight years, until their great victory conquering the fortress at Bacalar. For the latter part of the 19th century, the Maya in and around Chan Santa Cruz were virtually independent of governments in Mexico City and Mérida.

A military campaign by the Mexican government retook the city and the surrounding area at the beginning of the 20th century (see War of the Castes in Facts about the Yucatán), and the talking cross's shrine was desecrated. Many of the Maya fled to small villages in the jungle and kept up the fight into the 1930s; some resisted even into the 1950s.

Carrillo Puerto today remains a center of Mayan pride. The talking cross, hidden away in the jungle for many years following the Mexican takeover, has been returned to its shrine, and Maya from around the region still come to visit it, especially on May 3, the day of the Holy Cross.

Information

A **Bital bank** *(cnr Calles 70 & 69)* with ATM and money exchange lies two blocks east of the **post office** *(Calle 69; open 9am-4pm)*. **Balam Nah** *(Calle 65; open 8am-midnight daily)*, on the plaza, offers good, cheap

Internet connections in a smoke-free, air-con environment.

The **Santuario de la Cruz Parlante** (Sanctuary of the Talking Cross) is five blocks west of the gas station on Hwy 307. There's no sign at the site, but you can't miss the stone wall with a gate. Some of the town's residents do not like strangers in the sanctuary, and may try to take your camera if they see you using it here. The building, a thatch roof set over walls, is next to a small cenote and set on a rock slope. A sign on the door says no one may enter wearing a hat or shoes.

More accessible is the **Centro Cultural Chan Santa Cruz** (*open daily*), on the plaza, which has art exhibitions, workshops, and the occasional exhibit on the War of the Castes. Be sure to check the mural outside, expressing the conviction that the war is not lost, and displaying accomplishments of Mayan culture.

Places to Stay & Eat

Hotel Esquivel (☎ 834-0344, fax 834-0313; e hotelesquivelfcp@todito.com; Calle 65 No 746; doubles with fan M$140-170, with air-con M$220) is around the corner from the plaza and bus terminal. The air-con rooms are a good deal, with very clean bathrooms and tile floors, while the fan rooms have good beds and showers, but no insect screens. The hotel has a much older annex across the street. The rooms, surrounding a large courtyard, are a bit odd but have good beds and air-con.

El Faisán y El Venado (☎ 834-0702; cnr Av Juárez & Calle 69; doubles M$220) has 30 air-conditioned rooms with firm mattresses, TV and ceiling fans (as always, check the air-con before taking a room). Its adjacent restaurant has good, reasonably priced food; try the enormous shrimp ceviche (M$77) or the good *poc chuc* (grilled pork strips, M$60).

Restaurant 24 Horas (Av Juárez; mains M$35-50; open 6:30am-4am daily) is a friendly spot a few dozen meters south with food a bit cheaper than El Faisán's.

Parrilla Galerías (☎ 834-0313; Calle 65; mains M$36-50), on the plaza, has the look of a more upscale spot, but serves beer for M$12 and tacos for M$6. The house specialty is a *parrilla* (mixed grill) with lots of accompaniments (M$130 for three people).

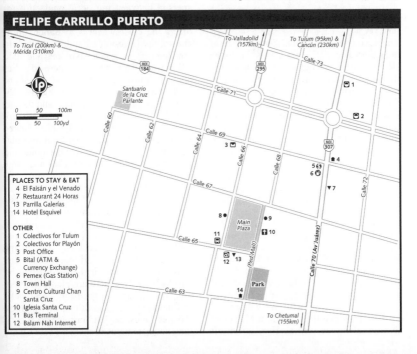

FELIPE CARRILLO PUERTO

To Ticul (200km) & Mérida (310km)

To Valladolid (157km)

To Tulum (95km) & Cancún (230km)

MEX 184

MEX 295

Calle 73

Santuario de la Cruz Parlante

Calle 71

🖃 1

Calle 60

Calle 62

Calle 64

Calle 69

Calle 66

MEX 307

🖃 2

3 🖃

Calle 68

5 🔆
6 ⊙

■ 4

Calle 72

Calle 67

▼ 7

PLACES TO STAY & EAT
4 El Faisán y el Venado
7 Restaurant 24 Horas
13 Parrilla Galerías
14 Hotel Esquivel

8 ●

Main Plaza

● 9

OTHER
1 Colectivos for Tulum
2 Colectivos for Playón
3 Post Office
5 Bital (ATM & Currency Exchange)
6 Pemex (Gas Station)
8 Town Hall
9 Centro Cultural Chan Santa Cruz
10 Iglesia Santa Cruz
11 Bus Terminal
12 Balam Nah Internet

Calle 65

11 🖃

🖃 10

12 ▼ 13

Calle 70 (Av Juárez)

(Pedl Mall)

Calle 63

14 ■

Park

To Chetumal (155km)

0 50 100m
0 50 100yd

Getting There & Away

Most buses serving Carrillo Puerto are *de paso* (they don't originate there).

Cancún M$80 to M$103, 3½ to four hours, 230km; nine 1st-class buses, hourly 2nd-class buses to 9pm

Chetumal M$56 to M$68, two to three hours, 155km; four 1st-class and 14 2nd-class buses

Mérida M$112, 5½ hours, 310km; 11 2nd-class buses

Playa del Carmen M$60 to M$72, 2½ hours, 159km; nine 1st-class buses, hourly 2nd-class buses to 9pm

Ticul M$81, 4½ hours, 200km; 11 2nd-class buses; change there or at Muna for Uxmal

Tulum M$36 to M$42, 1½ hours, 95km; nine 1st-class buses, hourly 2nd-class buses to 9pm

Shared vans leave for Playa del Carmen (M$55, two hours) and Tulum (M$35, one hour) from Hwy 307 just south of Calle 73.

Drivers: check your fuel tank before heading to or leaving Carrillo Puerto. There are no gas stations between it and the following cities: Valladolid (Hwy 295 north), Chetumal (Hwy 307 south), Tulum (Hwy 307 north) and José María Morelos (Hwy 184 west).

MAHAHUAL & THE COSTA MAYA

The area extending south from the edge of the Reserva de la Biósfera Sian Ka'an to the sleepy fishing village of Xcalak has been dubbed the Costa Maya. Among the attractions on offer here are a vast coral atoll dotted with shipwrecks, the ever-present barrier reef and its numerous diving opportunities, an array of wildlife and some lovely beaches and places to stay. Get it while it lasts though, as plans for development in the area are rolling ahead.

Private investors and the Mexican government have been sinking a lot of money into attracting tourism (and further investment) to the area. Their efforts center around the town of Mahahual (also spelled Majahual; population 200 in 2000), which now has an airport and more than a hundred housing units for service workers, but no bank. North of town, a cruise-ship dock and shopping complex (exclusively for passengers) is already receiving several ships a week, and has capacity for many more.

Work to widen the road from Mahahual to Hwy 307 – as well as Hwy 307 itself

south to Chetumal – to four lanes was due to be finished by mid-2003. Hwy 307 north to Tulum was scheduled to receive the same treatment immediately afterward. Hotels are to be built north of Mahahual up to the edge of the biosphere reserve, and boosters project a population of 150,000 for the town by 2013. Time will tell.

On the bright side, the town gets a waste-treatment plant and 24-hour electricity. Also, laws prohibit construction of anything higher than three floors in town. Outside of town, the limit is two floors, with a density restriction of 10 rooms per hectare. So megaresorts are out. Technically.

That said, Mahahual is presently a quiet little coastal town, not yet inundated by cruisers. They were mostly being whisked off on expensive tours to the archaeological zones of Chacchobén and Kohunlich (suckers, it's more than 170km away!), four-wheeling in the jungle, or having a 'Mayan cultural experience.' Some opt for local biking or kayaking excursions, but they're bound to be good sorts.

South of town along the rough coastal road are a few decent places to stay, interspersed between the occasional 'Lot for Sale' signs. More significantly, Mahahual offers the closest access to **Banco Chinchorro**, the largest coral atoll in the Northern Hemisphere. Some 45km long and up to 14km wide, Chinchorro's western edge lies about 30km off the coast, and dozens of ships have fallen victim to its barely submerged ring of coral. The atoll and its surrounding waters were made a biosphere reserve (the Reserva de la Biósfera Banco Chinchorro) to protect them from depredation. But the reserve lacks the personnel and equipment needed to patrol such a large area, and many abuses go undetected.

Lots of the wrecks lie in water too shallow to dive, and many of the most interesting diveable wrecks require ideal conditions to be approached safely (June and July are the best months); others are too far from shore to be reached on a day trip. At the time of writing it was all moot, as the director of the reserve had issued a ban on wreck dives. But there are plenty of other things to see around the bank: coral walls and canyons, rays, turtles, giant sponges, grouper, tangs, eels and in some spots reef, tiger and hammerhead sharks. There's good snorkeling as well, including **40 Cannons**, a wooden ship in 5m to 6m of water. Looters have left it with far fewer than 40 guns, and it can only be visited in ideal conditions, but the prohibition on wrecks doesn't apply to snorkelers.

Blue Ha Diving Center (W www.blue hadiving.com; Hwy 307 Km 2.7) runs trips to Chinchorro and to stretches of the barrier reef a few hundred meters from shore, which has some excellent spots as well. It takes a maximum of eight passengers to the bank, 10 to local spots. Blue Ha also offers PADI courses, and the operator, Douglas Campbell-Smith, speaks English, Spanish and German.

Places to Stay & Eat
All but the last of the following places are south of town. Addresses are given as distances from the military checkpoint at the north entrance to town.

Coco Ha (Km 1.8; doubles with shared bathroom M$130; tent or hammock sites M$35) is located three blocks south of the entrance and rents five cabanas. They're quite basic, but have cement floors and are right on the beach. A few coconut trees provide shade.

Las Cabañas del Doctor (☎ 983-832-2102; Km 2; cabanas with shared/private bathroom M$150/200) is across the street from the beach, about 100m south of the previous entry. It offers several fairly simple dwellings. Prices rise to M$200 and M$300 December and Easter week.

La Cabaña del Tío Phil (☎ 983-835-7166; Km 2; cabanas M$300) is a big step up. The wooden-floored cabanas sleep up to four people, and have hot-water bathrooms, good screening and ventilation as well as fans. The restaurant serves three meals a day (you can catch your own fish if you like).

Casa del Mar (Km 2; open 7am-midnight), next door to the Doctor, is a friendly German-run café serving coffee (including great cappuccino), applecakes, whole-wheat bread and other delights. The owners plan to begin serving breakfasts.

Lonchería Marí is right in town, behind the big yellow Hotel Mahahual. It's very simple and clean, and serves tasty fish fillets prepared in various styles, accompanied by beans and tortillas.

Getting There & Around
Mahahual is 68km south of Felipe Carrillo Puerto, 5km south of Limones and 46km north of Bacalar. Though locals hope bus service will improve with the better road, public transit currently consists of either cabs from Limones (about M$250) or dilapidated buses that run from Chetumal's main bus terminal to Limones, then Mahahual and Xcalak. Thus you can catch a bus from points north (Felipe Carrillo Puerto or Tulum, for example) to Limones and intercept one of the Mahahual buses (M$25). The buses arrive (barring breakdowns) in Limones at about 6am, 7:30am and 5:30pm. Schedules fluctuate; try to get to Limones with plenty of lead time. If you're driving, expect to be stopped at least once at a military checkpoint; they're only searching for contraband. A gas station was being constructed in Mahahual at last pass.

Bicycles work well for getting around here. **Casa del Mar** (see Places to Stay & Eat) rents them for M$50 a day.

XCALAK
The small fishing village of Xcalak (shka-**lak**), with its quiet atmosphere, decaying Caribbean-style wooden homes, swaying palms and pretty beaches is removed from Mahahual by 65km of paved road (and about 50km of potholed dirt track if you take the coastal road). It too offers access to the wonders of the nearby barrier reef, and to Banco Chinchorro, although the boat ride to the latter is several kilometers longer than from Mahahual.

The mangrove stretching inland from the coastal road hides some large lagoons and forms tunnels that invite the kayaker to explore them. It and the drier forest teem with wildlife, and as well as the usual herons, egrets and other waterfowl, you can see agouti, jabiru (storks), iguanas, javelinas (peccaries), parakeets, kingfishers, alligators and more. Unfortunately, the mangrove also breeds mosquitoes and some vicious *jejenes* (sand flies).

With luck, Xcalak's distance from the center of the planned boom will spare it from severe impact. So far it shows no signs of getting a bank or a gas station, so stock up before you come.

The paved road enters town about four blocks south of its central plaza/basketball court, which lies just across the street from the water.

Aventuras Xcalak to Chinchorro Dive Center *(☎ 983-831-0461;* W *www.xcalak .com.mx)*, about 300m north of town on the coast road, offers dive and snorkel trips to the wondrous barrier reef just offshore, and to Banco Chinchorro. They also rent equipment and do PADI, NAUI and SDI instruction, as well as fishing and birding tours.

Places to Stay & Eat

Hotel Caracol *(no tel; doubles M$110)*, a six-room hotel about three blocks south of the plaza and one block inland, is the town's only cheap place to stay. It offers decently screened rooms with basic beds, a fan and cold-water bathroom. The electricity is on from 6pm to 11:30pm. Look for the owner, Sra Mauricia Garidio, in the blue house next door to the hotel.

The following places are among a handful on the old coastal road leading north from town (mostly run by Americans or Canadians). All have purified drinking water, ceiling fans, 24-hour electricity (from solar or wind with generator backup), bikes and/or sea kayaks for guest use, and private hot-water bathrooms. The first three have docks to swim off, and most arrange fishing excursions.

High season here is mid-December to mid-April (with very slight variations). Most places don't accept credit cards without prior arrangements, and are best contacted through their websites or via email. Addresses here are expressed in kilometers from town.

Costa de Cocos *(☎ 983-831-0110;* W *www .costadecocos.com; Km 1.5; singles/doubles/ triples/quads low season US$73/110/134/ 144, high season US$84/134/168/207; closed October)* has wide, spacious, palm-studded grounds and 16 appealing, slightly spare, thatched cabanas with tile floors, slat blinds and hammocks in addition to beds. The restaurant–bar is attractive, and breakfast and dinner are included in the price, though kayak use isn't. A full dive shop with three boats rounds out the package.

Hotel Tierra Maya *(☎ 983-831-0404, in USA ☎ 800-480-4505;* W *www.tierramaya .net; Km 2; small/large doubles low season US$67/78, high season US$84/95)* is a modern beachfront hotel featuring six lovely rooms (three quite large), each tastefully appointed and with many architectural details. Each of the rooms has mahogany furniture and a balcony facing the sea – the bigger rooms even have small refrigerators. Single rates are about US$5 less, and air-con (available in some rooms) is US$15 extra per night. Mains at the pleasant restaurant (dinner only) are around US$10.50. Rates include a light buffet breakfast.

Casa Carolina *(☎ 983-831-0444;* W *www .casacarolina.net; Km 2.5; doubles low/high season US$65/84)* has four guestrooms with large, hammock-equipped balconies facing the sea. Each room has a kitchen with fridge, and the bathrooms try to outdo one another with their beautiful Talavera tile. All levels of scuba instruction (NAUI) are offered here, as well as recreational dives at the barrier reef. Rates include continental breakfast.

Villas La Guacamaya *(☎/fax 983-831- 0334;* e *villaslaguacamaya@yahoo.com; Km 10; doubles low/high season US$50/70)* is 10km north of Xcalak. It has two rooms that face the sea and share use of a fully equipped gourmet kitchen. Each room has a double and a single bed. There's also a separate apartment with kitchen set back from the beach, and a fourth, smallish room with a double bed and a lovely bathroom. One of the friendly owners is a family nurse practitioner and certified diving medical technician; she speaks English, Spanish and Portuguese. The other takes guests on guided kayak expeditions. They also offer free (limited) Internet access, and not only bikes and kayaks for guest use but snorkel gear as well.

Grocery trucks ply the coast road, and Xcalak centro has a few restaurants, some keeping sporadic hours.

Lonchería Silvia's *(mains M$35-65; open 8:30am-10pm daily)* is about three blocks south of the plaza and a block in from the coast. It has a half-sand, half-concrete floor, good food and sanitation and a very local atmosphere. Silvia serves mostly fish fillets and ceviche, and keeps pretty regular hours.

Restaurant Bar Xcalak Caribe *(mains M$45-60; open noon-whenever daily)* is an American-run place about two blocks south of the plaza and just across the street from the beach. Diners (and drinkers) sit on the 2nd floor under a *palapa* to eat burgers, fries, fish fingers and fillets. Alan closes anywhere between 8pm and midnight.

Getting There & Around

Getting to Xcalak entails much the same procedure as to Mahahual (see Getting There & Around under Mahahual & The Costa Maya earlier). Cabs from Limones cost about M$500 (including to the northern hotels). Buses cost M$25, the same as to Mahahual even though they travel an hour longer.

Driving from Limones, turn right (south) after 55km and follow the signs to Xcalak (another 60km). Keep an eye out for the diverse wildlife frequenting the forest and mangrove; a lot of it runs out into the road.

A taxi now works the town, serving the northern hotels for M$100 and available for hire for excursions to farther destinations.

LAGUNA BACALAR

A clear, turquoise freshwater lake more than 60km long and with a bottom of gleaming white sand, Laguna Bacalar comes as a surprise in this region of tortured limestone and scrubby jungle. It offers opportunities for camping, swimming, kayaking, birdwatching and lazing. A growing number of foreigners (chiefly Americans and Canadians) have been buying up lakeside lots.

The small, sleepy town of Bacalar lies east of the highway, 125km south of Felipe Carrillo Puerto and 39km north and east of Chetumal. It's the only settlement of any size on the lake, and is noted mostly for its old Spanish fortress and popular *balneario* (swimming facility).

The fortress was built above the lagoon to protect citizens from raids by pirates and Indians. It served as an important outpost for the whites in the War of the Castes. In 1859 it was seized by Maya rebels, who held the fort until Quintana Roo was finally conquered by Mexican troops in 1901. Today, with formidable cannons still on its ramparts, the fortress remains an imposing sight. It houses a **museum** exhibiting colonial armaments and uniforms from the 17th and 18th centuries, but at the time of research it had not opened yet following a prolonged remodeling job, in spite of a ribbon-cutting ceremony.

The **balneario** *(admission M$5; open 10am-7pm daily)* lies a few hundred meters north along the *costera* (waterfront avenue) below the fort. There are some small restaurants along the avenue and near the *balneario,* which is very busy on weekends.

La Costera South

The *costera* (also known as Calle 1) winds south several kilometers along the lakeshore from Bacalar town to Hwy 307 at Cenote Azul. All the following places to stay and eat are on it, listed from north to south.

Casita Carolina *(☎/fax 983-834-2334;* W *www.casitacarolina.com; doubles M$250-450; palapa M$400)* is a delightful place about 1½ blocks south of the fort. It has a large lawn leading down to the lake, five fan rooms and a deluxe *palapa* that sleeps up to four. Guests can explore the lake in the casita's kayaks. It's best reached by taking a bus into Bacalar and walking or catching a taxi.

Hotel Laguna *(☎ 983-834-2206, fax 983-834-2205; doubles M$380)* is clean, cool and hospitable, and boasts a small swimming pool, a restaurant, a bar and excellent views of the lake, directly below the hotel. Some rooms are showing their age. It's 2km south of Bacalar town along the *costera* and only 150m east of Hwy 307, so traveling on the highway you can ask a bus driver to stop at the turnoff.

La Casa de la Laguna *(☎ 983-834-2519; Costera 169; box lunches M$20, set meals M$32),* 200m south of Hotel Laguna, serves good food to take away or eat on the terrace overlooking the lake. Run by a charming couple, it's a ring-the-bell-on-the-gate sort of place, but serves three meals.

Los Coquitos *(campsites per person M$40),* 500m south of the previous listing, is a nice camping area on the lakeshore, run by a family who live in a shack on the premises. You can camp in the dense shade of the palm trees, enjoy the view of the lake from the *palapas* and swim from the grassy banks. Water and soft drinks are sometimes for sale.

Just shy of the south end of the costera is **Cenote Azul**, a 90m-deep natural pool on the southwest shore of the lake. It's 200m east of Hwy 307, so many buses will drop you nearby. **Restaurant Cenote Azul** *(mains M$45-115; open 8am-7pm daily)* overlooks the cenote, and has a ladder leading down into it for those who'd like a swim.

Getting There & Away

Southbound 2nd-class buses go through Bacalar town on Calle 7, passing a block uphill from the central square *(el parque),* which is just above the fort and has a taxi stand. Northbound 2nd-class buses run along Calle 5, a block downhill from Calle 7. Most 1st-class buses don't enter town, but many will drop you along Hwy 307 at the turnoffs to Hotel Laguna and Cenote Azul; check before you buy your ticket to be sure.

Minibuses from Chetumal to the town of Bacalar (M$13, 45 minutes, 39km) depart from the terminal on Primo de Verdad at Hidalgo about once an hour from 5am to 9pm.

If you're driving from the north and want to reach the town and fort, take the first Bacalar exit and continue several blocks before turning left (east) down the hill. From Chetumal, head west to catch Hwy 307 north; after 25km on the highway you'll reach the signed right turn for Cenote Azul and the costera.

AROUND BACALAR

A few kilometers north of Bacalar town, right next to the highway, is **Puerto del Cielo Hotel y Restaurante** *(☎/fax 983-837-0413; rooms M$300)*, which offers 12 air-con rooms with hot-water bathrooms and TV. A swimming pool on the grounds overlooks Laguna Bacalar. The restaurant specializes in chicken and fish dishes.

Farther north, and 3.2km off the highway, is **Federico's Laguna Azul** *(fax 983-834-2035; ⓦ www.laguna-azul.de;campsites M$35 per person, screened palapas M$150, cabanas M$250)*, a serene, secluded spot located on the north end of Laguna Bacalar. It has a variety of accommodations, including three well-built and - screened cabanas with good private bathrooms, perfect mattresses, tile floors and a hammock; places to pitch tents or hammocks; eight RV sites with hookups; and immaculate shared bathrooms with hot and cold water. You can rent kayaks here, and eat at the family-style restaurant (you generally eat what's cooking, though they often will prepare other, simple dishes).

The German owner speaks Spanish and very good English, and checks for incoming faxes and email at least once a week. The unpaved road in comes off the east side of Hwy 307, 200m south of the southernmost *tope* in Pedro A Santos, which is about 6km south of the Mahahual junction. You can ask to be let off 2nd-class buses either at the speed bump (and walk the 3.2km in) or in Pedro Santos itself, to take the town's one taxi.

CHETUMAL

☎ 983 • pop 129,000

Quintana Roo's capital is the jumping-off point for travelers heading to Belize and Guatemala. It offers a superb Mayan museum and a pleasant bayside esplanade, but little else of interest to the visitor.

Before the Spanish conquest, Chetumal was a Mayan port for shipping gold, feathers, cacao and copper to the northern Yucatán Peninsula. After the conquest, the town was not actually settled until 1898, when it was founded to put a stop to the illegal trade in arms and lumber carried on by the descendants of the War of the Castes rebels. Dubbed Payo Obispo, the town changed its name to Chetumal in 1936. In 1955, Hurricane Janet virtually obliterated it.

The rebuilt city is laid out on a grand plan with a grid of wide boulevards along which traffic speeds (be careful at stop signs).

Shoppers from Belize flock to Chetumal to load up on foodstuffs and other goods, as the variety is much greater and the prices much lower than in their tiny country.

Orientation & Information

Despite Chetumal's sprawling layout, the city center is largely manageable on foot, and it contains several hotels and restaurants.

The **tourist information kiosk** *(open 9am-8pm daily)* in the bus terminal is usually staffed by an English-speaker and offers a map of the city and information on hotels. A **city tourist office** *(☎ 835-0500; cnr Av 5 de Mayo & Carmen Ochoa de Merino; open 9am-6pm daily)* near the waterfront dispenses advice.

There are several banks and ATMs around town, including an ATM in the bus terminal and a Bital **currency exchange counter** *(open 8am-6pm Mon-Sat for US$, Mon-Fri for traveler's checks, euros and other currency)* with adjacent ATM in the San Francisco de Asís supermarket just east of the terminal. **Cambalache** *(Av de los Héroes between Elías Calles & Zaragoza)* is a currency exchange downtown.

The **post office** *(☎ 832-0057; cnr Plutarco Elías Calles & 5 de Mayo; open 9am-4pm*

CHETUMAL

PLACES TO STAY
6 Hotel Ucum
8 Holiday Inn Chetumal Puerta Maya
13 Hotel Los Cocos
25 Hotel María Dolores; Restaurant Sosilmar
27 Hotel Caribe Princess
28 Instituto Quintanarroense de la Juventud (Youth Hostel)

PLACES TO EAT
7 Restaurant Pantoja
15 Restaurant Vegetariano La Fuente
20 El Taquito de Don Julio
22 Café-Restaurant Los Milagros
24 Pollo Brujo
26 Sergio's Pizzas
30 Euro Buffet
34 Panadería y Pastelería La Invencible
36 Café Espresso

OTHER
1 Minibus Terminal
2 Public Library
3 ADO Bus Ticket Office
4 Taxi Stand; Combis to Bus Terminal & Immigration Office
5 Museo de la Cultura Maya
9 Hospital Morelos
10 Cruz Roja
11 Web Center
12 Museo de la Ciudad

14 Telmex
16 BBV Bancomer (ATM)
17 Aviacsa
18 Banorte; BanCrecer (ATM)
19 Post Office
21 Cambalache (Casa de Cambio)
23 BBV Bancomer (ATM)
29 Teatro Constituyentes
31 Bital
32 City Tourist Office
33 Pemex Station
35 Palacio de Gobierno

To Bus Terminal & Tourist Information Kiosk (2km) & Immigration Office (3km)

To Nuevo Mercado Lázaro Cárdenas (Buses to Belize) (1km)

Av Primo de Verdad

General Heriberto Lara
Felipe Carrillo Puerto
José María Luis Moya
Francisco Márquez
Elberto Frías

Cristóbal Colón

Av Belice

Av de los Héroes

Av Independencia

Av Benito Juárez

Av 16 de Septiembre

Av Miguel Hidalgo

Calzada Veracruz

Juan Esculta

Parking

3 ●
4
5
Park (Ped Mall)

Av Mahatma Gandhi

Av José María Morelos

Av Francisco I Madero

6 ▲
▼ 7

Juan de la Barrera

Mercado Ignacio Manuel Altamirano

▲ 8

Augustin Melgar

Efraín Aguilar

Francisco Márquez

To Belizean Consulate (1km)

9 ✚
✚ 10

🛏 11

Fernando Montes

Calzada Tampico

Héroes de Chapultepec

12 🏛

Héroes de Chapultepec

13 ▲

14 🖂

Lázaro Cárdenas

16 ☉

▼ 15

17 ●

18 ☉

Plutarco Elías Calles

✉ 19

▼ 20

☉ 21
22 ▼

Ignacio Zaragoza

To Airport (2km), Belize & Zona Libre (10km), Escárcega (273km) & Cancún (382km)

Av Álvaro Obregón

Av de los Héroes

Av 5 de Mayo

Av 16 de Septiembre

Av Miguel Hidalgo

Av Reforma

Calzada Veracruz

Av Cozumel

23 ☉ 24 ▼ ▲ 25

▼ 26

27 ▲

Heroica Escuela Naval

▲ 28

🖂 29

Othón P Blanco

▼ 30

Park

☉ 31

Carmen Ochoa de Merino

☉ 32
33 ●

34 ▼

22 de Enero

35 🏛 (Ped Mall)

36 ▼

Blvd Bahía

Blvd Bahía

Clock Tower ▲

Bahía Chetumal

0   100   200m
0   100   200yd

Mon-Fri) is quite central, while the **immigration office** *(☎ 832-6353; Av de los Héroes; open 9am-1pm Mon-Fri)* is far north of downtown, on the left about four blocks north of Av Insurgentes (and the bus terminal). It's open for tourist-card extensions and such.

There is no shortage of public telephones around town, from which you can place international calls. However, it's possible to place long-distance calls and send faxes from the **Telmex** *(Calle Lazaro Cárdenas; open 8am-6pm Mon-Fri),* between Avs Independencia and Juárez. **Web Center** *(Efraín Aguilar between Avs Belice & de los Héroes; open 8am-2am daily)* has lightning-fast Internet access for M$8 per hour.

The **Cruz Roja** *(☎ 832-0571; cnr Avs Independencia & Héroes de Chapultepec)* and **Hospital Morelos** *(☎ 832-4595),* just northeast in the same block, handle medical emergencies.

Museo de la Cultura Maya

This museum *(☎ 832-6838; Av de los Héroes between Colón & Av Gandhi; admission M$50; open 9am-7pm Tues-Thur & Sun, 9am-8pm Fri-Sat)* is the city's claim to cultural fame – a bold showpiece beautifully conceived and executed.

The museum is organized into three levels, mirroring Mayan cosmology. The main floor represents this world, the upper floor the heavens, and the lower floor Xibalbá, the underworld. The various exhibits (labeled in Spanish and English) cover all of the Mayab (lands of the Maya), not just Quintana Roo or Mexico, and seek to explain the Mayan way of life, thought and belief. Scale models show the great Mayan buildings as they may have appeared, including a temple complex set below plexiglass you can walk over. Though artifacts are in short supply there are replicas of stelae and a burial chamber from Copán, Honduras, reproductions of the murals found in Room 1 at Bonampak and much more. Ingenious mechanical and computer displays graphically illustrate the Mayas' complex calendrical, numerical and writing systems.

The museum's **courtyard** *(admission free)* has salons for temporary exhibits of modern artists (such as Rufino Tamayo), paintings reproducing Mayan frescoes and a *cine-museo* giving free film showings. In the middle of the courtyard is a Mayan thatched house with implements of daily life on display: gourds, grinders, a metate. Just walk past the ticket window.

Look for a bronze bust in the middle of Av de los Héroes, just east of the museum's entrance. It depicts Jacinto Pat, one of the Mayan leaders who planned to insurrection that became the War of the Castes.

Museo de la Ciudad

The local history museum *(Héroes de Chapultepec between Avs de los Héroes & Juárez; admission M$10; open 9am-7pm Mon-Sat)* is small but neatly done, displaying historic photos, military artifacts and old-time household items (even some vintage telephones and a television). All labels are in Spanish, but even if you don't read the language, it's worth visiting for 15 minutes of entertainment.

Places to Stay

Instituto Quintanarroense de la Juventud *(☎ 832-3465; Heroica Escuela Naval between Calzada Veracruz & Av Cozumel; campsites per person M$20, dorm beds M$30),* just past the eastern end of Av Obregón, is out-of-the-way and kind of shabby, but it's the cheapest place in town. It has single-sex dorms (four bunks to a room) and lockers (bring your own lock). The doors close at 11pm but the night person will let you in later.

Hotel María Dolores *(☎ 832-0508; Av Álvaro Obregón 206; singles M$150, doubles M$165-190),* west of Av de los Héroes, is good for the price. The beds are a bit saggy, but some of the fan-cooled rooms are a good size and there's off-street parking.

Hotel Ucum *(☎ 832-0711, 832-6186; Av Mahatma Gandhi 167; doubles with fan M$180-200, with air-con M$250)* is a fine budget, motel-like place with many rooms around a central courtyard/parking lot. It has a swimming pool and a restaurant serving good, inexpensive food.

Hotel Caribe Princess *(☎/fax 832-0900; Av Álvaro Obregón 168; singles/doubles/triples M$336/388/459)* is a quiet, well-run place. All rooms have air-con, phone and TV, and there's off-street parking.

Hotel Los Cocos *(☎ 832-0544, fax 832-0920; e hotelcocos@correoweb.com; cnr Av de los Héroes & Calle Héroes de Chapultepec; doubles with air-con & TV M$670)* has a nice swimming pool, a guarded parking lot and a popular sidewalk restaurant. Rooms are good and have fridges.

Holiday Inn Chetumal Puerta Maya (☎ 835-0400, fax 832-1676; W www.holiday -inn.com/chetumalmex; Av de los Héroes 171; doubles M$1109) is the best in town, with comfortable rooms overlooking a small courtyard, a swimming pool set amid tropical gardens and a restaurant and bar.

Places to Eat

Across from the Holiday Inn is the **Mercado Ignacio Manuel Altamirano** and its row of small, simple eateries serving inexpensive meals. Similar is the upstairs area in the **Nuevo Mercado Lázaro Cárdenas** (Calzada Veracruz).

Restaurant Sosilmar (Av Álvaro Obregón 206; breakfasts M$25-40, mains M$44-60; open 8am-10:30pm Mon-Sat), beneath the Hotel María Dolores, is a bright and simple place serving filling platters of seafood or meat, as well as sandwiches and burgers (M$7 to M$30).

Panadería y Pastelería La Invencible (Calle Carmen Ochoa de Merino; open 7am-9pm Mon-Sat), west of Av de los Héroes, is a bakery producing excellent pastries, of a quality well above the usual Mexican standard.

Pollo Brujo (☎ 837-4747; Av Álvaro Obregón 208; open 10am-10pm daily) is west of the Sosilmar. A roasted half chicken costs M$33, a whole one M$66; take it with you or dine in the air-con salon.

Restaurant Vegetariano La Fuente (☎ 832-5373; Lázaro Cárdenas 222; sandwiches M$12-18, set meals M$40; open Mon-Sat) is a tiny, tidy meatless restaurant and health-food store next to a homeopathic pharmacy. It serves mock-meat dishes made from wheat gluten, delicious veggie and fruit drinks (M$6-21), tofu, brown rice and more.

Euro Buffet (Blanco between Avs Juárez & Othón P Independencia; open 11am-5pm Mon-Fri), another good vegetarian find, offers build-your-own salads accompanied by free bread rolls. Priced by the kilo, a huge salad can be yours for M$27.

Café-Restaurant Los Milagros (☎ 832-4433; Calle Ignacio Zaragoza between Avs 5 de Mayo & de los Héroes; breakfast M$25-50, mains M$30-50; open 7:30am-10pm Mon-Sat, 7:30am-1pm Sun) serves espresso and food indoors and outdoors. A favorite with

Chetumal's student and intellectual set, it's a great place to drink coffee, chat and observe a local radio program being broadcast from one of the tables.

Restaurant Pantoja (☎ 832-3957; cnr Av Mahatma Gandhi & 16 de Septiembre; mains M$30-70; open 7am-9pm daily) is a popular, family-run restaurant serving breakfasts, enchiladas and a variety of meat dishes.

Café Espresso (☎ 833-3013; cnr 22 de Enero & Av Miguel Hidalgo; breakfast M$25-35, sandwiches M$24-38, mains M$60-85; open 8am-midnight daily), facing the bay, has an upscale ambience and a good selection of omelets and other breakfasts; the *huevos chetumaleños* (eggs, cheese, chaya – a spinach-like green – tomato and onion, M$32) are excellent. A full range of espresso drinks rounds out the morning meal. Among the other offerings are sandwiches, salads and various cuts of meat.

El Taquito de Don Julio (Plutarco Elías Calles 220; tacos M$7-12, mains M$50) is an airy, simple dining room and is a good spot for night owls. The small tacos cost slightly more with cheese added; other menu offerings include cheap snacks, *tortas* and vegetarian brochettes (M$22).

Sergio's Pizzas (☎ 832-0892; cnr Avs Álvaro Obregón & 5 de Mayo; pizza M$42-123, mains M$50-90) is a well air-conditioned place serving pizzas and cold beer in frosted mugs, plus Mexican and continental dishes, steaks and seafood, complemented by an extensive wine list.

Supermercado San Francisco de Asís, just east of the bus terminal, has a wide selection of groceries, and is a full department store besides.

Getting There & Away

Air Chetumal's small airport is less than 2km northwest of the city center along Av Obregón.

Aviacsa (☎ 832-7765, fax 832-7654, airport ☎ 832-7787, fax 832-7698; cnr Lázaro Cárdenas & Av 5 de Mayo) flies to Mexico City once a day Sunday to Friday.

For flights to Belize City (and on to Flores, to reach Tikal) or to Belize's cayes, cross the border into Belize and fly from Corozal.

Bus The main bus terminal is about 2km north of the center, near the intersection of

Avs Insurgentes and Belice. Deluxe Omnitur del Caribe, Maya de Oro and Super Expresso; ADO and Cristóbal Colón 1st-class; and 2nd-class TRT, Sur and Mayab (a cut above), among others, provide service. The terminal has lockers (in the store against the east wall, near the pay toilets), a bus information kiosk (open until 3pm), an ATM, international phone and fax services, a cafeteria and shops. East of the terminal is a huge San Francisco de Asís department store with a good Bital exchange counter.

You can also buy tickets for some lines and get information about most bus services at the **ADO office** (Av Belice; open 6am-10pm daily), just west of the Museo de la Cultura Maya.

Many local buses, and those bound for Belize, begin their runs from the **Nuevo Mercado Lázaro Cárdenas** (Calzada Veracruz at Confederación Nacional Campesina – also called Segundo Circuito), about 10 blocks north of Av Primo de Verdad. From this market, most 1st-class Belize-bound buses continue to the long-distance terminal and depart from there 15 minutes later; the 2nd-class buses don't. Tickets can be purchased on board the buses or (1st-class only) at the main terminal. There's usually a Belizean driver who can give information (in English and Spanish) at the café on the corner of the market parking lot.

The **minibus terminal** (cnr Avs Primo de Verdad & Hidalgo), has services to Bacalar and other nearby destinations. Departures listed below are from the main terminal unless otherwise noted.

Bacalar M$13 to M$15, 45 minutes, 39km; hourly minibuses from the minibus terminal; many Mayab buses departing from the main terminal

Belize City, Belize M$55 to M$70, three to four hours, 160km; 18 1st- and 2nd-class Novelo's and Northern buses, departing from Nuevo Mercado between 4:30am and 6:30pm, some departing main terminal 15 minutes later

Campeche M$158 to M$195, 6½ to nine hours, 422km; one ADO bus at noon, TRT buses at 4:15am and 2:15pm

Cancún M$142 to M$170, 5½ to 6½ hours, 382km; many buses

Corozal, Belize M$15 to M$20, one hour with border formalities, 30km; 18 1st- and 2nd-class Novelo's and Northern buses, departing from Nuevo Mercado between 4:30am and

6:30pm, some departing main terminal 15 minutes later

Escárcega M$102 to M$124, four to six hours, 273km; nine buses between 4:15am and 10:30pm

Felipe Carrillo Puerto M$56 to M$68, two to three hours, 155km; many buses

Flores, Guatemala (for Tikal) M$200, eight hours, 350km; five Servicio San Juan and Mundo Maya buses between 6:20am and 2:30pm

Mahahual M$40, four hours, 145km; 2nd-class buses at 4am, 6am and 3:15pm

Mérida M$155 to M$185, six to eight hours, 456km; eight Omnitur del Caribe and Super Expresso buses, three Mayab buses

Orange Walk, Belize M$30 to M$35, 2¼ hours, 91km; 18 1st- and 2nd-class Novelo's and Northern buses, departing from Nuevo Mercado between 4:30am and 6:30pm, some departing main terminal 15 minutes later

Palenque M$189 to M$221, seven to eight hours, 485km; four Altos and Colón buses

Playa del Carmen M$116 to M$140, 4½ to six hours, 315km; many buses

Ticul M$123, six hours, 352km; six Mayab buses

Tulum M$94 to M$111, 3½ to four hours, 251km; many buses

Valladolid M$112, six hours, 357km; six Mayab buses

Veracruz M$489, 16 hours, 1037km; two ADO buses

Villahermosa M$259, seven to nine hours, 565km; five ADO buses

Xcalak M$50, five hours, 210km; 2nd-class buses at 4am, 6am and 3:15pm

Xpujil M$47 to M$56, two to three hours, 120km; nine buses between 4:15am and 10:30pm

Getting Around

Taxis from the stand at the bus terminal charge M$9 to M$10 to the center (depending on your destination; agree on the price before getting in, as some will try to charge per person). If you can't get a fair price, walk to the street (Av Insurgentes), turn left (east), and walk a little over a block to the traffic circle at Av de los Héroes to hail a taxi. From here you can also catch the cheapest ride to the center (M$2 per person), in an eastbound ('Santa María' or 'Calderitas') combi. The route will be circuitous. To reach the terminal from the center, head for the combi and taxi stands on Av Belice behind the Museo de la Cultura Maya. If you're traveling by combi, ask to be dropped off at the *glorieta* (traffic circle) at Av Insurgentes. Head left (west) to reach the terminal. You can reach the immigration office via the same combis; it's about 800m north of the *glorieta* (ask for the *'oficina de inmigración'*).

ZONA LIBRE

A bustling free-trade zone sprawling over 24 muddy hectares in a no-man's land between the borders of Belize and Mexico, the Zona Libre draws thousands of Mexicans seeking cheap liquor and cigarettes, knock-off clothing and CDs and other shiny things. Before Christmas time and at other busy shopping periods, up to 18,000 vehicles a day line up to enter the Zone, including charter buses from Mérida and even as far as Mexico City. Two casinos should draw even more people when they open.

East Indian, Chinese, Korean, Vietnamese and other merchants hawk 'Reabox' shoes, 'Sorny' boom-boxes, T-shirts and some genuine-brand goods. About the only real bargains are on liquor and cigarettes, though if you look hard you can sometimes find fair hiking boots, trousers with zip-off legs and the like. Mountain-type bicycles with shocks and gears can be had for as little as M$400. At that price, when it breaks you can just give it away.

Minibuses depart from their terminal in Chetumal at the corner of Avs Primo de Verdad and Hidalgo about every half hour between 6am and 9pm, charging M$8 for the 20-minute trip. If traffic is bad at the border you can get off and walk over the bridge, then turn left; you can't miss it. Walking back you may need to show your passport, but usually officials will just ask where you've been and wave you through.

SOUTH TO BELIZE & GUATEMALA

Corozal, 18km south of the Mexico–Belize border, is a fairly laid-back town and an appropriate introduction to Belize. It has several hotels and restaurants catering to a full range of budgets.

Buses run directly from Chetumal's market to Belize City via Corozal and Orange Walk; all connect with buses to Melchor de Mencos in Guatemala. From there continue onward to Flores, Tikal and other points in Guatemala. There are also buses from Chetumal to Flores (Tikal is an hour beyond Flores). See the Chetumal Getting There & Away section for details.

THE CORREDOR ARQUEOLÓGICO

The Corredor Arqueológico comprises the archaeological sites of **Dzibanché** and **Kohunlich** *(admission M$32; open 8am-5pm daily)*. At the time of research, one admission ticket got you into both. As at most Mayan sites charging an entry fee, the use of a video camera requires you to pay an extra M$30 at the first site visited, which gives you a slip you can use all day, at as many sites as you can reach.

Dzibanché

Though it's a chore to get to, this site is definitely worth a visit for its secluded, semiwild nature and forest setting (plus some cool temples). Dzibanché ('writing on wood') was a major city extending more than 40 sq km, and on the road in you pass huge mounds covered in trees. The site itself is only partially cleared of brush, and contains many trees, some bearing Spanish moss, bromeliads, parasitic cacti or a combination of same. These and the flocks of parrots that fly screeching around the ruins add to the charm; if you're quiet, you may see shy agoutis foraging.

At the time of research, visitors were allowed to climb nearly all the structures; expect this to change when the site is developed further or someone gets killed. The site sees groups of 70 to 80 cruise-ship passengers roll in once a week or more. Get there earlier in the day for a chance to see more wildlife.

The first restored structure you come to is Edificio 6, the Palacio de los Dinteles (Palace of the Lintels), which gave the site its name. This is a perfect spot to orient yourself for the rest of the site: facing the palacio's steps, you are looking east. It's a pyramid topped by a temple with two vaulted galleries; the base dates from the early Classic period (AD 300–600), while the temple is from the late Classic period (AD 600–900). Climb the steps and stand directly under the original lintel on the right (south) side of the temple. Looking up you can see a Mayan calendrical inscription with the date working out to AD 733. This is some old wood.

On descending, head to your left (south) and thread between a mound on the right and a low, mostly restored, stepped structure on the left. This structure is Edificio 16, Palacio de los Tucanes; in the center from the side you approach on are the visible remains of posts that bore a mask. But the threading brings you into Plaza Gann. Circling it counterclockwise takes you past Edificio 14 (stuck onto the north side of a larger building), decorated at the base with 'tamborcillos' (little drums), in late Classic Río Bec style – look up the dirt hill to see them. The larger building to the south is Edifico 13, Templo de los Cautivos, so named for the carvings in its steps of captives submitting to whatever captives submitted to in those days. This seems to be the dominant (if you'll pardon the pun) theme in most Mayan stelae.

On the east side of the plaza is Dzibanché's highest structure, the Templo de los Cormoranes (Cormorants; Edificio 2), whose upper structure has been restored, while the lower part remains covered in greenery. A vaulted passage beckons halfway up, but at last pass it was forbidden to climb the temple.

Exit the plaza by climbing the stone steps to the north of Edificio 2, noting the imposing *copó* tree (source of the fragrant copal incense) on your left growing out of the corner of the Palacio Norte. At the top of the stairs is Plaza del Xibalbá (Plaza of the Underworld) though it's higher than Plaza Gann.

Opposite Palacio Norte is, of course, Palacio Sur, and you can now see more of Edificio 2, but the most notable building is across the plaza: Edificio 1, the Templo del Buho (Temple of the Owl). It had an inner chamber with a stairway leading down to another chamber, in which were found the remains of a Very Important Personage (VIP) and burial offerings. The nearly 360-degree views from the very top of the temple (it's a bit dicey, so be careful) are quite impressive. You can see Grupo Lamay to the west and may spot Kinich-Ná, more than 2km to the northwest.

Kinich-Ná Part of Dzibanché but well removed from the main site, Kinich-Ná consists of one building. But what a building: the megalithic Acrópolis held at least five

temples on three levels, and a couple more dead VIPs with offerings. The site's name derives from the frieze of the Mayan sun god once found at the top of the structure. It's an easy drive of 2km along a narrow but good road leading north from near Dzibanchés visitors center.

Kohunlich

The most accessible of the corridor's ruins has nearly 200 mounds still covered in vegetation. The surrounding jungle is thick, but the archaeological site itself has been cleared selectively and is now a delightful forest park and very compact. Drinks are sometimes sold at the site, and it has toilets.

The ruins, dating from the late pre-Classic (AD 100–200) and the early Classic (AD 250–600) periods, are famous for the great **Templo de los Mascarones** (Temple of the Masks), a pyramid-like structure with a central stairway flanked by huge, 3m-high stucco masks of the sun god. The thick lips and prominent features are reminiscent of Olmec sculpture. Of the eight original masks, only two are relatively intact following the ravages of archaeological looters.

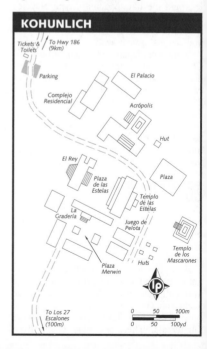

KOHUNLICH

The masks themselves are impressive, but the large thatch coverings that have been erected to protect them from further weathering obscure the view; you can see the masks only from close up. Try to imagine what the pyramid and its masks must have looked like in the old days as the Maya approached it across the sunken courtyard at the front.

A few hundred meters southwest of Plaza Merwin are the **27 Escalones** (27 Steps), the remains of an extensive residential area, with photogenic trees growing out of the steps themselves.

The hydraulic engineering used at Kohunlich was a great achievement; 90,000 of the site's 210,000 sq meters were cut to channel rainwater into Kohunlich's once enormous reservoir.

Getting There & Away

The turnoff for Dzibanché from Hwy 186 is about 50km east of Chetumal. From there it's another 24km north and east along a very pot-holed road. It's quite passable in a passenger car, but slow going at times (this may improve in the future).

Kohunlich's turnoff is 3km west along Hwy 186 from the Dzibanché turnoff, and the site lies at the end of a paved 8.5km road.

At the time of writing, there was no public transportation running directly to either of the sites. They're best visited by car, though Kohunlich could conceivably be reached by taking an early bus to the village of Francisco Villa near the turnoff, then either hitching or walking the 8.5km to the site. To return by bus to Chetumal or head west to Xpujil or Escárcega you must hope to flag down a bus on the highway; not all buses will stop.

Another means is to travel to Xpujil and book a tour from there. For about M$300 per person you can visit Kohunlich and Dzibanché (see Xpujil in the Campeche State chapter).

Yucatán State

The state of Yucatán is a pie slice at the top of the Yucatán Peninsula. Until the development of Cancún in neighboring Quintana Roo, it was the peninsula's economic engine. While Quintana Roo's tourist-driven economy has surpassed Yucatán's in recent years, historically and culturally Yucatán remains paramount. Here you'll find the peninsula's most impressive Mayan ruins (Chichén Itzá and Uxmal), its finest colonial cities (Mérida and Valladolid) and two coastal communities nationally famous for their wild red flamingos.

As a tourist destination, traditional Yucatán complements commercial Quintana Roo extremely well, and travel between the two states is convenient and affordable. A high-speed highway served by numerous 1st-class buses links Cancún and Mérida, and the trip to one of Mexico's oldest cities following a visit to one of its most modern resorts is highly recommended.

Mérida

☎ 999 • pop 690,000

Mérida has been a center of Mayan culture in the Yucatán region since before the conquistadors arrived. Today the Yucatán-state capital is a prosperous city of narrow streets, colonial buildings and shady parks. Every night of the week something's on: folkloric dance and music, theatre, film showings.

There are hotels and restaurants of every class and price range and good transportation services to any part of the peninsula and the country, and the city makes a good base for numerous excursions around the region.

Mérida's drawbacks are traffic, pollution and heat. Noisy buses pump clouds of noxious fumes into the air, and the region's high temperatures seem even higher here, where buildings catch and hold the heat. These factors and the crowded, narrow sidewalks have prompted calls to ban buses from the colonial center, a move that would enhance the city's already considerable charm.

HISTORY

Francisco de Montejo the Younger founded a Spanish colony at Campeche, about 160km

Highlights

- Mérida, a city of opulent architecture and abundant cultural events
- Chichén Itzá, the great Maya-Toltec ceremonial center
- Río Lagartos, home to Mexico's largest flamingo colony
- Uxmal and the Ruta Puuc's fascinating variety of Mayan sites
- The Grutas de Calcehtok, a vast and little-known cave system

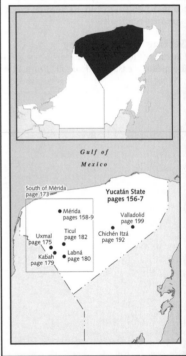

to the south, in 1540. From this base he took advantage of political dissension among the Maya, conquering T'hó (now Mérida) in 1542. By the end of the decade, Yucatán was mostly under Spanish colonial rule.

When Montejo's conquistadors entered T'hó, they found a major Mayan settlement of lime-mortared stone that reminded them of Roman architectural legacies in Mérida, Spain. They promptly renamed the city and proceeded to build it into the regional colonial capital, dismantling the Mayan structures and using the materials to construct a cathedral and other stately buildings. Mérida took its colonial orders directly from Spain, not from Mexico City, and Yucatán has had a distinct cultural and political identity ever since.

During the War of the Castes, only Mérida and Campeche were able to hold out against the rebel forces. On the brink of surrender, the ruling class in Mérida was saved by reinforcements sent from central Mexico in exchange for Mérida's agreement to take orders from Mexico City. Although Yucatán is certainly part of Mexico, there is still a strong feeling in Mérida and other parts of the state that the local people stand a breed apart.

Mérida today is the peninsula's center of commerce, a bustling city that has benefited greatly from the maquiladoras that opened in the 1980s and 1990s and the tourism that picked up during those decades.

ORIENTATION

The Plaza Grande, as *meridanos* call the main square, has been the city's heart since Mayan times. Though Mérida now sprawls several kilometers in all directions, most of the services and attractions for visitors are within five blocks of the Plaza Grande. Following the classic colonial plan, the square, holding the cathedral and seats of government, is ringed by several barrios (neighborhoods). Each barrio has its park and church (side by side), usually bearing the same name: Iglesia de Santiago is next to Parque de Santiago in Barrio de Santiago. Locals orient themselves and often give directions referring to the barrios.

Odd-numbered streets run east–west, and their numbers increase by increments of two going from north to south (eg, Calle 61 is one block north of Calle 63); even-numbered streets run north–south, and increase by two from east to west. House numbers may increase very slowly, and addresses are usually given in this form: 'Calle 57 No 481 x 56 y 58' (between Calles 56 and 58).

From 8pm Saturday to 11pm Sunday, Calles 60 and 62 are closed to motor vehicles between Plaza Grande and Calle 55.

INFORMATION
Tourist Offices

The **tourist information booths** at the airport and the main bus terminal, Terminal CAME, are not of much use beyond supplying some coupons for lodging discounts. Three tourist offices downtown have more current information, brochures and maps.

The **city tourist office** (☎ 928-2020 ext 833; Calle 62 on Plaza Grande; open 8am-8pm daily), just south of the main entrance to the Palacio Municipal, is staffed with helpful English speakers who provide probably the best city information of the three, and can give hotel and shopping recommendations.

The **state tourist office** (☎ 930-3101; Calle 61 on Plaza Grande; open 8am-9pm daily) is in the entrance to the Palacio de Gobierno. It usually has an English speaker on hand and provides city and state information.

Less than two blocks north, on the southwest edge of the Teatro Peón Contreras, is an **information office** (☎ 924-9290; cnr Calles 60 & 57A; open 8am-8pm daily) used for training tourism students. The verbal information is so-so, but it has a good supply of brochures, maps of downtown Mérida and the peninsula, and a list of hotels. There's always an English-speaker on hand, and sometimes a speaker of Italian or French.

Money

Casas de cambio (exchange houses) offer faster service and longer hours than banks, but often with poorer rates. Try **Money Marketing** (Parque Hidalgo), in the Gran Hotel; a nameless money exchange just south of the cathedral; **Cambistas Peninsulares** (Calle 60 between Calles 55 & 57); or **Central Cambiaria** (Calle 65 between Calles 62 & 60).

Banks and ATMs are scattered throughout the city. There is a cluster of both along Calle 65 between Calles 60 and 62, one block south of the Plaza Grande. Most are open 9am to 4pm Monday to Friday, and some are also open 9am to 1pm or 2pm Saturday. See the Mérida map for other locations.

Post & Communications

At the time of research, the **main post office** (☎ 921-2561; Calle 65 between Calles 56 & 56A; open 9am-4pm Mon-Fri, for stamps only 9am-1pm Sat) was just north of the market, but if plans to redo the market area proceed, it will become a museum. There

YUCATÁN STATE

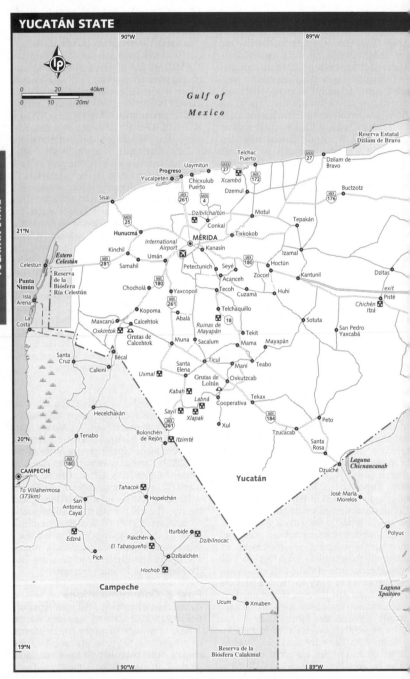

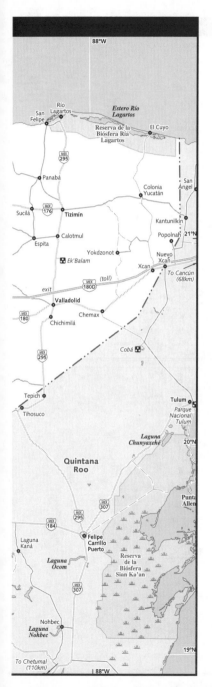

are **postal service booths** *(open Mon-Fri)* at the airport and bus terminal.

Card phones can be found throughout the city. Most Internet places around town charge M$15 per hour and allow use in smaller increments of time. The following have good connections and air-con. **Cybernet** *(Calle 57A between Calles 58 & 60; open 9am-9pm Mon-Sat)* has several terminals and is conveniently located. **Cibercafé Santa Lucí@** *(cnr Calles 62 & 55; open 8am-11pm daily)* has free coffee while you surf, and various pastries and snacks (including microwave popcorn) for sale. **La Net@** *(cnr Calles 58 & 57; open Mon-Sat)* is upstairs and keeps somewhat irregular hours.

Travel Agencies

It's out of the way in the north of town, but **Nómadas Travel** *(☎ 948-1187; ⓦ www.nomadastravel.com.mx; Prolongación Paseo de Montejo No 370, Colonia Benito Juárez Norte)* books flights, selling both SATA (student discount) and IATA (regular) tickets. You can also make itinerary changes and buy the ISIC (international student identity card) and ITIC (for teachers), and get help with ISIS (student insurance) matters.

Bookstores

Librería Dante *(☎ 928-3674; Calle 59 between Calles 60 & 62; open 8am-9:30pm Mon-Sat)* has a small selection of paperbacks in English, as well as some guidebooks, and a large selection of archaeology books in English, French, German and Spanish. The company has other stores throughout the city. **Arte Maya** *(Calle 57 between Calles 62 & 60; open 9am-9pm daily)* has stacks of used books in several languages, predominantly paperbacks in English. Most are M$30, or you can trade two for one, or one plus M$10 for one.

Laundry

Lavandería La Fe *(☎ 924-4531; Calle 64 between Calles 55 & 57; open 8am-6pm Mon-Fri, 8am-2pm Sat)* charges M$40 per 3kg load (less for smaller loads) to wash and dry. You also can drop off your clothing at **Lavandería Flamingo** *(Calle 57 between Calles 56 & 58; open 8am-5pm Mon-Fri, 8am-3pm Sat & Sun)* and pick it up in the late afternoon. It charges per item (eg, M$3 for a T-shirt, M$1 for each undergarment or

MÉRIDA

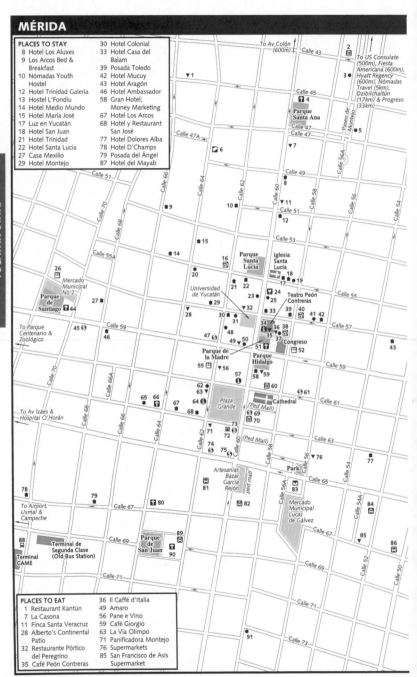

PLACES TO STAY
8 Hotel Los Aluxes
9 Los Arcos Bed & Breakfast
10 Nómadas Youth Hostel
12 Hotel Trinidad Galería
13 Hostel L'Fondiu
14 Hotel Medio Mundo
15 Hotel María José
17 Luz en Yucatán
18 Hotel San Juan
21 Hotel Trinidad
22 Hotel Santa Lucía
27 Casa Mexilio
29 Hotel Montejo
30 Hotel Colonial
33 Hotel Casa del Balam
39 Posada Toledo
42 Hotel Mucuy
43 Hotel Aragón
46 Hotel Ambassador
58 Gran Hotel; Money Marketing
67 Hotel Los Arcos
68 Hotel y Restaurant San José
77 Hotel Dolores Alba
78 Hotel D'Champs
79 Posada del Ángel
87 Hotel del Mayab

PLACES TO EAT
1 Restaurant Kantún
7 La Casona
11 Finca Santa Veracruz
28 Alberto's Continental Patio
32 Restaurante Pórtico del Peregrino
35 Café Peón Contreras
36 Il Caffé d'Italia
49 Amaro
56 Pane e Vino
59 Café Giorgio
63 La Vía Olimpo
71 Panificadora Montejo
76 Supermarkets
85 San Francisco de Asís Supermarket

OTHER
2 Museo Regional de
   Antropología (Palacio
   Cantón)
3 Mexicana
4 Iglesia de Santa Ana
5 Aerocaribe
6 Consulate of Netherlands
16 Cibercafé Santa Luci@
19 Turitransmérida
20 Lavandería La Fe
23 Budget Car Rental
24 El Establo; Other Bars
25 Hertz & National Car
   Rental Offices; Cambistas
   Peninsulares
26 Cines Rex
31 Arte Maya
34 Tourist Information Center
37 México Rent A Car
38 Cybernet
40 La Net@
41 Lavandería Flamingo
44 Iglesia de Santiago
45 Bital (ATM)
47 BBVA ATM
48 Camisería Canul
50 Miniaturas; Librería Dante
51 Iglesia de Jesús
52 Plaza Cine Internacional;
   Supersónicos Internet
53 Iglesia La Mejorada
54 Museo Nacional de Arte
   Popular
55 Teatro Mérida
57 State Tourist Office;
   Palacio de Gobierno
60 Museo de la Ciudad
61 BBVA Bancapromex (ATM)
62 Centro Cultural Olimpo
64 Palacio Municipal; City
   Tourist Office
65 Casa de las Artesanías
66 Iglesia de Monjas
69 Money Exchange
70 Museo de Arte
   Contemporáneo Ateneo
   de Yucatán (Macay)
72 Casa de Montejo
   (Banamex)
73 Bancrecer ATM
74 Central Cambiaria
75 Bital (Money Exchange,
   ATM)
80 Iglesia Nuestra Señora de
   la Candelaria
81 Progreso Bus Terminal
82 Shared Taxis to Progreso
83 Main Post Office
84 Shared Taxis to Tizimín
86 Noreste Bus Terminal
88 Airport Bus Stop
89 Shared Taxis to
   Dzibilchaltún
90 Iglesia de San Juan
91 Hamacas El Aguacate

a pair of socks), which works out to be very inexpensive, especially for smaller loads.

Most hotels in the mid-range category and above offer overnight laundry service.

Medical Services

The largest hospital in Mérida is **Hospital O'Horán** (☎ 924-4800; Av de los Itzáes), near the Parque Zoológico Centenario. For most treatments (including prescriptions and consultations) you're best off going to a private clinic. Ask at your consulate or hotel for a recommendation. In an emergency, call the **Cruz Roja** (Red Cross; ☎ 924-9813).

Dangers & Annoyances

Guard against pickpockets, bag-snatchers and bag-slashers in the market district and in any crowd. Buses drive fast along the narrow streets and don't slow down for anything; sidewalks are often narrow and crowded. Touts in Mérida have some of the least polished come-ons you'll encounter on the peninsula. One line often used on foreigners of height is 'you're so tall.' Some touts will angle up to you like a coyote trying to separate a lamb from the flock, physically blocking your path, and if spurned, spouting vague threats. Report the more obnoxious ones to Mérida's **Policía Turística** (Tourist Police; ☎ 925-2555 ext 260), who wear brown-and-white uniforms; during the day you can almost always find an officer at the Palacio de Gobierno or elsewhere on the Plaza Grande.

PLAZA GRANDE

This large but at times surprisingly intimate square is the most logical place to start a tour of Mérida. Also known as 'El Centro' (as in the center of town) or the Plaza Principal, the Plaza Grande was the religious and social center of ancient T'hó; under the Spanish it was the Plaza de Armas, the parade ground, laid out by Francisco de Montejo the Younger. The plaza is surrounded by some of the city's most impressive colonial buildings, and its carefully tended laurel trees provide welcome shade. On Sunday hundreds of *meridanos* take their *paseo* (stroll) here. Various events take place around the plaza on weekly schedules.

Cathedral

On the plaza's east side, on the former site of a Mayan temple, is Mérida's hulking, severe

YUCATÁN STATE

cathedral *(open 6am-noon & 4pm-7pm daily)*, begun in 1561 and completed in 1598. Some of the stone from the Mayan temple was used in its construction. The massive crucifix behind the altar is **Cristo de la Unidad** (Christ of Unity), a symbol of reconciliation between those of Spanish and Maya heritage. To the right over the south door is a painting of Tutul Xiú, cacique of the town of Maní, paying his respects to his ally Francisco de Montejo at T'hó (de Montejo and Xiú jointly defeated the Cocomes; Xiú converted to Christianity, and his descendants still live in Mérida).

In the small chapel to the left of the altar is Mérida's most famous religious artifact, a statue called **Cristo de las Ampollas** (Christ of the Blisters). Local legend says the statue was carved from a tree that was hit by lightning and burned for an entire night without charring. It is also said to be the only object to have survived the fiery destruction of the church in the town of Ichmul (though it was blackened and blistered from the heat). The statue was moved to the Mérida cathedral in 1645.

Other than these, the cathedral's interior is largely plain, its rich decoration having been stripped away by angry peasants at the height of anticlerical feeling during the Mexican Revolution.

Around the Cathedral

South of the cathedral, housed in the former archbishop's palace, is the **Museo de Arte Contemporáneo Ateneo de Yucatán** *(Macay; ☎ 928-3236; Calle 60 between Calles 61 & 63; admission M$20, free Sun; open 10am-5:30pm Wed-Mon)*. This attractive museum holds permanent exhibits of Yucatán's most famous painters and sculptors, changing exhibits of local arts and crafts, and a cafeteria. In December 2002 the museum held its first *bienal* (biennial exhibition), which attracted top-quality entries from all over the state and the republic. When will the next one happen? Well, let's see…

The **Casa de Montejo** *(Palacio de Montejo; open 9am-4pm Mon-Fri, 10am-2pm Sat)* is on the south side of the Plaza Grande and dates from 1549. It originally housed soldiers but was soon converted into a mansion that served members of the Montejo family until 1970. These days it shelters a bank, and you can enter and look around during bank hours. At other times, content yourself with a close look at the facade, where triumphant conquistadors with halberds hold their feet on the necks of generic barbarians (though they're not Maya, the association is inescapable). Typical of the symbolism in colonial statuary, the vanquished are rendered much smaller than the victors; works on various churches throughout the region feature big priests towering over or in front of little Indians. Also gazing across the plaza from the facade are busts of Montejo the Elder, his wife and his daughter.

Across the square from the cathedral is Mérida's **Palacio Municipal** (City Hall). Originally built in 1542, it was twice refurbished, in the 1730s and the 1850s. Adjoining it is the **Olimpo**, Mérida's municipal cultural center. Attempts to create a modern exterior for the building were halted by government order, to preserve the colonial character of the plaza. The ultramodern interior serves as a venue for music and dance performances as well as other exhibitions. Schedules for performances and frequent film showings are posted outside.

On the north side of the plaza, the **Palacio de Gobierno** *(admission free; open 8am-9pm daily)* houses the state of Yucatán's executive government offices (and one of its tourist information offices). It was built in 1892 on the site of the palace of the colonial governors. Be sure to have a look inside at the **murals** painted by local artist Fernando Castro Pacheco. Completed in 1978, they were 25 years in the making and portray a symbolic history of the Maya and their interaction with the Spaniards.

MUSEO DE LA CIUDAD

The city museum *(☎ 923-6869; Calle 61 between Calles 58 & 60; admission free; open 10am-2pm & 4pm-8pm Tues-Fri, 10am-2pm Sat & Sun)* is small but very worthwhile, with artifacts, exhibits and good photos of the city and region. Signs in English explain such subjects as Mayan traditions, history and the process of henequen production (for further information on henequen, see the boxed text 'Henequen: A Smelly, Bitter Harvest' later in this chapter).

CALLE 60

A block north of the Plaza Grande, beyond shady Parque Hidalgo, rises the 17th-century **Iglesia de Jesús**, also called Iglesia de la Ter-

Peeling a mango, Mérida

Grilling *costillas* (ribs), Cozumel

Selling traditional woven rugs, Tulum

Pirates' grave, Dzilam de Bravo

Produce market, Oxkutzcab

Horse-drawn cart, Izamal

cera Orden. Built by the Jesuits in 1618, it is the sole surviving edifice from a complex of buildings that once filled the entire city block.

North of the church is the enormous bulk of the **Teatro Peón Contreras** *(cnr Calles 60 & 57; open to visitors 9pm-6pm Tues-Sat)*, built between 1900 and 1908, during Mérida's henequen heyday. It boasts a main staircase of Carrara marble, a dome with faded frescoes by Italian artists and various paintings and murals throughout the building.

Across Calle 60 from the theater is the main building of the **Universidad de Yucatán**. The modern university was established in the 19th century by Governor Felipe Carrillo Puerto and General Manuel Cepeda Peraza.

A block north of the university is pretty little **Parque Santa Lucía** *(cnr Calles 60 & 55)*, with arcades on the north and west sides. When Mérida was a lot smaller, this was where travelers would get on or off the stagecoaches that linked towns and villages with the provincial capital. The **Bazar de Artesanías**, the local handicrafts market, is held here at 11am on Sunday.

To reach the Paseo de Montejo (see the following section), walk four blocks north and two east.

PASEO DE MONTEJO

The Paseo de Montejo was an attempt by Mérida's 19th-century city planners to create a wide boulevard similar to the Paseo de la Reforma in Mexico City or the Champs Élysées in Paris. Though more modest than its predecessors, the Paseo de Montejo is still a beautiful swath of green, relatively open space in an urban conglomeration of stone and concrete.

Europe's architectural and social influence can be seen along the paseo in the fine mansions built by wealthy families around the end of the 19th century. The greatest concentrations of surviving mansions are north of Calle 37, which is three blocks north of the Museo Regional de Antropología, and on the first block of Av Colón west of Paseo de Montejo.

MUSEO REGIONAL DE ANTROPOLOGÍA

The great white Palacio Cantón houses the Regional Anthropology Museum of the Yucatán *(☎ 923-0557; cnr Paseo de Montejo &*

Calle 43; admission M$32; open 8am-8pm Tues-Sat, 8am-2pm Sun). Construction of the mansion lasted from 1909 to 1911, and its owner, General Francisco Cantón Rosado (1833–1917), lived here for only six years before his death. The palacio's splendor and pretension make it a fitting symbol of the grand aspirations of Mérida's elite during the last years of the porfiriato, the period from 1876 to 1911 when Porfirio Díaz held despotic sway over Mexico.

Signs o' the Times

Visitors to Mérida will notice small, artistic plaques on the corners of some buildings beside major intersections. The brown-on-white ceramic plaques are located about 3m above the sidewalk – about where you'd expect to see a street sign if signposts weren't used.

Indeed, the plaques, which feature paintings of people, animals and other subjects with their Spanish names underneath, are old-fashioned Mérida street signs. For example, on the building housing a Burger King (Calle 59 at Calle 60), you'll see a painted figure of a dog and, just below it, the words *el perro* (the dog).

Signs like this one were placed on corner buildings during colonial days by conquistadors trying to teach the native populace some Spanish. The signs reflected the streets' local names. Unfortunately, all of the original plaques disappeared over time; the several dozen you see today were affixed to buildings relatively recently by city officials hoping to increase tourism and maintain a piece of history. Although new, the plaques are said to closely resemble the originals, and their locations are supposedly historically accurate.

A sign on the corner of Calles 65 and 60, for example, shows an old lady. The sign was posted at that particular location because local people knew the street as 'the old lady's street' on account of an elderly woman who had once worked in a bakery near the corner.

Likewise, the 'two faces' sign found at the intersection of Calles 65 and 58 has its origin in a liar who lived nearby. The 'headless man' street (look for the sign on Calle 67 at Calle 60) took its name from a man who had the misfortune of being under a window when it broke and was beheaded by a falling piece of glass.

The museum covers the peninsula's history since the age of mastodons. Exhibits on Mayan culture include explanations (many in Spanish only) of such cosmetic practices as forehead-flattening (done to beautify babies) causing eyes to cross and sharpening teeth and implanting them with tiny jewels. If you plan to visit archaeological sites near Mérida, you can study the exhibits here – some with plans and photographs – covering the great Mayan cities of Mayapán, Uxmal and Chichén Itzá, as well as lesser-known sites such as the marvelous Ek' Balam. There's also a good bookstore with many archaeological titles.

PARQUE CENTENARIO

About 12 blocks west of the Plaza Grande lies the large, verdant Parque Centenario *(admission free; open 6am-6pm Tues-Sun)*, bordered by Av de los Itzáes, which leads to the airport and becomes the highway to Campeche. The park's **zoo** *(admission free; open 8am-5pm Tues-Sun)* features the fauna of Yucatán, as well as some exotic species. To get there, take a bus west along Calle 61 or 65.

MUSEO NACIONAL DE ARTE POPULAR

The National Museum of Popular Art *(Calle 59 between Calles 48 & 50; admission M$10; open 9am-5pm Tues-Sat)* is six blocks northeast of the Plaza Grande and holds displays of the best of local arts and crafts. It will satisfy your curiosity about the embroidering of colorful *huipiles* (woven dresses), carving of ceremonial masks, weaving of hammocks and hats, turning of pottery and construction of musical instruments.

Next door to the museum is **Iglesia La Mejorada**, a large 17th-century church. The building just north of it was a monastery (el Convento de La Mejorada) until the late 19th century. It now houses an architectural school, but visitors are sometimes allowed to view the grounds.

ORGANIZED TOURS

The **city tourist office** *(☎ 928-2020 ext 833; Calle 62 on Plaza Grande)* offers free daily guided walking tours of the historic center, concentrating on the Plaza Grande. They depart at 9:30am from in front of the Palacio Municipal.

Transportadora Turística Carnaval *(☎ 927-6119)* conducts two-hour guided tours of Mérida in English on its Paseo Turístico bus (M$75) departing from Parque Santa Lucía (on the corner of Calles 55 and 60) at 10am, 1pm, 4pm and 7pm Monday to Saturday, and 10am and 1pm Sunday. Seating capacity is 30 people. You can buy your tickets ahead of time at the nearby Hotel Santa Lucía, among other places.

Turitransmérida *(☎/fax 924-1199; W www .turitransmerida.com.mx; cnr Calles 55 & 58)* is one of the largest of the many agencies offering group tours to sites around Mérida. Some of their offerings include Celestún with flamingo tour (M$440), Chichén Itzá (M$330; with drop-off in Cancún M$440), Uxmal and Kabah (M$330), Uxmal sound-and-light show (M$330), Ruta Puuc (Puuc Route, M$300) and Izamal (M$300). All prices are per person and most include transportation, guide and lunch.

Many hotels will book these tours, as will **Nómadas Youth Hostel** *(☎/fax 924-5223; e nomadas1@prodigy.net.mx; Calle 62 No 433)*, which also arranges a variety of other tours, from do-it-yourself trips in your rented car or on public transportation (with written instructions) to nearly all-inclusive (some meals) trips in private buses. Many include lodging at other hostels as well as insurance. Nómadas will help to match up travelers into groups for sharing cars and such. It also does an interesting excursion to cenotes on the grounds of an old henequen estate in Cuzamá that involves a ride on a horse-drawn cart on rails.

SPECIAL EVENTS

For most of February the Universidad de Yucatán celebrates its anniversary with free performances by the Ballet Folklórico, concerts of Afro-Cuban music and *son* (Mexican folk music that blends elements of indigenous, Spanish and African musical styles) and other manifestations of Yucatán's cultural roots.

Prior to Lent, in February or March, Carnaval features colorful costumes and nonstop festivities. It is celebrated with greater vigor in Mérida than anywhere else in Yucatán state. Also during the last days of February or the beginning of March (the dates vary) is Ki-huic, a market that fills the Plaza Grande with handicraft artisans from all over Mexico.

Between September 22 and October 14, *gremios* (guilds or unions) venerate the Cristo de las Ampollas (Christ of the Blisters) statue in the cathedral with processions.

Another big religious tradition is the Exposición de Altares de los Muertos held on the night of November 1. Throughout Mexico families prepare shrines to welcome the spirits of loved ones back onto the earth. Many Maya prepare elaborate dinners outside their homes, and Mérida observes the occasion with festivities and displays in the center of town from 11am on November 1 until 11am the next day.

PLACES TO STAY

At the time of research, many of Mérida's hotels had reversed their inflationary trends in the face of decreased tourism and were offering true bargains on quality accommodations. From about December 15 to January 6, and during Easter week, many mid-range and top-end hotels raise prices by 10% to 20%. These times and July and August (which also see price increases at some places) tend to be the busiest; it's wise to book ahead. Rates quoted in the following listings are for the low season.

When business is slow many places will discount, some without being asked (it never hurts to ask for a *descuento* if they don't, but don't be cruel). If you're arriving at the CAME (1st-class) bus terminal, check at the tourism desk for flyers offering hotel discounts.

Budget

Rooms in this category have fans unless otherwise noted; spending the extra money for air-conditioning is worth it in the hotter months.

Nómadas Youth Hostel (☎/fax 924-5223, ☎ 800-800-2625; ☒ www.hostels.com.mx; Calle 62 No 433 at Calle 51; hammocks with mosquito net or tents with air mattress M$48, dorm beds with/without HI card or ISIC M$63/68, singles/doubles with shared bathroom M$120/145, with private bathroom M$160/195; triples/quads with private bathroom M$250/280) has a total of 46 beds in mixed and women's dorms and six private rooms. All rates include breakfast, and guests have use of a full kitchen with fridge and purified water, 24-hour hot showers and hand-laundry facilities. Basic foods are provided on an honor system, as is good Internet access. Luggage lockers are free while you stay, M$10 a day while you travel. Bring mosquito repellent and earplugs, as the front rooms can get traffic noise.

Hotel y Restaurant San José (☎ 928-6657; Calle 63 between Calles 62 & 64; singles/doubles/triples/quads with shared bathroom M$85/100/110/120, with private bathroom M$100/120/140/160) is about 30m west of the southwest edge of the Plaza Grande. It has 30 clean, good-sized rooms, set well off the street. The doubles with good private bathrooms have two decent beds. The place offers value and is a favorite with visiting Mennonites.

Hotel Los Arcos (☎ 924-9728; Calle 63 between Calles 62 & 64; singles/doubles/triples M$120/140/160), just down the street from the Hotel y Restaurant San José, offers secure on-site parking, and fairly quiet rooms with OK bathrooms and beds, good screens and nice decor for the price. The friendly management supplies free morning coffee.

Hotel del Mayab (☎ 928-5174, fax 928-6047; Calle 50 No 536A between Calles 65 & 67; doubles/triples/quads with fan M$150/175/200, with air-con & TV M$235/270/305), not far from the Noreste bus terminal, is clean and low-key. Streetside rooms can be noisy, but interior rooms are quiet, and the hotel has a swimming pool.

Hostel L'Fondiu (☎/fax 924-0005; ☒ www.lfondiu.8m.com; Calle 52 between Calles 53 & 51; doubles M$170), a little gem of a place, had four rooms at the time of research, and the owner had plans to build more, as well as a pool and bar. The light, airy rooms are on two floors at the back of the garden, and have tile floors, screen doors and hammocks (in addition to the regular doors and beds), and an unusual setup of toilet, shower and sink all surrounded by a shower stall. The owner catches rainwater in a cistern, irrigates the garden with gray water and has tanks underground in which the hostel's sewage is processed. Guests can use laundry facilities and the restaurant serves very inexpensive food.

Hotel Mucuy (☎ 928-5193, fax 923-7801; Calle 57 No 481 between Calles 56 & 58; singles/doubles/triples M$180/200/220) has 24 tidy rooms on two floors facing a long, narrow garden courtyard and comes recommended. The señora and her daughter speak English and French as well as Spanish.

Posada del Ángel (☎ 923-2754; *Calle 67 No 535 between Calles 66 & 68; singles/ doubles/triples/quads with fan M$160/230/ 300, with air-con M$220/300/380/460)* is a 30-room, neocolonial hotel three blocks northeast of Terminal CAME. Rooms have good beds and it's quieter here than at most other hotels in the area.

Hotel Aragón (☎ 924-0242, fax 924-1122; ⓦ *www.hotelaragon.com; Calle 57 No 474 between Calles 52 & 54; 1-/2-bed doubles M$240/300)* offers 18 very clean air-con rooms on three floors overlooking a charming little courtyard. Room rates include a continental breakfast and purified water; tea and coffee are available free 24 hours.

Hotel Trinidad Galería (☎ 923-2463, fax 924-2319; ⓦ *www.hoteltrinidadgaleria.com; Calle 60 No 456 near Calle 51; singles/doubles M$200/225)* began as a grand home, did a spell as an appliance showroom, and is now a 'post-modern museum hotel,' filled with wild pieces done in various mediums. It has a bar, a swimming pool, an art gallery and a courtyard that when we visited had lost its enormously shady tree to Hurricane Isidore but was showing signs of recovery. Both the public areas and the presentable, fan-cooled rooms offer up a multitude of visual delights.

Hotel Montejo (☎ 928-0390, fax 928-0277; ⓦ *www.hotelmontejo.com; Calle 57 between Calles 62 & 64; singles/doubles M$200/265, with air-con M$255/265)* has a central courtyard loaded with 400-year-old stone columns. Big, clean rooms with classic colonial doors and tiled bathrooms are distributed around it on two floors. The Montejo's bar–restaurant serves Yucatecan and continental dishes.

Hotel Dolores Alba (☎ 928-5650, 800-849-5060, fax 928-3163; ⓦ *www.dolores alba.com; Calle 63 between Calles 52 & 54; doubles M$270-380, triples/quads M$440/ 480)* is a longtime Mérida institution. Rooms have air-con and are on three floors (with an elevator) around two large courtyards. Those in the new, modern wing are quite large, have good beds and TVs and face the lovely, chlorine-free pool. The hotel has secure parking and is quiet, well managed and friendly (no credit cards).

Posada Toledo (☎/fax 923-2256, ☎ 923-1690; ⓔ *hptoledo@pibil.finred.com.mx; Calle*

58 *No 487 at Calle 57; doubles with fan/air-con M$280/327)* is a colonial mansion offering free parking, small, somewhat modernized rooms arranged on two floors around the classic courtyard, and a dining room (breakfast only) straight out of the 19th century. The newer, upstairs rooms are larger than the ground-floor rooms.

Hotel Trinidad (☎ 924-9806, fax 924-1122; ⓦ *www.hoteltrinidad.com; Calle 62 No 464 between Calles 55 & 57; dorm beds with/without HI card or ISIC M$60/75, doubles with shared/private bathroom M$230/290)* occupies a colonial house and a newer wing, and has a variety of rooms, each with its own unique decor and charm. Some have good kitchenettes, most have air-con, and one of the four-bed dorms in the colonial wing has its own bathroom. The Trini has great common areas (including two courtyards, one with a lovely garden), a book exchange, a small café, luggage storage, 24-hour tea, and guests have use of the pool at the nearby Hotel Trinidad Galería. All rates include continental breakfast.

Hotel Santa Lucía (☎/fax 928-2672, ☎ 928-2662; *Calle 55 No 508 between Calles 60 & 62; singles/doubles/triples M$320/350/410),* across from the park of the same name, is clean, secure and popular. It has a smallish pool and 51 air-con rooms with TV and telephone.

Hotel María José (☎ 928-7037; ⓦ *www .hotelmariajose.com.mx; Calle 64 between Calles 53 & 55; doubles M$350)* is a modern, clean place in an old, recently refurbished building. The 18 cheery air-con rooms have decent beds and good bathrooms, and the hotel's restaurant serves three meals.

Hotel San Juan (☎/fax 924-17-42; *Calle 55 No 497A; singles/doubles/triples/quads M$327/375/425/446),* near Calle 58, offers a pool, parking and 63 very clean, relatively quiet and roomy units with phone, TV, and aging air-con.

Mid-Range

Compared with many parts of the peninsula, many of Mérida's mid-range places provide surprising levels of comfort for the price.

Luz en Yucatán (☎ 924-0035; ⓦ *www .luzenyucatan.com; Calle 55 between Calles 58 & 60; apartments M$250-500)* gets high marks from several readers. It has a welcoming and homey atmosphere, with abundant local Mexican art and crafts. Furnishings are attractive and comfortable, and hammocks hang in the rooms and garden. The seven apartments rent by the day, week or month; larger ones have air-con. Five apartments have full kitchenettes; guests in the other two share a separate kitchen, and all have use of the small pool and some excellent common spaces, including the large dining room downstairs. Rates vary seasonally and are discounted for longer stays; the large units are M$400 for much of the year. Luz also offers massage, facials, manicures, pedicures, and classes in Spanish language, salsa dancing and yoga.

Hotel Medio Mundo (☎/fax 924-5472; W www.hotelmediomundo.com; Calle 55 No 533 between Calles 64 & 66; doubles with fan US$35-40, with air-con US$50; triples/quads with fan US$47/54, with air-con US$57/64) is another highly recommended place. The former private residence has been completely remodeled and painted in lovely colors. Its 10 ample, simply furnished rooms have super-comfortable beds (one king or two queens), tile floors, beautiful sinks, great bathrooms and plenty of natural light. One of the two courtyards has a small swimming pool, the other a fountain. The well-traveled, charming hosts prepare large, delicious breakfasts (US$7) and make their guests feel like part of the family.

Gran Hotel (☎ 924-7730, fax 924-7622; W www.granhoteldemerida.com.mx; Calle 60 No 496 between Calles 59 & 61; singles/doubles M$510/560, triples & quads M$760) was indeed a grand hotel when built in 1901; it's a bit faded now but retains many elegant and delightful decorative flourishes. The 28 air-con rooms have period furnishings; some of them overlook Parque Hidalgo.

Hotel D'Champs (☎ 924-8655, 800-849-0934, fax 923-6024; Calle 70 No 543 at Calle 67; doubles M$585), just a block from the two main bus terminals, is in a classy old building with a modernized interior. It has a massive open courtyard with a pool and trees, a restaurant and 90 decent-sized rooms with TV, air-con and phones.

Casa Mexilio (☎/fax 928-2505, in USA ☎ 800-538-6802; e casamexilio@prodigy .net.mx; Calle 68 No 495 between Calles 57 & 59; rooms M$430-830) is a charming

small hotel. It occupies a well-preserved, historical house with a maze of quiet, beautifully appointed rooms (some with fan, some air-con), a small bar and a compact pool with Jacuzzi. All room rates include a good breakfast in the period dining room, and the hotel serves dinner as well.

Hotel Colonial (☎ 923-6444, fax 928-3961, in USA ☎ 888-886-2982; W www .hotelcolonial.com.mx; Calle 62 No 476 between Calles 57 & 59; doubles/triples M$617/730) features 73 comfortable air-con rooms in a fairly modern building with a small pool.

Los Arcos Bed & Breakfast (☎ 928-0214; W www.losarcosmerida.com; Calle 66 between Calles 49 & 53; 1-/2-bed doubles US$65/85) is a lovely, gay-friendly B&B with two guestrooms at the end of a drop-dead-gorgeous garden and pool area. The rooms are decorated with an eclectic assortment of art and antiques, have excellent beds and bathrooms, and come stocked with CD players, bathrobes and sarongs. The American owners are very accommodating and have filled the elegant main house with an incredible collection of antiques and objets d'art from various corners of the globe. They rent a third room there, with canopy bed, for US$65, and give all guests access to the Internet and a huge CD library. Room rates include breakfast.

Hotel Ambassador (☎ 924-2100, fax 924-2701; W www.ambassadormerida.com; Calle 59 No 546; doubles/triples/suites M$770/840/960), near Calle 68, offers 100 comfortable, modern rooms with satellite TV and minibars. The multistory building also has a pool, a pleasant courtyard and a travel agency and car-rental outfit. Try asking for a discount.

Top End

If you reserve a top-end room through your travel agent at home, you're likely to pay international-class rates. But if you walk in and ask about *promociones* (promotional rates) or – even better – look through local newspapers and handouts for special rates aimed at a local clientele, you can often lower your lodging bill substantially.

Hotel Los Aluxes (☎ 924-2199, 800-712-0444, fax 923-3858; W www.aluxes.com.mx; cnr Calles 60 & 49; doubles US$100) is a very modern and comfortable hotel with 109

YUCATÁN STATE

rooms, parking, a pool, restaurant and nightclub; it's popular with tour groups.

Hotel Casa del Balam *(☎ 924-2150, fax 924-5011, in USA or Mexico ☎ 800-624-845;* Ⓦ *www.yucatanadventure.com.mx; Calle 60 No 488; doubles M$1185)*, near Calle 57, is wearing at the edges a bit, but it's centrally located and has a great pool and large, quiet rooms with powerful central air-con. The Balam often offers hefty discounts during quiet times.

Fiesta Americana Mérida *(☎ 942-1111, 800-504-500, fax 942-1112, in USA ☎ 800-343-7821;* Ⓔ *ventasmd@fiestaamericana.com.mx; Calle 56A No 451; doubles from M$1630)*, an enormous, modern neocolonial hotel, boasts luxurious, marble-floored rooms with safes, coffeemakers, hairdryers and minibars. Also on offer are a gym, tennis court and spa, and a complex below the hotel houses shops, travel agencies, airline offices and restaurants. Though the official address doesn't indicate it, the hotel occupies a large stretch of Av Colón just off swanky Paseo de Montejo north of the colonial center.

Hyatt Regency Mérida *(☎ 942-0202, fax 925-7002;* Ⓦ *www.hyatt.com; Av Colón 344; doubles from M$1660)* is not far from the Fiesta Americana. The 17-story Hyatt is Mérida's most expensive hotel, offering 300 rooms, tennis courts, a gym and steam bath, and a great pool with swim-up bar.

PLACES TO EAT

As in other touristed areas of the Yucatán Peninsula, many restaurants in Mérida have begun adding a service charge (usually 10%) to the bill. Check the menu carefully before you order to see if this is official policy.

Budget

Mérida's least-expensive eateries are in the **Mercado Municipal Lucas de Gálvez** *(Calle 56A)*; most are open from early morning until early evening. Upstairs joints have tables and chairs and more varied menus; main-course platters of beef, fish or chicken go for as little as M$12. Downstairs at the north end are some cheap *taquerías* where you sit on a stool at a narrow counter, while near the south end are *coctelerías* serving shrimp, octopus and conch cocktails and ceviches starting at around M$20.

A less crowded, but still cheap and good market is **Mercado Municipal No 2** *(Calle*

57) on the north side of Parque de Santiago, packed with juice stalls, *loncherías* and even a cheap ice-cream place.

For good, cheap breakfasts, try a selection of *panes dulces* (sweet rolls and breads) from one of Mérida's several bakeries, such as **Panificadora Montejo** on the southwest corner of the main plaza. A full bag of goodies usually costs no more than M$25.

A few blocks east of the Plaza Grande are side-by-side **supermarkets** *(Calle 56 between Calles 63 & 65)* as well as a branch of **San Francisco de Asís** *(cnr Calles 67 & 54A)*, a market–department store chain.

Mid-Range

At last pass, **Il Caffé d'Italia** *(☎ 925-9452; Calle 57A between Calles 58 & 60; open 8am-11pm)* was serving good espresso drinks and a selection of ice-cream. It was on the verge of offering breakfasts, Italian-style sandwiches and dishes such as grilled eggplant.

Finca Santa Veracruz *(☎ 924-2450; cnr Calles 60 & 51; salads & sandwiches M$21-34)* offers all varieties of espresso drinks (including the straight stuff for M$9 a shot, excellent cappuccinos, and concoctions with ice cream and/or booze). It also serves salads and good sandwiches made with bagels, baguettes or croissants and salami, manchego cheese and other tasty fillings.

La Vía Olimpo *(☎ 923-5843; Calle 62 between Calles 61 & 63; breakfasts M$47-49, mains M$51-85; open 24hr)* is an upscale and trendy restaurant-café on the west side of the Plaza Grande, closed only between 11pm Monday and 7am Tuesday. Among the choices are salads, sandwiches, steaks and breakfasts. Try the *baguette de pavo lomo ahumado* (smoked turkey sandwich, M$55). Don't try the Internet connections.

Cafe Peón Contreras *(Calle 57A between Calles 58 & 60; breakfast M$40-50, mains M$35-65; open 7am-1am daily)* has indoor and outdoor tables and a long, varied menu, including a combination plate of Yucatecan specialties for around M$90.

Pop Cafetería *(☎ 928-6163; Calle 57 between Calles 60 & 62; breakfasts M$23-45, mains M$35-60; open 7am-midnight Mon-Sat, 8am-midnight Sun)* may be plain to look at, but the air-con works great. The restaurant serves up cheap breakfast combinations and a good variety of Mexican dishes; try the chicken in dark, rich mole (M$35).

Café Giorgio *(Calle 60 between Calles 59 & 61; breakfasts M$35-50, mains M$45-60; open 7am-10pm daily)*, on the edge of Parque Hidalgo, serves generous, reasonably priced breakfasts, as well as ample portions of pasta and other dishes, including mediocre pizza. The outdoor tables offer prime people-watching opportunities, and guarantee you'll be targeted by hammock vendors.

Amaro *(☎ 928-2452; Calle 59 between Calles 60 & 62; mains M$40-70; open 11am-1am daily)* makes a romantic dining spot, especially at night, when there's usually a duo performing ballads. Amaro is set in the courtyard of the house in which Andrés Quintana Roo – poet, statesman and drafter of Mexico's Declaration of Independence – was born in 1787. The service and food are good (but check your bill carefully), and the menu includes Yucatecan dishes and a variety of vegetarian plates, as well as some continental dishes, crepes and pizzas.

Pane e Vino *(☎ 928-6228; Calle 62 between Calles 59 & 61; mains M$50-80; open 6pm-midnight Tues-Sun)* is an Italian-run place serving tasty antipasti and salads (with olive oil and balsamic vinegar if you wish), lasagna, fish, meat and a selection of respectable wines by the glass or bottle. The star attraction is the fresh handmade pastas, including ravioli, gnocchi and a heavenly fettuccine al pesto (M$55). Don't scrimp; pair it with a glass of Montepulciano (M$30). Ahhhh.

Restaurante Kantún *(☎ 923-4493; Calle 45 between Calles 64 & 66; mains M$42-87; open 12:30pm-6pm daily)* serves some of the best seafood in town. Main dishes are all prepared to order and delicately seasoned or sauced; try the *filete Normanda,* a fillet stuffed with smoked oysters and topped with anchovies (M$70). There are a few meat offerings for nonfishy types, and you can eat very well for under M$100. Service is friendly and attentive, if almost formal at times. The family that runs the place lives next door and will open up in the evening if you phone before coming over.

Top End

Readers highly recommend **Restaurante Pórtico del Peregrino** *(☎ 928-6163; Calle 57 between Calles 60 & 62; mains M$60-120; open noon-midnight daily)*, which has several pleasant, traditional-style dining rooms

(some air-con) surrounding a small courtyard. Yucatecan dishes such as *pollo pibil* (chicken flavored with *achiote* sauce, wrapped in banana leaves and baked till tender) are its forte, but you'll find many international dishes and a broad range of seafood and steaks as well.

La Casona *(☎ 923-9996; Calle 60 between Calles 47 & 49; mains M$47-108; open 1pm-1am daily)* is in a fine old house, decorated with abundant antiques. Tables set out in a lush, lovely courtyard with dim lighting lend an air of romance – but use repellent if you're eating outside at night. You can choose from excellent Italian dishes – such as lasagna, pizza and handmade pastas – or steak, seafood and a few Yucatecan dishes. Two very colonial private dining rooms (one air-con) and a collection of vintage clocks round things out.

Alberto's Continental Patio *(☎ 928-5367; cnr Calles 64 & 57; salads M$40-60, mains M$110-150, set dinners M$235-270; open 11am-11pm daily)* offers yet more colonial-courtyard (as well as indoor) dining. The setting is extremely atmospheric, chock-a-block with religious artifacts, Mayan ceramic figures and greenery. Middle Eastern dishes such as hummus, babaganoush and tabbouleh are served with pita bread, and can be a welcome change from Mexican food. The steaks, poultry and seafood are also good, as is the service.

ENTERTAINMENT

The **Centro Cultural Olimpo** *(☎ 928-2020 ext 477; cnr Calles 62 & 61)* has something on nearly every night, from films to concerts to art installations.

Mérida offers many folkloric and musical events in parks and historic buildings, put on by local performers of considerable skill. Admission is free except as noted. Check with one of the tourist information offices to confirm schedules and find out about special events.

Monday *Vaquerías* (traditional Yucatecan dances) are performed to live music in front of the Palacio Municipal (west side of Plaza Grande) from 9pm to 10pm (arrive early to get a good seat; this is one of the most popular events). The dance and music reflect a mixture of Spanish and Mayan cultures, and date from the earliest days of the Vaquería Regional, a local festival that celebrated the branding of cattle on neighboring haciendas.

Tuesday In Parque de Santiago, on the corner of Calles 59 and 70, from 8:30pm to 10:30pm a big band plays dance music from the '40s and '50s for couples to whirl to.

Wednesday Open-air *teatro regional* (regional theater), behind the Palacio Municipal from 9pm to 10pm, gives performers the opportunity to air political and social issues and lambaste the government (or anyone else, for that matter!) with impunity (in Spanish only). The issues and references may be obscure, but it's always a lively – and often uproarious – time. Other theater performances take place in different parts of the city.

Thursday Traditional Yucatecan serenades (featuring dance, poetry and Yucatecan musical trios) are performed in the Parque Santa Lucía (on the corner of Calles 55 and 60) at 9pm.

Friday Diviértete Mérida (which translates as Have Some Fun, Mérida) features musical performances and other entertainment in various neighborhoods of the city. The University of Yucatán's Ballet Folklórico (☎ 924-6429), rated number three in the country, is performed in the university's main courtyard. Performances are held from 9am to 10pm except during Semana Santa and August. Admission costs M$20.

Saturday 'Mexican Night,' at the southern end of Paseo de Montejo (where it meets Calle 47), features mariachi and other Mexican (as opposed to Yucatecan) music and folkloric dances. The festivities last from 7pm to midnight and are very well attended. There are usually fireworks around 10:30pm.

Sunday Mejor Mérida Mejor Domingo is a series of concerts and special events taking place between 9am and 9pm in various venues around the Plaza Grande, including Parque Santa Lucía.

Mérida has several cinemas, most of which show first-run Hollywood fare in English, with Spanish subtitles (ask *'¿inglés?'* if you need to be sure), as well as other foreign films and Mexican offerings. Cinema tickets cost about M$32 for evening shows, M$21 for matinees. Try the central **Plaza Cine Internacional** *(cnr Calles 59 & 58)* or **Cines Rex** *(Calle 57 between Calles 70 & 72)*, located on the north side of Parque Santiago's market. It's a modern twin theater showing first-run films. **Teatro Mérida** *(Calle 62 between Calles 59 & 61)* often shows classic Hollywood and international flicks.

El Establo *(☎ 924-2289; Calle 60 between Calles 57 & 55; open 9pm-2:30am daily)* is one of a cluster of bars on this block that have live

music and dancing from Thursday through Sunday nights in busy times, Friday and Saturday nights when slow. The crowd is fairly young, with a mix of locals and visitors.

SHOPPING

Mérida is a fine place for buying Yucatecan handicrafts. Purchases to consider include guayaberas and traditional Mayan clothing such as the colorful embroidered *huipiles*, panama hats woven from palm fibers and of course the wonderfully comfortable Yucatecan hammocks.

Mercado Municipal Lucas de Gálvez, Mérida's main market, is bounded by Calles 56 and 56A at Calle 67, southeast of the Plaza Grande. Plans are in the works to relocate the market slightly and turn much of the area into a pedestrian zone, but there's a lot of resistance. Whatever happens, the surrounding streets are all part of the large market district, lined with shops selling everything one might want. Guard your valuables extra carefully in the market area. Watch for pickpockets, purse-snatchers and bag-slashers. The crush of people around Christmas and other busy periods can be intense.

Handicrafts

One place to start looking for handicrafts is **Casa de las Artesanías** *(☎ 928-6676; Calle 63 between Calles 64 & 66; open 9am-8pm Mon-Sat, 9am-1:30pm Sun)*, a government-supported market for local artisans selling just about everything: earthenware, textiles, wicker baskets, sandals, vases, ceramic dolls, wind chimes, purses and pouches, figurines of Mayan deities and bottles of locally made liqueurs. Prices are fixed and a bit high; you can have a look at the stuff here, then try to bargain down independent sellers elsewhere, but it may not be worth the amount you save. **Artesanías Bazar García Rejón** *(cnr Calles 65 & 60)* concentrates a wide variety of products into one area of shops.

At **Miniaturas** *(☎ 928-6503; Calle 59 between Calles 60 & 62; open 10am-2pm & 4pm-8pm daily)* you'll find lots of small Día de los Muertos tableaux, tinwork and figurines of every sort, from ceramics to toy soldiers. They all have one thing in common: they're easy to pack! The store is definitely fun to browse and prices are fixed at a fair rate so you needn't worry about bargaining. Its hours are *'más o menos'* ('more or less'), according to the sign.

Clothing

A good place for guayaberas and *huipiles* is **Camisería Canul** (☎ 923-5661; Calle 62 between Calles 59 & 57; open 8:30am-8pm Mon-Sat, 10am-1pm Sun). It has been in business for years, offers fixed prices and does custom tailoring.

Hammocks

You will be approached by peddlers on the street wanting to sell you hammocks about every hour throughout your stay in Mérida (every five minutes in the Parque Hidalgo). Check the quality of the hammocks carefully. See the boxed text 'Yucatecan Hammocks: The Only Way to Sleep' for details.

Panama Hats

Locally made panama hats are woven from jipijapa palm leaves in caves, where humid conditions keep the fibers pliable when the hat is being made. Once exposed to the relatively dry air outside, the panama hat is surprisingly resilient and resistant to crushing. The Campeche town of Bécal is the center of the hat-weaving trade, but you can

---

Yucatecan Hammocks: The Only Way to Sleep

The fine strings of Yucatecan hammocks make them supremely comfortable. In the sticky heat of a Yucatán summer, most locals prefer sleeping in a hammock, where the air can circulate around them, rather than in a bed. Many inexpensive hotels used to have hammock hooks in the walls of all guestrooms, though the hooks are not so much in evidence today.

Yucatecan hammocks are normally woven from strong nylon or cotton string and dyed in various colors. There are also natural, undyed cotton versions. Some sellers will try to fob these off as henequen (also called sisal) or jute, telling you it's much more durable (and valuable) than cotton, and even that it repels mosquitoes. Don't be taken in; real henequen hammocks are very rough and not something you'd want near your skin. The finest, strongest, most expensive hammocks are woven from silk, but these are very rare and usually available only by special order (whatever you do, don't pay silk prices for nylon!).

Hammocks come in several widths (each shop seems to have slightly different names and numbers for them), and though much is made of the quantity of pairs of end strings they possess, a better gauge of a hammock's size and quality is its weight. The heavier the better. A *sencilla* (for one person) should run about 500g to 700g and cost from M$120 to M$150. The *doble* goes about 750g to 1000g and costs roughly M$150 to M$200. Next come the *matrimonial* at 1100g to 1250g (M$180 to M$250), and *familiar* (up to about 1500g, M$240 to M$300). They go beyond this, to extra, king and other designations. *De croché* (very tightly woven) hammocks can take several weeks to produce and cost double or triple the prices given here.

When selecting a hammock, you must check to be sure that you're really getting the width you're paying for. Because they fold up small and the larger hammocks are more comfortable (though more expensive), consider the bigger sizes. A good store will let you do more than just look; if you ask *'¿puedo probar?'* they'll string it up and let you have a lie-down.

During your first few hours in Mérida you will be approached on the street by hammock peddlers. They may quote very low prices, but a low price is only good if the quality is high, and street-sold hammocks are mediocre at best. Check the hammock very carefully.

You can save yourself a lot of trouble by shopping at a hammock store with a good reputation. Getting away from the heavily touristed areas helps. **Hamacas El Aguacate** (☎ 928-6469; cnr Calles 58 & 73) has quality hammocks and decent prices, and there's absolutely no hard sell.

Some of the best (and best-priced) hammocks are produced in prisons, but a less-depressing excursion is to venture out to the nearby village of Tixcocob to watch hammocks being woven. Sharpies here are on the lookout for tourists and you need to use the same caution in buying that you would in downtown Mérida. A bus runs regularly from the Progreso bus station, Calle 62 No 524, between Calles 65 and 67 south of the main plaza.

buy good examples of the hatmaker's art in Mérida.

The best quality hats have a fine, close weave of slender fibers. The coarser the weave, the lower the price should be. Prices range from a few dollars for a hat of basic quality to US$80 or more for top quality. The Casa de las Artesanías has only very low-quality examples; the Bazar García Rejón is a much better bet.

GETTING THERE & AWAY
Air
Mérida's modern airport is a 10km, 20-minute ride southwest of the Plaza Grande off Hwy 180 (Av de los Itzáes). It has car rental desks, an ATM and currency exchange booth and a tourist office that can help with hotel reservations.

Most international flights to Mérida are connections through Mexico City or Cancún. Nonstop international services are provided by Aeroméxico (daily from Los Angeles, thrice weekly from Miami), Continental and Northwestern (both from Houston, total eight times weekly). Scheduled domestic flights are operated mostly by smaller regional airlines, with a few flights by Aeroméxico and Mexicana.

Aerocaribe (☎ 928-6790) Paseo de Montejo 500B. Flies between Mérida and Cancún, Veracruz and Villahermosa, with connections to Tuxtla Gutiérrez, Havana and other destinations.
Aeroméxico (☎ 920-1260) Hotel Fiesta Americana, Av Colón at Paseo Montejo. Flies to Mexico City, Los Angeles and Miami.
Aviacsa (☎ 800-006-2200, at Hotel Fiesta Americana ☎ 925-6890, at airport ☎ 946-1850) Flies to Mexico City.
Continental Airlines (☎ 800-900-5000) Paseo Montejo No 437 at Calle 29. Flies nonstop between Houston and Mérida.
Mexicana (☎ 924-6910) Paseo de Montejo 493. Nonstop flights to Mexico City.

Bus
Mérida is the bus transportation hub of the Yucatán Peninsula. Take care with your gear on night buses and those serving popular tourist destinations (especially 2nd-class buses); Lonely Planet has received many reports of theft on the night runs to Chiapas and of a few daylight thefts on the Chichén Itzá route and other lines.

Bus Terminals Mérida has a variety of bus terminals, and some lines operate out of (and stop at) more than one terminal. Tickets for departure from one terminal can often be bought at another, and destinations overlap greatly among lines. Some lines offer round-trip tickets to nearby towns that bring the fare down quite a bit. Following are some of the stations, bus lines operating out of them and areas served.

Hotel Fiesta Americana Av Colón near Calle 56A. A small 1st-class terminal on the west side of the hotel complex aimed at guests of the luxury hotels on Av Colón, far from the center. Don't catch a bus to here unless you'll be staying at the Fiesta or Hyatt. ADO GL and Super Expresso services run between here and Cancún, Campeche, Chetumal and Playa del Carmen.
Parque de San Juan Calle 69 between Calles 62 and 64. From all around the square and church, vans and Volkswagen combis depart for Dzibilchaltún Ruinas, Muna, Oxkutzcab, Petó, Sacalum, Tekax, Ticul and other points.
Progreso Calle 62 No 524 between Calles 65 and 67. Progreso has a separate bus terminal here.
Terminal CAME (ka-meh; reservations ☎ 924-8391) Calle 70 between Calles 69 and 71. Sometimes referred to as the 'Terminal de Primera Clase,' Mérida's main terminal is seven blocks southwest of the Plaza Grande. Come here for (mostly 1st-class) buses to points around the Yucatán Peninsula and well beyond, for example, Campeche, Cancún, Mexico City, Palenque, San Cristóbal de Las Casas and Villahermosa. Lines include ADO, Altos (providing *directo económico* service, with air-con and few stops, but no bathroom; watch your belongings), and the deluxe lines ADO GL, Maya de Oro, Super Expresso and UNO. CAME has card phones and an ATM and runs counters for tourist, bus and hotel information. The baggage check is open 6am to midnight daily and charges M$5 for storage from 6am to noon, M$10 for all day.
Terminal de Segunda Clase Calle 69. Also known as Terminal 69 (Sesenta y Nueve) or simply Terminal de Autobuses, this terminal is located just around the corner from CAME. ATS, Mayab, Oriente, Sur, TRP and TRT run mostly 2nd-class buses to points in the state and around the peninsula. The terminal has a luggage checkroom (open 7am to 11pm daily; M$3 per bag per hour).
Terminal Noreste Calle 67 between Calles 50 and 52. LUS, Occidente and Oriente use the Noreste bus line's terminal. Destinations served from here include many small towns in the northeast

part of the peninsula, including Tizimín and Río Lagartos; frequent service to Cancún and points along the way; as well as small towns south and west of Mérida, including Celestún (served by Occidente), Ticul and Oxkutzcab. Some Oriente buses depart from Terminal 69 and stop here, others leave directly from here (eg, those to Izamal and Tizimín).

Bus Routes Destinations served from Mérida include the following:

Campeche (long route via Uxmal) M$72, four hours, 250km; five 2nd-class Sur buses between 6:05am and 5:05pm
Campeche (short route via Bécal) M$72 to M$103, 2½ to 3½ hours, 195km; many ADO buses, two ADO GL buses, ATS 2nd-class bus every 30 minutes to 7:15pm
Cancún M$114 to M$165, four to six hours, 320km; 16 2nd-class Oriente buses, 20 deluxe Super Expresso buses and many other buses
Celestún M$34, two hours, 95km; 15 2nd-class Occidente buses from Terminal Noreste
Chetumal M$147 to M$185, six to eight hours, 456km; four Super Expresso buses from Terminal CAME, five 2nd-class Mayab buses, four super-deluxe Caribe Express buses from Terminal de Segunda Clase
Chichén Itzá M$43 to M$62, 1¾ to 2½ hours, 116km; three Super Expresso and 16 2nd-class Oriente Cancún-bound buses stop at Chichén Itzá during open hours, otherwise at nearby Pisté
Cobá M$78 to M$106, 3½ to four hours, 270km; Super Expresso bus at 1pm, Oriente bus at 5:20am
Escárcega M$123 to M$158, five to 5½ hours, 345km; one Altos, five ADO and many 2nd-class Sur buses
Felipe Carrillo Puerto M$107 to M$112, 5½ to six hours, 310km; six Mayab and five TRP buses
Izamal M$26, 1½ hours, 72km; frequent 2nd-class Oriente buses from Terminal Noreste
Mayapán Ruinas M$15 (M$26 round trip), 1½ hours, 48km; 15 LUS buses between 5:30am & 8pm from Noreste terminal; continuing to Oxkutzcab
Mexico City (Norte) M$759, 19 hours, 1514km; ADO bus at 12:05pm
Mexico City (TAPO) M$733 to M$831, 20 hours, 1504km; four ADO buses between 10am and 9:15pm, ADO GL bus at 2pm and 5:30pm
Palenque M$233 to M$276, eight to nine hours, 556km; one deluxe Maya de Oro bus at 9:30pm, three ADO buses, one Altos bus at 7:15pm

Playa del Carmen M$196 to M$230, 4½ to eight hours, 385km; 10 deluxe Super Expresso buses, one ADO GL bus at 1:30pm, other buses
Progreso M$12, one hour, 33km; buses leave every 20 minutes, 8am to 9pm, from the Progreso bus terminal; for the same ticket price, shared vans (some with air-con) take off from a parking lot located on Calle 60 between Calles 63 and 65
Río Lagartos M$57 to M$71, three to four hours, 261km; three 1st- and 2nd-class Noreste buses from 9am
Ticul M$30 to M$34, 1¾ hours, 85km; frequent Mayab buses, some TRP buses; frequent direct *colectivo* combis and vans from Parque de San Juan (M$27, 1¼ hours) from 5am to 10pm
Tizimín M$51 to M$72, 2½ to four hours, 210km; six 1st-and 2nd-class Noreste
Tulum M$126, four hours, 320km (via Cobá); Super Expresso bus at 6:30am, 11am and 1pm; there is 2nd-class service to Tulum, but it takes much longer
Tuxtla Gutiérrez M$356 to M$453, 13 to 16 hours, 820km; one deluxe Maya de Oro bus at 9:30pm, one Altos bus at 7:15pm; or change at Palenque or Villahermosa
Valladolid M$57 to M$83, 2½ to 3½ hours, 160km; many buses, including Super Expresso, 2nd-class Oriente and ATS
Villahermosa M$293 to M$486, eight to nine hours, 560km; 11 ADO buses, direct superdeluxe UNO bus at 9:30pm and 11pm, direct ADO GL bus at 5:30pm

Car

The optimal way to tour the many archaeological sites south of Mérida is by rental car, especially if you have two or more people to share costs. Assume you will pay a total of M$400 to M$600 per day (tax, insurance and gas included) for short-term rental of the cheapest car offered, which is usually a bottom-of-the-line Volkswagen or Nissan. Getting around Mérida's sprawling tangle of one-way streets and careening buses is better done on foot or on a careening bus, so hold off renting your car until you've seen most of the city, or at least gotten well oriented.

México Rent A Car (☎ 923-3637, fax 927-4916, ✉ mexicorentacar@hotmail.com; Calle 57A between Calles 58 & 60; open 8am-12:30pm & 6pm-8pm Mon-Sat, 8am-12:30pm Sun) offers rates the big-name agencies often can't touch, especially if you're paying cash. In slow seasons it's sometimes possible to get a VW Beetle for as little as M$250 a day, and long-term rentals can bring prices lower than that, even on higher-quality cars. The rental cars are in very good condition, and the friendly managers speak English well.

Several other agencies have branches at the airport as well as on Calle 60 between 55 and 57, including **Budget** *(☎ 928-6759, 800-712-0324)*, **National** *(☎ 923-2493)* and **Hertz** *(☎ 924-2834, 800-709-5000)*.

See the Getting There & Away section under Cancún in the Quintana Roo chapter for a warning about the overpriced toll highway between Mérida and Cancún.

GETTING AROUND
To/From the Airport

Bus 79 (Aviación) travels between the airport and the city center every 15 to 30 minutes until 9pm, with occasional service until 11pm. The half-hour trip (M$4) is via a very roundabout route; the best place to catch the bus to the airport is on Calle 70 just south of Calle 69, near the corner of the CAME terminal.

Transporte Terrestre *(☎ 946-1529)* provides speedy service between the airport and the center, charging M$100 per carload (same price for hotel pick-up). A taxi from the center to the airport should run about M$60 (but it's hard to get this price *from* the airport).

Bus

Most parts of Mérida that you'll want to visit are within five or six blocks of the Plaza Grande and are thus accessible on foot. Given the slow speed of city traffic, particularly in the market areas, travel on foot is also the fastest way to get around.

City buses are cheap at M$4, but routes can be confusing. Most start in suburban neighborhoods, meander through the city center and terminate in another distant suburban neighborhood. To travel between the Plaza Grande and the upscale neighborhoods to the north along Paseo de Montejo, catch the Ruta 10 on the corner of Calles 58 and 59, half a block east of the Parque Hidalgo, or catch a 'Tecnológico,' 'Hyatt' or 'Montejo' bus on Calle 60 and get out at Av Colón. To return to the city center, catch any bus heading south on Paseo de Montejo displaying the same signs and/or 'Centro.' Many will let you off on Calle 58 north of Calle 61.

Taxi

Taxis in Mérida are not metered. Rates are fixed, with an outrageous M$30 minimum fare, which will get you from the bus terminals to all downtown hotels. Most rides within city limits do not exceed M$55. Taxi stands can be found at most of the barrio parks, or dial ☎ 928-5322 or ☎ 923-1221; service is available 24 hours (dispatch fees are an extra M$10 to M$20).

South of Mérida

HACIENDA YAXCOPOIL

Hacienda Yaxcopoil *(☎ 999-927-2606; admission M$40; open 8am-6pm Mon-Sat, 9am-1pm Sun)* is on the west side of Hwy 261, 33km southwest of central Mérida. A vast estate that grew and processed henequen, its numerous French Renaissance–style buildings have been restored and turned collectively into a museum of the 17th century. Frequent buses pass Yaxcopoil running between Mérida and Ticul.

HACIENDA OCHIL

This lovely hacienda *(☎ 999-950-1275; Hwy 261 Km 176; admission free; open 10am-6pm daily)* lies about 44km south of Mérida and provides a fascinating look at how henequen was grown and processed. From the parking lot follow the 'truck' tracks – used by the small wheeled carts to haul material to and from the processing plant – to the right around the parklike, restored portion of the hacienda. You'll pass workshops where you might see locals fashioning handicrafts for sale and a henequen museum with exhibits illustrating the cultivating, harvesting and processing of the plant. These include pieces of machinery and photos of hacienda life.

The *casa de máquinas* (machine house) and smokestack still stand, and Ochil also has a **restaurant** *(mains M$68-76)* and bar, a small cenote and a henequen patch. It is a fairly classy place overall and well worth a visit. Mayab and Sur (among others) run 2nd-class buses between Mérida and Muna that will drop you at Ochil's parking lot (M$22, one hour from Mérida).

GRUTAS DE CALCEHTOK

Though some may dispute it, the Calcehtok caves comprise the longest dry cave system on the Yucatán Peninsula. More than 4km have been explored so far, and two of the caves' 25 vaults exceed 100m in diameter (one has a 30m-high 'cupola'). The caves hold abundant and impressive natural formations, human and animal remains and plenty of artifacts, including many *haltunes* (stone basins carved by the Mayas to catch water). Archaeologists have found and removed ceramic arrowheads, quartz hammers and other tools, and you can still see low fortifications built by Mayas who sheltered here during the War of the Castes.

The opening of the main entrance is an impressive 30m in diameter and 40m deep, ringed by vegetation often thronging with bees. It's about 1m deep in bat guano at the bottom (some visitors wear dust masks to avoid infection from a fungus that grows on guano). There's nothing to stop you from exploring on your own (and possibly getting lost), but you'd be wise to employ one of the six guides, all members of the Cuy family, whose great grandfather rediscovered the caves in 1840. They carry Coleman lanterns and flashlights and know their way around.

You can opt for a low-key tour or an adventure package, one that involves belly-crawling, rope descents to see human skeletons, and possibly the 7m long by 20cm wide 'Pass of Death,' or *'El Parto'* (The Birth: you figure it out). Tours last one to six hours and can cost as little as M$100 for 10 people. Wear sturdy shoes.

The caves are a few kilometers south of the town of Calcehtok, which lies between

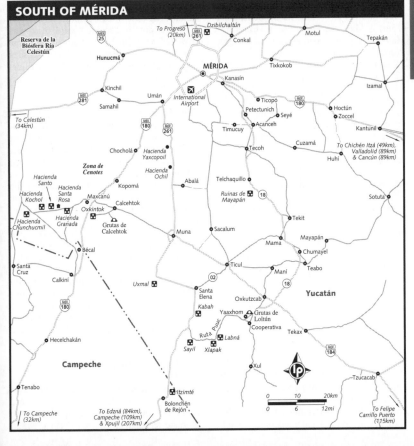

SOUTH OF MÉRIDA

YUCATÁN STATE

Hwys 184 and 261 a little less than 8km east of Maxcanú and 28km west of Muna – about 75km southwest of Mérida in all. At the time of research, they were best reached by car.

OXKINTOK

Archaeologists have been excited about the ruins of Oxkintok (admission M$29; open 8am-5pm daily) for several years. Inscriptions found at the site contain some of the oldest known dates in the Yucatán, and indicate the city was inhabited from the pre-Classic to the post-Classic period (300 BC to AD 1500), reaching its greatest importance between 475 and 860 BC. Three main groups of the approximately 8-sq-km site have been restored thus far, all very near the site entrance. Though much of the rebuilding work looks like it was done with rubble, you can see examples of Oxkintok, Proto-Puuc and Puuc architecture. The highest structure (15m) is Ma-1, **La Pirámide**, in Grupo Ah-May, which provides good views of the area. Probably the most interesting structure is Palacio Chich (Estructura Ca-7), in the Ah-Canul Group, for its original stonework and the two columns in front carved with human figures in elaborate dress.

The ruins are reached by taking a west-leading fork off the road to the Grutas de Calcehtok; for information on getting to the Grutas de Calcehtok, see the end of that section earlier.

RUINAS DE MAYAPÁN

These ruins (admission M$24; open 8am-5pm daily) are some 50km southeast of Mérida, on Yucatán state Hwy 18. Though far less impressive than many Mayan sites, Mayapán is historically significant, its main attractions are clustered in a compact core, and visitors usually have the place to themselves.

Don't confuse the ruins of Mayapán with the Mayan village of the same name, some 40km southeast of the ruins, past the town of Teabo.

History

Mayapán was supposedly founded by Kukulcán (Quetzalcóatl) in 1007, shortly after the former ruler of Tula arrived in Yucatán. His dynasty, the Cocom, organized a confederation of city-states that included Uxmal, Chichén Itzá and many other notable

cities. Despite their alliance, animosity arose between the Cocomes of Mayapán and the Itzáes of Chichén Itzá during the late 12th century, and the Cocomes stormed Chichén Itzá, forcing the Itzá rulers into exile. The Cocom dynasty emerged supreme in all of northern Yucatán.

Cocom supremacy lasted for almost 2½ centuries, until the ruler of Uxmal, Ah Xupán Xiú, led a rebellion of the oppressed city-states and overthrew Cocom hegemony. The great capital of Mayapán was utterly destroyed and remained uninhabited ever after.

But struggles for power continued in the region until 1542, when Francisco de Montejo the Younger conquered T'hó and established Mérida. At that point the current lord of Maní and ruler of the Xiú people, Ah Kukum Xiú, proposed to Montejo a military alliance against the Cocomes, his ancient rivals. Montejo accepted, and Xiú was baptized as a Christian, taking the name Francisco de Montejo Xiú. The Cocomes were defeated and – too late – the Xiú rulers realized that they had signed the death warrant of Mayan independence.

The Site

The city of Mayapán was large, with a population estimated to be around 12,000; it covered 4 sq km, all surrounded by a great defensive wall. More than 3500 buildings, 20 cenotes and traces of the city wall were mapped by archaeologists working in the 1950s and in 1962. The late post-Classic workmanship is inferior to that of the great age of Mayan art.

Among the structures that have been restored is the **Castillo de Kukulcán**, a climbable pyramid with fresco fragments around its base and, at its rear side, friezes depicting decapitated warriors. The **Templo Redondo** (Round Temple) is vaguely reminiscent of El Caracol at Chichén Itzá. Close by is Itzmal Chen, a cenote that was a major Mayan religious sanctuary. Excavation and restoration continue at the site.

Getting There & Away

The Ruinas de Mayapán are just off Hwy 18, a few kilometers southwest of the town of Telchaquillo. LUS runs 15 2nd-class buses between 5:30am and 8pm from the Noreste terminal in Mérida (M$15, M$25 round trip, 1½ hours) that will let you off near the entrance to the ruins, and pick you up on your way back.

UXMAL

Some visitors rank Uxmal *(oosh-***mahl***; admission M$87 Mon-Sat, M$37 Sun & holidays; open 8am-5pm daily)* among the top Mayan archaeological sites. While this may be stretching things, it is a large site with some fascinating structures in good condition and bearing a riot of ornamentation. Adding to its appeal is Uxmal's setting in the hilly Puuc region, which lent its name to the architectural patterns in this area. *Puuc* means 'hills,' and these, rising up to about 100m, are the first relief from the flatness of the northern and western portions of the peninsula.

History

Uxmal was an important city in a region that encompassed the satellite towns of Sayil, Kabah, Xlapak and Labná. Although Uxmal means 'Thrice Built' in Mayan, it was actually constructed five times.

That a sizable population flourished in this dry area is yet more testimony to the engineering skills of the Maya, who built a series of reservoirs and *chultunes* (cisterns) lined with lime mortar to catch and hold water during the dry season. First settled about AD 600, Uxmal was influenced by highland Mexico in its architecture, most likely through contact fostered by trade. This influence is reflected in the town's serpent imagery, phallic symbols and columns. The well-proportioned Puuc architecture,

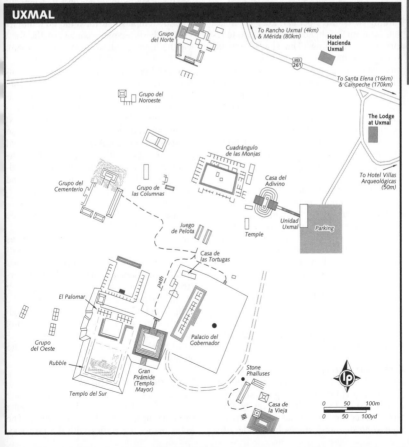

UXMAL

Grupo del Norte
Grupo del Noroeste
Grupo del Cementerio
Grupo de las Columnas
Cuadrángulo de las Monjas
Casa del Adivino
Juego de Pelota
Temple
Unidad Uxmal
Parking
Casa de las Tortugas
El Palomar
path
Grupo del Oeste
Rubble
Gran Pirámide (Templo Mayor)
Palacio del Gobernador
Templo del Sur
Stone Phalluses
Casa de la Vieja

To Rancho Uxmal (4km) & Mérida (80km)
Hotel Hacienda Uxmal
MEX 261
To Santa Elena (16km) & Campeche (170km)
The Lodge at Uxmal
To Hotel Villas Arqueológicas (50m)

0   50   100m
0   50   100yd

with its intricate, geometric mosaics sweeping across the upper parts of elongated facades, was strongly influenced by the slightly earlier Río Bec and Chenes styles.

The scarcity of water in the region meant that Chac, the rain god or sky serpent, carried a lot of weight. His image is ubiquitous at the site in the form of stucco masks protruding from facades and cornices. There is much speculation as to why Uxmal was abandoned in about AD 900; drought conditions may have reached such proportions that the inhabitants had to relocate.

Rediscovered by archaeologists in the 19th century, Uxmal was first excavated in 1929 by Frans Blom. Although much has been restored, there is still a good deal to discover.

Information

Parking costs M$10 per car; keep the ticket you get from the attendant if you want to return in the evening. The site is entered through the modern Unidad Uxmal building, which holds an air-con restaurant, a small museum, shops selling souvenirs and crafts, an auditorium, bathrooms, an ATM and a left-luggage facility. Also here is Librería Dante, a bookstore that stocks an excellent selection of travel and archaeological guides and general-interest books on Mexico in English, Spanish, German and French; the imported books are very expensive.

The price of admission, if you retain the wristband-ticket, includes a 45-minute sound-and-light show, beginning nightly at 8pm in summer and 7pm in winter. It's in Spanish, but you can rent devices for listening to English, French, German or Italian translations (beamed via infrared) for M$25. Specify the language you need or it may not be broadcast. The cost for the show only is M$30, which goes toward the next day's site admission.

As you pass through the turnstile and climb the slope to the ruins, the rear of the Casa del Adivino comes into view.

Casa del Adivino

This tall temple (the name translates as 'Magician's House'), 39m high, was built in an unusual oval shape. It gives rather a bad first impression of Uxmal to the visitor, consisting of round stones held rudely together with lots of cement. What you see is a restored version of the temple's fifth incarnation. Four earlier temples were completely covered in the final rebuilding by the Maya, except for the high doorway on the west side, which remains from the fourth temple. Decorated in elaborate Chenes style (which originated further south), the doorway proper forms the mouth of a gigantic Chac mask.

Climbing the temple was not allowed when we visited.

Cuadrángulo de las Monjas

The 74-room, sprawling Nuns' Quadrangle is directly west of the Casa del Adivino. Archaeologists guess variously that it was a military academy, royal school or palace complex. The long-nosed face of Chac appears everywhere on the facades of the four separate temples that form the quadrangle. The northern temple, grandest of the four, was built first, followed by the southern, then the eastern and then the western.

Several decorative elements on the exuberant facades show signs of Mexican, perhaps Totonac, influence. The feathered-serpent (Quetzalcóatl, or in Mayan, Kukulcán) motif along the top of the west temple's facade is one of these. Note also the stylized depictions of the *na* (traditional Mayan thatched hut) over some of the doorways in the northern and southern buildings. Take plenty of time to look around here; the amount of detail is almost overwhelming.

Passing through the corbeled arch in the middle of the south building of the quadrangle and continuing down the slope takes you through the **Juego de Pelota** (ball court). From here you can turn left and head up the steep slope and stairs to the large terrace. If you've got time and energy, you could instead turn right to explore the **Grupo del Cementerio** (which, though largely unrestored, holds some interesting square blocks carved with skulls in the center of its plaza), then head for the stairs and terrace.

Casa de las Tortugas

To the right at the top of the stairs is the House of the Turtles, which takes its name from the turtles carved on the cornice. The Maya associated turtles with the rain god,

Beach, Xcaret

Sound-and-light show, Uxmal

Boat tour, Reserva de la Biósfera Ría Celestún

Cenote, Ik Kil Parque Ecoarqueológico

Ball court, Chichén Itzá

Cenote dive, Tulum

Chac. According to Mayan myth, when the people suffered from drought so did the turtles, and both prayed to Chac to send rain.

The frieze of short columns, or 'rolled mats,' that runs around the temple below the turtles is characteristic of the Puuc style. On the west side of the building a vault has collapsed, affording a good view of the corbeled arch that supported it.

Palacio del Gobernador

This *palacio,* the Governor's Palace, with its magnificent facade nearly 100m long, has been called 'the finest structure at Uxmal and the culmination of the Puuc style' by Mayanist Michael D Coe. Buildings in Puuc style have walls filled with rubble, faced with cement and then covered in a thin veneer of limestone squares; the lower part of the facade is plain, the upper part festooned with stylized Chac faces and geometric designs, often lattice-like or fretted. Other elements of Puuc style are decorated cornices, rows of half-columns (as in the House of the Turtles) and round columns in doorways (as in the palace at Sayil). The stones forming the corbeled vaults in Puuc style are shaped somewhat like boots.

Gran Pirámide

Though it's adjacent to the Governor's Palace, a sign by the steps of the Gran Pirámide (Great Pyramid) warns 'it is dangerous to go up' from the rear of the palace. Most visitors ignore the sign and take the shortcut from the palace's southwest corner. If you don't feel right doing this, retrace your route to go back down the hillside stairs and then keep turning left to follow the foot of the platform until you reach the pyramid's steps.

The 32m-high pyramid has been restored only on its northern side. Archaeologists theorize that the quadrangle at its summit was largely destroyed in order to construct another pyramid above it. That work, for reasons unknown, was never completed. At the top are some stucco carvings of Chac, birds and flowers.

El Palomar

West of the Great Pyramid sits a structure whose roofcomb is latticed with a pattern reminiscent of the Moorish pigeon houses built into walls in Spain and northern Africa – hence the building's name, which means the Dovecote or Pigeon House. The nine honeycombed triangular 'belfries' sit on top of a building that was once part of a quadrangle. The base is so eroded that it is hard for archaeologists to guess its function.

Casa de la Vieja

Off the southeast corner of the Palacio del Gobernador's platform is a small complex, largely rubble, known as the Casa de la Vieja (Old Woman's House). In front of it is a small *palapa* (thatched-roof shelter) sheltering several large phalluses carved from stone. Don't get any ideas; the sign here reads 'Do not sit.'

Places to Stay & Eat

There is no town at Uxmal, only the archaeological site and several top-end hotels, so for most cheap food and lodging you need to head up or down the road a ways. Two options listed are in the village of Santa Elena, 16km southeast of Uxmal and 8km north of Kabah – for details of bus services, see Getting There & Away later.

Camping Bungalows Sacbé (☎ 985-858-1281; e sacbebungalow@hotmail.com; campsites per person M$30, dorm beds with/without HI card or ISIC M$60/65, doubles M$150-175, triples M$200) is a quiet, well-kept HI affiliate on the south side of Santa Elena. It offers camping in a parklike setting, four simple but pleasant and clean doubles (one can accommodate a third person) with spotless bathrooms and two four-bed, single-sex dorms with separate bathrooms. All rooms have fans, good screens and good beds. The two dorms have lockers (with locks) and share a wonderful little kitchen with fridge, stove and even a blender. Sacbé is also convenient to the Ruta Puuc ruins, and the friendly owners speak French, English and Spanish, and serve good, cheap breakfasts and dinners (with vegetarian options). Ask the bus driver for the *campo de béisbol* (baseball field) *de Santa Elena.* It's about 200m south of the town's southern entrance.

Rancho Uxmal (☎ 997-977-6254; doubles with fan M$250) is a friendly place 4km north of the ruins on Hwy 261 (the road to Mérida). It has 23 basic, serviceable guestrooms with good ventilation, a swimming pool, and a shaded, welcoming restaurant serving three meals at reasonable prices.

There are more budget lodgings 30km east of Uxmal in Ticul (see that section later in this chapter).

The Flycatcher Inn (W *www.mexonline .com/flycatcherinn.htm; doubles M$300, suite M$400)* is on the southeastern edge of Santa Elena. It features three squeaky-clean rooms and an enormous master suite. All have terraces, super-comfy, imported beds (two queens in doubles, a king in the suite) plus hammocks, excellent screenage and great bathrooms – those in the suites are done in marble quarried from nearby Ticul. Breakfast, included in the room rates, consists of homemade breads, tropical fruit and tea or coffee. The owners, a local Mayan and his American wife, have kept most of the five hectares of land around the inn undeveloped, and a number of bird and animal species can be seen here, including the flycatchers that gave their name to the place. The inn's driveway is less than 100m north of the town's southern entrance and on the 'west' side of the highway; there's a bus stop just across the highway from it, near Restaurant El Chac-Mool.

Hotel Villas Arqueológicas Uxmal *(☎/fax 997-976-2020, 800-514-8244, in USA ☎ 800-258-2633, in France ☎ 801-80-28-03;* e *villa uxm@sureste.com; doubles M$616)* is an attractive Club Med–run hotel with a swimming pool, tennis courts, a restaurant and air-con guestrooms, not far from the ruins entrance.

The Lodge at Uxmal *(☎ 997-976-2010, fax 997-976-2102, in USA ☎ 800-235-4079;* W *www.mayaland.com; rooms May-Oct US$134-188, Nov-Apr US$194-228)*, Mayaland Resorts' lodge, is Uxmal's newest and most luxurious hotel. Rooms have two queens or one king bed, a minibar, coffeemaker and great bathrooms. Some have stained-glass windows and other pretty touches. The hotel offers meal plans and has two pools and a restaurant-bar. Walk-in rates are sometimes lower than the official rates quoted here. It's just opposite the entrance to the archaeological site.

Hotel Hacienda Uxmal *(☎ 997-976-2012, fax 997-976-2011, in USA ☎ 800-235-4079;* W *www.mayaland.com; doubles with fan M$32, doubles with air-con May-Oct US$115, Nov-Apr US$165)* is another Mayaland Resort,

500m from the ruins and across the highway. It housed the archaeologists who explored and restored Uxmal. Wide, tiled verandas, high ceilings, great bathrooms and a beautiful swimming pool make this a very comfortable place to stay. The fan-cooled rooms are in the much more modest annex, right by the highway. It's decaying a bit, but the screens and bathrooms are good, and the beds are OK. The Hacienda also has a restaurant and offers meal plans.

Restaurant El Chac-Mool *(☎ 999-996-2025; mains M$38-40; open 8am-8pm daily)*, on Hwy 261 at the south entrance to Santa Elena, is a friendly place serving Yucatecan food that includes a hearty vegetarian plate of rice, beans, fried bananas, *chayote* (a green vegetable a bit like winter melon) and squash.

Getting There & Away

Uxmal is 80km (1½ hours) from Mérida. The inland route between Mérida and Campeche passes Uxmal, and most buses coming from either city will drop you there, at Santa Elena, Kabah or the Ruta Puuc turnoff. But when you want to leave, passing buses may be full (especially on Saturday and Monday).

ATS buses depart Mérida's Terminal de Segunda Clase at 8am daily on a whirlwind excursion to the Ruta Puuc sites plus Kabah and Uxmal, heading back from Uxmal's parking lot at 2:30pm. This 'tour' is transportation only; you pay all other costs. The time spent at each site is enough to get only a nodding acquaintance, though some say the two hours at Uxmal is sufficient, if barely. The cost is M$100 for the whole deal, or M$60 if you only want to be dropped off at Uxmal in the morning and picked up in the afternoon.

Organized tours of Uxmal and other sites can be booked in Mérida (see Organized Tours in the Mérida section earlier).

If you're going from Uxmal to Ticul, first take a northbound bus to Muna (M$5, 20 minutes) then catch one of the frequent buses from there to Ticul (M$8, 30 minutes).

KABAH

The ruins of Kabah *(admission M$29; open 8am-5pm daily)*, just over 23km southeast of Uxmal, are right astride Hwy 261. The guard shack–souvenir shop (selling snacks and cold drinks) and the bulk of the restored ruins are on the east side of the highway.

On entering, head to your right to climb the stairs of the structure closest to the highway, **El Palacio de los Mascarones** (Palace of Masks). Standing in front of it is the Altar de los Glifos, whose immediate area is littered with many stones carved with glyphs. The palace's facade is an amazing sight, covered in nearly 300 masks of Chac, the rain god or sky serpent. Most of their huge curling noses are broken off; the best intact beaks are at the building's south end. These noses may have given the palace its modern Mayan name, Codz Poop (Rolled Mat; it's pronounced more like 'Codes Pope' than some Elizabethan curse).

When you've had your fill of noses, head north and around to the back of the Poop to check out the two restored **atlantes** (an atlas – plural 'atlantes' – is a male figure used as a supporting column). These are especially interesting, as they're some of a very few three-dimensional human figures you'll see at the Mayan sites covered in this book. One is headless and the other wears a jaguar mask atop his head. Two more atlantes stand in a storage shed near the office, though when we were there it looked like

they were about to be packed up and shipped off to a museum, as has happened with others that have been discovered here.

Descend the steps near the atlantes and turn left, passing the small **Pirámide de los Mascarones**, to reach the plaza containing **El Palacio**. The palace's broad facade has several doorways, two of which have a column in the center. These columned doorways and the groups of decorative *columnillas* (little columns) on the upper part of the facade are characteristic of Puuc architectural style.

Steps on the north side of El Palacio's plaza put you on a path leading about 200m through the jungle to the **Templo de las Columnas** (watch out for the 'tourist trap' on the way – a person-sized hole in the middle of the path). This building has more rows of decorative columns on the upper part of its facade.

West of El Palacio, across the highway, a path leads up the slope and passes to the south of a high mound of stones that was once the **Gran Pirámide** (Great Pyramid). The path curves to the right and comes to a large restored **monumental arch**. It's said that the *sacbé*, or cobbled and elevated ceremonial road, leading from here goes through the jungle all the way to Uxmal, terminating at a smaller arch; in the other direction it goes to Labná. Once, all of the Yucatán Peninsula was connected by these marvelous 'white roads' of rough limestone.

At present, nothing of the *sacbés* is visible, and the rest of the area west of the highway is a maze of unmarked, overgrown paths leading off into the jungle.

There's good, affordable lodging about 8km north of Kabah at **Camping Bungalows Sacbé** and **The Flycatcher Inn**; for more details, see Places to Stay & Eat under Uxmal earlier.

Getting There & Away

Kabah is 104km (about two hours) from Mérida. See Getting There & Away under Uxmal for details on transport. Kabah gets particularly short shrift – about 25 minutes – from the ATS excursion bus.

Buses will usually make flag stops at the entrance to the ruins. Many visitors come to Kabah by private car and may be willing to give you a lift, either back to Mérida or south and east on the Ruta Puuc.

KABAH

To Santa Elena (8km), Uxmal (24km) & Mérida (104km)

MEX 261

– – Suggested Route

Templo de las Columnas

Shed (Atlantes)

Office

Parking

To Arch

El Palacio

Pirámide de los Mascarones

Statues (Atlantes)

El Palacio de los Mascarones (Codz Poop)

MEX 261

To Sayil (Ruta Puuc, 10km) & Campeche (146km)

0   25   50m
0   25   50yd
Approximate Scale

YUCATÁN STATE

RUTA PUUC

Just 5km south of Kabah on Hwy 261, a road branches off to the east and winds past the ruins of Sayil, Xlapak and Labná, eventually leading to the Grutas de Loltún. This is the Ruta Puuc (Puuc Route), and its sites offer some marvelous architectural detail and a deeper acquaintance with the Puuc Mayan civilization.

See the Uxmal and Ticul Getting There & Away sections for details on catching the ATS excursion bus, the only regularly scheduled public transport on the route. Though during the busy winter season it's usually possible to hitch rides from one site to the next, the best way year-round to appreciate the sites is by rented car.

Sayil

The ruins of Sayil *(admission M$29; open 8am-5pm daily)* are 4.5km from the junction of the Ruta Puuc with Hwy 261.

Sayil is best known for **El Palacio**, the huge three-tiered building with a facade some 85m long and reminiscent of the Minoan palace on Crete. The distinctive columns of Puuc architecture are used here over and over, as supports for the lintels, as decoration between doorways and as a frieze above them, alternating with huge stylized Chac masks and 'descending gods.' Ascending the palacio beyond its first level is not allowed.

Taking the path south from the palace for about 400m and bearing left, you come to the temple named **El Mirador**, whose roosterlike roofcomb was once painted a bright red. About 100m beyond El Mirador, beneath a protective *palapa*, is a stela bearing the relief of a fertility god with an enormous phallus, now badly weathered.

Xlapak

From the entrance gate at Sayil, it's 6km east to the entrance gate at Xlapak *(shla-***pak***; admission M$24; open 8am-5pm daily)*. The name means 'Old Walls' in Mayan and was a general term among local people for ancient ruins.

If you're going to skip any of the Ruta Puuc sites, Xlapak should be it. The ornate **palace** at Xlapak is smaller than those at Kabah and Sayil, measuring only about 20m in length. It's decorated with the inevitable Chac masks, columns and colonnettes and

fretted geometric latticework of the Puuc style. The building is slightly askew, looking as though it doesn't know which way to fall. There's not much else here.

Labná

If Xlapak is the skippable Puuc site, Labná *(admission M$29; open 8am-5pm daily)* is the one not to miss. Its setting on a flat, open area is striking, and if no one has been through before you for a while, at each doorway you approach you're likely to startle groups of long-tailed mot-mots (clock birds) into flight. Between the birds and the vegetation growing atop the Palacio, you can almost imagine yourself one of the first people to see the site in centuries. OK, you may need to squint a bit to ignore the trimmed grass.

Archaeologists believe that at one point in the 9th century, some 3000 Maya lived at Labná. To support such numbers in these arid hills, water was collected in *chultunes*. At Labná's peak there were some 60 *chultunes* in and around the city; several are still visible. From the entrance gate at Xlapak, it's 3.5km east to the gate at Labná.

El Palacio The first building you come to at Labná is one of the longest in the Puuc region, and much of its interesting decorative carving is in good shape. On the west corner of the main structure's facade,

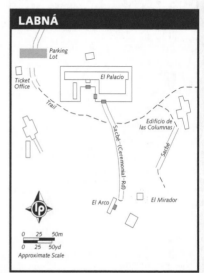

straight in from the big tree near the center of the complex, is a serpent's head with a human face peering out from between its jaws, the symbol of the planet Venus. Toward the hill from this is an impressive Chac mask, and nearby is the lower half of a human figure (possibly a ballplayer) in loincloth and leggings.

The lower level has several more well-preserved Chac masks, and the upper level contains a large *chultún* that still holds water. The view of the site and the hills beyond from there is impressive.

From the palace a limestone-paved *sacbé* leads to El Arco.

El Arco Labná is best known for its magnificent arch, once part of a building that separated two quadrangular courtyards. It now appears to be a gate joining two small plazas. The corbeled structure, 3m wide and 6m high, is well preserved, and the reliefs decorating its upper facade are exuberantly Puuc in style.

Flanking the west side of the arch are carved *na* (thatched structures) with multi-tiered roofs. Also on these walls, the remains of the building that adjoined the arch, are lattice patterns atop a serpentine design. Archaeologists believe a high roofcomb once sat over the fine arch and its flanking rooms.

El Mirador Standing on the opposite side of the arch and separated from it by the *sacbé* is a pyramid known as El Mirador, topped by a temple. The pyramid itself is largely stone rubble. The temple, with its 5m-high roofcomb, is well positioned to be a lookout, thus its name.

GRUTAS DE LOLTÚN
North and east of Labná some 15km, a sign points out the left turn to the Grutas de Loltún, 5km further northeast. The road passes through lush orchards and some banana and palm groves, an agreeable sight in this dry region.

The Grutas de Loltún (*Loltún Caverns; admission M$49; open 9am-5pm daily*), one of the largest dry cave systems on the Yucatán Peninsula, provided a treasure trove of data for archaeologists studying the Maya. Carbon dating of artifacts found here reveals that the caves were used by humans 2500 years ago. Chest-high murals of hands,

faces, animals and geometric motifs were apparent as recently as 20 years ago, but so many people have touched them that scarcely a trace remains, though some handprints have been restored, a few pots are displayed in a niche, and an impressive bas-relief, El Guerrero, guards the entrance. Other than that, you'll see mostly floodlit limestone formations, or the poorly aimed floodlights shining into your eyes.

To explore the labyrinth, you must take a scheduled guided tour at 9:30am, 11am, 12:30pm, 2pm, 3pm or 4pm, but they may depart early if enough people are waiting, or switch languages if the group warrants it (tours are usually in Spanish). The services of the guides are included in the admission price, though they expect a small tip afterwards. Tours last about one hour and 20 minutes, with lots of lengthy stops. Some guides' presentations are long on legends (and jokes about disappearing mothers-in-law) and short on geological and historical information.

When we last visited, the restaurant near the cave exit was not operating, but food was available at the **parador turístico** across the highway from the caves' parking lot (which costs M$10 to park in).

Getting There & Away
At the time of research, LUS had at least temporarily discontinued its service from the Noreste terminal in Mérida to the Grutas, but still offered service to Oxkutzcab (osh-kootz-**kahb**; M$32, three hours) via Ticul, with departures at 5:30am, 6:30am, 7:30am, 9:30am and 11am. Loltún is 7km southwest of Oxkutzcab, and there is usually some transportation along the road. *Camionetas* (pickups) and *camiones* (trucks) charge M$10 for a ride (the locals' price of M$6 may be hard to get). A taxi from Oxkutzcab may charge M$60 or so, one way.

If you're driving from Loltún to Labná, turn right out of the Loltún parking lot and take the next road on the right. Do not take the road marked for Xul. After 5km turn right at the T-intersection to join the Ruta Puuc to the west.

TICUL
☎ 997 • pop 27,000
Ticul, 30km east of Uxmal and 14km northwest of Oxkutzcab, is the largest town in this ruin-rich region. It has decent hotels

and restaurants and good transportation. Although there is no public transportation to the Ruta Puuc from Ticul, it is possible to stay the night here and take an early morning bus to Muna or a *colectivo* to Santa Elena, arriving there in time to catch a tour bus to the Ruta Puuc ruins; see Getting There & Away. Ticul is also a center for fine *huipil* weaving, and ceramics made here from the local red clay are renowned throughout the Yucatán Peninsula.

Orientation & Information

Ticul's main street is Calle 23, sometimes called the Calle Principal, going from the highway northeast past the market and the town's best restaurants to the main plaza, or Plaza Mayor. A **post office** *(open 8am-2:30pm Mon-Fri)* faces the plaza, as do two banks with ATMs. The bus terminal is less than 100m away. Catercorner to the Plaza Mayor is the recently built Plaza de la Cultura, which is all cement and stone but nevertheless an agreeable place to take the evening breeze, enjoy the view of the church and greet passing townspeople.

Things to See & Do

Because of the number of Mayan ruins in the vicinity from which to steal building blocks and the number of Maya in the area needing conversion to Christianity, Francis-

can friars built many churches in the region that is now southern Yucatán state. Among them is Ticul's **Iglesia de San Antonio de Padua**, construction of which dates from the late 16th century. Although looted on several occasions, the church has some original touches, among them the stone statues of friars in primitive style flanking the side entrances and a Black Christ altarpiece ringed by crude medallions.

Saturday mornings in Ticul are picturesque: Calle 23 in the vicinity of the public market is closed to motorized traffic, and the street fills with three-wheeled cycles transporting shoppers between the market and their homes.

Places to Stay

Hotel San Miguel *(Calle 28 No 215D; singles/doubles M$81/105)* is near Calle 23 and the market. The friendly management offers worn, simple rooms (some musty) with fan and bathroom.

Hotel Sierra Sosa *(☎/fax 972-0008; Calle 26 No 199A; singles M$120, 1-/2-bed doubles M$150/170, air-con extra M$45)* is just northwest of the plaza. It's clean and friendly, and has good beds, bathrooms and natural light in the front and back rooms. The optional air-con is good as well.

Hotel San Antonio *(☎ 972-1983; cnr Calles 25A & 26; singles M$176, 1-/2-bed*

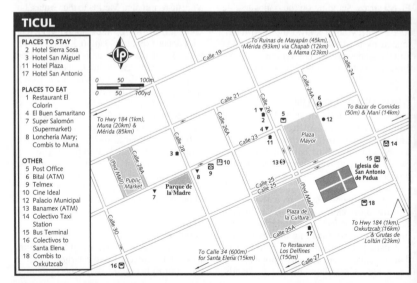

TICUL

PLACES TO STAY
2 Hotel Sierra Sosa
3 Hotel San Miguel
11 Hotel Plaza
17 Hotel San Antonio

PLACES TO EAT
1 Restaurant El
   Colorín
4 El Buen Samaritano
7 Super Salomón
   (Supermarket)
8 Lonchería Mary;
   Combis to Muna

OTHER
5 Post Office
6 Bital (ATM)
9 Telmex
10 Cine Ideal
12 Palacio Municipal
13 Banamex (ATM)
14 Colectivo Taxi
   Station
15 Bus Terminal
16 Colectivos to
   Santa Elena
18 Combis to
   Oxkutzcab

To Ruinas de Mayapán (45km),
Mérida (93km) via Chapab (12km)
& Mama (23km)

To Bazar de Comidas
(50m) & Maní (14km)

To Hwy 184 (1km),
Muna (20km) &
Mérida (85km)

Plaza
Mayor

Public
Market

Parque de
la Madre

Plaza
de la Cultura

Iglesia de
San Antonio
de Padua

To Hwy 184 (1km),
Oxkutzcab (16km)
& Grutas de
Loltún (23km)

To Calle 34 (600m)
for Santa Elena

To Restaurant
Los Delfines
(150m)

doubles M\$234/293) was the new kid on the block and the best value when we visited. It has good air-con, OK beds and good bathrooms in all rooms, plus TV, telephones, parking and its own restaurant.

Hotel Plaza *(☎ 972-0484, fax 972-0026;* ⓦ *www.hotelplazayucatan.com; cnr Calles 23 & 26; doubles/triples with fan M\$260/360, with air-con M\$300/400)*, once the best hotel in town, is feeling the pressure from the competition. Rooms have good beds and bathrooms, and the hotel's courtyard boasts a shady mango tree. Air-con rooms have telephone and cable TV.

Places to Eat

Ticul's lively **public market** *(Calle 28A between Calles 21 & 23)* provides all the ingredients for picnics and snacks. It also has lots of those wonderful eateries where the food is good, the portions generous and the prices low. Stalls at the new **Bazar de Comidas** *(cnr Calles 25 & 24)* serve inexpensive prepared food.

Super Salomón *(Calle 23)*, across from the public market, is a small supermarket with a big variety of groceries and household items.

El Buen Samaritano *(Calle 23)* is west of Calle 26 and bakes bread and sweet rolls.

Restaurant El Colorín *(☎ 972-0094; Calle 26 No 199B; set meals M\$27; open 8am-6pm daily)* is a cheap restaurant, half a block northwest of the plaza. Try it for a homemade meal.

Lonchería Mary *(Calle 23)*, east of Calle 28, is a clean, family-run place.

Restaurant Los Delfines *(Calle 27)*, just west of Calle 28, was temporarily closed when we visited, but people say it's the best in town.

Getting There & Away

Bus & Colectivo Ticul's **bus terminal** *(Calle 24)* is behind the massive church. Mayab runs frequent 2nd-class buses between Mérida and Ticul (M\$30, 1½ hours) from 4:30am to 9:45pm. Mayab and TRP run 11 buses to Felipe Carrillo Puerto (M\$81 to M\$86, four hours), frequent ones to Oxkutzcab (M\$6 to M\$7) and five a day to Chetumal (M\$123, six hours). There are also seven Mayab buses to Cancún each day (M\$166, six hours), three of which also serve Tulum (M\$118) and Playa del Carmen

(M\$140). TRP and Super Expresso have less frequent 2nd- and 1st-class services, respectively, to some of these destinations.

Colectivo vans direct to Mérida's Parque de San Juan (M\$27, 1½ hours) depart from their shiny new **terminal** *(cnr Calles 24 & 25)* as soon as they're full between 5am and 7:30pm. Combis for Oxkutzcab (M\$7, 30 minutes) leave from Calle 25A on the south side of the church between 7am and 8:30pm.

Colectivos to Santa Elena (M\$8, 15km), the village between Uxmal and Kabah, depart from Calle 30 just south of Calle 25 between 6:15am and 7:30pm. They take Hwy 02 and drop you to catch another bus northwest to Uxmal (15km) or south to Kabah (3.5km). You can take a combi or bus to Muna on Hwy 261 and then south to Uxmal (16km).

Ruta Puuc–bound travelers can catch one of the early-morning buses from Ticul to Muna and pick up the ATS tour bus (M\$50) for Labná, Sayil, Xlapak, Kabah and Uxmal at 9am on its way from Mérida. It returns to Muna at 3pm. Any of the buses leaving Ticul between 6am and 8am for Muna (M\$9) will get you there in time to catch the Ruta Puuc bus (all 2nd-class Mérida-bound buses stop in Muna). Combis for Muna (M\$8) leave from in front of Lonchería Mary on Calle 23 near Calle 28. Another route would be to catch a *colectivo* from Ticul to Santa Elena then walk a few blocks to Hwy 261, cross it, and wait for the Ruta Puuc bus to come by at 9:30am.

Car The quickest way to Uxmal, Kabah and the Ruta Puuc sites is via Santa Elena. From central Ticul, go west to Calle 34 and turn south (left); it heads straight to Santa Elena as Hwy 02.

Those headed east to Quintana Roo and the Caribbean coast by car can take Hwy 184 from Ticul through Oxkutzcab to Tekax, Tzucacab and José María Morelos (which has a gas station). At Polyuc, 130km from Ticul, a road turns left (east), ending after 80km in Felipe Carrillo Puerto, 210km from Ticul. The right fork of the road goes south to the region of Laguna Bacalar.

Between Oxkutzcab and Felipe Carrillo Puerto or Bacalar there are few restaurants or gasoline stations, and no hotels. Mostly you see small, typical Yucatecan villages, with their traditional Mayan thatched houses, *topes* (speed bumps) and agricultural activity.

TICUL TO VALLADOLID

The 239km route from Ticul to Valladolid via Tihosuco, in Quintana Roo, is seldom traveled by tourists. The highways that link the three cities variously pass through farmland and jungle and occasionally offer travelers a glimpse of Mayan life that has changed little in recent centuries. Indeed, the Maya in these parts entered the 21st century continuing to honor the gods of rain, wind and agriculture, and to hold religious ceremonies in their fields presided over by a wise man, just as their ancestors had done before them.

Along this route it's still possible to find hamlets of thatched wooden huts nearly identical to those used by the ancient Maya a millennium ago. The homes of today's rural Maya are still rectangular-shaped, wood-framed huts with lean-to roofs of palm. The walls are made of bamboo poles or branches, and the spaces between the poles are often filled with mud to keep rats and other pests out.

The typical Mayan home is generally no bigger than a two-car garage, and the dwelling may be divided into two rooms by a curtain or wall, with one room used as a kitchen and the other as a living room and sleeping area. Contemporary Maya prefer hammocks to beds, just like their ancestors.

Anywhere from a stone's throw to an hour's walk from the hut is a *milpa*, or corn field. Corn tortillas remain a staple of the Mayan diet, but the Maya also raise pigs and turkeys and produce honey, squash and other crops, which they sell in town markets.

Except in the towns of Oxkutzcab, Tekax and Tihosuco, which offer budget accommodations, there are no hotels to be found along roads connecting Ticul, Tihosuco and Valladolid. Beyond Oxkutzcab, the towns along this route are linked by combis and, less frequently, local buses; they may be hailed from the roadside.

Oxkutzcab

Located 16km southeast of Ticul, Oxkutzcab is renowned for its daily produce market and colonial church. Markets were the principal means of trade for the ancient Maya, and the peninsula's indigenous people still travel from the countryside to central communities to exchange produce at stalls beside a main square. Oxkutzcab is such a community.

Here, alongside Hwy 184, which becomes a slow-moving, two-lane road as it passes through central Oxkutzcab, the visitor can't miss seeing the magnificent Franciscan mission at the center of town, out front of which is the sprawling produce market.

The church is remarkable mostly for its ornamental facade, at the center of which is a stone statue of St Francis, the mission patron. Two large belfries flank the statue of the saint, and worn statues of friars stand between the bell openings. The church, which was constructed at a snail's pace from 1640 to 1693, is also remarkable for its magnificent altarpiece. Indeed, it's one of only a few baroque altarpieces in the Yucatán to survive the revolts that have occurred since its construction. Among the many finely detailed features of the altarpiece are six relief panels that illustrate the main events in the lives of Christ and the Virgin. Images of friars and saints surround the Virgin, and tokens of thanks appear at the foot of the shrine.

A mural in the plaza across from the market depicts inquisitor Friar Diego de Landa burning idols and codices while Mayas cling to his hassock, vainly pleading for him to stop. This took place in Maní, 8km to the north, in 1562 (see History in the Facts about the Yucatán chapter).

Tekax

Unlike the church at Oxkutzcab, the one in Tekax has been looted a couple of times, initially during the War of the Castes and later during the Mexican Revolution. Still, it's worth a visit if you happen to be in the area.

Situated in an increasingly prosperous area, due to a successful crop switch from corn to sugarcane and citrus, Tekax in recent years replaced the church's damaged floor with a beautiful tiled floor and added a lovely new stone altar. The interior was whitewashed and looks probably as good as it ever did. According to *Maya Missions: Exploring the Spanish Colonial Churches of Yucatán*, a fabulous book by Richard and Rosalind Perry, during construction of the church one of the church's belfries collapsed, burying (and presumably crushing) the many indigenous laborers beneath it under tons of rubble. Miraculously, as local legend has it, no one lost their life in the collapse, and construction thereafter continued uneventfully until completion.

Also noteworthy is the shape of the church, which undoubtedly was constructed of materials taken from nearby Mayan temples. The general form of the church is that of a three-tiered pyramid. Possibly the architecture took the shape from the Mayan structure from which the building blocks were taken.

Certainly not 'borrowed' from the Maya are the Moorish belfries at the front corners of the building, and a framed relief of the Franciscan coat of arms situated atop an elaborately decorated doorway. Inside, only the simply carved scalloped basins are original; everything else that could have been destroyed or removed with ease is gone.

Tihosuco

Tihosuco, located several kilometers inside the state of Quintana Roo, was a major military outpost for the Spanish during the late 16th century and for 300 years thereafter. During this time, the town came under numerous Mayan assaults, and in 1686 it was attacked, though not sacked, by pirates led by legendary Dutch buccaneer Lorencillo.

During many of those attacks, the Spaniards retreated to the heavily fortified 17th-century church at the center of town, which for much of its life served as both a house of God and an arsenal and stronghold. At one time it was quite beautiful, with ornamental details throughout and a colonnaded facade that was pure artwork.

But the town and church fell to rebel hands in 1866 following a long siege, and much of the magnificent building was gutted. Today, a third of the curved roof is gone, as is more than half of the facade. What remains of the once-great church is still worth investigating if time permits; it's quite impressive even with the roof missing. Services are still held inside, as in many other roofless churches in the region.

Also in Tihosuco, housed in an 18th-century building one block straight ahead of the church, is the **Museo de la Guerra de Castas** *(Museum of the War of the Castes; admission M$5; open 10am-6pm Tues-Sun)*. It does a good job of detailing the more than three centuries of oppression suffered by the Mayas on the peninsula, and their several uprisings against it. The descriptions of

social and economic divisions in the Yucatán supply a broader context. Only a couple of explanations are translated into English, but the dioramas, paintings, photos and artifacts (including various weapons and a collection of old coins and bills) are interesting all the same. The grounds also hold a botanical garden with a variety of medicinal plants, and you can buy products made from them, as well as honey and postcards.

From Tihosuco, it's a fast ride up Hwy 295 to Valladolid. Along the way you can expect the usual traffic stop and questions by military personnel as you cross the border back into Yucatán state.

North & West of Mérida

DZIBILCHALTÚN

Situated about 17km due north of downtown Mérida, Dzibilchaltún *(Place of Inscribed Flat Stones; admission M$57 Mon-Sat, M$37 Sun & holidays; open 8am-5pm daily)* was the longest continuously utilized Mayan administrative and ceremonial city, serving the Maya from 1500 BC or earlier until the European conquest in the 1540s. At the height of its greatness, Dzibilchaltún covered 15 sq km. Some 8500 structures were mapped by archaeologists in the 1960s; only a few of these have been excavated and restored.

Enter the site along a nature trail that terminates at the modern, air-con **Museo del Pueblo Maya** *(open 8am-4pm Tues-Sun)*, featuring artifacts from throughout the Mayan regions of Mexico, including some superb colonial-era religious carvings and other pieces. Exhibits explaining Mayan daily life and beliefs from ancient times until the present are labeled in Spanish and English. Beyond the museum, a path leads to the central plaza, where you'll find an open chapel that dates from early Spanish times (1590–1600). At the time of research, half the museum was still closed due to damage from Hurricane Isidore, but repairs were under way.

The **Templo de las Siete Muñecas** (Temple of the Seven Dolls), which got its name from seven grotesque dolls discovered here during excavations, is a 1km walk from the central plaza. It is most unimpressive but for its precise astronomical orientation: the rising and setting sun of the equinoxes 'lights up' the temple's windows and doors, making them blaze like beacons and signaling this important turning point in the year.

The **Cenote Xlacah**, now a public swimming pool, is more than 40m deep. In 1958 a National Geographic Society diving expedition recovered more than 30,000 Mayan artifacts, many of ritual significance, from the cenote. The most interesting of these are now on display in the site's museum. South of the cenote is **Estructura 44**, at 130m one of the longest Mayan structures in existence.

Parking costs M$10. Minibuses and *colectivo* taxis depart frequently from Mérida's **Parque de San Juan** *(Calle 69 between Calles 62 & 64)* for the village of Dzibilchaltún Ruinas (M$8, 15km, 30 minutes), a little over 1km from the museum.

PROGRESO
☎ 969 • pop 46,000

If Mérida's heat has you dying for a quick beach fix, or you want to see the longest wharf (7km) in Mexico, head to Progreso (also known as Puerto Progreso). Otherwise there's little reason to visit this dual-purpose port-resort town. The beach is fine, well groomed and long, but except for the small *palapas* (thatched shelters) erected by restaurants it's nearly shadeless and is dominated by the view of the wharf, giving it a rather industrial feel. Winds hit here full force off the Gulf in the afternoon and can blow well into the night. As with other Gulf beaches, the water is murky; visibility even on calm days rarely exceeds 5m. None of this stops meridanos from coming in droves on weekends, especially in the summer months. Even on spring weekdays it can be difficult to find a room with a view.

In the fall of 2002, a combination car-ferry–cruise-ship service began between Tampa (Florida) and Progreso. Even before this service began, regular cruise lines were bringing passengers to the port, though at the time of research several cruises had been canceled due to passenger complaints about the town.

Downtown Progreso's streets got new signs in anticipation of the foreign tourist boom, and its confusing dual numbering system was largely changed. Even-numbered streets run east–west and decrease by increments of two eastward; odd ones decrease by two northward. The **bus terminal** *(Calle 29)* is west of Calle 82, a block north (toward the water) from the main plaza. From the plaza on Calle 80, it is six short blocks to the waterfront *malecón* (boulevard; Calle 19) and *muelle* (wharf); along the way are two Banamex banks, one with an ATM.

Places to Stay & Eat
All hotels and restaurants listed are no more than a total of 11 blocks north and east of the station.

Hotel Miralmar *(☎ 935-0552; Calle 27 No 124 at Calle 76; 1-/2-bed doubles with fan M$130/200; doubles with air-con M$280)*, four blocks inland, has mostly good beds, decent bathrooms and good natural light. Rooms on the upper floor offer better ventilation and baths.

Hotel Tropical Suites *(☎ 935-1263, fax 935-3093; cnr Malecón & Calle 70; 1-/2-bed doubles with fan M$200/250, with air-con M$280/300)* is a seaside hotel with 21 tidy rooms, some with sea views.

Hotel Real del Mar *(☎ 935-0798; doubles M$180-330)*, across the street from Tropical Suites, features 15 air-conditioned rooms with various configurations of beds and views.

Restaurant Los Pelícanos *(☎ 935-0798; cnr Malecón & Calle 70; mains M$45-150; open 8am-11pm daily)*, by the Hotel Real del Mar, has a shady terrace, sea views, a good menu and moderate prices, considering its location.

Restaurant Mary Doly *(Calle 25 between Calles 74 & 76; breakfasts M$15-25, lunch & dinner mains M$35-55; open 7am-5pm Mon-Sat, 7am-5pm Sun)*, near the Hotel Miralmar, is a homey place with good, cheap seafood, meat and breakfasts.

Restaurant El Cordobes *(☎ 935-2621; cnr Calles 80 & 31; mains M$35-55; open 6am-11:30pm daily)*, also near Hotel Miralmar, is on the north side of the plaza in a 100-year-old building with character.

Getting There & Away
Progreso is 33km due north of Mérida along a fast four-lane highway that's basically a continuation of the Paseo de Montejo. If you're driving, head north on the Paseo and follow the signs for Progreso. For bus

information see the Mérida Getting There & Away section earlier in the chapter.

For information on ferry services between Progreso and Tampa (Florida), see Sea in the Getting There & Away chapter.

EAST OF PROGRESO

Heading east from Progreso, Hwy 27 parallels the coast for 70km, to Dzilam de Bravo, before turning inland. Taking a few twists and turns the road continues a further 100km east and north to hit the coast again at the charming fishing village of San Felipe (see that section later). The most interesting bits of this area are relatively close to Progreso and are best explored by car.

The coastal stretch to Dzilam de Bravo was one of the areas hit hardest by Hurricane Isidore, which battered fishing fleets and destroyed or damaged many structures. Indeed, at last pass a new channel between lagoon and sea still cut the road beyond Chabihau, at Km 57, making it entirely impassable.

For the first 16km from Progreso to Uaymitún the beach is separated from the road by a solid line of condos, hotels, restaurants and summer homes of *meridanos*. To the south of the road is mangrove, lagoon, marsh and other wetland, part of a strip that stretches nearly uninterrupted from just north of the city of Campeche all the way around the top of the peninsula nearly to Cancún.

At Uaymitún a tall wooden observation tower at the edge of the lagoon allows you to watch flamingos, as well as ibis, herons, spoonbills and other waterfowl. You can rent binoculars for the purpose.

The buildings thin out beyond Uaymitún, and about 16km east of it a road heads south from the coast some 3km across the bird-riddled Laguna Rosada (Pink Lagoon) to the turnoff for the ruins of Xcambó, which was a Mayan salt-distribution center. It's a mostly unremarkable site, and much looks to be reconstructed entirely from scratch.

Following the road south beyond the ruins turnoff takes you into grassy marshland with cattails and scatterings of palm trees, a beautiful landscape providing ample opportunities for bird-spotting without even getting out of the car.

Continuing south on this road takes you back to civilization at Motul, from where you can head in any number of directions: east and south to Izamal, west and north to the Dzibilchaltún ruins, or west and south to Mérida via Conkal, whose Convento de San Francisco de Asís now houses the new **Museo de Arte Sacro** *(admission free; open 9am-6pm Tues-Sat, 9am-2pm Sun)*. This is a small but well-done museum of religious art and artifacts, including 18th- and 19th-century altarpieces and carvings of saints, good historical and archaeological exhibits detailing the foundation (and later restoration) of Yucatán's monasteries, and contemporary profane and religious artwork. Some of the latter is surprisingly racy. All labeling is in Spanish. Be sure to check out the architecture of the convent itself, including the *noria* (irrigation system) out back.

CELESTÚN

☎ 988 • pop 6200

Celestún, to the west of Mérida, is in the middle of the Reserva de la Biósfera Ría Celestún, a wildlife sanctuary abounding in resident and migratory waterfowl, with flamingos as the star attraction. It makes a good beach-and-bird day trip from Mérida, and it's also a great place to kick back and do nothing for a few days, especially if you've become road-weary. Fishing boats dot the appealing white-sand beach that stretches to the north for kilometers, and afternoon breezes cool the town on most days.

Though the winds can kick up sand and roil the sea, making the already none-too-clear water unpleasant for swimming, they are less intense than in Progreso. Celestún is sheltered by the peninsula's southward curve, resulting in an abundance of marine life. It's a fine place to watch the sun set into the sea, and if you are from a west coast anywhere you'll feel perfectly oriented. If you're not from a west coast, all you need to know is that Calle 11 is the road into town (it comes due west from Mérida), ending at Calle 12, the road paralleling the beach along which lie most of the restaurants and hotels.

Flamingo Tours

The 591-sq-km Reserva de la Biósfera Ría Celestún is home to a huge variety of animal life, including a large flamingo colony.

The best months to see the flamingos are from March or April to about September, outside the season of the *nortes* (winds and rains arriving from the north). Morning is the best time of day, though from 4pm onward the birds tend to concentrate in one area after the day's feeding, which can make for good viewing. You can hire a boat for bird-watching either from the bridge on the highway into town (about 1.5km inland) or from the beach itself.

Tours from the beach last 2½ to three hours and begin with a ride south along the coast for several kilometers, during which you can expect to see egrets, herons, cormorants, sandpipers and many other species of bird. The boat then turns into the mouth of the ría (estuary) and passes through a 'petrified forest,' where tall coastal trees once belonging to a freshwater ecosystem were killed by saltwater intrusion long ago and remain standing, hard as rock.

Continuing up the ría takes you under the highway bridge where the other tours begin and beyond which lie the flamingos. Depending on the tide, the hour and the season, you may see hundreds or thousands of the colorful birds. Don't encourage your captain to approach them too closely; a startled flock taking wing can result in injuries and deaths (for the birds). In addition to taking you to the flamingos, the captain will wend through a 200m mangrove tunnel and visit one or both (as time and inclination allow) of the freshwater cenote–springs welling into the saltwater of the estuary, where you can take a refreshing dip.

Tours cost about M$150 per passenger with a minimum of six (boats carry up to eight passengers if it's not too rough). You can try for M$900 per boatload, but this may take some doing. Boats depart from several beachside spots, including from outside Restaurant Celestún, at the foot of Calle 11. The restaurant's beachfront *palapa* is a pleasant place to wait for a group to accumulate.

Tours from the bridge, where there is a parking lot, ticket booth and a place to wait for fellow passengers, are cheaper and last about 1¼ hours. For M$400 per boat (maximum six passengers) plus M$20 per passenger, you get to see the flamingos, mangrove tunnel and spring. It's also possible to add a trip from the bridge south to the 'petrified forest,' for an additional M$400 and a total time of about 2½ hours.

With either operation, bridge or beach, your captain may or may not speak English. An English-speaking guide can be hired at the bridge for about M$200 for the short tour; this reduces the maximum possible number of passengers, of course. Bring snacks, water and sunscreen for the longer tours, and cash for any of them. There is no bank in town, and neither credit cards nor traveler's checks are accepted by the tour operators.

Beach & Birding

North of town, beyond the small navy post, you'll find more secluded stretches of beach. In the same area, but inland of the road, lies a large section of scrub stretching east to the estuary that provides good birding opportunities. South and east of town, toward the abandoned Hacienda Real de Salinas, is another good area for natural observation. Flamingos, white pelicans, cormorants, anhingas and many other species frequent the shores and waters of the ría. The hacienda itself makes an interesting excursion as well.

Hacienda Real de Salinas

This abandoned hacienda a few kilometers south and east of town once produced dyewood and salt, and served as a summer home for a family from Campeche. It's about 5km in from the mouth of the estuary. Out in the ría you can see a cairn marking an *ojo de agua dulce* (freshwater spring) that once supplied the hacienda.

The buildings are decaying in a most scenic way; you can still see shells in the wall mixed into the building material, as well as pieces of French roof tiles that served as ballast in ships on the way from Europe and were sold. Many intact tiles with the brickworks' name and location, Marseille, are still visible in what's left of the roofs. The hacienda makes a good bicycle excursion from town. Coming south, go left at the Y, or turn right to reach El Lastre (The Ballast), a peninsula between the estuary and its western arm. Flamingos, white pelicans and other birds are sometimes seen here. Marco, at the hostel in town, does bicycle tours to the area.

Places to Stay

Celestún's hotels are all on Calle 12, within a short walk of one another. The following list runs from north to south. Try to book ahead if you want a sea view, especially on weekends.

Eco Hotel Flamingos Playa *(☎ 916-2133, in Mérida ☎ 999-928-5708;* ⓔ *drivan@ sureste.com; Calle 12; doubles M$300-400)* is the newest hotel in town, about three blocks north of Calle 11. It has decent rooms (sea views cost more) with air-con, fan, TV, purified water and very good bathrooms. It has tile all over the place and a small beachside pool, restaurant and bar.

Hotel San Julio *(☎ 916-2062, in Mérida ☎ 999-923-6309; Calle 12; 1-/2-bed doubles M$120/150)*, also north of Calle 11, is old and a little beat-up but has its own charm. It's right on the beach, and the eight fan-cooled rooms are clean, and have good bathrooms and screens. The owner replaces the mattresses regularly, and is remodeling some of the rooms into 'minisuites,' with glass windows instead of wooden louvers, and possibly air-con. A pity!

Hotel Sofía *(in Mérida ☎ 999-990-7707; Calle 12; doubles/triples M$80/150)*, across the street and a bit south of Hotel San Julio, is a whitewashed place with eight spotless, well-maintained good-value rooms with fans. It also has secure parking and the owners let guests use the (hand) laundry facilities.

Hostel Ría Celestún *(☎ 916-2170;* ⓔ *hostelriacelestun@hotmail.com; cnr Calles 12 & 13; dorm beds M$65)*, south of Calle 11, was officially opened shortly after our last pass. It promises to be a good cheap sleep, offering single-sex fan-cooled dorms, full kitchen and laundry facilities, a courtyard and TV room for common areas, bicycle rentals and Internet access. The owner offers bicycle tours of local sights, including the very interesting Hacienda Real de Salinas nearby. Rates include a continental breakfast.

Hotel María del Carmen *(☎/fax 916-2170; cnr Calles 12 & 15; doubles with fan/air-con M$200/280)* has 14 clean and pleasant beachfront rooms; those on the upper floors have balconies facing the sea. Prices drop when things are slow. The owners rent bicycles for M$50 a day, and offer Internet access for M$15 an hour.

Places to Eat

Celestún's specialties are crab, octopus, small shrimp from the lagoon and, of course, fresh fish. Service and decor vary from restaurant to restaurant in Celestún, but the menu for the most part does not, and most places have outdoor areas on the beach. Eat early (by 7:30pm or so) on weeknights or you may find all seafood restaurants closed.

Prices vary, but expect to pay about M$50 for either the catch of the day, delicious ceviche, or crab prepared in a variety of ways, and M$25 for a conch, shrimp, crab or octopus cocktail.

La Playita, a few doors north of the foot of Calle 11, offers large portions of good food, as well as good service.

Restaurante Chivirico *(cnr Calles 11 & 12)* is another good place, and the English translations on its menu are absolutely hilarious. The *ensalada de jaiba* (crab salad, M$50) is delicious.

El Lobo *(open 7am-noon & 7pm-midnight daily)*, a block inland on the southwest edge of the plaza, is a tiny place with a rooftop terrace. It's run by a Dutch couple who serve breakfasts (good cappuccino, bad hotcakes), pizza and pasta.

Getting There & Away

Buses from Mérida head for Celestún (M$37, two hours) 17 times daily between 5am and 8pm from the terminal on Calle 50 between Calles 67 and 65. The route terminates at Celestún's plaza, a block inland from Calle 12. Returning to Mérida, buses run from 5am to 8pm.

See Organized Tours under Mérida for agencies that do day trips to the flamingos for around M$440, leaving Mérida at 9am and returning at 5pm. Tour prices include transportation, a guide, boat tour and lunch.

By car from Mérida, the best route to Celestún is via the new road out of Umán. At last pass the gas station on the east edge of Celestún was closed. Another Pemex station lies on the southeastern edge of town, at the *puerto de abrigo* (a shallow port sheltering the fishing fleet).

RUINED HACIENDAS ROUTE

A fascinating alternative return route if you're driving out of Celestún is to turn right (south) off Hwy 281 about 19km east of town, where a sign points to Chunchucmil. The road has some potholes along the 25km stretch to Chunchucmil, which is the name of both a ruined henequen hacienda and a nearby Mayan archaeological site. The hacienda serves as headquarters for archaeologists excavating the site. After here the road is in good shape (look for the covered Mayan mounds as you drive away), and about every 5km passes another ruined hacienda all the way to Hacienda Granada, shortly before the road hits old Hwy 180.

You can have a look at most of the five haciendas (ask permission at Granada; the owner lives there). An exception is **Hacienda Santa Rosa** (☎ 999-910-4852; W www.star wood.com/luxury; rooms US$250-500) which has been marvelously restored and turned into a luxurious hotel. The 11 rooms show amazing variety; some have private walled gardens with bathtubs or plunge pools. It's very slow-paced and a good place to unwind.

Eastern Yucatán State

IZAMAL
☎ 988 • pop 14,400

In ancient times, Izamal was a center for the worship of the supreme Mayan god, Itzamná, and the sun god, Kinich-Kakmó. A dozen temple pyramids were devoted to these or other gods. Perhaps these bold expressions of Mayan religiosity are why the Spanish colonists chose Izamal as the site for an enormous and impressive Franciscan monastery, which today stands at the heart of this town just under 70km east of Mérida.

The Izamal of today is a quiet, colonial gem of a provincial town, nicknamed La Ciudad Amarilla (The Yellow City) for the traditional yellow that most buildings are painted. It is easily explored on foot and makes a great day trip from Mérida. Horse-drawn carriages add to the city's charm.

The monastery's front entrance faces west; it's flanked by Calles 31 and 33 on the north and south, respectively, and 28 and 30 on the east and west.

Things to See & Do
When the Spaniards conquered Izamal, they destroyed the major Mayan temple, the Ppapp-Hol-Chac pyramid, and in 1533 began to build from its stones one of the first monasteries in the Western Hemisphere. Work on **Convento de San Antonio de Padua** (admission free; open 6am-8pm daily) was finished in 1561. Under the

monastery's arcades, look for building stones with an unmistakable mazelike design; these were clearly taken from the earlier Mayan temple.

The monastery's principal church is the **Santuario de la Virgen de Izamal**, approached by a ramp from the main square. The ramp leads into the **Atrium**, a huge arcaded courtyard in which the fiesta of the Virgin of Izamal takes place each August 15.

At some point, the 16th-century **frescoes** beside the entrance of the sanctuary were completely painted over. For years they lay concealed under a thin layer of whitewash until a maintenance worker who was cleaning the walls discovered them a few years ago. The church's original altarpiece was destroyed by a fire believed to have been started by a fallen candle. Its replacement, impressively gilded, was built in the 1940s. In the niches at the stations of the cross are some superb small figures.

In the small courtyard to the left of the church, look up and toward the Atrium to see the original sundial projecting from the roof's edge. A small **museum** at the back commemorates Pope John Paul II's 1993 visit to the monastery. He brought with him a silver crown for the statue of the patron saint of Yucatán, the Virgin of Izamal.

The best time to visit is in the morning, as the church is occasionally closed during the afternoon siesta.

Three of the town's original 12 Mayan **pyramids** have been partially restored so far. The largest is the enormous **Kinich-Kakmó**, three blocks north of the monastery. You can climb it for free.

Places to Stay & Eat
Hotel Canto (Calle 31; doubles M$150), in front of the monastery, has rather musty but clean rooms. Tiny skylights and once-colorful murals help brighten them, and far at the back of the property is one of Izamal's pyramids. A restaurant at the front serves cheap meals.

Macan-Ché (☎/fax 954-0287; W www .macanche.com; Calle 22 No 305; doubles M$250-500) is about three long blocks east of the monastery (take Calle 31 toward Cancún and turn right on Calle 22). The charming hotel has a cluster of cottages and a small pool in a woodsy setting, with 12 pretty rooms in all. The most expensive has

Henequen: A Smelly, Bitter Harvest

Henequen (*Agave fourcroydes*), also called sisal, is a common plant in Yucatán and indeed in most of Mexico. Its stalk grows almost 2m high in the wild, about 1m high in cultivation, and has lance-shaped leaves up to 2m long and 10cm to 15cm wide, edged with thorns. The plant's evil-smelling flowers are borne on a central stalk, which grows straight up to heights of 6m. Agaves flower periodically but infrequently, some species only once in a century.

A cultivated henequen plant yields about 25 leaves annually from the fifth to the 16th year after planting. The leaves are cut off by a worker with a machete, taken to a factory, and crushed between heavy rollers. The pulpy vegetable matter is scraped away to reveal fiber strands up to 1.5m in length, which are slightly stretchable and resistant to marine organisms.

Around Izamal and en route from Mérida to Celestún, as well as in several other locations, you pass through or near the henequen fields that gave rise to Yucatán's affluence in the 19th century, when workers toiled on the haciendas under what was basically a feudal system. Prosperity in these parts reached its high point during WWI, when the demand for rope was great and synthetic fibers had not yet been invented.

Sometimes you can smell the grayish, spike-leafed henequen plants before you can see them, as they emit a putrid, excremental odor. Once planted, henequen can grow virtually untended for seven years. Thereafter, the plants are annually stripped for fiber. A plant may be productive for upwards of two decades.

These days great quantities of henequen are imported from Brazil and processed into rope and other products in the maquiladoras of Yucatán state. Growing henequen on the peninsula is still economically viable, if barely; synthetic fibers and cheap imported henequen have greatly diminished the profits. The decline has been hard on the few Mayan farm workers who still struggle to keep the defibering machines operating on a few former haciendas.

air-con and a kitchenette. Rates include a big breakfast.

Restaurant Kinich-Kakmó (☎ *954-0489; Calle 27 between Calles 28 & 30; mains M$50; open 11:30am-5pm daily*), three blocks north of the monastery, is casual and extremely friendly, offering fan-cooled patio dining beside a garden. It specializes in traditional Yucatecan food, and you can have an absolute feast for less than M$80.

Several *loncherías* occupy spaces in the market on the monastery's southwest side.

Getting There & Away

Oriente operates frequent buses between Mérida and Izamal (M$26, 1½ hours) from the 2nd-class terminal. There are buses from Valladolid (M$26 to M$32, two hours) as well. Coming from Chichén Itzá you must change buses at Hoctún. Izamal's bus terminal is two short blocks west of the monastery.

Other services from Izamal include buses to Tizimín (M$50, 2½ hours) and Cancún (M$86, six hours). Shared vans leave from Calle 31 a block north of Hotel Canto for Mérida; they charge M$20 and arrive in Mérida on the corner of Calles 67 and 50.

Driving from the west, turn north at Hoctún to reach Izamal; from the east, turn north at Kantunil.

CHICHÉN ITZÁ

The most famous and best restored of the Yucatán Peninsula's Mayan sites, Chichén Itzá (*Mouth of the Well of the Itzáes; admission M$87 Mon-Sat, M$37 Sun & holidays; open 8am-5:30pm daily winter, 8am-6pm daily summer*) will awe even the most jaded visitor. Many mysteries of the Mayan astronomical calendar are made clear when one understands the design of the 'time temples' here. Other than a few minor passageways, El Castillo is now the only structure at the site you're allowed to climb or enter.

At the vernal and autumnal equinoxes (March 20 to 21 and September 21 to 22), the morning and afternoon sun produces a light-and-shadow illusion of the serpent ascending or descending the side of El Castillo's staircase. Chichén is mobbed on these dates, however, making it difficult to get close enough to see, and after the spectacle, parts of the site are sometimes closed to the public. The illusion is almost as good

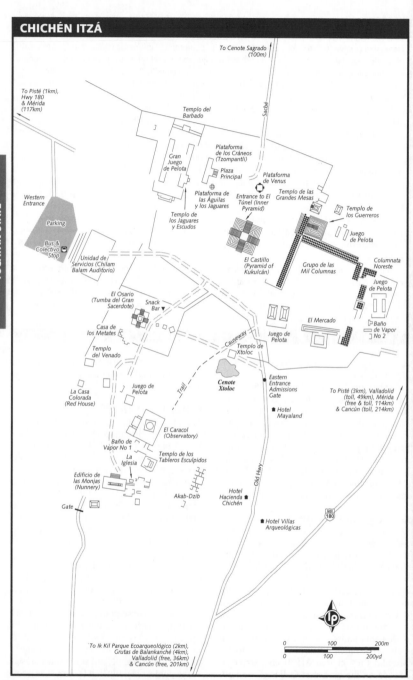

CHICHÉN ITZÁ

To Cenote Sagrado (100m)

To Pisté (1km), Hwy 180 & Mérida (117km)

Templo del Barbado

Sacbé

Plataforma de los Cráneos (Tzompantli)

Plaza Principal

Plataforma de Venus

Templo de las Grandes Mesas

Gran Juego de Pelota

Plataforma de las Águilas y los Jaguares

Entrance to El Túnel (Inner Pyramid)

Templo de los Guerreros

Templo de los Jaguares y Escudos

Juego de Pelota

Western Entrance

Parking

Bus & Colectivo Stop

Unidad de Servicios (Chilam Balam Auditorio)

El Castillo (Pyramid of Kukulcán)

Grupo de las Mil Columnas

Columnata Noreste

Juego de Pelota

El Osario (Tumba del Gran Sacerdote)

Snack Bar

El Mercado

Baño de Vapor No 2

Casa de los Metates

Templo del Venado

Juego de Pelota

Causeway

Templo de Xtoloc

La Casa Colorada (Red House)

Juego de Pelota

Trail

Cenote Xtoloc

Eastern Entrance Admissions Gate

To Pisté (3km), Valladolid (toll, 49km), Mérida (free & toll, 114km) & Cancún (toll, 214km)

Hotel Mayaland

El Caracol (Observatory)

Baño de Vapor No 1

La Iglesia

Templo de los Tableros Esculpidos

Edificio de las Monjas (Nunnery)

Akab-Dzib

Old Hwy

Gate

Hotel Hacienda Chichén

Hotel Villas Arqueológicas

MEX 180

To Ik Kil Parque Ecoarqueológico (2km), Grutas de Balankanché (4km), Valladolid (free, 36km) & Cancún (free, 201km)

0   100   200m
0   100   200yd

YUCATÁN STATE

in the week preceding and following each equinox, and is re-created nightly in the light-and-sound show year-round.

Heat, humidity and crowds can be fierce; try to spend the night nearby and do your exploration of the site (especially climbing El Castillo) either early in the morning or late in the afternoon. In Pisté town, vendors of all ages hawk plaster casts of Mayan statuettes painted to look like carved wood. They become so numerous and persistent at times that you may feel like one of the besieged protagonists in *Night of the Living Dead.*

History

Most archaeologists agree that the first major settlement at Chichén Itzá, during the late Classic period, was pure Mayan. In about the 9th century, the city was largely abandoned for reasons unknown. It was re-settled around the late 10th century, and shortly thereafter it is believed to have been invaded by the Toltecs, who had migrated from their central highlands capital of Tula, north of Mexico City. Toltec culture was fused with that of the Maya, incorporating the cult of Quetzalcóatl (Kukulcán, in Mayan). You will see images of both Chac, the Mayan rain god, and Quetzalcóatl, the plumed serpent, throughout the city.

The substantial fusion of highland central Mexican and Puuc architectural styles makes Chichén unique among the Yucatán Peninsula's ruins. The fabulous El Castillo and the Plataforma de Venus are outstanding architectural works built during the height of Toltec cultural input.

The warlike Toltecs contributed more than their architectural skills to the Maya. They elevated human sacrifice to a near obsession, and there are numerous carvings of the bloody ritual in Chichén demonstrating this. After a Maya leader moved his political capital to Mayapán while keeping Chichén as his religious capital, Chichén Itzá fell into decline. Why it was subsequently abandoned in the 14th century is a mystery, but the once-great city remained the site of Mayan pilgrimages for many years.

Orientation

Most of Chichén's lodgings, restaurants and services are arranged along 1km of highway in the village of Pisté, to the western

(Mérida) side of the ruins. It's 1.5km from the ruins' main (west) entrance to the first hotel (Pirámide Inn) in Pisté, and 2.5km from the ruins to Pisté village plaza, which is shaded by a huge tree. Buses generally stop at the plaza; you can make the hot walk to and from the ruins in 20 to 30 minutes.

On the eastern (Cancún) side, it's 1.5km from the highway along the access road to the eastern entrance to the ruins; three top-end hotels line the road, the closest being only about 100m from the entrance.

Information

As at most sites, filming with a video camera costs M$30 extra, and tripods require a special permit from Mexico City. Hold on to your wristband ticket; it gives you in-and-out privileges and admission to that evening's sound-and-light show. Parking costs M$10. Explanatory plaques around the site are in Spanish, English and Mayan.

The main, western entrance has a large parking lot and a big visitors center, the **Unidad de Servicios** (☎ 985-851-0124; open 8am-9pm). The Unidad has a small but worthwhile **museum** (open 8am-5pm) with sculptures, reliefs, artifacts and explanations of these in Spanish, English and French.

The **Chilam Balam Auditorio**, next to the museum, sometimes has video shows about Chichén and other Mexican sites. The picture quality can be truly abominable, but the air-con is great. In the central space of the Unidad stands a scale model of the archaeological site, and off toward the toilets is an exhibit on Edward Thompson's excavations of the Sacred Cenote. Facilities include two **bookstores** with a good assortment of guides and maps, a restaurant serving decent if somewhat pricey food, a Banamex ATM, Telmex card phones, excellent free bathrooms and, around the corner from the ticket counter, a free *guardaequipaje* (room for storing luggage) where you can leave your belongings while you explore the site.

The 45-minute **sound-and-light show** in Spanish begins each evening at 8pm in summer and 7pm in winter. It costs M$30 if you don't have a ruins wristband, and it's applicable toward the admission price the following day. Devices for listening to English, French, German or Italian translations (beamed via infrared) rent for M$25. Specify the language you need or it may not be broadcast.

Exploring The Ruins

El Castillo As you approach from the turnstiles at the Unidad de Servicios into the archaeological zone, El Castillo (also called the Pyramid of Kukulcán) rises before you in all its grandeur. The first temple here was pre-Toltec, built around AD 800, but the present 25m-high structure, built over the old one, has the plumed serpent sculpted along the stairways and Toltec warriors represented in the doorway carvings at the top of the temple.

The pyramid is actually the Mayan calendar formed in stone. Each of El Castillo's nine levels is divided in two by a staircase, making 18 separate terraces that commemorate the 18 20-day months of the Vague Year. The four stairways have 91 steps each; add the top platform and the total is 365, the number of days in the year. On each facade of the pyramid are 52 flat panels, which are reminders of the 52 years in the Calendar Round.

To top it off, during the spring and autumn equinoxes, light and shadow form a series of triangles on the side of the north staircase that mimic the creep of a serpent (note the carved serpent's heads flanking the bottom of the staircase).

The older pyramid *inside* El Castillo boasts a red jaguar throne with inlaid eyes and spots of jade; also lying behind the screen is a Chac-Mool figure. The entrance to **El Túnel**, the passage up to the throne, is at the base of El Castillo's north side; it's open only from 11am to 3pm and 4pm to 4:45pm. The dank air and steep, narrow stairway can make the climb a sweltering, slippery, claustrophobic experience.

Gran Juego de Pelota The great ball court, the largest and most impressive in Mexico, is only one of the city's eight courts, indicative of the importance the games held here. The court is flanked by temples at either end and is bounded by towering parallel walls with stone rings cemented up high.

There is evidence that the ball game may have changed over the years. Some carvings show players with padding on their elbows and knees, and it is thought that they played a soccerlike game with a hard rubber ball, the use of hands forbidden. Other carvings show players wielding bats; it appears that if a player hit the ball through one of the stone hoops, his team was declared the winner. It may be that during the Toltec period the losing captain, and perhaps his teammates as well, were sacrificed.

Along the walls of the ball court are stone reliefs, including scenes of decapitations of players. The court exhibits some interesting acoustics – a conversation at one end can be heard 135m away at the other, and a clap produces multiple loud echoes.

Templo del Barbado & Templo de los Jaguares y Escudos The structure at the northern end of the ball court, called the Temple of the Bearded Man after a carving inside of it, has some finely sculpted pillars and reliefs of flowers, birds and trees. The Temple of the Jaguars and Shields, built atop the southeast corner of the ball court's wall, has some columns with carved rattlesnakes and tablets with etched jaguars. Inside are faded mural fragments depicting a battle.

Plataforma de los Cráneos The Platform of Skulls (*tzompantli* in Náhuatl) is between the Templo de los Jaguares and El Castillo. You can't mistake it, because the T-shaped platform is festooned with carved skulls and eagles tearing open the chests of men to eat their hearts. In ancient days this platform held the heads of sacrificial victims.

Plataforma de las Águilas y los Jaguares Adjacent to the tzompantli, the carvings on the Platform of the Eagles and Jaguars depict those animals gruesomely grabbing human hearts in their claws. It is thought that this platform was part of a temple dedicated to the military legions responsible for capturing sacrificial victims.

Cenote Sagrado A 300m rough stone road runs north (a five-minute walk) to the huge sunken well that gave this city its name. The Sacred Cenote is an awesome natural well, some 60m in diameter and 35m deep. The walls between the summit and the water's surface are ensnared in tangled vines and other vegetation. There are ruins of a small steam bath next to the cenote, as well as a modern drinks stand (charging M$12 for a small bottle of water) with toilets. See the boxed text 'Dredging Chichén's Sacred Cenote' for the historical details.

Grupo de las Mil Columnas This group behind El Castillo takes its name, which means 'Group of the Thousand Columns', from the forest of pillars stretching south and east. The star attraction here is the **Templo de los Guerreros** (Temple of the Warriors), adorned with stucco and stone-carved animal deities. At the top of its steps is a classic reclining Chac-Mool figure – you're no longer allowed to ascend to it, though you might be able to snap a tele-photo shot from up on El Castillo. Many of the columns in front of the temple are carved with figures of warriors. Archaeologists working in 1926 discovered a Temple of Chac-Mool lying beneath the Temple of the Warriors.

You can walk through the columns on its south side to reach the Columnata Noreste, notable for the 'big-nosed god' masks in its facade. Some have been reassembled on the ground around the statue. Just to the south are the remains of the **Baño de Vapor** (Steam Bath or Sweat House) with an underground oven and drains for the water. The sweat houses were regularly used for ritual purification.

El Osario The Ossuary, otherwise known as the Bonehouse or the Tumba del Gran Sacerdote (High Priest's Grave), is a ruined pyramid southwest of El Castillo. As with most of the buildings in this southern section, the architecture is more Puuc than Toltec. It's notable for the beautiful serpent heads at the base of its staircases. A square shaft at the top of the structure leads into a cave beneath it that was used as a burial chamber; seven tombs with human remains were discovered inside. These days a snack bar with phone and toilets stands nearby.

El Caracol Called El Caracol (The Snail) by the Spaniards for its interior spiral staircase, this observatory is one of the most fascinating and important of all the Chichén Itzá buildings (but you can't go into it). Its circular design resembles some central highlands structures, although, surprisingly, not those of Toltec Tula. In a fusion of architectural styles and religious imagery, there are Mayan Chac rain-god masks over four external doors facing the cardinal directions. The windows in the observatory's dome are aligned with the appearance of certain stars at specific dates. From the dome the priests decreed the times for rituals, celebrations, corn-planting and harvests.

Edificio de las Monjas & La Iglesia Thought by archaeologists to have been a palace for Mayan royalty, the so-called Edificio de las Monjas (Nunnery), with its myriad rooms, resembled a European convent to the conquistadors, hence their name for the building. The building's dimensions are imposing: its base is 60m long, 30m wide and 20m high. The construction is Mayan rather than Toltec, although a Toltec sacrificial stone stands in front. A smaller adjoining building to the east, known as La Iglesia (The Church), is covered almost entirely with carvings.

Akab-Dzib On the path east of the Nunnery, the Puuc-style Akab-Dzib is thought by some archaeologists to be the most

---

Dredging Chichén's Sacred Cenote

In around 1900 Edward Thompson, a Harvard professor and US consul to Yucatán, bought the hacienda that included Chichén Itzá for US$75. No doubt intrigued by local stories of female virgins being sacrificed to the Mayan deities by being thrown into the cenote, Thompson resolved to have the cenote dredged.

He imported dredging equipment and set to work. Gold and jade jewelry from all parts of Mexico and as far away as Colombia was recovered, along with other artifacts and a variety of human bones. Many of the artifacts were shipped to Harvard's Peabody Museum, but some have since been returned to Mexico.

Subsequent diving expeditions in the 1920s and 1960s turned up hundreds of other valuable artifacts. It appears that all sorts of people, including children and old people, the diseased and the injured, and the young and the vigorous, were forcibly obliged to take an eternal swim in Chichén's Sacred Cenote.

ancient structure excavated here. The central chambers date from the 2nd century. The name means 'Obscure Writing' in Maya and refers to the south-side annex door, whose lintel depicts a priest with a vase etched with hieroglyphics that have never been translated.

Chichén Viejo Old Chichén comprises largely unrestored ruins, scattered about and hidden in the bush south of the Nunnery. The predominant architecture is Mayan, with Toltec additions and modifications. At the time of research, the public was not allowed to enter the area.

Cenote Ik Kil

About 3km east of the eastern entrance to the ruins is the turnoff for Ik Kil Parque Ecoarqueológico (☎ 985-858-1525; adult/child M$40/20; open 9am-5:30pm daily), whose cenote has been developed into a divine swimming spot. Small cascades of water plunge from the high limestone roof, which is ringed by greenery. A good buffet lunch runs an extra M$50 (beverages extra). Get your swim in by no later than 1pm to beat the tour groups. The grounds also hold five lovely cabanas with air-con and Jacuzzi that rent for M$900 each.

In late 2002 two Japanese visitors were killed by falling rock when a section of the cenote, saturated by the heavy rains of Hurricane Isidore, collapsed. It's believed that dynamite blasting during construction of the cenote's staircase created fissures that weakened the rock and allowed the water to seep in.

Grutas de Balankanché

In 1959 a guide to the Chichén ruins was exploring a cave on his day off when he came upon a narrow passageway. He followed the passageway for 300m, meandering through a series of caverns. In each, perched on mounds amid scores of glistening stalactites, were hundreds of ceremonial treasures the Maya had placed there 800 years earlier: ritual metates and *manos* (grinding stones), incense burners and pots. In the years following the discovery, the ancient ceremonial objects were removed and studied. Eventually most of them were returned to the caves, and placed exactly where they were found.

The turnoff for the caverns (admission Mon-Sat M$47, Sun M$20; ticket booth open 9am-5pm daily) is 5km east of the ruins of Chichén Itzá (about 5km southeast of the Hotel Dolores Alba and Cenote Ik Kil) on the highway to Cancún. Second-class buses heading east from Pisté toward Valladolid and Cancún will drop you at the Balankanché road. The entrance to the caves is 350m north of the highway.

Outside the caves you'll find a good botanical garden (displaying native Yucatecan flora with information on the medicinal and other uses of the trees and plants), a small museum, a shop selling cold drinks and souvenirs, and a ticket booth with free luggage check. The museum features large photographs taken during the exploration of the caves, and descriptions (in English, Spanish and French) of the Mayan religion and the offerings found in the caves. Also on display are photographs of modern-day Mayan ceremonies called Ch'a Chaac, which continue to be held in all the villages on the Yucatán Peninsula during times of drought and consist mostly of praying and making numerous offerings of food to Chac.

Compulsory 40-minute tours (minimum six people, maximum 30 people) have melodramatic recorded narration that is nearly impossible to make out and is not very informative, but if you'd like it in a particular language, English is at 11am, 1pm and 3pm; Spanish is at 9am, noon, 2pm and 4pm; and French is at 10am.

Be warned that the cave is unusually hot, and ventilation is poor in its farther reaches. The lack of oxygen (and abundance of carbon dioxide, especially after a few groups have already passed through) makes it difficult to draw a full breath until you're outside again.

Places to Stay

No matter what you plan to spend on a bed, don't hesitate to haggle in the off-season (May, June, September and October), when prices should be lower. Hwy 180 is known as Calle 15A on its way through Pisté.

Budget Camping is allowed at **Pirámide Inn** (☎ 985-851-0115, fax 985-851-0114; ⓦ www .piramideinn.com; Calle 15A No 30; hammock or tent sites per person M$40), an agreeable place on the west side of Pisté (see

Mid-Range, following, for more details). You can pitch a tent or hang a hammock under a *palapa*, enjoy the inn's pool and watch satellite TV in the lobby. Campers have use of tepid showers, clean shared toilet facilities and a safe place to stow gear.

Hotel Posada Maya (☎ 985-851-0211; *Calle 8 between Calles 15 & 10; hammock sites M$40, singles/doubles M$130/160)*, just north of the highway (look for the sign), around the corner from the Oriente ticket office, has clean fan rooms with decent beds, but poor screens. It's a very modest place.

Posada Olalde (☎ 985-851-0086; *Calle 6 at Calle 17; singles/doubles M$135/200, bungalows M$180)*, two blocks south of the highway by Artesanías Guayacán, is the best of Pisté's several small pensiones. It offers five clean, quiet and attractive rooms and four rustic but charming and decent-sized bungalows. All accommodations are fan-cooled, and the friendly manager speaks Spanish and English, as well as some German and Mayan.

Posada Poxil (☎ 985-851-0116; *Calle 15A; doubles/triples/quads M$200/250/300)*, at the western end of Pisté, has relatively clean, quiet fan rooms with good light and ventilation and an inexpensive restaurant serving big breakfasts (M$25) and Yucatecan dishes. The pool was being repaired at last pass.

Posada Chac-Mool (☎ 985-851-0270; *Calle 15A; singles/doubles/triples with fan M$160/180/220, with air-con M$300/330/360)*, just east of the Hotel Chichén Itzá and on the opposite (south) side of the highway in Pisté, has fairly basic doubles with good screens. All are available with good air-con to augment the fans.

Mid-Range All rooms in this category have air-con.

Hotel Chichén Itzá (☎ 985-851-0022, fax 985-851-0023; W *www.mayaland.com; Calle 15A No 45; doubles M$400-600)*, on the west side of Pisté, has 42 pleasant rooms with tile floors and old-style brick-tile ceilings. Rooms in the upper range face the pool and the nicely landscaped grounds. The restaurant serves a M$60 buffet lunch from 11am to 5pm daily.

Pirámide Inn (☎ 985-851-0115, fax 985-851-0114; W *www.piramideinn.com; Calle 15A No 30; doubles M$410)* is next to the eastern bus stop in Pisté. The 42 spacious rooms have good bathrooms and two OK double beds. The hotel also has a book exchange, a deep swimming pool and a Mayan ruin on its gardened grounds, and a restaurant serving international and vegetarian cuisine. Here you're as close as you can stay to the archaeological zone's western entrance.

Hotel Dolores Alba (☎ 985-858-1555, in Mérida ☎ 999-928-5650, fax 999-928-3163; W *www.doloresalba.com; Hwy 180 Km 122; doubles/triples/quads M$350/410/470)* is across the highway from Cenote Ik Kil, just over 3km east of the eastern entrance to the ruins and 2km west of the Grutas de Balankanché. Its 40 rooms have a simple but pleasing decor and face two inviting swimming pools, one with a partial natural limestone bottom, and both with high-tech, nonchemical filtration. The hotel also has a good restaurant and plenty of tourist information, and staff will transport you to the Chichén ruins.

Top End All these hotels have air-con, swimming pools, restaurants, bars, well-kept tropical gardens, comfortable guestrooms and tour groups coming and going. They're very close to the eastern entrance to the archaeological zone.

Hotel Mayaland (☎ 985-851-0100, fax 985-851-0129, in USA ☎ 800-235-4079; W *www.mayaland.com; doubles May-Oct US$103, Nov-Apr US$162, bungalows May-Oct from US$157, Nov-Apr from US$227)* is less than 100m from the ruins' entrance – from the lobby and front rooms you can look out at El Caracol. The hotel was built around 1923 and is the most gracious in Chichén's vicinity, with multiple pools and restaurants and vast, beautifully green grounds. Rooms and garden bungalows are very nicely built and appointed.

Hotel Hacienda Chichén (in Mérida ☎ 999-924-2150, fax 999-924-5011, in USA ☎ 800-624-8451; W *www.haciendachichen.com; doubles US$120-140)*, about 300m from the ruins' entrance, is on the grounds of a 16th-century estate. The hacienda's elegant main house and ruined walls make a great setting. The archaeologists who excavated Chichén during the 1920s lived here in bungalows, which have been refurbished and augmented with new ones. Readers give it and the restaurant high marks. The same outfit runs the Casa del Balam in Mérida, so if you telephone, be sure to specify which location you're calling about.

Hotel Villas Arqueológicas (☎ 985-851-0034, fax 985-851-0018, in USA ☎ 800-258-2633, in France ☎ 801-80-28-03; ⓔ chicchef 01@clubmed.com; doubles/triples M$616/766), a Club Med hotel, is 300m from the east entrance. It is an exact clone of the villas at Cobá and Uxmal, a walled hacienda-style complex sporting a profusion of red floor tiles, a library with billiard table, and 40 smallish but comfortable rooms recently upgraded with nice touches of marble and tile.

Places to Eat
Besides the restaurants mentioned in the preceding sections, the highway through Pisté is lined with more than 20 eateries, large and small. The cheapest are the market stalls on the main plaza opposite the large tree. Other places are ranged along the highway from the town square to the Pirámide Inn. **Los Pájaros** and **Cocina Económica Chichén Itzá**, facing each other on opposite sides of the highway, serve sandwiches, omelets, enchiladas and quesadillas for around M$35, or a whole grilled chicken with salad, rice or soup for M$50/70 take away/dine in.

Lonchería Sayil (mains M$20; open 7am-9pm daily), a touch west of Posada Chac-Mool, is a very no-frills place serving a small range of Yucatecan dishes and a couple of other items.

Restaurant Hacienda Xaybe'h (☎ 985-851-0039; buffet lunch & dinner M$90; open 11:30am-6pm daily), set a block back from the highway opposite the Hotel Chichén Itzá, is a large, rather fancy place with nice grounds. Readers have praised the food; the selection of salads makes this a good option for vegetarians. Diners can use the swimming pool free of charge.

Getting There & Away
At the time of research, Aerocaribe/Aerocozumel operated Tuesday and Thursday flights between Cancún and Chichén Itzá, via Cozumel, but its future was uncertain. Other than that, the large, modern and underutilized airport about 14km east of Pisté receives only local charter flights.

When they're running on schedule (which is rare), Oriente's 2nd-class buses pass through Pisté bound for Mérida (M$43, 2½ hours) hourly between 8:15am and 4:15pm. Hourly Oriente buses to Valladolid (M$15, 50 minutes) and Cancún (M$71, 4½ hours) pass between 8:30am and 5:30pm.

At the time of research, 1st-class buses served Mérida (M$62, 1¾ hours) at 2:25pm and 5pm, Cancún (M$110, 2½ hours) at 4:30pm, and Cobá (M$48, 1½ hours) and Tulum (M$73, 2½ hours) at 8am and 4:30pm. The last two continued to Playa del Carmen (M$140, 3½ hours).

Shared vans to Valladolid (M$16, 40 minutes) pass through town regularly.

Getting Around
Oriente has ticket offices near the east and west sides of Pisté, and 2nd-class buses passing through town stop most anywhere along the way. Many 1st-class buses only hit the ruins and the west side of town, close to the toll highway.

During Chichén Itzá's opening hours 1st- and 2nd-class buses serve the ruins (check with the driver), and they will take passengers from town for about M$6 when there's room. For a bit more, 2nd-class buses will also take you to the Hotel Dolores Alba/Cenote Ik Kil and the Grutas de Balankanché (be sure to specify your destination when buying your ticket). If you plan to see the ruins and then head directly to another city by 1st-class bus, buy your bus ticket in the Unidad de Servicios before hitting the ruins, for a better chance of getting a seat.

There is a taxi stand near the west end of town; the price to the ruins is M$25. There are usually cabs at Chichén's parking lot.

VALLADOLID
☎ 985 • pop 39,000
Valladolid is relatively small, manageable and affordable, with an easy pace of life, many handsome colonial buildings and several good hotels and restaurants. It's a fine place to stop and spend a day or three getting to know the real Yucatán, and it makes a good base from which to visit the surrounding area, including Chichén Itzá.

History
Valladolid was once the Mayan ceremonial center of Zací (sah-**kee**). The initial attempt at conquest in 1543 by Francisco de Montejo, nephew of Montejo the Elder, was

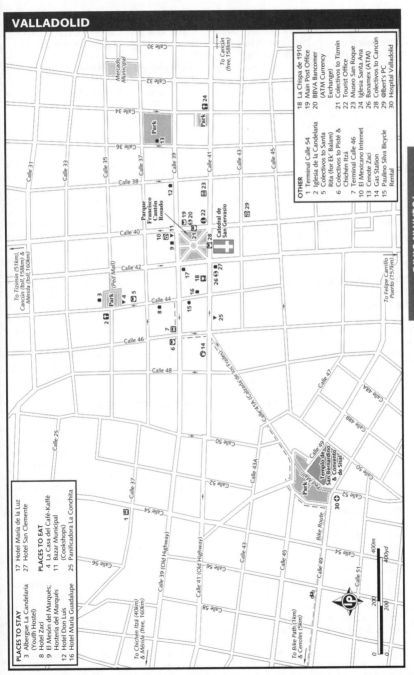

VALLADOLID

YUCATÁN STATE

PLACES TO STAY
3 Albergue La Candelaria (Youth Hostel)
8 Hotel Zací
9 El Mesón del Marqués; Hostería del Marqués
12 Hotel Don Luis
16 Hotel María Guadalupe
17 Hotel María de la Luz
27 Hotel San Clemente

PLACES TO EAT
4 La Casa del Café-Kaffé
11 Bazar Municipal (Cookshops)
25 Panificadora La Conchita

OTHER
1 Terminal Calle 54
2 Iglesia de la Candelaria
5 Colectivos to Santa Rita (for Ek' Balam)
6 Colectivos to Pisté & Chichén Itzá
7 Terminal Calle 46
10 El Mexicano Internet
13 Cenote Zací
14 Gas Station
15 Paulino Silva Bicycle Rental
18 La Chispa de 1910
19 Main Post Office
20 BBVA Bancomer (ATM Currency Exchange)
21 Colectivos to Tizimín
22 Tourist Office
23 Museo San Roque
24 Iglesia Santa Ana
26 Banamex (ATM)
28 Colectivos to Cancún
29 @lbert's PC
30 Hospital Valladolid

thwarted by fierce Mayan resistance, but the Elder's son Montejo the Younger ultimately took the town. The Spanish laid out a new city on the classic colonial plan.

During much of the colonial era, Valladolid's physical isolation from Mérida kept it relatively autonomous from royal rule. The Maya of the area suffered brutal exploitation, which continued after Mexican independence. Barred from entering many areas of the city, the Maya made Valladolid one of their first points of attack following the 1847 outbreak of the War of the Castes in Tepich. After a two-month siege, the city's defenders were finally overcome. Many fled to the safety of Mérida; the rest were slaughtered.

Today Valladolid is a prosperous seat of agricultural commerce, augmented by some light industry and a growing tourist trade. Many *vallisetanos* speak Spanish with the soft and clear Mayan accent.

Orientation & Information

The old highway passes through the center of town, though most signs urge motorists toward the toll road north of town. To follow the old highway eastbound, take Calle 41; westbound, take Calle 39. To preserve the colonial flavor of the center, Valladolid has limited the posting of signs by businesses to those approved by the city. This can sometimes make it difficult to find an establishment; you need to keep a keen eye out for small cardboard signs on open doors.

Most hotels are on the main plaza, called Parque Francisco Cantón Rosado, or within a block or two of it. The **tourist office** (☎ 856-1865; open 9am-9pm Mon-Sat, 9am-2pm Sun), on the east side of the plaza, is frequently unattended and provides mediocre information, but you can pick up maps and enjoy the photographs of town on display.

A few doors north is the **main post office** (open 8:30am-3pm Mon-Fri). Various banks (most with ATMs) near the center of town are generally open 9am to 5pm Monday to Friday and 9am to 1pm Saturday.

The main plaza has banks of Telmex **card phones** in each corner. Two good Internet places are **El Mexicano** (Calle 40; open 9am-11:30pm daily), with passable connections for M$10 per hour, and **@lbert's PC** (Calle 43 No 200G; open 9am-10:30pm Mon-Sat, 9am-4pm Sun), which charges M$12 per hour and gives faster access.

Hospital Valladolid (☎ 856-2883; cnr Calles 49 & 52), near the Convento de Sisal, handles emergencies 24 hours a day.

Templo de San Bernardino & Convento de Sisal

The Church of San Bernardino de Siena (open 8am-noon & 5pm-9pm daily) and the Convent of Sisal are just less than 1km southwest of the plaza. They were constructed between 1552 and 1560 to serve the dual functions of fortress and church.

You may have to knock on the church's left-hand door to gain admittance. Its charming decoration includes some recently uncovered 16th-century frescoes and a small image of the Virgin on the altar. These are about the only original items; the grand wooden *retablo* (altarpiece) dates from the 19th century. The adjacent convent is often closed to the public; your best bets of gaining entrance to it are during the vacation periods of Easter Week, August and Christmas (December 14 to January 6). It's well worth a visit. The walled grounds hold a cenote with a vaulted dome built over it and a system of channels that once irrigated the large garden.

If you're arriving by bicycle, note that it's prohibited to ride on the wide concrete paths leading from the street to the church.

Museo San Roque

This church turned museum (Calle 41 between Calles 38 & 40; admission free; open 9am-9pm daily) is less than a block east of the plaza. Models and exhibits relate the history of the city and the region, and other displays focus on various aspects of traditional Mayan life, including religious offerings and ceremonies, masks and instruments, medicines, handicrafts and food.

Cenotes

Among the region's several underground cenotes is **Cenote Zací** (Calle 36, enter from Calle 39; admission M$5; open 8am-6pm daily), set in a park that also holds traditional stone-walled thatched houses and a small zoo. People swim in Zací, though being mostly open it has some dust and algae.

A bit more enticing but less accessible is **Cenote Dzitnup** (Xkekén; admission M$20; open 7am-6pm daily), 7km west of the plaza. It's artificially lit and very swimmable, and a massive limestone formation dripping with stalactites hangs from its ceiling. Across the road about 100m closer to town is **Cenote Samulá** (admission M$10; open 7am-6pm daily), a lovely cavern pool with *álamo* roots stretching down many meters from the middle of the ceiling to drink from it. At last pass, Samulá was more appealing than Dzitnup, which was roughed up a bit by Hurricane Isidore. The *ejido* (indigenous communal landholding) that developed and maintains both cenotes charges M$30 for use of a video camera in either one, and will be raising Samulá's admission price once it improves the site.

Pedaling a rented bicycle (see Getting Around later) to the cenotes takes about 20 minutes. By bike from the center of town take Calle 41A (Calzada de los Frailes), a street lined entirely with colonial architecture, which leads past the Templo de San Bernardino and the convent. Keep them to your left as you skirt the park, then turn right on Calle 49. This opens into tree-lined Av de los Frailes and hits the old highway. Turn left onto the *ciclopista* (bike path) paralleling the road to Mérida. Turn left again at the sign for Dzitnup and continue for just under 2km; Samulá will be off this road to the right and Dzitnup a little farther on the left.

Shared vans from in front of Hotel María Guadalupe (on Calle 44 south of Calle 39) go to Dzitnup for M$10. Taxis from Valladolid's main plaza charge M$85 for the round-trip excursion to Dzitnup and Samulá, with an hour's wait. You also can hop aboard a westbound bus; ask the driver to let you off at the Dzitnup turnoff, then walk the final 2km (20 minutes) to the site. Dzitnup has a restaurant and drinks stand.

Mercado Municipal

This is a good, authentic Mexican market where locals come to shop for cheap clothing, housewares, meat, produce and whathave-you, and to eat at inexpensive *taquerías*. The east side is the most colorful, with flowers and stacks of fruit and vegetables on offer. Most of the activity takes place between 6am and 2pm.

Places to Stay

Budget HI-affiliated **Albergue La Candelaria** (☎/fax 856-2267; e fidery@chichen .com.mx; Calle 35 No 201F; dorm beds

with/without hostel card or ISIC M$60/65, doubles M$160/175) is in a classic old house on the north side of the park across from Iglesia de la Candelaria. It has a full kitchen, self-service laundry area, a cable TV room, lockers, Internet access and a lush, serene back area with hammocks to relax in. The 36 dorm beds are in eight- and 10-bed rooms (single-sex and mixed), and the four double rooms have shared bathrooms. The owners rent bicycles to guests for M$5 an hour, arrange tours and provide loads of information on the area, both for sightseers and those seeking cultural insights.

Hotel María Guadalupe (☎ 856-2068; Calle 44 No 198A; doubles/triples M$130/ 150), reader-recommended, has eight simple and clean fan-cooled rooms. Beds are slightly springy, but the management is friendly and provides purified water.

Hotel Don Luis (☎ 856-2008, cnr Calles 39 & 38; singles/doubles/triples/quads M$130/ 160/190/220), a motel-style structure, has acceptable fan-cooled rooms, a palmshaded patio, a somewhat murky swimming pool and a restaurant that serves three meals.

Mid-Range & Top End All of the hotels listed here have restaurants, free secure parking facilities and swimming pools.

Hotel María de la Luz (☎/fax 856-2071; w www.mariadelaluzhotel.com; Calle 42 No 193; doubles/triples/quads M$270/320/350), at the northwest corner of the plaza, offers good value for money with serviceable air-con rooms around an excellent pool. The restaurant puts on a buffet breakfast for M$44.

Hotel Zací (☎/fax 856-2167; Calle 44 No 191; singles/doubles/triples/quads with fan M$187/257/304/351, with air-con M$257/ 304/351/398), a well-kept place, has 50 rooms with mock-colonial decor around a green courtyard.

Hotel San Clemente (☎/fax 856-2208; w www.hotelsanclemente.com.mx; Calle 42 No 206; singles/doubles/triples/quads M$280/ 330/382/436) offers good value and boasts 64 air-con rooms with decor nearly identical to the Zací's. It's on the corner of the plaza, across from the cathedral.

El Mesón del Marqués (☎ 856-2073, fax 856-2280; e h_marques@chichen.com.mx; Calle 39 No 203; standard/deluxe doubles

M$395/495), the most expensive hotel in town, seems to be constantly expanding behind its colonial facade. All rooms are aircon and decently appointed, but the deluxe 'junior suites' in the older, rear wing are much nicer and offer far better value. The hotel has a charming old courtyard.

Places to Eat

Valladolid has a few good bakeries, including **Panificadora La Conchita** (*Calle 41 between Calles 44 & 46; open 7am-1pm & 3pm-9pm Mon-Sat*) two blocks west of the plaza.

Bazar Municipal (*cnr Calles 39 & 40*) is a collection of market-style cookshops at the plaza's northeast corner, popular for their big, cheap breakfasts. At lunch and dinner some offer *comidas corridas* (set meals) – check the price before you order. **El Amigo Casiano** on the left side nearly at the back, is good, super-cheap and always crowded; it's closed for the day by 2pm. **Lonchería Canul**, at the very back, stays open much later and serves good food accompanied by tasty salsas.

La Casa del Café-Kaffé (*☎ 856-2879; Calle 44; dishes M$12-18; open 8am-1pm & 6pm-midnight daily*) serves espresso, cappuccino and other coffee variations, as well as Chilean-style empanadas (baked, not fried; if you don't know them, think pasties with minced meat and egg), hotcakes and egg dishes. It has indoor and outdoor seating, on the pleasant Parque La Candelaria.

Hostería del Marqués (*☎ 856-2073; Calle 39 No 203; mains M$42-95; open 7am-11pm daily*), probably the best restaurant in town for lunch and dinner, is in the Hotel El Mesón del Marqués. You can dine in the tranquil colonial courtyard with its bubbling fountain, or the air-con salon looking onto it. Try the *pan de cazón* (dogfish – a small shark – in layers of tortillas, M$52), a specialty of Campeche. The restaurant also offers some vegetarian choices, and steaks priced by weight.

Entertainment

Following a centuries-old tradition, **dances** are held in the main plaza from 8pm to 9pm Sunday, with music by the municipal band or other local groups. This is not activity aimed at tourists, though they're more than welcome.

La Chispa de 1910 (*☎ 856-2668; Calle 41 No 201; open 6pm-1am Mon-Thur, 5pm-3am*

Fri-Sun) is a bar/restaurant that often features live music.

Getting There & Away

Bus Valladolid has two bus terminals: the convenient **Terminal Calle 46** (*Calle 39 at Calle 46*), two blocks from the plaza, and a **Terminal Calle 54** (*Calle 37 at Calle 54*) five blocks farther northwest. All buses going through town stop at both, except those to Izamal and Chiquilá, which serve only Terminal Calle 54. Most 1st-class buses running between Cancún and Mérida don't go into town at all but drop and pick up passengers at the *isleta* near the toll highway's off-ramp, which is served by shuttle buses from town (included in the ticket price).

The principal services are Oriente, Mayab and Expresso (2nd class) and ADO and Super Expresso (1st class).

Cancún M$57 to M$79, two to three hours, 158km; many buses

Chetumal M$112, six hours, 357km; five Mayab buses

Chichén Itzá/Pisté M$15, 45 minutes, 40km; 17 Oriente Mérida-bound buses between 7:30am and 6pm, stop near ruins during opening hours

Chiquilá (for Isla Holbox) M$60, 2½ hours, 155km; Oriente bus at 1:30am

Cobá M$19 to M$25, 45 minutes, 60km; four buses

Izamal M$26 to M$32, two hours, 115km; three buses

Mérida M$57 to M$79, two to three hours, 160km; many buses

Playa del Carmen M$60 to M$97, 2½ to 3½ hours, 169km; eight buses

Tizimín M$19, one hour, 51km; 12 buses

Tulum M$40 to M$45, two hours, 106km; six buses

Colectivos Often faster, more reliable and more comfortable than 2nd-class buses are the shared vans that leave for various points as soon as their seats are filled. Most operate from 7am or 8am to about 7pm. Direct services to Mérida (from Calle 39 just east of Calle 46, M$50) and Cancún (from in front of the cathedral, M$60) take a little over two hours – confirm it's nonstop. *Colectivos* for Pisté and Chichén Itzá (M$15, 40 minutes) leave from Calle 46 north of Calle 39, and for Tizimín from the east side of the plaza.

Getting Around

Bicycles are a great way to see the town and get out to the cenotes. **Paulino Silva** *(Calle 44 between Calles 39 & 41; open 8:30am-8pm Mon-Sat, 8:30am-noon Sun)* is among a few places renting bikes for M$5 per hour. As always, check out any bike carefully before putting money down.

EK' BALAM

The turnoff for this fascinating archaeological site *(admission M$23; open 8am-5pm daily)* is due north of Valladolid, 17km along the road to Tizimín. Ek' Balam is another 10.5km east. There is usually someone at the site willing to act as a guide; tips are appreciated.

Vegetation still covers much of the area, but excavations and restoration continue to add to the sights, including an interesting ziggurat-like structure near the entrance, as well as a fine arch and a ball court.

Most impressive is the gargantuan **Acrópolis**, whose well-restored base is 160m long and holds a 'gallery,' actually a series of separate chambers. Built atop the base is Ek' Balam's massive main pyramid, reaching a height of 32m and sporting a huge jaguar mouth with 360° dentition. Below the mouth are stucco skulls, while above and to the right sits a figure with amazing expressivity of face and posture. On the right side stand unusual winged human figures (some call them Mayan angels), whose hands are poised in gestures looking for all the world like Hindu/Buddhist *mudras*. It's enough to make you wonder, either about connections between ancient civilizations or the artistic license taken by the restoration crew.

The view from the top of the pyramid is fantastic as well. Across the flat terrain you can make out the pyramids of Chichén Itzá and Cobá.

It's possible to catch a *colectivo* from Calle 44 between Calles 35 and 37 in Valladolid for the village of Santa Rita (M$10), a safe 2km walk from Ek' Balam; you may even be able to get the driver to go the rest of the way for a just a little bit more. The return service stops at 3pm or 4pm. A round-trip taxi ride from Valladolid with an hour's wait at the ruins will cost around M$200. Hostel La Candelaria in Valladolid can arrange tours.

TIZIMÍN

☎ 986 • pop 41,000

Many travelers bound for Río Lagartos, San Felipe and Isla Holbox change buses in Tizimín, a ranching center. There is little to warrant an overnight stay (other than a difficult or missed connection), but the tree-filled Parque Principal is pleasant, particularly at sundown. The city fills with people from outlying ranches during its annual fair, lasting from January 1 to 15.

Two great colonial structures – **Parroquia Los Santos Reyes de Tizimín** (Church of the Three Wise Kings) and its former Franciscan monastery (the ex-convento) – are worth a look while you're waiting to make your bus connection. They're on opposite sides of Calle 51, reached by walking two blocks south on Calle 48, which itself is a block west of the bus terminals.

The church fronts Tizimín's main plaza, the Parque Principal, which has a **Bital** with ATM and currency exchange on its southwest side. **Bancomer**, at Calles 48 and 51 behind the church, also has an ATM.

Places to Stay & Eat

Posada María Antonia *(☎ 863-2384, fax 863-2857; Calle 50 No 408; air-con rooms M$175)*, just south of the church, has 12 fairly basic rooms, each holding up to four people. You can place international calls at the reception desk.

Pizzería César's *(Calle 50; pizzas M$26-89, steaks M$70-110; open 5am-3am daily)*, a popular joint near the Posada María Antonia, serves inexpensive pasta, sandwiches and burgers in addition to pizza and steak.

The **market** *(cnr Calles 47 & 48)*, half a block west of the Noreste terminal, has the usual cheap eateries.

Getting There & Away

Oriente and Mayab, both 2nd-class, share a terminal on Calle 47 between Calles 48 and 46 (to the west and east, respectively) just east of the market. Noreste's 1st- and 2nd-class terminal is just around the corner on Calle 46.

Cancún M$70 to M$77, three to 3½ hours, 194km; 15 Mayab and Noreste buses between 3am and 8pm

Izamal M$52, 2½ hours, 109km; Oriente bus at 5:15am, 11:20am and 4pm

Mérida M$73 to M$75, 2½ to 3½ hours, 180km; 10 1st-class Noreste buses between 4:30am and 6:30pm, three Oriente buses

Río Lagartos M$20, one hour, 50km; eight Noreste buses between 6am and 7:45pm; some buses continue 12km west to San Felipe (same price)

Valladolid M$20, one hour, 51km; 10 Oriente buses between 5:30am and 7pm

Taxis to Río Lagartos or San Felipe charge M$200, and leave from outside both bus terminals.

RÍO LAGARTOS
☎ 986 • pop 2200

The densest concentration of flamingos in Mexico warrants a trip to this fishing village, 103km north of Valladolid, 52km north of Tizimín and lying within the Reserva de la Biósfera Ría Lagartos. The mangrove-lined estuary also shelters 334 other species of resident and migratory birds, including snowy egrets, red egrets, tiger herons and snowy white ibis, as well as a small number of the once-numerous crocodiles that gave the town its name, Río Lagartos (Alligator River).

The Maya knew the place as Holkobén and used it as a rest stop on their way to Las Coloradas, a shallow part of the vast estuary that stretches east almost to the border of Quintana Roo. There they extracted precious salt from the waters, a process that continues on a much vaster scale today. Spanish explorers mistook the narrowing of the *ría* (estuary) for a *río* (river) and the crocs for alligators, and the rest is history.

Less than 1km east of town, on the edge of the estuary, a natural *ojo de agua dulce* has been developed into a swimming hole.

Flamingo, Shorebird & Wildlife Tours

The brilliant orange-red flamingos can turn the horizon fiery when they take wing. For their well-being, however, please ask your boat captain not to frighten the birds into flight. You can generally get to within 100m of the birds before they walk or fly away. Depending on your luck, you'll see either hundreds or thousands of them. The best months for viewing them are June to August.

The four primary haunts, in increasing distance from town, are Punta Garza, Yoluk,

Necopal and Nahochín (all flamingo feeding spots named for nearby mangrove patches). Prices vary with boat, group size (maximum five) and destination. The lowest you can expect to pay is around M$400; a full boat to Nahochín runs as much as M$650. In addition, the reserve charges visitors a M$20 admission fee.

You can negotiate with one of the eager men in the waterfront kiosks near the entrance to town; it's nearly impossible to get through town without being approached. They speak English and will connect you with a captain (who usually doesn't).

A good alternative is to seek out Ismael and Diego, licensed guides with formal training both as guides and naturalists. They speak English and Italian and are up to date on the area's fauna and flora, including the staggering number of bird species, for which they have books and the official Yucatán Peninsula checklist.

Besides their flamingo expeditions, **Ismael Navarro** (☎ 862-0000; 🖳 *www.ismael navarro.gobot.com*) takes four-hour shorebird tours along the mudflats in winter. **Diego Núñez Martínez** (☎ 862-0202; 🖃 *diego 2909@yahoo.com*) takes catch-and-release fly fishing for tarpon and snook, and can help with lodgings reservations. They also offer land tours for birding as well as night rides looking for crocodiles and, from May to September, sea turtles. Driving into town, turn left on Calle 19 at the sign for Restaurante-Bar Isla Contoy and follow it to the restaurant at the end. From the bus terminal, head to the water and turn left (west).

Special Events

La Feria de Santiago, the patron saint festival of Río Lagartos, is held around July 18 to 25 every year, and it's a blast. A bullfight (really bullplay) ring is erected in the middle of town during the weeklong event, and every afternoon anyone who wishes is able to enter it and play matador with a young bull. The animal is not killed or even injured, just a little angry at times. Don't turn your back to it or it will knock you down.

Day one of the festival begins with a big dance that lasts all night. On day two, the bullplay sessions start; also on this day there's a procession that winds from the entrance of town and goes to the bullfight ring, where a ceiba tree is planted in the center of the ring. During each of the remaining days the festivities begin with Mass at the town church followed by a procession; each procession is led by a guild (one day it's the ranchers, another day it's the fishermen, another day it's the farmers, and so on).

The fair begins the Saturday prior to July 25, Patron Saint Day, and lasts at least a week. If the Saturday before July 25 falls on July 23 or July 24, then the celebration actually begins two Saturdays before the 25th. The festival always lasts at least a week, but never more than nine days. Yes, it's confusing, and the residents of Río Lagartos don't always follow this rule.

Another big annual event in Río Lagartos is the Día de la Marina (Day of the Marine Force), which is always June 1. On this day, following 9am Mass, a crown of flowers is dedicated to the Virgin and is carried from the church to a boat, where it is then taken 4km out to sea and placed in the water as an offering to all the fishermen who have perished at sea.

What's remarkable about this is that virtually every boat in this fishing town goes to the sea site, and scores of fishermen sing en route to the honored site and pray there before a selected queen lays the gorgeous wreath in the water. For one minute after the wreath is placed in the water, there is a moment of total silence in honor of the lost fishermen. After the service, everyone heads back to town and celebrates with dancing, drinking and games. The queen dances with every fisherman to bring him good luck.

The boats, not incidentally, are heavily decorated on this day, and tourists are welcome to ride to the site for free. Just ask if you can go, and be friendly and respectful. At the sea service, keep your chatter to a minimum and simply observe. Doing so will encourage the fishermen to welcome tourists to join them year after year. A tip for their kindness, following the service, is always appreciated (M$50 to M$100 per person).

Places to Stay & Eat

Most residents aren't sure of the town's street names, and signs are few. The road into town is the north–south Calle 10, which ends at the waterfront Calle 13.

Cabañas Dos Hermanos (☎ 862-0146; 1-/2-bed cabanas M$150/200) is near the school at the east edge of town, almost on the waterfront. It offers four spacious, good-value cabanas with fans and simple bathrooms. The friendly owners speak some English (their children are fluent).

Posada Leyli (☎ 862-0106; cnr Calles 14 & 11; singles with shared/private bathroom M$120/150, doubles with private bathroom M$200), two blocks south of Calle 10, has six pleasant, fan-cooled rooms. La encargada (the manager) often needs to be sought out; you can ask a neighbor or at the waterfront kiosks.

Hotel Villas de Pescadores (☎ 862-0020; Calle 14; doubles M$35) is two blocks north of the Leyli, near the water's edge, and offers 12 very clean rooms, each with good cross-ventilation (all face the estuary), two beds and a fan. Upstairs rooms have balconies. The owner rents bicycles and canoes as well; if he's not around, ask for his neighbor Benigno.

Restaurante-Bar Isla Contoy (Calle 19; mains M$40-55), a popular eating spot at the waterfront, is a good place to meet other travelers and form groups for the boat tours.

Getting There & Away

Several buses by Noreste run daily between Tizimín (M$20, one hour), Mérida (M$57 to M$71, three to four hours) and San Felipe (M$10, 20 minutes). Noreste and Mayab also serve Cancún (M$69, three to four hours) several times daily.

EAST OF RÍO LAGARTOS

If you have a car, turning east at the junction about 2km south of Río Lagartos (turning west would take you to San Felipe) will lead you to some interesting sights. About 8km from the junction, on the south side of the road, is the beginning of a 1km interpretive trail to Petén Tucha (a petén is a hummock or rise often forming around a spring, and rich in diverse flora and fauna). You should register at the biosphere reserve's office near the junction before walking the trail.

Continuing east on the road 4km beyond the trailhead you'll reach a bridge over a very narrow part of the estuary. Fishermen cast nets here, and you can sometimes see crocs lurking in the water (look for dead horseshoe crabs on the bridge). Another 6km beyond this is Las Coloradas, a small town housing workers who extract salt from the vast shallow lagoons of the same name that stretch eastward for kilometers on the south side of the road. The salt is piled in gleaming mounds that look like snowdrifts, up to 15m high.

The road turns to sand after Las Coloradas, but is usually in good shape and leads another 20km or so to the fishing town of El Cuyo, which is also something of a local resort in summer months. Along the way you're never far from the beach (though it's often separated from the road by a raised berm) on the north or the lagoons on the south. The area is rich in birdlife, and the unique vegetation includes many century plants, an agave species that lives quietly for decades before a last hurrah of sending up a tall stalk with blossoms and expiring.

From El Cuyo the road turns paved again and heads south through broad expanses of grassy savanna with palms and some huge-trunked trees, passing the site of the original founding of Valladolid, in 1543. At Colonia Yucatán, a little over 30km south of El Cuyo, you can head east to pick up the road to Chiquilá and Isla Holbox (or in the opposite direction to Hwy 180) or west to Tizimín and from there south to Ek' Balam and Valladolid.

SAN FELIPE
☎ 986 • pop 1600
This is a seldom-visited fishing village 12km west of Río Lagartos, notable for its orderly streets and painted wooden houses. San Felipe makes a nice day or overnight trip. Its beach lies across the mouth of the estuary, at Punta Holohit, and the mangroves there and on the west edge of town are a bird-watcher's paradise. Just looking out the windows of the town's one hotel you can see white and brown pelicans, terns, cormorants, great blue herons, magnificent frigate birds and jabirus (storks).

The beach, though not great, usually has *palapas* providing shade (when we visited, they and most of the mangroves' leaves were gone with the wind of Isidore). Lancheros charge M$40 per boatload (round trip) to take passengers across, or M$150 an hour for fishing trips.

Hotel San Felipe de Jesús *(☎ 862-2027, fax 862-2036; e sanfelip@prodigy.net.mx; doubles M$246-351, triples M$281-351)* is a friendly, clean and cleverly constructed hotel at the edge of San Felipe's harbor. To get there, turn left at the water and proceed about 200m. Six of the 18 rooms are large and have private balconies and water views; those in the top-floor rooms are reached by their own staircases inside the room. All rooms have fans and good cross-ventilation; the large upper ones are especially good bargains. The restaurant offers tasty seafood at low prices.

Six buses from Tizimín pass through Río Lagartos and continue to San Felipe (M$20, 1½ hours) each way. The bus ride (M$10, 12km) from Río Lagartos itself takes about 20 minutes. You can take a taxi from Tizimín to San Felipe for M$200, but there are no cabs around to make the return trip.

Campeche State

Although it's the least visited of the Yucatán's three states, Campeche is rushing toward a place among Mexico's top destinations, as excavation, restoration, preservation and reconstruction work proceed rapidly at many locations throughout the state. Visitors can enjoy the uncrowded Mayan archaeological sites of Edzná, Calakmul and Chicanná; the impressive walled city of Campeche, with its colonial fortifications and architecture; and the Reserva de la Biósfera Calakmul, Mexico's largest biosphere reserve.

The 56,000-sq-km state has the highest average altitude of the peninsula's three states. Hills begin not far inland from much of its coastline, and in the southern part of the state the land rises gradually from west to east, reaching heights in the interior exceeding 365m. And unlike other parts of the peninsula, which contain largely light forest and brush, 30% of Campeche is covered with jungle. Marshlands, ponds and inlets are common along the state's coastline, which faces the dark and generally uninviting waters of the Gulf of Mexico, and several sizable above-ground rivers are located in the southern part of the state, which borders Guatemala and Tabasco.

CAMPECHE
☎ 981 • pop 198,000

In 1999 Unesco added the city of Campeche to its list of World Heritage sites. *Campechanos* are rightly proud of this and are doing an excellent job of improving the colonial heart of the city while retaining the best of the old (Mérida take note!). Many structures have been restored, repainted or, in some cases, reconstructed from scratch, and the work is ongoing. At the same time the city puts on concerts, theatre, dance performances and other events most nights of the week.

During Campeche's heyday, wealthy Spanish families built mansions, many of which still stand. Two segments of the city's famous wall have survived the times as well, as have no fewer than seven of the *baluartes* (bastions or bulwarks) that were built into it. Two perfectly preserved colonial forts guard the city's outskirts. One of them, Fuerte de San Miguel, contains a

Highlights

• Campeche city's rich history, colonial center, pirate-proof fortifications and Mayan museum

• Edzná, a picturesque ancient Mayan site

• Calakmul, a vast ancient city with an enormous pyramid, surrounded by a sea of forest

• Becán, 'Path of the Snake,' a moated Mayan city atop a rock outcrop

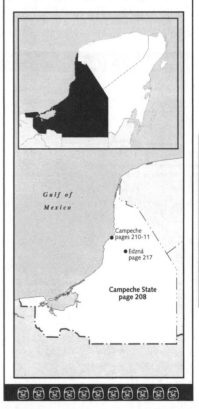

Gulf of Mexico

Campeche pages 210-11

Edzná page 217

Campeche State page 208

small archaeological museum with world-class pieces.

Adding to Campeche's charm is its location on the Gulf of Mexico. A broad waterfront boulevard provides the perfect place for cloud- and sunset-watching; add a

CAMPECHE STATE

thunderstorm rolling in off the gulf and you have a sound-and-light show nonpareil. In clear weather, sunsets over the water turn the sky an amazing shade of gold, bathing the city in soft, diffused light and turning the colonial center even more picturesque. By night the charm continues as the yellow-hued floodlights (which now seem to be *de rigueur* in World Heritage cities) illuminate the cathedral and other landmarks.

History

Once a Mayan trading village called Ah Kim Pech (Lord Sun Sheep-Tick), Campeche was first approached by the Spaniards in 1517. The Maya resisted, and for nearly a quarter of a century the Spaniards were unable to fully conquer the region. Colonial Campeche was founded in 1531, but later abandoned due to Mayan hostility. By 1540 the conquistadors had gained sufficient control, under the leadership of Francisco de Montejo the Younger, to found a settlement here that survived. They named it the Villa de San Francisco de Campeche.

The settlement soon flourished as the major port of the Yucatán Peninsula, but was subject to pirate attacks from an early date (see the boxed text 'Pirates!'). After a particularly appalling attack in 1663 that left the city in ruins, the king of Spain ordered construction of Campeche's famous bastions, which put an end to the periodic carnage.

Today the local economy is largely driven by shrimping and offshore petroleum

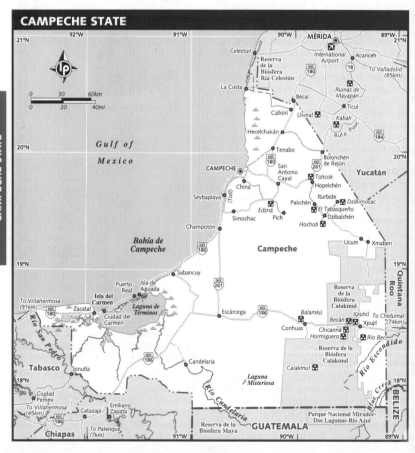

extraction, and the prosperity brought by these activities has helped fund the downtown area's renovation.

Orientation

Though the bastions still stand, the city walls themselves have been mostly razed and replaced by Av Circuito Baluartes, which rings the city center just the way the walls once did. Many of the streets making up the circuit are paved with stone taken from the demolished wall. In the classic colonial plan, the center is ringed by several barrios (neighborhoods or quarters), each with its own church and square. Particularly charming are San Román, Guadalupe and Santa Ana, which host weekly serenatas of music and dance.

According to the compass, Campeche is oriented with its waterfront to the northwest, but be aware that locals giving directions usually follow tradition and convenience, which dictate that the water is to the west, inland is east.

A multilane boulevard with bicycle and pedestrian paths on its seaward side extends several kilometers in either direction along Campeche's shore, changing names a few times. The stretch closest to the city center is named Av Adolfo Ruiz Cortínez and is commonly referred to as el malecón (the waterfront drive). It's graced by several art installation or monuments symbolic of various aspects of Campeche's history and culture.

Information

The **city tourist desk** (☎ 816-1782; Calle 57 No 6; open 9am-9pm daily) is in the Centro Cultural Casa Número 6, on the southeast side of the Parque Principal. Its friendly staff have brochures and information on cultural events, tourist activities and the city's architectural attractions.

The state-run **Secretaría de Turismo** (☎ 816-6767; Plaza Moch-Couoh; open 8am-8pm daily; closed holidays), just off Av Ruiz Cortínez, was at last pass fairly useless, with a very poor selection of literature.

Campeche has numerous banks (with ATMs), open 9am to 4pm Monday to Friday, 9am to 1pm Saturday. See the map for some locations.

The **central post office** (cnr Av 16 de Septiembre & Calle 53; open 9am-3pm Mon-Fri) is in the Edificio Federal (Federal Building). There are plenty of card phones around town. The **Telmex office** (Calle 8) is near Calle 51.

Air-conditioned **Café Internet** (cnr Calles 10 & 61; open 9am-10pm daily) charges M$12 an hour for Internet access.

Lavandería Campeche (Calle 55 between Calles 12 & 14; open 8am-4pm Mon-Sat) takes in laundry in the morning and usually

Pirates!

As early as the mid-16th century, Campeche was flourishing as the Yucatán Peninsula's major port under the careful planning of Viceroy Hernández de Córdoba. Locally grown timber, chicle and dyewoods were major exports to Europe, as were gold and silver mined from other regions and shipped from Campeche.

Such wealth did not escape the notice of pirates, who arrived only six years after the town was founded. For two centuries, the depredations of pirates terrorized Campeche. Not only were ships attacked, but the port itself was invaded, its citizens robbed, its women raped and its buildings burned. In the buccaneers' Hall of Fame were the infamous John Hawkins, Diego the Mulatto, Laurent de Gaff, Barbillas and the notorious 'Pegleg' (Pata de Palo) himself. In their most gruesome assault, in early 1663, the various pirate hordes set aside their rivalries to converge as a single flotilla upon the city, where they massacred many of Campeche's citizens.

This tragedy finally spurred the Spanish monarchy to take preventive action, but it was not until five years later, in 1668, that work on the 3.5m-thick ramparts began. After 18 years of building, a 2.5km hexagon incorporating eight strategically placed baluartes, or bastions, surrounded the city. A segment of the ramparts extended out to sea so that ships literally had to sail into a fortress, easily defended, to gain access to the city.

With Campeche nearly impregnable, the pirates turned their attention to other ports and ships at sea. In 1717, the brilliant naval strategist Felipe de Aranda began a campaign against the buccaneers, and eventually made this area of the gulf safe from piracy.

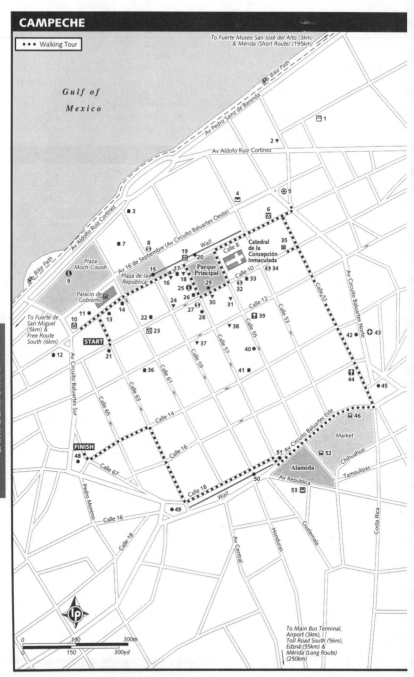

CAMPECHE

••• Walking Tour

Gulf of Mexico

gets it back cleaned, dried and folded by the afternoon, charging about M$45 for a large load. **Lave Klin** *(Av Circuito Baluartes Norte between Calles 14 & 16; open 9am-6pm Mon-Sat)* is a bit cheaper.

In an emergency, call **Hospital Dr Manuel Campos** *(☎ 811-1142; Av Circuito Baluartes Norte between Calles 14 & 16)* or the **Cruz Roja** *(Red Cross; ☎ 815-2411)*.

The center's smooth cobblestone streets are slippery even when dry. When the slightest bit wet they can be like ice. Additionally, some sidewalks are quite high and have abrupt drops in odd places. Tread carefully!

Walking Tour

Seven of the eight bulwarks still stand, and all can be visited on a 2km walk around Av Circuito Baluartes, taking in other sights on the way. Because of traffic, some of the walk is not very pleasant; you might want to limit your excursion to the first three or four *baluartes* described, which house museums and gardens.

Start at the **ex-Templo de San José** *(cnr Calles 10 & 63)*, which is a visual delight. Its facade is covered in striking blue and yellow tiles, and one spire is topped by a lighthouse complete with weather vane. Begun in 1735 and completed in 1799, it's truly a multipurpose building, having served as a church, library, warehouse and now concert and exposition space.

Walk a block northwest along Calle 63 to the bizarre, ultramodern **Palacio Legislativo** *(Congress Building; Calle 8)*. Undoubtedly meant to evoke a *baluarte* with slitted windows, it looks more like the mothership landing. Just southwest is its colonial inspiration, the **Baluarte de San Carlos** *(Calle 8; admission free; open 9am-2pm Mon, 8am-8pm Tues-Sat, 8am-2pm Sun)*, which contains the modest Museo de la Ciudad. The museum has a good scale model of the old city, historical photos, specimens of dyewood and the like. You can visit the dungeon downstairs and climb to the roof to look out over the sea.

Head northeast back along Calle 8 to its intersection with Calle 59 to see the **Puerta del Mar** *(Sea Gate; cnr Calles 8 & 59)*, which provided access to the city from the sea before the surrounding area was filled in. The gate was demolished in 1893 but rebuilt in

CAMPECHE STATE

1957 when its historical value was realized. If you're in a shopping mood, duck through the gate for a look at the handicrafts on offer in the Plaza de la República.

A short section of re-erected wall connects the gate to the **Baluarte de Nuestra Señora de la Soledad**, which holds the **Museo de Estelas Maya** *(admission M$22, free Sun; open 8am-7:30pm Tues-Sun)*. Many of the Mayan artifacts here are badly weathered, but the precise line drawing next to each stone shows you what the designs once looked like. You can visit the roof here as well.

Just northeast of the Baluarte de Nuestra Señora is a replica of the original Palacio Municipal, housing a public library (still waiting for its books to arrive at last pass). Across Calle 8 from the library is the **Parque Principal**, Campeche's main plaza. It's a pleasant place where locals go to sit and think, chat, smooch, plot, snooze, have their shoes shined or stroll and cool off after the heat of the day. Come for the free evening concerts (see Entertainment later in this section).

On the park's southwest side is **Centro Cultural Casa Número 6** *(Calle 57; admission free; open 9am-9pm Sun-Fri, 9am-10pm Sat)*, an 18th-century building furnished with pieces from the 18th and 19th centuries. It gives a good idea of how the city's high society lived back then; be sure to visit the grand kitchen. The center also has a bookstore, and on Saturday evenings hosts a lively game of *lotería,* Mexico's version of bingo. Free guided tours of the building are conducted in Spanish only.

Construction was begun on the imposing **Catedral de la Concepción Inmaculada**, on the northeast side of the plaza, in the mid-16th century shortly after the conquistadors established the town, but it wasn't finished until 1705.

Back on Calle 8 head northeast again for two blocks beyond the park to **Baluarte de Santiago** *(admission free; open 9am-3pm & 5pm-8pm Mon-Fri, 9am-1pm & 4pm-8pm Sat, 9am-1pm Sun)*. It houses a minuscule yet lovely tropical garden, the **Jardín Botánico Xmuch Haltún**, with 250 species of tropical plants set around a courtyard with fountain and pool.

Walk back on Calle 8 a few steps and turn left (inland) onto Calle 51. Walk a block and turn right on Calle 10 to reach **Mansión Carvajal**, once the city residence of a wealthy *hacendado* (landowner). It now houses government offices, but if you tell the guard you're a tourist he'll usually let you wander around the courtyard a bit, at least.

When you've had your fill or been tossed out, return to Calle 51 and follow it inland to Calle 18, passing the **Iglesia de San Juan de Dios** (1652) on the way. The **Baluarte de San Pedro** *(cnr Calles 16 & 51; admission free; open 9am-3pm & 5pm-9pm daily)* is in the middle of a complex traffic intersection at the beginning of Av Gobernadores. Within the bulwark are the Exposición Permanente de Artesanías, a regional crafts sales center, and an agency that will book tours of the city and region.

If you're still game, head southwest from the Baluarte de San Pedro along Av Circuito Baluartes Este to the **Baluarte de San Francisco** (closed at last pass) and a block farther to the **Puerta de Tierra** *(Land Gate; Calle 59; admission free; open 8am-9pm daily)*. It contains a small room with artifacts on display, and for M$5 you can ascend and walk along the top of Campeche's other stretch of wall, as far as the **Baluarte de San Juan**. After that, diehard bulwarks fans can head in the direction of the sea on Calle 63 (more pleasant than the circuito) for two blocks and turn left on Calle 14, heading another two blocks to the **Baluarte de Santa Rosa** *(cnr Calles 14 & 67; admission free; open 9am-8:30pm daily)*. Here you'll be rewarded with bathrooms, the occasional temporary art exhibition, and the satisfaction of a job well done.

Evening Stroll

To see some beautiful houses, many painted in cheerful pastels, walk through Campeche's streets – especially Calles 55, 57 and 59 – in the evening, when the sun is not blazing, and interior lighting illuminates courtyards, salons and alleys. When conditions are right, starting your walk as the sun is setting will yield views of a centro awash in a serene, almost surreal glow of diffused natural light.

Museo Arqueológico & Fuerte de San Miguel

Four kilometers southwest of Plaza Moch-Couoh a road turns left off the *malecón* and climbs to the Fuerte de San Miguel, a colonial fort now home to the excellent archaeological museum (☎ 044-982-10973; admission M$24; open 8:30am-7:30pm Tues-Sun). Here you can see objects found at the ancient Mayan sites of Calakmul, Edzná and Jaina, an island north of the city once used as a burial site for Mayan aristocracy.

Among the objects on display are stunning pieces of jade jewelry and exquisite vases, masks and plates. The star attractions are the jade burial masks from Calakmul. Also displayed are stelae, arrowheads, weapons, seashell necklaces and clay figurines.

The fort is itself a thing of beauty. In mint condition, it's compact and equipped with a dry moat and working drawbridge, and it's topped with several cannons. The views are great too.

For M$3, buses marked Lerma or Playa Bonita depart from the market (at the southeast edge of the center) and travel counterclockwise around the circuito before heading down the *malecón*, making stops along the way. Tell the driver you're going to the Fuerte de San Miguel. The turnoff for the fort, Av Escénica, is across from the old San Luis artillery battery. You'll have to walk about 700m up the hill from the coastal road (bear left when the way forks). To avoid the strenuous walk, you can take a taxi or the *tranvía* (see Organized Tours).

Fuerte Museo San José del Alto

San Miguel's northern counterpart is also a museum (admission M$24; open 8am-8pm Tues-Sun) housing some old weapons, nice models of ships, and modest exhibits of import and export items. The small fort itself is in great shape and has a drawbridge over a (dry) moat. You get good views of the gulf and city, but the modern sections of town are not as appealing as what's visible from Fuerte San Miguel.

If you're driving, take the coast road, turn right at the sign, and pray (go up the hill and head left; it gets tricky). You can also take the tram and just get off at the fort or, for M$3, catch a local, green 'Josefa,' 'Bellavista' or 'Morelos' bus from the side of the market. These get you within easy walking distance.

Organized Tours

Three different tours by motorized *tranvía* (trolley) depart from Calle 10 beside the Parque Principal daily; all cost a pricey M$70 and last about 45 minutes. Hourly between 9am and 9pm, the Tranvía de la Ciudad heads off on a tour of the principal neighborhoods of the historic town center. On the same schedule, El Guapo goes to the Fuerte de San Miguel. You don't get enough time to take in the archaeological museum; if it's your goal, just use the tram to get there, and then walk down the hill. The third tour has departures at 9am and 5pm, to the Fuerte de San José, the Fuerte de San Miguel's very well-preserved twin on the north side of the city. Again, the tram tour doesn't give you time to visit.

Buy tram tickets (and check on the variable schedules) at the *tranvía* ticket booth just inside the parque from the trolley stop.

Servicios Turísticos Xtampak (☎ 812-6485; e xtampak@elfoco.com; Calle 57 between Calles 10 & 12) offers archaeological tours to Edzná, the Chenes sites, Calakmul, and the various sites around Xpujil in eastern Campeche, among other places. **Monkey Hostel** (☎ 811-6500; cnr Calles 10 & 57) offers shuttle services to Mayan sites Edzná and Kin-Há (M$150 for both); Calakmul, Becán, Chicanná and Xpuhil (M$350 to M$550, visiting all sites), and the Ruta Puuc sites (M$288 to M$491). Prices are per person, and vary according to group size.

Places to Stay

Budget Originally called the Campeche Hostal, **Monkey Hostal** (☎ 811-6500; w www.hostalcampeche.com; cnr Calles 10 & 57; dorm beds M$70), is almost too nice to be a hostel. It occupies the upstairs of a grand old building directly overlooking the Parque Principal, and has a rooftop terrace with a bar and superb views of the parque and cathedral. Besides the usual lockers, kitchen and laundry facilities, it also offers a book exchange, high-speed Internet access (M$15 per hour), a multilingual staff who dispense travel advice, and inexpensive shuttle service to many Mayan sites in the region. A good breakfast is included in the price, as is bottled water. One double room is available (M$160, also including breakfast) in addition to the one co-ed and two single-sex dorms with six or eight beds. The hostel rents bicycles cheaply. Reservations recommended.

Hotel Reforma (☎ 816-4464; Calle 8 between Calles 57 & 59; singles/doubles/triples/quads M$85/105/125/145) is centrally located, just off the Parque Principal. The 400-year-old building has 22 clean, simple rooms with fans and decent bathrooms. Upstairs rooms are roomier, generally.

Hotel Castelmar (*☎ 816-2886; Calle 61 No 2; rooms M$88*) feels like the kind of seedy place the protagonist in a noir novel might hole up in. Rooms are huge and musty, with old tile floors. Potted plants ring the courtyard and pigeon droppings coat the doors, rounding out the hotel's decrepit charm.

Hotel Roma (*☎ 816-3897; Calle 10 No 254; rooms with/without bathroom M$120/90*) has fairly dumpy, fan-cooled rooms.

Hotel Colonial (*☎ 816-2222; Calle 14 No 122; singles M$147, doubles M$176-199, triples M$234*) is popular with budget travelers. Some readers have complained of noise, but others recommend it highly. Housed in what was once the mansion of Doña Gertrudis Eulalia Torostieta y Zagasti, former Spanish governor of Tabasco and Yucatán, the rooms have good showers with hot water and a fan. Air-con (available in three rooms) costs M$76 extra.

Mid-Range & Top End Try the **Posada del Ángel** (*☎ 816-7718; Calle 10 No 307; singles/doubles/triples/quads with fan M$234/269/304/340, with air-con M$316/351/386/421*) for good bathrooms and air-con, but somewhat springy beds. Rooms tend to be spacious if sparsely furnished.

Hotel López (*☎/fax 816-3344; e lopezh@elsitio.com; Calle 12 No 189; doubles/triples/quads with air-con M$304/337/421*), remodeled in early 2003, has three floors of clean, agreeable (if small) rooms around three pretty courtyards.

Hotel del Paseo (*☎ 811-0100, fax 811-0097; w www.hoteldelpaseo.8k.com; Calle 8 No 215; singles/doubles/triples M$415/475/565*) has 48 like-new rooms, very reasonably priced. All have air-con, cable TV and phone, and good bathrooms and beds. The hotel has a restaurant and bar as well.

Hotel Baluartes (*☎ 816-3911, fax 816-2410; w www.baluartes.com.mx; Av 16 de Septiembre No 128; singles/doubles/triples M$550/590/670*) performed many upgrades in 2002, and though it still shows some rough edges, the beds are super-comfy, the air-con is good and tiled bathrooms are clean and well-stocked. Each room has an

electronic safe and cable TV. Get a room on the top floor if possible, with a good view of the sea or the city. The hotel has a large pool, a restaurant (with impossible service) and a café (a much better bet), as well as a business center with Internet facilities and offstreet parking. Enter the premises from Calle 61.

Hotel del Mar (*☎ 811-9191, fax 811-1618; e delmarcp@camp1.telmex.net.mx; Av Ruiz Cortínez No 51; rooms with city/sea view M$882/1080*), the former Ramada hotel, boasts 126 large, modern and comfortable rooms. Seaview rooms have balconies. It also has two restaurants, a bar, pool, gym and offstreet parking.

Places to Eat

While in town, be sure to try the regional specialty *pan de cazón,* which is dogfish (a small shark) cooked between layers of tortillas in a sauce sometimes rich, dark and mole-like, sometimes tomato-based. If it smells like ammonia, though, send it back; the shark has gone bad. Another regional specialty is *camarones al coco,* consisting of shrimp rolled in ground coconut and fried. It's often served with marmalade and when done right tastes much better than it sounds.

San Francisco de Asís, across Av Ruiz Cortinéz and north of the Baluarte de Santiago, is the local branch of the supermarket chain.

Panificadora Nueva España (*cnr Calles 10 & 59; open 7:30am-9pm daily*) has a large assortment of fresh baked goods at very low prices.

Restaurant Marganzo (*☎ 811-3898; Calle 8 between Calles 57 & 59; breakfast M$25-47, lunch & dinner mains M$45-80; open 7am-11pm daily*) is a popular, upscale air-conditioned restaurant facing the Baluarte de Nuestra Señora. It serves good breakfasts and juices (carrot and beet among them), plus espresso drinks, and has an extensive seafood menu.

Restaurant Campeche (*☎ 816-2128; Calle 57; mains M$40-80; open 6:30am-midnight daily*), opposite the Parque Principal, is in the building that saw the birth of Justo Sierra, founder of Mexico's national university. It offers a wide selection of dishes and is often filled with locals.

Nutri Vida (*Calle 12 No 167; open 8am-2pm & 5:30pm-8:30pm Mon-Fri, 8am-2pm*

Sat) is a health-food store serving up soy burgers and the like.

Natura 2000 *(☎ 816-2303; Calle 12 between Calles 55 & 57; open 8:30am-9pm Mon-Fri, 9am-2pm Sat)*, another health-food store, also has soy burgers. And soy milk and soy hot dogs, and soy on.

Restaurant-Bar Familiar La Parroquia *(☎ 816-2350; Calle 55 No 8; breakfast M$27-35, mains M$31-70; open 24 hr)* is the complete family restaurant–café hangout. Breakfast is served from 7am to 10am. Substantial lunches and dinners of traditional and regional dishes are also on offer, including a passable *pan de cazón*, plus swordfish and ceviches (seafood marinated in lime juice). Service can be spotty at times.

La Casa Vieja *(☎ 811-8016; Calle 10 No 310, 2nd floor; mains M$45-98; open 9am-1am Tues-Sun)* offers good food, excellent service and a perfect vantage point for observing the parque's evening scene. Ignore the indoor seating and grab a table outdoors on the gallery. Order some pâté and a glass of wine from the decent list (may we recommend the Casillero del Diablo?) and soak in the views of the cathedral and the square below. On concert nights you can watch and hear the bands while enjoying a super *flan de coco* (coconut flan).

Entertainment

From September to May, the tourism authorities sponsor free performances of folkloric music and dancing. Performances are held on Saturdays at 7pm (weather permitting) in the Plaza de la República, and Thursdays at 8:30pm in the Centro Cultural Casa Número 6. Wednesday through Sunday nights at 8pm there's always something on in the Parque Principal, be it jazz, rock, marimba groups or the Banda del Estado (State Band). There's no cost to attend and it's a pleasant way to pass time. Arrive early for a good seat.

Saturday night from 6pm to 10pm the Centro Cultural holds *la lotería*, a bingo-like game of European origin that uses numbered figures such as *el Sol*, *el Borracho*, *la Muerte* (the Sun, the Drunk, Death). Stephens' *Incidents of Travel in Yucatan* has a good description of the game as he observed it played at a fiesta in Mérida in 1841. The action may not be as heated now as he describes, but the old folks can get pretty excited when one of them fills a card.

Getting There & Away

Air The airport is at the end of Av López Portillo (reached by Av Central), 3.5km southeast of Plaza Moch-Couoh. **Aeroméxico** *(☎ 800-021-4000)* flies to Mexico City at least once daily.

Bus At the time of going to press, Campeche's **main bus terminal** (sometimes called the ADO or 1st-class terminal) was moving from its location on Av Gobernadores to the corner of Av Patricio Trueba (also known as Av Central) and Av Casa de la Justicia, about 20 blocks south of Av Circuito Baluartes Este via Av Central. The 2nd-class terminal may follow suit, though this was unknown at the time. To get to the new terminal, catch any 'Flores,' 'Linda Vista,' 'Casa de Justicia,' 'SEP' or 'SECUD' bus from the stop by the post office. This will drop you directly across Av Trueba from the terminal.

Though most of its buses leave from the main terminal, Sur has a **terminal** *(Av República)* for buses to Champotón across from the Alameda (which is south of the market). Rural buses for Edzná and other parts depart from here as well.

There have been reports of theft on night buses, especially to Chiapas; keep a close eye on your bags.

Destinations accessible from Campeche include:

Bolonchén de Rejón M$47, three to four hours, 116km; four 2nd-class buses

Cancún M$215 to M$251, six to seven hours, 512km; two 1st-class ADO direct buses, one 2nd-class TRP bus via Mérida

Chetumal M$158 to $M190, 6¼ to nine hours, 422km; 1st-class ADO bus at noon, 2nd-class buses at 8:15am & 10pm

Edzná M$18, 1½ hours, 55km; buses leave at 7am and 10am, then roughly hourly until 6pm, from the Sur Champotón terminal; see the Edzná section for further information

Escárcega M$57 to M$73, two to three hours, 150km; five 1st-class ADO buses, many 2nd-class buses

Hopelchén M$34, two hours, 86km; several 2nd-class buses

Mérida (via Bécal) M$72 to M$87, 2½ to three hours, 195km; many 1st-class ADO buses, ATS bus every 30 minutes to 2:30pm

Mérida (via Uxmal) M$72, four hours, 250km; five 2nd-class Sur buses between 6:05am and 5:05pm

Mexico City (TAPO) M$648 to M$782, 18 hours, 1360km; four 1st-class ADO buses, one deluxe ADO GL bus

Palenque M$166 to M$228, five hours, 362km; one deluxe Maya de Oro bus at midnight, three 1st-class ADO buses; some Villahermosa-bound buses can drop you at Catazajá (the Palenque turnoff), 27km north of Palenque town

San Cristóbal de Las Casas M$305, 14 hours, 820km; one deluxe Maya de Oro bus at midnight

Villahermosa M$243 to M$260, six hours, 450km; eight 1st-class buses

Xpujil M$112 to M$140, six to eight hours, 306km; 1st-class ADO bus at noon, four 2nd-class Sur buses including one via Hopelchén

Car & Motorcycle If you're heading for Edzná, the long route to Mérida or the fast toll road going south, take Av Central and follow signs for the airport and either Edzná or the *cuota* (toll road). For the free route south you can just head down the *malecón*. For the short route to Mérida head north on the *malecón*; it curves right eventually and hits the highway at a Pemex station.

Coming *to* Campeche from the south via the *cuota*, turn left at the roundabout signed for the *universidad*, and follow that road straight the coast. Turn right up the *malecón* and you will arrive instantly oriented.

Getting Around

Local buses all originate at the market or across the Av Circuito Baluartes from it. Most charge M$3 and go at least partway around the circuito before heading to their final destinations. Ask a local where along the circuito you can catch the bus you want.

Taxis have set prices for destinations on a sign posted in the back seat, but agree on a price with the driver before you go. By the hour they are M$75. A booth in the airport terminal sells tickets for taxis to the center at M$70 per cab. *Colectivo* taxis from the airport to the Parque Principal charge M$30 per person.

Monkey Hostal (see Places to Stay) rents bicycles at M$20 for two hours and M$5 for each additional hour.

CAMPECHE TO MÉRIDA VIA HIGHWAY 180

The *ruta corta* is the fastest way to get between the two cities, and it's the road more traveled by buses. If you'd prefer to go the long way via Kabah and Uxmal, ask for a seat on one of the less-frequent long-route buses. If you'd like to stop at one of the towns along the short route, catch a 2nd-class bus.

Hecelchakán

At Hecelchakán, about 65km northeast of Campeche, you'll find an archaeology museum and a historic church, both facing the central plaza. The **Museo Arqueológico del Camino Real Hecelchakán** (*admission M$22; open 9am-6pm Tues-Sat*) houses burial artifacts from Isla Jaina as well as ceramics and jewelry from other sites. There are also many artists' renditions of ancient Maya going about their daily lives. It's a fairly impressive museum that's worth a stop if you have your own wheels, but the attendant seems to take long siestas and you may have to hunt him down to open up the museum. It's on the far left side of the plaza when you're facing the church.

The **Iglesia de San Francisco** dates from the 16th century, but its dramatic features – a massive octagonal dome and a pair of monumental bell towers – are 18th-century additions. It's the center of festivities on October 4 when townsfolk celebrate the feast of St Francis. From August 9 to 18, the popular Novenario festival is held in town, with bullfights, dancing and refreshments. The town is one hour by bus (M$21) from Campeche.

Bécal

Bécal is 32km from Hecelchakán, just before you enter the state of Yucatán. It's a center of the Yucatán's panama hat trade. The soft, pliable hats, called jipijapas by the locals, have been woven by townsfolk from the fibers of the huano palm tree in humid limestone caves since the mid-19th century. The caves – there's at least one on every block, generally reached by a hole in the ground in someone's backyard – provide just the right atmosphere for shaping the fibers, keeping them pliable and minimizing breakage. Each cave is typically no larger than a bedroom. About a third of the adult population make their living weaving hats, which cost from around M$40 for very coarsely woven ones to well over M$800 for very fine work. Keep an eye out for the statue in the plaza: giant cement jipijapas leaning against one another.

From Bécal (M$33, three hours by bus from Campeche) it's 85km to Mérida.

CAMPECHE TO MÉRIDA VIA HIGHWAY 261

Most travelers take this long route from Campeche to Mérida in order to visit the various ruin sites on the way. It's often referred to as the Ruta Chenes (Chenes Route), for the *chenes* (wells) that give the region its name.

Edzná

The closest major ruins to Campeche are about 53km to the southeast. Edzná *(admission M$32; open 8am-5pm daily)* covered more than 17 sq km and was inhabited from approximately 600 BC to the 15th century AD. Most of the visible carvings date from AD 550 to 810. Though it's a long way from such Puuc hills sites as Uxmal and

Kabah, some of the architecture here has elements of the Puuc style. What led to Edzná's decline and gradual abandonment remains a mystery.

Beyond the ticket office is a *palapa* (thatched, palm-leaf-roofed shelter) protecting carvings and stelae from the elements, and holding a gift shop that sells film, postcards, coffee cups and reproductions of ceramics. A path from the *palapa* leads about 400m through vegetation (follow the signs for the Gran Acrópolis) and then through the patio next to the **Plataforma de los Cuchillos** (Platform of the Knives), which got its name from the offering of chert knives found within it. On top of the platform it's still possible to see several walls that once formed rooms which

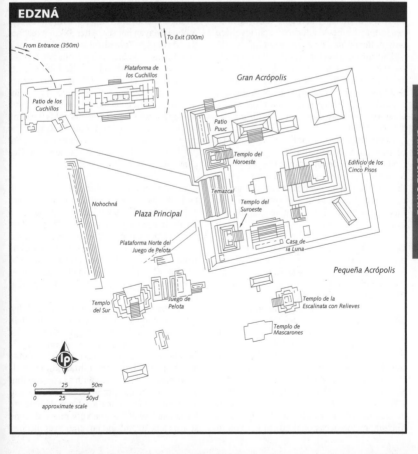

EDZNÁ

From Entrance (350m)

To Exit (300m)

Plataforma de los Cuchillos

Gran Acrópolis

Patio de los Cuchillos

Patio Puuc

Templo del Noroeste

Edificio de los Cinco Pisos

Temazcal

Nohochná

Plaza Principal

Templo del Suroeste

Casa de la Luna

Plataforma Norte del Juego de Pelota

Pequeña Acrópolis

Templo del Sur

Juego de Pelota

Templo de la Escalinata con Relieves

Templo de Mascarones

0   25   50m
0   25   50yd
approximate scale

archaeologists suspect were used by high-ranking figures. The zone's big draw, the Plaza Principal, is 160m long, 100m wide and surrounded by temples. On your right as you enter from the north is the **Nohochná** (Big House), a massive, elongated structure that was topped by four long halls likely used for administrative tasks, such as the collection of tributes and the dispensation of justice. The built-in benches facing the main plaza clearly were designed to serve spectators of special events in the plaza.

Across the plaza is the Gran Acrópolis, a raised platform holding several structures, including Edzná's major temple, the 31m-high **Edificio de los Cinco Pisos** (Five-Story Building). It rises five levels from its base to the roofcomb and contains many vaulted rooms. A great central staircase of 65 steps goes right to the top. Some of the weathered carvings of masks, serpents and jaguars' heads that formerly adorned each level are now in the *palapa* near the ticket office.

The current structure is the last of four remodels and was done primarily in the Puuc architectural style. Scholars generally agree that this temple is a hybrid of a pyramid and a palace. The impressive roofcomb is a clear reference to the sacred buildings at Tikal in Guatemala.

In the Pequeña Acrópolis to the southeast of the Plaza Principal is the *palapa*-protected **Templo de Mascarones** (Temple of Masks), which features carved portrayals of the sun god. The central motif is the anthropomorphic head of a Maya man whose face has been modified to give him the appearance of a jaguar.

Getting There & Away From Campeche, dilapidated rural buses leave from outside the Sur Champotón terminal at 7am and 10am, then hourly until 6pm (M$18, 1½ hours, 55km). Most drop you 200m from the site entrance; ask before boarding. The last bus returning to Campeche passes the site around 3pm, so if you're coming here on a day trip from the city you'll want to catch one of the two early buses leaving Campeche. These schedules vary; so check the day before.

Coming from the north and east, get off at San Antonio Cayal and hitch or catch a bus 20km south to Edzná. If you're headed north on leaving Edzná, you'll have to depend on hitching or the occasional bus to get you to San Antonio Cayal, where you can catch a Ruta Chenes bus north to Hopelchén, Bolonchén de Rejón and ultimately Uxmal.

Coming by car from Campeche, take Av Central out of town and follow the signs to the airport and Edzná. If you drove to Edzná from the north and are headed to Campeche city, don't retrace your route to San Antonio Cayal; just bear left shortly after leaving the parking lot and follow the signs westward.

Shuttle service from Campeche to Edzná and the site of Kin-Há costs M$150. Tours of Edzná from Campeche start at about M$200 per person. See Organized Tours in the Campeche city section for further information on both.

Bolonchén de Rejón & Xtacumbilxunaan

The road east from San Antonio Cayal passes citrus orchards and villages with many traditional Mayan houses. After 38km it reaches the Mayan site **Tohcok** (also called Tahacok), one ruined structure dating from late Classic times, on the north side of the highway. Its decoration is a blend of Puuc and Chenes styles; not exciting, but it's free. Two kilometers east is a gasoline station and the town of Hopelchén, where Hwy 261 splits, heading north toward Uxmal and south to Xpujil. The road to the latter is in very poor condition, but passes near the fascinating Mayan site of Hochob (see the following section).

Hopelchén contains no attractions, but it does offer travelers a friendly, decent hotel, **Hotel Arcos** (☎ 996-812-0123; singles/doubles M$70/100), with a restaurant serving three meals. It's on the plaza and around the corner from the bus terminal. The terminal is served by 2nd-class Sur buses: 17 daily to Campeche from 4:45am to 7:45pm (M$34), four to Mérida (M$45), 11 to Dzibalchén from 8:30am to 8pm (M$19), and one to Xpujil at 8pm (M$55).

The next town to appear out of the hilly, green countryside to the north is Bolonchén de Rejón, after 34km. Its local festival of the Santa Cruz is held each year on May 3. Bolonchén is about 3km north of the **Grutas de Xtacumbilxunaan** (shtaa-koom-beel-shoo-**nahn**). This cavern with a cenote within was closed at the time of research, having suffered severe damage from Hurricane Isidore in late 2002. In a very rare move the storm came inland and hovered over the area for more than 20 hours, savaging it with winds and drenching it with rain. When the *gruta* is open, you descend steps leading down to a barely visible cenote, beyond which a passage leads 100m farther. There are few stalactites or stalagmites, but the climb back up to the green forest surrounding the cave is dramatic, and with future improvements the cenote may be visible.

Hwy 261 continues north into Yucatán state to Uxmal, with a side road leading to the ruins along the Ruta Puuc. See Uxmal and Ruta Puuc in the Yucatán State chapter for more information.

El Tabasqueño & Hochob

These two Mayan sites are relatively easy to access if you're on your way between Hopelchén and Xpujil in your own vehicle, a bit more difficult as a side trip from Hopelchén, due to the condition of Hwy 261 going south. When they're developed further, an entrance fee will undoubtedly be charged.

Northwest of Dzibalchén, El Tabasqueño *(admission free)* boasts a temple-palace (Estructura 1) with a striking monster-mouth doorway flanked by Chac masks. The doorway is similar to the one atop the Magician's House at Uxmal, though in Chenes style. Estructura 2 is a solid freestanding tower, an oddity in Mayan architecture. To reach El Tabasqueño, go south from Hopelchén 30km, turn right (south) to the village of Pakchén and follow an unpaved road 4km to the site.

Five kilometers south of Chencoh is Hochob *(admission free)*, which, though small, is among the most beautiful and impressive of Chenes-style sites. The Palacio Principal (Estructura 2) is faced with an amazingly elaborate Chenes monster-mouth doorway in surprisingly good condition. Estructura 1 is similar, though in worse condition. Estructura 5, on the east side of the plaza, retains part of its roofcomb. Estructura 6, to the west, is in ruins. To reach Hochob, turn right (south) about 500m west of Dzibalchén and drive the 9km to Chencoh on a rocky road, then the remaining 5km on a rough dirt road.

SOUTH FROM CAMPECHE

Two roads head south from Campeche: a free coastal route and a much faster toll road (M$45). The *cuota* ends after about 40km, merging with the free road some 20km north of the fishing village of

Champotón. Hwy 180 continues southwest along the coast, eventually reaching Ciudad del Carmen, bridging the Laguna de Términos at the southern tip of Isla del Carmen and passing into the state of Tabasco. There is little along this route to draw one's attention, and most people traveling from Campeche who see the area do so through the window of a bus bound for Villahermosa or points north and west.

The other road, Hwy 261, leads 84km due south to **Escárcega**, an unprepossessing crossroads town between Campeche, Palenque and Quintana Roo. Unless you must break your journey to rest or change buses, there is no reason to stay here. The bus terminal is located on the north side of Hwy 186 near the east edge of town. **Hotel Posada Escárcega** *(☎ 982-824-0079; Calle 25 No 15; singles/doubles/triples with fan M$180/200/250, with air-con M$270/300/350)* is a block east of the bus terminal and about 50m north on Calle 25. It has decent rooms and a restaurant.

All buses from Escárcega are *de paso* (originating elsewhere and passing through on approximate schedules); some arrive and leave full. Destinations include:

Campeche M$57 to M$73, two to three hours; five 1st-class and many 2nd-class buses
Chetumal M$102 to M$124, four to six hours; five 1st-class and four 2nd-class buses
Palenque M$98 to M$105, four hours; five 1st-class buses
Xpujil M$55 to M$68, two to three hours; 11 1st- and 2nd-class buses

ESCÁRCEGA TO XPUJIL

Hwy 186 heads nearly due east across southern-central Campeche state, climbing gradually from east of Escárcega to a broad, jungly plateau and descending again to finally reach Chetumal, in Quintana Roo, a total distance of 261km. The highway passes near several fascinating Mayan sites and through the ecologically diverse and archaeologically rich Reserva de la Biósfera Calakmul. The largest settlement on the road between Escárcega and Chetumal – and the only one with accommodations – is Xpujil, on Hwy 186 about 20km west of the Campeche–Quintana Roo border. The only gasoline station in the same stretch is about 5km east of Xpujil.

Many of the numerous archaeological sites between Escárcega and Xpujil are still being excavated and restored. The most significant historically is Calakmul, which is also one of the most difficult to reach (60km from the highway, with no buses). It and most of the other sites in this section can be visited by taxis hired in Xpujil or tours booked either in Xpujil or with companies in the city of Campeche (see Organized Tours in the Campeche section). The sites are listed in order from west to east, and their distances from Xpujil (a possible base for exploration) are given as well.

The predominant architectural styles of the region's archaeological sites are Río Bec and Chenes. The former is characterized by long, low buildings that look as though they're divided into sections, each with a huge serpent or 'monster' mouth for a door. The facades are decorated with smaller masks, geometric designs (with many X forms) and columns. At the corners of the buildings are tall, solid towers with extremely small, steep, nonfunctional steps and topped by small false temples. Many of these towers have roofcombs. The Chenes style shares most of these characteristics except for the towers.

Balamkú

Balamkú (Chunhabil; admission M$24; open 8am-5pm daily) is 60km west of Xpujil (or 98km east of Escárcega), then just under 3km north of the highway along a paved (though deeply fissured) road. Discovered only in 1990, the site boasts an exquisite, ornate stucco frieze showing a jaguar flanked by two large mask designs and topped with images of a king in various forms. Another section has figures as well (look for the toad). The unusual design bears little resemblance to any of the known decorative elements in the Chenes and Río Bec styles and has mystified archaeologists.

The frieze is well preserved and still bears traces of its original painted colors; the solid stone that hid it for centuries has been replaced with an artfully designed new structure with slit windows that let in a little light. The door is kept locked, but the site custodian or an assistant will usually appear to open it up and give you a flashlight tour (no flash photography is allowed). The structure bearing the frieze is about 400m in from the ticket booth.

A round-trip taxi ride from Xpujil with a one-hour visit costs about M$250 plus M$50 an hour waiting time, but can usually be combined with a visit to Calakmul at nearly the same cost as Calakmul alone.

Calakmul

Calakmul (Adjacent Mounds; admission M$34; open 8am-5pm daily) was a major Mayan city. Discovered in 1931 by American botanist Cyrus Lundell, it's larger than Tikal, in Guatemala. A central chunk of its 100-sq-km expanse has been consolidated and partially restored, but owing to ecological considerations, clearing has been kept to a minimum. Architectural purists complain that this doesn't allow the buildings to communicate with one another, or to serve their astronomical functions of solstice observation and the like, but many others find it makes for a romantic setting. Most of the city's more than 6500 buildings lie covered in jungle; exploration and restoration are ongoing. The turnoff to Calakmul is 59km west of Xpujil, and the site is 59km south of the highway at the end of a paved road.

Lying at the heart of the vast, untrammeled Reserva de la Biósfera Calakmul (one of the two Unesco-designated biosphere regions on the Yucatán Peninsula; Sian Ka'an is the other), the ruins are surrounded by rain forest, which is best viewed from the top of one of the several pyramids. Visiting the site is a good opportunity to explore the area without the risk of getting lost in the jungle. Visitors are likely to see wild ocellated turkeys, parrots and toucans, and may come across peccaries, agoutis, spider and howler monkeys and others of the huge number of species living within the reserve. Jaguars, ocelots, margays and other cats, as well as long-snouted tapirs, are around, but seldom seen. The earlier you come, the more you're likely to spot.

From about AD 250 to 695, Calakmul was the leading city in a vast region known as the Kingdom of the Serpent's Head. Its perpetual rival was Tikal, and its decline began with the power struggles and internal conflicts that followed the defeat by Tikal of Calakmul's King Garra de Jaguar (Jaguar Claw).

As at Tikal, there are indications that construction occurred over a period of more than a millennium. Beneath Edificio VII, archaeologists discovered a burial crypt with some 2000 pieces of jade, and tombs continue to yield spectacular jade burial masks; many of these objects are on display in Campeche city's Museo Arqueológico. The cleared area of Calakmul holds at least 120 carved stelae, though many are eroded.

A toll of M$40 per car (more for heavier vehicles) and M$20 per person is levied by the *municipio* (township) of Calakmul at the turnoff from Hwy 186, nominally to fund road maintenance, but at last pass the bushes on either side of the road were sorely in need of trimming back. You'll need to register at the Semarnat post 20km in from the highway; it isn't staffed until about 6am. About 7km beyond it is an interpretive trail leading to a small lake, a good place for observing wildlife.

From the ticket booth at the end of the road to the ruins is about a 1km walk. It's worth spending M$8 at the entrance to buy a little brochure with a map of the site and copying onto it the tracks shown on the big map posted at the beginning of the path in. Signage around the site itself is skimpy (though it contains very good information on the zoological and botanical features of the site), and the many arrows placed in attempts to indicate the way only confuse things.

The Gran Plaza, with loads of stelae in front of its buildings (Estructura V has the best ones), makes a good first stop, and climbing the enormous **Estructura II**, at the south side of the plaza, is a must. Each of this pyramid's sides is 140m long, giving it a footprint of just under 2 hectares – the largest known Mayan structure. After a good climb you'll reach a temple occupying what appears to be the top of the building, but don't be fooled; you have to go around it to the left to reach the real apex. From here, more than 50m above the forest floor, you can see views, views, views and a few trees. The back side of the structure has been left in jungle; if you face it and look to the right slightly you'll be sighting toward the Mayan city El Mirador, in neighboring Guatemala, but without binoculars it's very difficult to pick out that site's towering pyramid.

A path on the left (east) side of Estructura II leads past **Estructura III**, with its many chambers and passages. Archaeologists found a tomb inside the 5th-century structure that contained the body of a male ruler of Calakmul, surrounded by offerings of jade,

ceramics and shell beads, and wearing not one, but three jade mosaic masks (one each on his face, chest and belt). Winding southeast and southwest past a low structure brings you to the Plaza Central and **Estructura I**, which was still being restored at the time of research. The view from atop it is less obstructed by trees than the view from Estructura I.

A trail leading north from Estructura I's steps around the back of Estructura II to the Gran Acrópolis wasn't quite finished at last pass, but made for an interesting walk and scramble. A quicker way to the Gran Acrópolis is to retrace your steps to the Gran Plaza and follow the signs west.

If you've seen enough after exploring the Acrópolis, with its 'open construction' ball court (no hoops or markers), you can turn around and retrace your path to the ticket booth. For a bit more adventure, head through the largely uncleared western end of the Acrópolis and turn right. When you reach a complex of labyrinthine structures (residences of the elite) bear right through them until you reach a road that leads a few hundred meters to the main path in. Turn left on it and go against the arrows.

Places to Stay & Eat Rangers allow camping at the Semarnat post; they appreciate a donation if you use the shower and toilets. They've built a small, screened *palapa* that you can sometimes rent and pitch your hammock (or unroll your sleeping bag) in. People have been known to sleep in the parking lot near the site itself. Bear in mind that it can get chilly on this plateau in winter months – up to three blankets' worth.

Villas Puerta Calakmul (*e* *puertacalakmul@hotmail.com; cabanas M$600-800*) is about 300m east of the access road, just in from the highway. It has 15 lovely and very spacious fan-cooled cabanas hidden in the jungle; their walls (except around the bathroom) are nearly all screen, with curtains for privacy. The hotel also has a screened-in restaurant serving good food at reasonable prices (including a very passable chicken cordon bleu), and a small swimming pool (closed at last pass due to lack of water). The decorator did an excellent job of making room and restaurant features look like organic parts of the landscape, going so far as to make the wiring look like vines.

Getting There & Away A full-day round-trip excursion by taxi from Xpujil costs about M$600 plus admission and road fees; you should be able to get a visit to Balamkú thrown in.

Chicanná

Almost 12km west of Xpujil and 500m south of the highway, Chicanná *(House of the Snake's Jaws; admission M$29; open 8am-5pm daily)* is a mixture of Chenes and Río Bec architectural styles buried in the jungle. The city was occupied from about AD 300 to 1100.

Enter through the modern *palapa* admission building, then follow the rock paths through the jungle to Grupo D and Estructura XX (AD 830), which boasts not one but two monster-mouth doorways, one above the other, the pair topped by a roofcomb.

A five-minute walk along the jungle path brings you to Grupo C, with two low buildings (Estructuras X and XI) on a raised platform; the temples bear a few fragments of decoration.

The buildings in Grupo B (turn right when leaving Grupo C) have some intact decoration as well, and there's a good roofcomb on Estructura VI.

Shortly beyond is Chicanná's most famous building, Estructura II (AD 750 to 770) in Grupo A, with its gigantic Chenes-style monster-mouth doorway, believed to depict the jaws of the god Itzamná, lord of the heavens, creator of all things. If you photograph nothing else here, you'll want a picture of this, best taken in the afternoon. Take the path leading from the right corner of Estructura II to reach nearby Estructura VI.

Chicanná Ecovillage Resort *(☎ 983-871-6075, fax 871-6074; e chicanna@campeche .sureste.com; singles/doubles/triples M$766/ 859/906)*, the former Ramada, is 500m north of the highway and directly across from the road to the ruins. Large, airy rooms with ceiling fans and very nice bathrooms are grouped mostly four to a bungalow and set amid well-tended grass lawns. The resort has a pool, and a small dining room–bar serving decent but expensive meals.

Río Bec Dreams *(☎ 983-871-6057; e info@ riobecdreams.com; Hwy 186 Km 142; cabanas with shared/private bathroom M$250/500)* was still getting up and running at last pass, but by the time you read this should offer five shared-bathroom 'jungalows,' two private-bathroom cabanas, a restaurant serving European cuisine, a bar and a gift shop. All were lovingly built by the Canadian and English owners and feature composting toilets, collected rainwater and solar electricity. The lodgings are in a wooded area full of bromeliads and orchids. Look for the various national flags on the north side of the highway 2km west of Chicanná.

Round-trip taxi fare from Xpujil to Chicanná is M$30 (plus M$50 per hour waiting).

Becán

Becán *(admission M$32; open 8am-5pm daily)* is 8km west of Xpujil and 500m north of the highway. It sits atop a rock outcrop; a 2km moat snakes its way around the entire city to protect it from attack. (Becán is Mayan for 'canyon,' 'moat' or, literally, 'path of the snake.') Seven causeways crossed the moat, providing access to the city. Becán was occupied from 550 BC until AD 1000.

This is among the most elaborate sites in the area. After dodging the numerous car-watchers (and other young would-be hustlers) and walking to the site itself, the first thing you'll come to is a plaza. Walk keeping it on your left to pass through a rock-walled passageway and beneath a corbeled arch. You will reach a huge twin-towered temple with cylindrical columns at the top of a flight of stairs. This is Estructura VIII, dating from about AD 600 to 730. The view from the top of this temple has become partially obscured by the trees, but on a clear day you may still be able to see structures at the Xpujil ruins to the east.

Northwest of Estructura VIII is Plaza Central, partially ringed by 30m-high Estructura IX (the tallest building at the site) and the more interesting Estructura X. At X's far south side, in early 2001, a stucco mask still bearing some red paint was uncovered. It is enclosed in a wooden shelter with window.

In the jungle to the west are more ruins, including the Plaza Oeste, which is surrounded by low buildings and a ball court. Much of this area is still being excavated and restored, so it's open to the public only intermittently.

Loop back east, through the passageway again, to the plaza; cross it diagonally to the right, climbing a stone staircase to the Plaza

Sureste. Around this are Estructuras I through IV; a circular altar (Estructura III-a) lies on the east side. Estructura I has the two towers typical of the Río Bec style. You can go around the plaza counterclockwise and descend the stone staircase on the southeast side or go down the southwest side and head left. Both routes lead to the exit.

A round-trip taxi visit from Xpujil will run about M$25 plus M$50 per hour of waiting time.

XPUJIL

The truck-stop hamlet of Xpujil (shpu-**heel**) lies at the junction of east–west Hwy 186 and Campeche Hwy 261 (not to be confused with Mexico Hwy 261), which leads north to Hopelchén and eventually Mérida. A good base from which to explore the area's sites, Xpujil grew rapidly at the end of the 20th century in anticipation of a tourist boom that still hasn't fully materialized. It has no bank or laundry, but the only gasoline station between Escárcega and Chetumal is 5km east of town. Several restaurants, a couple of hotels and a taxi stand are all within 1km of the bus depot.

From the junction, the Xpuhil ruins are less than 1km west, Becán is 8km west, Chicanná is 11.5km west, and Balamkú is 60km west.

Servidores Turísticos Calakmul (☎ 983-871-6064; ☑ calakmul@finred.com.mx), on the east edge of town, provides the services of trained local guides to visit sites in the area. All speak only Spanish (or Spanish and Mayan) except for one English-speaker. They specialize in flora, fauna and Mayan archaeology, and do bird-watching tours, photo safaris, camping trips and agricultural tourism (visits to beekeepers, reforestation projects and organic farms), among other things. As an example, camping trips to Calakmul run from M$700 for one person to M$1100 for five, including gear and transportation; admission and road fees are extra.

Ruins

Xpuhil (Cat's Tail; admission M$29; open 8am-5pm daily) flourished during the late Classic period from AD 400 to 900, though there was a settlement here much earlier. The site's entrance is on the west edge of town on the north side of Hwy 186, at the turnoff for the airport, less than 1km west of the junction.

One large building and three small ones have been restored. Estructura I in Grupo I, built about AD 760, is a fine example of the Río Bec architectural style, with its lofty towers. The three towers (rather than the usual two) have traces of the impractically steep ornamental stairways reaching nearly to their tops, and several fierce jaguar masks (go around to the back of the tower to see the best one). About 60m to the east is Estructura II, an elite residence.

Xpuhil is a far larger site than may be imagined from these buildings. Three other structure groups have been identified, but it may be decades before they are restored.

Places to Stay & Eat

Hotel y Restaurant Calakmul (☎/fax 983-871-6029; double cabins with shared bathroom M$200, doubles with air-con & private bathroom M$400) is about 350m west of the junction. The 14 rooms are large, modern and clean, with lots of tiles; each has its own sitting area outside with table and chairs. The shared-bathroom cabins have two rather springy double beds each, a floor fan and good bug screens. Service in the **restaurant** (open 6am to midnight daily) is grindingly slow.

El Mirador Maya (☎/fax 983-871-6005; double bungalows M$250, double rooms M$350), about 1km west of the junction, has eight bungalows and two rooms. The bungalows have fans, two good beds, OK bathrooms and nice porches, but are poorly screened. The rooms are fairly new and have air-con but are very small, and the air-con is poorly placed. The Mirador has a **restaurant** as well, open 6am to midnight daily.

Xpujil has a couple of modest restaurants besides those at the hotels, and one block east (toward the junction) from the Hotel Calakmul is a surprisingly well-stocked and economical **market**.

Getting There & Around

Xpujil is 220km south of Hopelchén, 153km east of Escárcega and 120km west of Chetumal. Stopping in Xpujil are 11 buses daily to Escárcega (M$55 to M$68, two to three hours), five to Campeche (M$112 to M$139, five to six hours), five to Chetumal (M$47 to M$56, 1½ to two hours) and two to Palenque (M$135, six hours). No buses originate in Xpujil, so you must hope to luck into a vacant seat on one passing through. The bus terminal is just east of the Xpujil junction, on the north side of the highway.

The Xpuhil ruins are within walking distance of Xpujil junction. You may be able to hitch a ride to the access roads for Becán, Chicanná and Balamkú, but for other sites you will need to book a tour or hire a cab; taxis wait on the north and south sides of the junction. Taxi fares to each site are given in the site's section; you may have to bargain some and pay a bit more. Waiting time is figured at M$50 an hour.

HORMIGUERO

This site *(admission M$24; open 8am-5pm daily)* is reached by heading 14km south from Xpujil junction, then turning right and heading 8km west on what was once a paved road, now still passable except following heavy rains. Hormiguero (Spanish for 'anthill') is an old site, with buildings dating as far back as AD 50. The city flourished during the late Classic period, however. Hormiguero has one of the most impressive buildings in the region. As you enter the site you will see the 50m-long **Estructura II**, which has a giant Chenes-style monster-mouth doorway with much of its decoration in fair condition. Walking around the back of the building you can see very good Mayan stonework still intact, a rare thing at many sites. Follow the arrows to reach **Estructura V**, 60m to the north. Walk keeping it on your left and loop around on the fainter path to get a good look at a mostly unexcavated structure and a good idea of how a lot of sites looked before restoration.

A round-trip taxi ride from Xpujil will run M$70 plus waiting time.

RÍO BEC

The entrance to the collective farm Ejido 20 de Noviembre is 10km east of the Xpujil junction and signed 'Río Bec.' The unpaved farm road south leads 5km to the collective itself and its U'lu'um Chac Yuk Nature Reserve. Look for the small store on the left side of the road, and ask there for guides to show you the various sites about 13km farther down the very rough road. 'Río Bec' is the designation for an agglomeration of small sites, 17 at last count, in a 50-sq-km area southeast of Xpujil. It gave its name to the prevalent architecture style in the region. Of these many sites, the most interesting is certainly Grupo B, followed by Grupos I and N. The best example is Estructura I at Grupo B, a late Classic building dating from around AD 700. Though not restored, Estructura I has been consolidated and is in a condition certainly good enough to allow appreciation of its former glory. At Grupo I look for Estructuras XVII and XI. At Grupo N, Estructura I is quite similar to the grand one at Grupo B.

At the time of research, a team of French archaeologists had begun excavation and restoration of some of the Río Bec ruins, in the past long neglected.

The road is passable only when dry, and even then you need a high-clearance vehicle. The way is unsigned as well; you're best off hiring a guide with or without a 4WD truck. It's possible to arrange this in Xpujil or at the *ejido* (collective farm). A taxi to the *ejido* will charge around M$35 for drop-off service; negotiate waiting time. Though it looks closer on the map, access to Río Bec from the road to Hormiguero is all but impossible.

Language

Spanish

Spanish is the official language of Mexico and is widely spoken on the peninsula. English is widely spoken in the major cities and at the better hotels and restaurants, but few people understand it in the smaller cities and in the rural towns and villages.

Pronunciation
Pronunciation of Spanish is not difficult, given that many Spanish sounds are similar to their English counterparts and there is a clear and consistent relationship between pronunciation and spelling. Unless otherwise indicated, the English words used below to approximate Spanish sounds take standard American pronunciation.

Vowels
a	as in 'father'
e	as in 'met'
i	as the 'i' in 'feet'
o	as in 'hot'
u	as in 'put'

Diphthongs
A diphthong is one syllable made up of two vowels, each of which conserves its own sound.

ai	as the 'i' in 'hide'
au	as the 'ow' in 'how'
ei	as the 'ay' in 'hay'
ia	as the 'ya' in 'yard'
ie	as the 'ye' in 'yes'
oi	as the 'oy' in 'boy'
ua	as the 'wa' in 'wash'
ue	as the 'we' in 'well'

Consonants
Many consonants are pronounced in much the same way as in English, but there are some exceptions:

c	as the 's' in 'sit' before e or i; elsewhere as 'k'
ch	as in 'choose'
g	as in 'gate' before a, o and u; before e or i it is a harsh, breathy sound like the 'h' in 'hit.' When g occurs before ue or ui, the u is silent, unless it has a dieresis (ü), when it functions much like the English 'w,' eg, guerra 'geh-rra' (war), güero 'gweh-ro' (blond)
h	always silent
j	a harsh, guttural sound similar to the 'ch' in Scottish loch
ll	as the 'y' in 'yellow'
ñ	a nasal sound like the 'ny' in 'canyon'
q	as the 'k' in 'kick'; always followed by a silent u
r	a very short rolled 'r'
rr	a longer rolled 'r'
x	like the English 'h' after e or i; elsewhere as the 'x' in 'taxi'
z	as the 's' in 'sit'; never as in 'zoo'

There are a few other minor pronunciation differences, but the longer you stay in Mexico, the easier they will become. The letter ñ is considered a separate letter of the alphabet and follows n in alphabetically organized lists, such as dictionaries and phone books; often although not always, this is also true for ll and ch.

Word Stress
For words ending in a vowel, -n or -s, the stress is on the penultimate (next-to-the-last) syllable, eg, naranja, 'na-rahn-ha' (orange). For words ending in a consonant other than n or s, the stress is on the final syllable, eg, ciudad, 'syoo-dahd' (city). Any deviation from these rules is indicated by an accent, eg, México, 'meh-hee-ko.'

Gender
Nouns in Spanish are either masculine (m) or feminine (f). Nouns ending in -o, -e or -ma are usually masculine. Nouns ending in -a, -ión or -dad are usually feminine. Some nouns take either a masculine or feminine form, depending on the ending; for example, viajero is a male traveler, viajera is a female traveler. An adjective usually comes after the noun it describes and must take the same gender as the noun.

Greetings & Civilities
Hello/Hi.	Hola.
Good morning/ Good day.	Buenos días.

Good afternoon.	*Buenas tardes.*
Good evening/ Good night.	*Buenas noches.*
Goodbye.	*Adiós.*
See you.	*Hasta luego.*
Pleased to meet you.	*Mucho gusto.*
How are you? (to one person)	*¿Como está?*
How are you? (to more than one person)	*¿Como están?*
I am fine.	*Estoy bien.*
Yes.	*Sí.*
No.	*No.*
Please.	*Por favor.*
Thank you.	*Gracias.*
You're welcome.	*De nada.*
Excuse me.	*Perdóneme.*

Small Talk

I am ...	*Soy ...*
American	*(norte)americano/ americana* (m/f)
Australian	*australiano/a* (m/f)
British	*británico/a* (m/f)
Canadian	*canadiense* (m & f)
English	*inglés/inglesa* (m/f)
French	*francés/ francesa* (m/f)
German	*alemán/ alemana* (m/f)
good/OK	*bueno/a* (m/f)
bad	*malo/a* (m/f)
better	*mejor*
best	*lo mejor*
more	*más*
less	*menos*
very little	*poco/a* (m/f) *poquito/a* (m/f)

People

I	*yo*
you (informal)	*tú*
you (polite)	*usted*
you (pl, polite)	*ustedes*
he/it	*el*
she/it	*ella*
we	*nosotros*
they	*ellos/ellas* (m/f)
Sir/Mr	*Señor*
Madam/Mrs	*Señora*
Miss	*Señorita*

my ...	*mi ...*
wife	*esposa*
husband	*esposo/marido*
sister	*hermana*
brother	*hermano*

Language Difficulties

I speak ...	*Yo hablo ...*
I don't speak ...	*No hablo ...*
Do you speak ...?	*¿Habla usted ...?*
Spanish	*español*
English	*inglés*
German	*alemán*
French	*francés*
I understand.	*Entiendo.*
I don't understand.	*No entiendo.*
Do you understand?	*¿Entiende usted?*
Please speak slowly.	*Por favor hable despacio.*
What did you say?	*¿Mande?* (colloq) *¿Cómo?*

Getting Around

Where is the ...?	*¿Dónde está ...?*
airport	*el aeropuerto*
bus station	*el terminal de autobuses/ la central camionera*
train station	*la estación del ferrocarril*
the ticket office	*la taquilla*
the waiting room	*la sala de espera*
the baggage check-in	*(recibo de) equipaje*
When does the ... leave/arrive?	*¿A qué hora sale/llega ...?*
bus	*el camión/el autobús*
minibus	*el colectivo/la combi*
plane	*la avión*
train	*el tren*

Signs

Entrada	**Entrance**
Salida	**Exit**
Información	**Information**
Abierto	**Open**
Cerrado	**Closed**
Prohibido	**Prohibited**
Comisaria	**Police Station**
Servicios/Baños	**Toilets**
Hombres	**Men**
Mujeres	**Women**

taxi	el taxi
departure	la salida
arrival	la llegada
platform	el andén
left-luggage room/ checkroom	la guardería (or la guarda) de equipaje

How far is ...?	¿A qué distancia está ...?
How long? (How much time?)	¿Cuánto tiempo?

Where is ...?	¿Dónde está ...?
the post office	el correo
the toilet	el sanitario
a long-distance phone	un teléfono de larga distancia

to the left	a la izquierda
to the right	a la derecha
forward, ahead	adelante
straight ahead	todo recto or derecho
this way	por aquí
that way	por allí
north	norte (Nte)
south	sur
east	este
east (in an address)	oriente (Ote)
west	oeste
west (in an address)	poniente (Pte)

avenue	la avenida
boulevard	el bulevar, boulevard
highway	la carretera
road	el camino
street	la calle
corner (of)	la esquina (de)
corner/bend	la vuelta
block	la cuadra

How much is a liter of gasoline?	¿Cuánto cuesta el litro de gasolina?
My car has broken down.	Se me ha descompuesto el carro.
I need a tow truck.	Necesito un remolque.
Is there a garage near here?	¿Hay un garaje cerca de aquí?

gasoline	la gasolina
fuel station	la tienda gasolinera
unleaded	sin plomo
fill the tank	llene el tanque; llenarlo
full	lleno or 'ful'
oil	el aceite

Highway Signs

Though Mexico mostly uses the familiar international road signs, you should be prepared to encounter these other signs as well:

Camino en Reparación	**Road Repairs**
Conserve Su Derecha	**Keep Right**
Curva Peligrosa	**Dangerous Curve**
Derrumbes	**Landslides/ Subsidence**
Despacio	**Slow**
Desviación	**Detour**
Disminuya Su Velocidad	**Slow Down**
Escuela	**School**
No Hay Paso	**Road Closed**
No Rebase	**No Overtaking**
Peligro	**Danger**
Prepare Su Cuota	**Have Toll Ready**
Puente Angosto	**Narrow Bridge**
Topes/Vibradores	**Speed Humps**
Vía Corta (often a toll road)	**Short Route**
Vía Cuota	**Toll Highway**

tire	la llanta
puncture	el agujero

Border Paperwork

birth certificate	certificado de nacimiento
border (frontier)	la frontera
car-owner's title	título de propiedad
car registration	registración
customs	aduana
driver's license	licencia de manejar
identification	identificación
immigration	inmigración
insurance	seguro
passport	pasaporte
temporary vehicle import permit	permiso de importación temporal de vehículo
tourist card	tarjeta de turista
visa	visado

Accommodations

hotel	hotel
guesthouse	casa de huéspedes
inn	posada

I'd like ...	*Quisiera ...*
Do you have ...?	*¿Tiene ...?*
a room with one bed	*un cuarto sencillo*
a room with two beds	*un cuarto doble*
a room for one	*un cuarto para una persona*
a room for two	*un cuarto para dos personas*
a double bed	*una cama matrimonial*
twin beds	*camas gemelas*

with bath	*con baño*
shower	*ducha/regadera*
hot water	*agua caliente*
air-conditioning	*aire acondicionado*
blanket	*manta/cobija*
towel	*toalla*
soap	*jabón*
toilet paper	*papel higiénico*
the check (bill)	*la cuenta*

What's the price?
  ¿Cuál es el precio?
Does that include taxes?
  ¿Están incluidos los impuestos?
Does that include service?
  ¿Está incluido el servicio?

Shopping

How much?	*¿Cuánto?*
How much is it worth?	*¿Cuánto vale?*
I want ...	*Quiero ...*
I'd like ...	*Quisiera ...*
Give me ...	*Dame ...*
What do you want?	*¿Qué quiere?*
Do you have ...?	*¿Tiene ...?*
Is/are there ...?	*¿Hay ...?*
How much does it cost?	*¿Cuánto cuesta?*
	¿Cuánto se cobra?

Money

I'd like to change some money.	*Quisiera cambiar dinero.*
What's the exchange rate?	*¿Cuál es el tipo de cambio?*
Is there a commission?	*¿Hay comisión?*
money	*el dinero*
travelers checks	*cheques de viajero*
bank	*el banco*
exchange bureau	*la casa de cambio*
credit card	*la tarjeta de crédito*

Emergencies

Help!	*¡Socorro!/¡Auxilio!*
Fire!	*¡Fuego!*
Call a doctor!	*¡Llama a un médico!*
Call the police!	*¡Llama a la policía!*
I'm ill.	*Estoy enfermo/a.* (m/f)
I'm lost.	*Estoy perdido/a.* (m/f)
Go away!	*¡Váyase!*

exchange rate	*el tipo de cambio*
ATM	*la caja permanente/ el cajero automático*

Telephones

letter	*carta*
parcel	*paquete*
postcard	*postal*
stamps	*estampillas, timbres*
airmail	*correo aéreo*
telephone	*teléfono*
telephone call	*llamada*
telephone number	*número telefónico*
telephone card	*tarjeta telefónica*
local call	*llamada local*
long-distance call	*llamada de larga distancia*
person to person	*persona a persona*
collect (reverse charges)	*por cobrar*
busy	*ocupado*
Don't hang up.	*No cuelgue.*

Times & Dates

What time is it?	*¿Qué hora es?*
yesterday	*ayer*
today	*hoy*
tomorrow (at some point, maybe)	*mañana*
morning	*mañana*
tomorrow morning	*mañana por la mañana*
afternoon	*tarde*
night	*noche*
right now (meaning in a few minutes)	*horita/ahorita*
already	*ya*

Monday	*lunes*
Tuesday	*martes*
Wednesday	*miércoles*
Thursday	*jueves*
Friday	*viernes*
Saturday	*sábado*
Sunday	*domingo*

Numbers

0	*cero*
1	*un, uno* (m), *una* (f)
2	*dos*
3	*tres*
4	*cuatro*
5	*cinco*
6	*seis*
7	*siete*
8	*ocho*
9	*nueve*
10	*diez*
11	*once*
12	*doce*
13	*trece*
14	*catorce*
15	*quince*
16	*dieciséis*
17	*diecisiete*
18	*dieciocho*
19	*diecinueve*
20	*veinte*
21	*veintiuno*
22	*veintidós*
30	*treinta*
31	*treinta y uno*
32	*treinta y dos*
40	*cuarenta*
50	*cincuenta*
60	*sesenta*
70	*setenta*
80	*ochenta*
90	*noventa*
100	*cien*
143	*ciento cuarenta y tres*
1000	*mil*

FOOD

Called 'the land of the pheasant and the deer' by its Maya inhabitants, the Yucatán Peninsula has always had a distinctive cuisine. This food section includes both general Mexican dishes and Yucatecan specialties. See Food and Drinks in the Facts for the Visitor chapter for more information.

At the Table

carta – menu (see also *lista*)
copa – glass (especially for wine)
cuchara – spoon
cuchillo – knife
cuenta – bill
lista – menu; short for *lista de precios* (see *menú*)

menú – fixed-price meal, as in *menú del día*; it's also coming to be used with its English meaning ('menu')
plato – plate/dish
propina – tip
servilleta – table napkin
taza – cup
tenedor – fork
vaso – drinking glass

Antojitos

Many traditional Mexican dishes are known as *antojitos* ('little whims') – savory or spicy concoctions that delight the palate.

burrito – any combination of beans, cheese, meat, chicken or seafood, seasoned with salsa or chili and wrapped in a wheat-flour tortilla
chilaquiles – scrambled eggs with chilies and bits of tortilla
chili relleno – stuffed *poblano* chili dipped in egg whites, fried and baked in sauce
empanada – small pastry with savory or sweet filling
enchilada – ingredients similar to those used in burritos wrapped in a corn tortilla, dipped in sauce and baked or fried
enfrijolada – soft tortilla in a bean sauce topped with cheese and onion
entomatada – soft tortilla in a tomato sauce topped with cheese and onion
frijol con puerco – Yucatecan-style pork and beans, topped with a grilled tomato sauce and decorated with bits of radish, slices of onion and fresh cilantro (coriander) leaves; served with rice
gordita – fried corn (maize) dough filled with refried beans, topped with cream, cheese and lettuce
guacamole – mashed avocados mixed with onion, chili, lemon and tomato
machaca – cured, dried and shredded beef or pork mixed with eggs, onions, cilantro and chilies
panuchos – fried handmade tortillas topped with shredded chicken and refried beans
papadzules – Yucatecan dish of tortillas with a filling of hard-boiled eggs, zucchini or cucumber seeds and topped with tomato sauce
quesadilla – flour tortilla topped or filled with cheese and heated
queso fundido – melted cheese served with tortillas

queso relleno – 'stuffed cheese,' a mild cheese filled with minced meat and spices

salbutes – fried handmade tortillas topped with shredded turkey, onion and slices of avocado

sincronizada –lightly grilled or fried tortilla 'sandwich,' usually filled with ham and cheese

sope – thick corn dough patty lightly grilled, served with green or red salsa and frijoles, onion and cheese

taco – corn tortilla wrapped or folded around the same filling as a burrito

tamal – steamed corn dough stuffed with meat, beans, chilies or nothing at all, wrapped in corn husks

torta – Mexican-style sandwich in a roll

tostada – flat, crisp tortilla, served as an accompaniment to ceviche or other dishes, or topped with meat or cheese, tomatoes, beans and lettuce as a dish by itself

Soups (Sopas)

birria – spicy-hot soup of meat, onions, peppers and cilantro, served with tortillas

chipilín – corn-based cheese and cream soup

gazpacho – chilled tomato-vegetable soup spiced with hot chilies

menudo – soup made with spiced tripe

pozole – hominy soup with meat and vegetables (sometimes spicy)

sopa de arroz – not a soup at all but a plate of rice, commonly served with lunch

sopa de lima – 'lime soup,' chicken stock flavored with lime and filled with pieces of crisped corn tortilla

sopa de pollo – bits of chicken in a thin chicken broth

Eggs (Huevos)

huevos estrellados – fried eggs

huevos fritos – fried eggs

huevos motuleños – local dish of Motul: fried eggs on a tortilla spread with refried beans, garnished with diced ham, green peas, shredded cheese and tomato sauce, with fried bananas on the side

huevos rancheros – ranch-style eggs: fried, laid on a tortilla and smothered with spicy tomato sauce

huevos revueltos – scrambled eggs

Seafood (Pescado/Mariscos)

abulón – abalone

almejas – clams

atún – tuna

cabrilla – sea bass

caguama – turtle (usually endangered; best avoided)

camarones – shrimp

camarones gigantes – prawns

cangrejo – large crab

cazón – dogfish (a small shark)

ceviche – parboiled seafood marinated in lime juice and mixed with onions, chilies, garlic, tomatoes and cilantro

dorado – dolphin fish

filete de pescado – fish fillet

huachinango – red snapper

jaiba – small crab

jurel – yellowtail

langosta – lobster

lenguado – flounder or sole

mariscos – shellfish

ostiones – oysters

pan de cazón – Campeche specialty of dogfish layered with corn tortillas in a rich, dark (or sometimes tomato) sauce

pargo – red snapper

pescado – fish as food (see *pez*)

pescado al mojo de ajo – fish fried in butter and garlic

pez – fish alive in the water (see *pescado*)

pez espada – swordfish

sierra – mackerel

tiburón – shark

tortuga – turtle

trucha de mar – sea trout

Meat & Poultry (Carnes y Aves)

asado – a roast

barbacoa – 'barbecued'; meat covered and placed under hot coals to cook

bistec – beefsteak; can mean any cut of meat, fish or poultry (*bistec de res* specifies beef)

bistec a la Mexicana – bits of beef sautéed with chopped tomatoes and hot peppers

borrego – sheep

cabra – goat

cabrito – kid (baby goat)

carne al carbón – charcoal-grilled meat

carne asada – tough but tasty grilled beef

carnitas – deep-fried pork

cerdo – pork

chaquaca – quail

chicharrones – deep-fried pork skin

chorizo – pork sausage

chuletas de cerdo – pork chops

cochinita – suckling pig

codorniz – quail

conejo – rabbit

cordero – lamb

costillas de cerdo – pork ribs or chops
empanizado – breaded
guajolote – turkey
hígado (encebollado) – liver (and onions)
jamón – ham
longaniza – spicy sausage
milanesa – crumbed/breaded
patas de puerco – pig's feet
pato – duck
pavo – turkey
pavo relleno – slabs of turkey meat layered
    with chopped, spiced beef and pork and
    served in a rich, dark sauce
pibil – Yucatecan preparation style: meat
    flavored with achiote sauce, wrapped in
    banana leaves and baked in a pit oven
pib pipián –Yucatecan preparation style:
    meat or fish is flavored with a sauce of
    ground squash seeds, wrapped in banana
    leaves and steamed
poc-chuc – slices of pork cooked in a tangy
    onion and sour orange or lemon sauce
pollo – chicken
pollo asado – grilled (not roasted) chicken
pollo con arroz – chicken with rice
pollo frito – fried chicken
puchero – a stew of pork, chicken, carrots,
    squash, potatoes, plantains and chayote
    (vegetable pear), spiced with radish, fresh
    cilantro and sour orange
puerco – pork
tampiqueño/tampiqueña – 'in the style of
    Tampico,' with spiced tomato sauce
tocino – bacon or salt pork
venado – venison

Fruit (Frutas)

Much of the ready-to-eat-fruit sold in the
Yucatán is offered with powdered chili,
lemon juice and salt (chili, limón y sal).
This may sound odd at first, but is in fact a
delightful combination of flavors.

coco – coconut
dátil – date
fresas – strawberries or any berries
guayaba – guava
higo – fig
limón – lime or lemon
mango – mango
melón – melon
naranja – orange
papaya – papaya
piña – pineapple
plátano – banana

toronja – grapefruit
uva – grape

Vegetables (Legumbres/Verduras)

aceitunas – olives
ajillo – a small onion akin to a scallion
calabaza – squash, marrow or pumpkin
cebolla – onion
champiñones – mushrooms
chícharos – peas
ejotes – green beans
elote – corn on the cob
hongos – mushrooms, also called champiñ-
    ones
jícama – root vegetable resembling a potato
    crossed with an apple; eaten fresh with a
    sprinkling of lime, chili and salt
lechuga – lettuce
papa – potato
tomate – tomato, also called jitomate
zanahoria – carrot

Desserts (Dulces)

flan – custard/crème caramel
helado – ice cream
nieve – Mexican equivalent of the American
    'snow cone': flavored ice with the con-
    sistency of ice cream
paleta – flavored ice on a stick
pan dulce – sweet rolls, usually eaten for
    breakfast
pastel – cake
postre – dessert

Condiments & Other Foods

achiote – a mild, tart spice paste colored
    red with annato seed and used widely in
    Yucatán cooking
azúcar – sugar
bolillo – French-style bread rolls
crema – cream
mantequilla – butter
mole poblano – sauce from Puebla, Mexico,
    made from up to 30 ingredients, includ-
    ing bitter chocolate, chilies and spices;
    often served over chicken or turkey
pimienta negra – black pepper
queso – cheese
sal – salt
salsa – sauce of chilies, onion, tomato, lemon
    or lime juice and spices; any kind of sauce

Drinks

agua – water
atole – hot drink made with corn, milk,
    cinnamon and sugar

café americano – black coffee with sugar
café con crema – coffee with cream served separately
café con leche – coffee with hot milk
café sin azúcar – coffee without sugar; ordering this keeps the waiter from adding heaps of sugar to your cup, but doesn't mean your coffee won't taste sweet – sugar is often added to and processed with the beans
café solo – black coffee with sugar
leche – milk
nescafé – instant coffee (also called *café instantáneo* or *café soluble*)
té de manzanilla – chamomile tea
té negro – black tea

Yucatec Maya

Yucatec Maya, spoken primarily in the Mexican states of Yucatán, Campeche and Quintana Roo, and in the northern and western parts of Belize, is part of the Amerind family of Native American languages. This means that Yucatec Maya (commonly called 'Yucatec' by scholars and 'Maya' by local speakers) is related to many languages spoken in the southeastern United States, as well as many of the indigenous languages of far-off California and Oregon (eg, Costanoan, Klamath, and Tsimshian). Yucatec is just one of 28 modern Mayan languages but it probably has the largest number of speakers, estimated at 750,000 people.

You can hear Yucatec spoken in the markets and occasionally by hotel staff in cities throughout the peninsula. If you really want to hear Yucatec spoken by monolingual Maya (and learn a lot about Maya culture besides!), you must travel to some of the peninsula's more remote villages. Maya speakers will not assume that you know any of their language. If you attempt to say something in Maya, people will usually respond quite favorably. So give it a try!

Pronunciation

Mayan vowels are similar to English vowels but the consonants can be a bit tricky.

c   always hard, as the 'k' in 'kick'
j   always an aspirated 'h' sound. So *abaj* is pronounced ah-**bahh**; to get the 'hh' sound, take the 'h' sound from 'half' and put it at the end of ah-**bahh**

u   as 'oo' except when it begins or ends a word, in which case it is like English 'w.' Thus *baktun* is 'bahk-**toon**,' but *Uaxactún* is 'wah-shahk-**toon**' and *ahau* is 'ah-**haw**'
x   as the 'sh' in 'ship'; a shushing sound

Mayan glottalized consonants (ie, those followed by an apostrophe: **b'**, **ch'**, **k'**, **p'**, **t'**), are similar to normal consonants, but are pronounced more forcefully and 'explosively.' However, an apostrophe following a vowel signifies a glottal stop (the sound between syllables in 'uh-oh'), not a more forceful vowel.

Maya is a pitch-accent language, which means that some words take on different meanings when pronounced with a high tone or a low tone. For example, *aak* said with a high tone means 'turtle,' but 'grass' or 'vine' when said with a low tone.

In many Mayan place names the stress falls on the last syllable. When these names are written out, Spanish rules for indicating stress are often followed (see earlier in this chapter). This practice varies; in this book we have tried to include accents as much as possible. Here are some pronunciation examples:

Abaj Takalik	ah-**bahh** tah-kah-**leek**
Acanceh	ah-kahn-**keh**
Dzibilchaltún	dzee-beel-chahl-**toon**
Hopelchén	ho-pel-**chen**
Oxcutzkab	ohsh-kootz-**kahb**
Pacal	pah-**kahl**
Pop	pope
Tikal	tee-**kahl**

Village Greetings

The most polite thing to do in a village setting is to greet the male head of the household first. You will probably have trouble figuring out who this is – see the Phrase Guide for help, or simply try to greet the oldest man around. Men should try to speak to other men or possibly older women. Approaching young women might give people a mistaken idea of your intentions. Women should try to greet the eldest man (as above), and any of the women you think are your age or older.

Uaxactún	wah-shahk-**toon**
Xcaret	sh-kah-**reht**
Yaxchilán	yahsh-chee-**lahn**

Phrase Guide

Words borrowed from Spanish tend to be stressed differently in Mayan. For example: *amigo* (Spanish for 'friend') is pronounced 'a-**mi**-go' in Spanish and '**aa**-mi-go' in Yucatec.

Hello.
  Hola.   **o**-la
Good day.
  Buenos dias.   **bwe**-nos **dee**-as
Good afternoon.
  Buenas tardes. **bwe**-nos **tar**-des
Good evening.
  Buenas noches. **bwe**-nos **no**-ches

You might also hear someone saying simply *buenos* to stand in for the full greeting; this isn't considered as improper to Maya speakers as it is for many Spanish speakers.

How are you?
  Bix a beel?   beesh ah bail?
  Bix yanikech? beesh yaw-nee-**kech**?
  (less formal)
OK/Well.
  Maalob.   **mah**-lobe
Bye/See you tomorrow.
  Hasta saamal. **ahs**-ta **sah**-mahl
Goodbye.
  Pa'atik kin bin. **pa'a**-teek keen been
Thank you.
  Gracias/   **grah**-see-as/
    Dios Bo'otik. dyose **boe'oh**-teek
Yes.
  Haah/He'ele.   haah/**heh'eh**-leh

Maya speakers often reiterate what is said to them, instead of saying 'yes'; eg, 'Are you going to the store?' 'I'm going.'

No.
  Ma'.   mah'
What's your name?
  Bix a k'aaba? beesh ah **k'aah**-bah?
My name is ...
  In kaabae'... een kah-bah-**eh'**
I understand English.
  Kin na'atik   keen **na**-'ah-teek
    ingles.   een-gles

I don't speak Maya.
  Ma tin na'atik mayat'aani.
    mah' teen **na**-'ah-teek ma-ya-**taah**-nee
Do you speak Spanish?
  Teche', ka t'aanik wa castellano t'aan?
    te-cheh', kah **t'ah**-neek wah
    cah-stay-**yah**-no t'ahn?
Who is the head of the house?
  Maax u pool u nahil?
    mahsh oo pole oo **na**-heel?

Where is the ...?
  Tu'ux yaan le ... **too**-'oosh yahn leh ...
  bathroom
    baño   ba'-nyo
  road to ...
    u beh ti'...   u beh tee ...
  hotel
    hotel   oh-**tel**
  doctor
    médico   **meh**-dee-ko
  Comisario
    Comis   ko-mees

How much is ...?
  Bahux ...?   bah-**hoosh** ...?
  this one
    lela'   leh-**lah'**
  that one
    lelo'   leh-**loh'**

expensive
  ko'oh   **ko**-'oh
not expensive
  mix ko'ohi   meesh **ko**-'o-hi
pretty
  ki'ichpam   **kee**-'eech-pahm

I'm hungry.
  Wiihen.   wee-**hen**
It's (very) tasty.
  (Hach) Ki'.   (hahch) kee'
I want to drink water.
  Tak in wukik ha'. tahk een woo-keek
                         hah'

1	*un peel*	oom pail
2	*ka peel*	kah pail
3	*ox peel*	ohsh pail

When counting animate objects, like people, replace *peel* with *tuul* (pronounced 'tool'). Beyond three, use Spanish numbers.

Glossary

Words specific to food, restaurants and eating are listed under Food in the Language chapter.

alux (s), **aluxes** (pl) – Mayan 'leprechauns,' benevolent 'little people'

Ángeles Verdes – 'Green Angels'; bilingual mechanics in green trucks who patrol major highways, offering breakdown assistance

ayuntamiento – commonly seen as *H Ayuntamiento (Honorable Ayuntamiento)* on the front of town hall buildings, it translates as 'municipal government'

baluartes – bastions or bulwarks
barrio – district, neighborhood
billete – bank note (unlike in Spain, where it's a ticket)
boleto – ticket (bus, train, museum etc)

cacique – Indian chief; also used to describe a provincial warlord or strongman
cafetería – literally 'coffee-shop,' it refers to any informal restaurant with waiter service; it is not usually a cafeteria in the American sense of a self-service restaurant
cajero automático – automated bank teller machine (ATM)
camión (s), **camiones** (pl) – truck; bus
camioneta – pickup
campechanos – citizens of Campeche
campesinos – countryfolk, farm workers
casa de cambio – currency exchange office; it offers exchange rates comparable to banks' and is usually much faster to use
caseta de larga distancia – long-distance telephone station, often shortened to *caseta*
cenote – a deep limestone sinkhole containing water
cerveza – beer
Chac – Mayan god of rain
chac-mool – Mayan sacrificial stone sculpture
chenes – name for cenotes (limestone pools) in the Chenes region
chilangos – natives of Mexico City
chultún (s), **chultunes** (pl) – Mayan cistern found at Puuc archaeological sites south of Mérida
cocina – cookshop (literally 'kitchen'), a small, basic restaurant usually run by one woman, often located in or near a municipal market; also seen as *cocina económica* (economical kitchen) or *cocina familiar* (family kitchen); see also *lonchería*

colectivo – literally, 'shared,' a car, van (VW combi, Ford or Chevrolet) or minibus that picks up and drops off passengers along its set route; also known as *taxi colectivo*
combi – a catch-all term used for taxi, van and minibus services regardless of van type
comida corrida – set meal, meal of the day
conquistador – explorer-conqueror of Latin America from Spain
correo, correos – post office
costera – waterfront avenue
criollo – a person of pure Spanish descent born in Spanish America
cuota – toll road

daños a terceros – third-party car insurance
de lujo – deluxe class of bus service
DNI – Derecho para No Inmigrante; non-immigrant fee charged to all foreign tourists and business travelers visiting Mexico

ejido – communal landholding, though laws now allow sale of *ejido* land to outside individuals
encomenderos – owners of Mayan lands divided into large estates
encomienda – a grant made to a conquistador, consisting of labor by or tribute from a group of indigenous people; the conquistador was supposed to protect and convert them, but usually treated them as little more than slaves

feria – fair or carnival, typically occurring during a religious holiday

gala terno – a straight, white, square-necked dress with an embroidered overyoke and hem, worn over an underskirt, which sports an embroidered strip near the bottom; fancier than a *huipil* and often accompanied by a hand-knitted shawl
gringo/a – male/female US or Canadian visitor to Latin America (sometimes applied to any visitor of European heritage); can be used derogatorily but more often is a mere statement of fact

gruta – cave, grotto
guardaequipaje – room for storing luggage (eg, in a bus terminal)
guayabera – man's thin fabric shirt with pockets and appliqued designs on the front, over the shoulders and down the back; often worn in place of a jacket and tie

hacendado – landowner
hacienda – estate; Hacienda (capitalized) is the Treasury Department
henequen – agave fiber used to make rope, grown particularly around Mérida
huipil (s), **huipiles** (pl) – indigenous women's sleeveless white tunic, usually intricately and colorfully embroidered

iglesia – church
INAH – Instituto Nacional de Arqueología e Historia; the body in charge of most ancient sites and some museums
INM – Instituto Nacional de Migración (National Immigration Institute)
Itzamná – lord of the heavens; a popular figure on the wooden panels of contemporary architecture
IVA – the *impuesto al valor agregado* or 'ee-bah,' a 15% value-added tax added to many items in Mexico
Ixchel – Mayan goddess of the moon and fertility

jarana – a folkloric dance that has been performed by Yucatecans for centuries
jipijapa – an alternative name for panama hats (the hats are made from jipijapa palm fronds)

Kukulcán – Mayan name for the Aztec-Toltec plumed serpent Quetzalcóatl

lagunas – lakes
larga distancia – long-distance; usually refers to telephones, often seen on signs outside *casetas* as 'Lada'
lavandería – laundry; a *lavandería automática* is a coin-operated laundry
lista de correos – general delivery in Mexico; literally 'mail list,' the list of addressees for whom mail is being held, displayed in the post office
lonchería – from English 'lunch'; a simple restaurant that may in fact serve meals all day (not just lunch), often seen near municipal markets. See also *cocina*.

lotería – Mexico's version of bingo

machismo – maleness, masculine virility or bravura
malecón – waterfront boulevard
manzana – apple; also a city block. A *supermanzana* is a large group of city blocks bounded by major avenues. Cancún uses *manzana* and *supermanzana* numbers as addresses.
mariachi – small ensemble of Mexican street musicians; strolling mariachi bands often perform in restaurants
más o menos – more or less, somewhat
meridanos – citizens of Mérida
mestizo – also known as ladino, a person of mixed Indian and European blood; the word now more commonly means 'Mexican'
metate – flattish stone on which corn is ground with a cylindrical stone roller
Montezuma's revenge – Mexican version of 'Delhi-belly' or travelers' diarrhea
mudéjar – Moorish architectural style
mulatto – a person of mixed white and black ancestry
municipios – townships

na – thatched Mayan hut
nortes – relatively cold storms bringing wind and rain from the north
Nte – abbreviation for *norte* (north), used in street names

oficina de correos – post office; also called *correo* or *correos*
Ote – abbreviation for *oriente* (east), used in street names

palacio de gobierno – building housing the executive offices of a state or regional government
palacio municipal – town or city hall; municipal government
palapa – thatched, palm-leaf-roofed shelter usually with open sides
Pemex – government-owned petroleum extraction, refining and retailing monopoly
pisto – colloquial Mayan term for money
plateresque – 'silversmith-like'; the architectural style of the Spanish renaissance (16th century), rich in decoration
Popol Vuh – painted Mayan book containing sacred legends and stories; similar to the Bible

porfiriato – the name given to the era of Porfirio Diaz's 35-year rule as president-dictator (1876–1911), preceding the Mexican Revolution

PRI – Partido Revolucionario Institucional (Institutional Revolutionary Party); the controlling force in Mexican politics for much of the 20th century

primera (1a) clase – 1st class of bus service

Quetzalcóatl – plumed serpent god of the Aztecs and Toltecs

retablo – altarpiece (usually an ornate gilded, carved wooden decoration in a church)

roofcomb – a decorative stonework lattice atop a Mayan pyramid or temple

sacbé (s), **sacbeob** (pl) – ceremonial limestone avenue or path between great Mayan cities

segunda (2a) clase – 2nd class of bus service

Semana Santa – Holy Week, the week from Palm Sunday to Easter Sunday; Mexico's major holiday period, when accommodations and transport get very busy

stela (s), **stelae** (pl) – standing stone monument, usually carved

supermercado – supermarket, ranging from a corner store to a large, US-style supermarket

sur – south; often seen in street names

templo – in Mexico, a church; anything from a wayside chapel to a cathedral

tequila – clear, distilled liquor produced, like pulque and mezcal, from the maguey cactus

Tex-Mex – Americanized version of Mexican food

típico – typical or characteristic of a region; particularly used to describe food

topes – speed bumps found in many Mexican towns, sometimes indicated by a highway sign bearing a row of little bumps

torito – a vivacious song that evokes the fervor of a bullfight

tranvía – tram or motorized trolley

viajero/a – male/female traveler

vulcanizadora – automobile tire repair shop

vaquería – a traditional Yucatecan party where couples dance in unison to a series of songs

War of the Castes – bloody 19th-century Mayan uprising in the Yucatán

xtabentún – a traditional Mayan spirit in the Yucatán; an anise-flavored liqueur made by fermenting honey

Xibalbá – in Mayan religious belief, the secret world or underworld.

LONELY PLANET

You already know that Lonely Planet produces more than this one guidebook, but you might not be aware of the other products we have on this region. Here is a selection of titles that you may want to check out as well:

Mexico
ISBN 1 74059 028 7
US$24.99 • UK£14.99

Latin American Spanish Phrasebook
ISBN 0 86442 558 9
US$6.95 • UK£4.50

Diving & Snorkeling Cozumel
ISBN 0 86442 574 0
US$14.95 • UK£8.99

Mexico's Pacific Coast
ISBN 1 74059 273 5
US$16.99 • UK£11.99

Belize Guatemala & Yucatán
ISBN 1 86450 140 5
US$19.99 • UK£13.99

Guatemala
ISBN 0 86442 684 4
US$16.99 • UK£10.99

Healthy Travel Central & South America
ISBN 1 86450 053 0
US$5.95 • UK£3.99

Green Dreams: Travels in Central America
ISBN 0 86442 523 6
US$12.95 • UK£6.99

Travel Photography
ISBN 1 86450 207 X
US$16.99 • UK£9.99

Baja California
ISBN 1 86450 198 7
US$16.99 • UK£10.99

Available wherever books are sold

LONELY PLANET
Guides by Region

Lonely Planet is known worldwide for publishing practical, reliable and no-nonsense travel information in our guides and on our Web site. The Lonely Planet list covers just about every accessible part of the world. Currently there are 16 series: Travel guides, Shoestring guides, Condensed guides, Phrasebooks, Read This First, Healthy Travel, Walking guides, Cycling guides, Watching Wildlife guides, Pisces Diving & Snorkeling guides, City Maps, Road Atlases, Out to Eat, World Food, Journeys travel literature and Pictorials.

AFRICA Africa on a shoestring • Botswana • Cairo • Cairo City Map • Cape Town • Cape Town City Map • East Africa • Egypt • Egyptian Arabic phrasebook • Ethiopia, Eritrea & Djibouti • Ethiopian Amharic phrasebook • The Gambia & Senegal • Healthy Travel Africa • Kenya • Malawi • Morocco • Moroccan Arabic phrasebook • Mozambique • Namibia • Read This First: Africa • South Africa, Lesotho & Swaziland • Southern Africa • Southern Africa Road Atlas • Swahili phrasebook • Tanzania, Zanzibar & Pemba • Trekking in East Africa • Tunisia • Watching Wildlife East Africa • Watching Wildlife Southern Africa • West Africa • World Food Morocco • Zambia • Zimbabwe, Botswana & Namibia
Travel Literature: Mali Blues: Traveling to an African Beat • The Rainbird: A Central African Journey • Songs to an African Sunset: A Zimbabwean Story

AUSTRALIA & THE PACIFIC Aboriginal Australia & the Torres Strait Islands •Auckland • Australia • Australian phrasebook • Australia Road Atlas • Cycling Australia • Cycling New Zealand • Fiji • Fijian phrasebook • Healthy Travel Australia, NZ & the Pacific • Islands of Australia's Great Barrier Reef • Melbourne • Melbourne City Map • Micronesia • New Caledonia • New South Wales • New Zealand • Northern Territory • Outback Australia • Out to Eat – Melbourne • Out to Eat – Sydney • Papua New Guinea • Pidgin phrasebook • Queensland • Rarotonga & the Cook Islands • Samoa • Solomon Islands • South Australia • South Pacific • South Pacific phrasebook • Sydney • Sydney City Map • Sydney Condensed • Tahiti & French Polynesia • Tasmania • Tonga • Tramping in New Zealand • Vanuatu • Victoria • Walking in Australia • Watching Wildlife Australia • Western Australia
Travel Literature: Islands in the Clouds: Travels in the Highlands of New Guinea • Kiwi Tracks: A New Zealand Journey • Sean & David's Long Drive

CENTRAL AMERICA & THE CARIBBEAN Bahamas, Turks & Caicos • Baja California • Belize, Guatemala & Yucatán • Bermuda • Central America on a shoestring • Costa Rica • Costa Rica Spanish phrasebook • Cuba • Cycling Cuba • Dominican Republic & Haiti • Eastern Caribbean • Guatemala • Havana • Healthy Travel Central & South America • Jamaica • Mexico • Mexico City • Panama • Puerto Rico • Read This First: Central & South America • Virgin Islands • World Food Caribbean • World Food Mexico • Yucatán
Travel Literature: Green Dreams: Travels in Central America

EUROPE Amsterdam • Amsterdam City Map • Amsterdam Condensed • Andalucía • Athens • Austria • Baltic States phrasebook • Barcelona • Barcelona City Map • Belgium & Luxembourg • Berlin • Berlin City Map • Britain • British phrasebook • Brussels, Bruges & Antwerp • Brussels City Map • Budapest • Budapest City Map • Canary Islands • Catalunya & the Costa Brava • Central Europe • Central Europe phrasebook • Copenhagen • Corfu & the Ionians • Corsica • Crete • Crete Condensed • Croatia • Cycling Britain • Cycling France • Cyprus • Czech & Slovak Republics • Czech phrasebook • Denmark • Dublin • Dublin City Map • Dublin Condensed • Eastern Europe • Eastern Europe phrasebook • Edinburgh • Edinburgh City Map • England • Estonia, Latvia & Lithuania • Europe on a shoestring • Europe phrasebook • Finland • Florence • Florence City Map • France • Frankfurt City Map • Frankfurt Condensed • French phrasebook • Georgia, Armenia & Azerbaijan • Germany • German phrasebook • Greece • Greek Islands • Greek phrasebook • Hungary • Iceland, Greenland & the Faroe Islands • Ireland • Italian phrasebook • Italy • Kraków • Lisbon • The Loire • London • London City Map • London Condensed • Madrid • Madrid City Map • Malta • Mediterranean Europe • Milan, Turin & Genoa • Moscow • Munich • Netherlands • Normandy • Norway • Out to Eat – London • Out to Eat – Paris • Paris • Paris City Map • Paris Condensed • Poland • Polish phrasebook • Portugal • Portuguese phrasebook • Prague • Prague City Map • Provence & the Côte d'Azur • Read This First: Europe • Rhodes & the Dodecanese • Romania & Moldova • Rome • Rome City Map • Rome Condensed • Russia, Ukraine & Belarus • Russian phrasebook • Scandinavian & Baltic Europe • Scandinavian phrasebook • Scotland • Sicily • Slovenia • South-West France • Spain • Spanish phrasebook • Stockholm • St Petersburg • St Petersburg City Map • Sweden • Switzerland • Tuscany • Ukrainian phrasebook • Venice • Vienna • Wales • Walking in Britain • Walking in France • Walking in Ireland • Walking in Italy • Walking in Scotland • Walking in Spain • Walking in Switzerland • Western Europe • World Food France • World Food Greece • World Food Ireland • World Food Italy • World Food Spain **Travel Literature:** After Yugoslavia • Love and War in the Apennines • The Olive Grove: Travels in Greece • On the Shores of the Mediterranean • Round Ireland in Low Gear • A Small Place in Italy

LONELY PLANET

Mail Order

Lonely Planet products are distributed worldwide. They are also available by mail order from Lonely Planet, so if you have difficulty finding a title please write to us. North and South American residents should write to 150 Linden St, Oakland, CA 94607, USA; European and African residents should write to 72-82 Rosebery Ave, London, EC1R 4RW, UK; and residents of other countries to Locked Bag 1, Footscray, Victoria 3011, Australia.

INDIAN SUBCONTINENT & THE INDIAN OCEAN Bangladesh • Bengali phrasebook • Bhutan • Delhi • Goa • Healthy Travel Asia & India • Hindi & Urdu phrasebook • India • India & Bangladesh City Map • Indian Himalaya • Karakoram Highway • Kathmandu City Map • Kerala • Madagascar • Maldives • Mauritius, Réunion & Seychelles • Mumbai (Bombay) • Nepal • Nepali phrasebook • North India • Pakistan • Rajasthan • Read This First: Asia & India • South India • Sri Lanka • Sri Lanka phrasebook • Tibet • Tibetan phrasebook • Trekking in the Indian Himalaya • Trekking in the Karakoram & Hindukush • Trekking in the Nepal Himalaya • World Food India **Travel Literature**: The Age of Kali: Indian Travels and Encounters • Hello Goodnight: A Life of Goa • In Rajasthan • Maverick in Madagascar • A Season in Heaven: True Tales from the Road to Kathmandu • Shopping for Buddhas • A Short Walk in the Hindu Kush • Slowly Down the Ganges

MIDDLE EAST & CENTRAL ASIA Bahrain, Kuwait & Qatar • Central Asia • Central Asia phrasebook • Dubai • Farsi (Persian) phrasebook • Hebrew phrasebook • Iran • Israel & the Palestinian Territories • Istanbul • Istanbul City Map • Istanbul to Cairo • Istanbul to Kathmandu • Jerusalem • Jerusalem City Map • Jordan • Lebanon • Middle East • Oman & the United Arab Emirates • Syria • Turkey • Turkish phrasebook • World Food Turkey • Yemen **Travel Literature**: Black on Black: Iran Revisited • Breaking Ranks: Turbulent Travels in the Promised Land • The Gates of Damascus • Kingdom of the Film Stars: Journey into Jordan

NORTH AMERICA Alaska • Boston • Boston City Map • Boston Condensed • British Columbia • California & Nevada • California Condensed • Canada • Chicago • Chicago City Map • Chicago Condensed • Florida • Georgia & the Carolinas • Great Lakes • Hawaii • Hiking in Alaska • Hiking in the USA • Honolulu & Oahu City Map • Las Vegas • Los Angeles • Los Angeles City Map • Louisiana & the Deep South • Miami • Miami City Map • Montreal • New England • New Orleans • New Orleans City Map • New York City • New York City City Map • New York City Condensed • New York, New Jersey & Pennsylvania • Oahu • Out to Eat – San Francisco • Pacific Northwest • Rocky Mountains • San Diego & Tijuana • San Francisco • San Francisco City Map • Seattle • Seattle City Map • Southwest • Texas • Toronto • USA • USA phrasebook • Vancouver • Vancouver City Map • Virginia & the Capital Region • Washington, DC • Washington, DC City Map • World Food New Orleans **Travel Literature**: Caught Inside: A Surfer's Year on the California Coast • Drive Thru America

NORTH-EAST ASIA Beijing • Beijing City Map • Cantonese phrasebook • China • Hiking in Japan • Hong Kong & Macau • Hong Kong City Map • Hong Kong Condensed • Japan • Japanese phrasebook • Korea • Korean phrasebook • Kyoto • Mandarin phrasebook • Mongolia • Mongolian phrasebook • Seoul • Shanghai • South-West China • Taiwan • Tokyo • Tokyo Condensed • World Food Hong Kong • World Food Japan **Travel Literature**: In Xanadu: A Quest • Lost Japan

SOUTH AMERICA Argentina, Uruguay & Paraguay • Bolivia • Brazil • Brazilian phrasebook • Buenos Aires • Buenos Aires City Map • Chile & Easter Island • Colombia • Ecuador & the Galapagos Islands • Healthy Travel Central & South America • Latin American Spanish phrasebook • Peru • Quechua phrasebook • Read This First: Central & South America • Rio de Janeiro • Rio de Janeiro City Map • Santiago de Chile • South America on a shoestring • Trekking in the Patagonian Andes • Venezuela **Travel Literature**: Full Circle: A South American Journey

SOUTH-EAST ASIA Bali & Lombok • Bangkok • Bangkok City Map • Burmese phrasebook • Cambodia • Cycling Vietnam, Laos & Cambodia • East Timor phrasebook • Hanoi • Healthy Travel Asia & India • Hill Tribes phrasebook • Ho Chi Minh City (Saigon) • Indonesia • Indonesian phrasebook • Indonesia's Eastern Islands • Java • Lao phrasebook • Laos • Malay phrasebook • Malaysia, Singapore & Brunei • Myanmar (Burma) • Philippines • Pilipino (Tagalog) phrasebook • Read This First: Asia & India • Singapore • Singapore City Map • South-East Asia on a shoestring • South-East Asia phrasebook • Thailand • Thailand's Islands & Beaches • Thailand, Vietnam, Laos & Cambodia Road Atlas • Thai phrasebook • Vietnam • Vietnamese phrasebook • World Food Indonesia • World Food Thailand • World Food Vietnam

ALSO AVAILABLE: Antarctica • The Arctic • The Blue Man: Tales of Travel, Love and Coffee • Brief Encounters: Stories of Love, Sex & Travel • Buddhist Stupas in Asia: The Shape of Perfection • Chasing Rickshaws • The Last Grain Race • Lonely Planet ... On the Edge: Adventurous Escapades from Around the World • Lonely Planet Unpacked • Lonely Planet Unpacked Again • Not the Only Planet: Science Fiction Travel Stories • Ports of Call: A Journey by Sea • Sacred India • Travel Photography: A Guide to Taking Better Pictures • Travel with Children • Tuvalu: Portrait of an Island Nation

Index

Bold indicates maps.

Bold indicates maps.

Boxed Text

MAP LEGEND

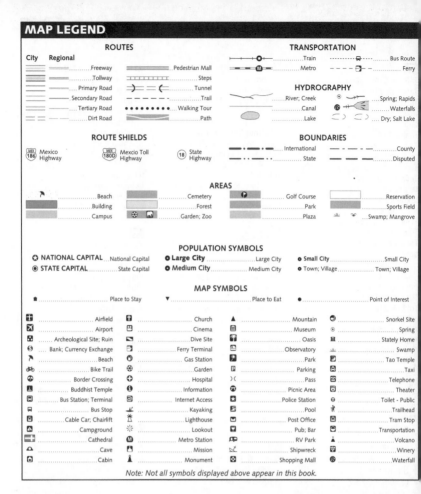

LONELY PLANET OFFICES

Australia
Locked Bag 1, Footscray, Victoria 3011
☎ 03 8379 8000 fax 03 8379 8111
email: talk2us@lonelyplanet.com.au

USA
150 Linden St, Oakland, CA 94607
☎ 510 893 8555 TOLL FREE: 800 275 8555
fax 510 893 8572
email: info@lonelyplanet.com

UK
72-82 Rosebery Ave, London, EC1R 4RW
☎ 020 7841 9000 fax 020 7841 9001
email: go@lonelyplanet.co.uk

France
1 rue du Dahomey, 75011 Paris
☎ 01 55 25 33 00 fax 01 55 25 33 01
email: bip@lonelyplanet.fr
www.lonelyplanet.fr

World Wide Web: www.lonelyplanet.com *or* AOL keyword: lp
Lonely Planet Images: www.lonelyplanetimages.com